'Winder is an engaging host . . . The Habsburgs were, latterly, authoritarian liberals. They survived by guile and luck, by sheer chance and cold expediency. With the exceptions of figures like Rudolf II, that melancholy devotee of the occult, there are few of them one can imagine a novelist wanting to explore. Yet Winder rightly enthuses over the contribution this odd political amalgam made to culture . . . *Danubia* is astoundingly smart and negotiates the Scylla of elegy and the Charybdis of denunciation with expert skill. It's also damn funny, and includes dodos, the banning of cribs, cockatrices and the entire history of Europe'
Scotland on Sunday

'Memorably funny . . . wonderfully readable and entertaining'
Sunday Times

'*Danubia* is a logical sequel to Simon Winder's quirky and delightful *Germania* . . . Political and military history supplies *Danubia* with its narrative line, but Simon Winder loves to explore the byways and odd corners of this rambling empire. He is excellent on architecture, painting and music. Never averse to putting himself at the centre of what he discovers on his travels, he has written a book that is every bit as entertaining and enlightening as *Germania* . . . Anyone with an interest in a part of Europe and a section of history largely ignored in our schools and universities will find this book richly rewarding'
Literary Review

'Funny and yet also fantastically informative'
Observer, Books of the Year

'Fascinating . . . Winder celebrates with amusing panache the tale of pluralist, anarchic, polyglot central Europe. Particularly poignant are his descriptions of the harrowing conditions that prevailed for centuries . . . Like the history it relates, the book is vast and chaotic and . . . as well as filling embarrassing historical gaps, the charm lies in being a treasure map stiff with leads to be pursued either by foot or by armchair . . . Winder's curiosity is infectious'
Country Life

'Absorbing . . . his learned enthusiasm for the sheer oddity of the vanished empire can be thrilling. He is particularly good on the empire's sense of political laissez-aller . . . few popular writers are as good as Winder at portraying Vienna as only one of several power centres'

Times Literary Supplement

'Winder gently but seriously emphasises that to think of the empire as a rational, centralising authority is completely to miss the point . . . Winder approaches his dementingly enormous subject more in the spirit of an amused and irreverent tourist, as his subtitle suggests: as much travel writer as historian . . . Winder plainly knows his way around the empire: he's not only more knowledgeable than he makes out about military history; he's also well-read and clever about art and music.'

Spectator

'The first historian of the Danube to try knockabout humour . . . His tales are spellbinding because he does not just sit in an archive or a library, but takes the reader out into the real world . . . there is an acute and agile intellect at work, allowing Winder to move effortlessly from the Big Picture to pointillist detail . . . Winder is the best-read cicerone imaginable. He never stops talking and rarely pauses for breath. Even then, however, you want to tell him: Forget about breathing and just go on talking. *Danubia* is a long book, yet this reader would not mind if it were longer still'

New York Times

'Winder's "personal history" of the Habsburg Empire takes the form of a journey across middle Europe, where the "plural, anarchic, polyglot" lands of old have given way to the "small and dirty cages of the new nation states." He finds humor and pathos in the history of the Habsburgs, who for five centuries ruled over territories stretching from the North Sea to Peru with a "dizzying blend of ineptitude, viciousness and occasional benignity." For every Emperor Maximilian I, an early adopter of the printing press and a patron of Albrecht Dürer, there is a King Carlos II of Spain, who could barely speak or eat, thanks to his family's incessant inbreeding'

New Yorker

DANUBIA

Simon Winder is the author of the
highly praised *The Man Who Saved Britain* and
the *Sunday Times* top ten bestseller *Germania*.
He works in publishing and lives in
Wandsworth Town.

Also by Simon Winder

The Man Who Saved Britain
Germania

AS EDITOR
Night Thoughts
Sea Longing
The Feast
'My Name's Bond . . .'

Simon Winder

DANUBIA

A Personal History of Habsburg Europe

PICADOR

First published 2013 by Picador

First published in paperback 2013 by Picador

This edition published 2014 by Picador
an imprint of Pan Macmillan, a division of Macmillan Publishers Limited
Pan Macmillan, 20 New Wharf Road, London N1 9RR
Basingstoke and Oxford
Associated companies throughout the world
www.panmacmillan.com

ISBN 978-0-330-52279-3

1 3 5 7 9 8 6 4 2

Visit www.picador.com to read more about all our books
and to buy them. You will also find features, author interviews and
news of any author events, and you can sign up for e-newsletters
so that you're always first to hear about our new releases.

For Martha Frances

What is 'known' in civilized countries, what people may be assumed to 'know', is a great mystery.

Saul Bellow, *To Jerusalem and Back*

The fat volunteer rolled onto the other straw mattress and went on: 'It's obvious that one day it will all collapse. It can't last forever. Try to pump glory into a pig and it will burst in the end.'

Jaroslav Hašek, *The Good Soldier Švejk*

Emperor of Austria

Apostolic King of Hungary

King of Bohemia, Dalmatia, Croatia, Slavonia, Galicia, Lodomeria, Illyria

King of Jerusalem, etc.

Archduke of Austria

Grand Duke of Tuscany, Kraków

Duke of Lorraine, Salzburg, Styria, Carinthia, Carniola, the Bukovina

Grand Prince of Transylvania

Margrave of Moravia

*Duke of Upper & Lower Silesia, Modena, Parma, Piacenza, Guastalla,
Auschwitz, Zator, Teschen, Friuli, Ragusa, Zara*

Princely Count of Habsburg, Tyrol, Kyburg, Gorizia, Gradisca

Prince of Trent, Brixen

Margrave of Upper & Lower Lusatia, in Istria

Count of Hohenems, Feldkirch, Bregenz, Sonnenberg, etc.

Lord of Trieste, Kotor, the Wendish March

Grand Voivode of the Voivodship of Serbia, etc. etc.

Franz Joseph I's titles after 1867, some of which are more in the nature
of brave assertions than indicators of practical ownership

Contents

Contents

Contents

Maps

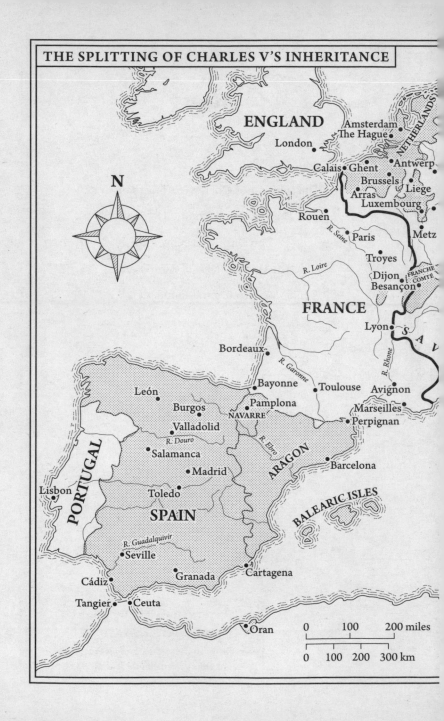

THE SPLITTING OF CHARLES V'S INHERITANCE

N

ENGLAND

NETHERLANDS

Amsterdam
The Hague
London
Antwerp
Calais Ghent
Brussels
Liège
Arras
Luxembourg
Rouen
Metz
R. Seine Paris
Troyes
FRANCHE-
Dijon COMTÉ
Besançon

FRANCE

R. Loire

Lyon

S A V

Bordeaux

R. Garonne

Bayonne Toulouse Avignon

Pamplona Marseilles
León NAVARRE Perpignan
Burgos
Valladolid
R. Douro R. Ebro ARAGON
Salamanca
Madrid Barcelona

PORTUGAL

Toledo BALEARIC ISLES

SPAIN

Lisbon

R. Guadalquivir
Seville
Cádiz Granada Cartagena
Tangier Ceuta
Oran

| 0 | 100 | 200 miles |
| 0 | 100 | 200 | 300 km |

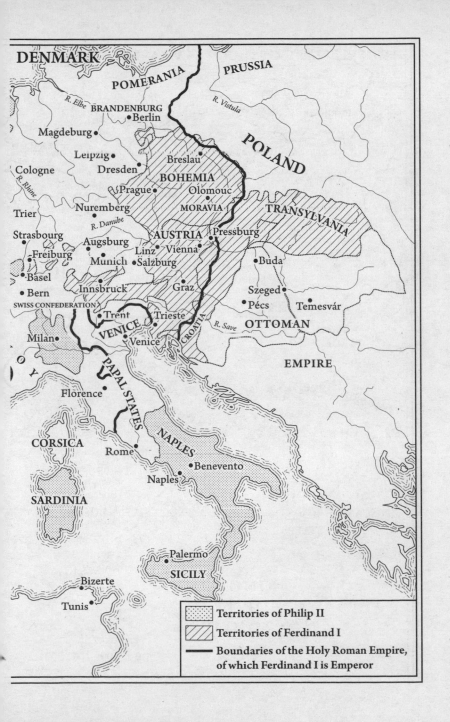

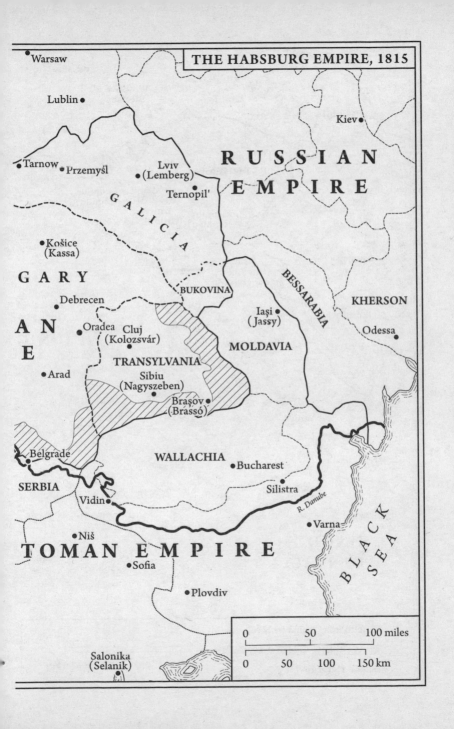

THE HABSBURG EMPIRE, 1815

Warsaw

Lublin

Kiev

Tarnow • Przemyśl • Lviv (Lemberg)

RUSSIAN

Ternopil'

EMPIRE

G A L I C I A

Košice (Kassa)

BUKOVINA

BESSARABIA

KHERSON

G A R Y

Debrecen

Iaşi (Jassy)

Odessa

A N E

Oradea • Cluj (Kolozsvár)

MOLDAVIA

E

TRANSYLVANIA

Arad

Sibiu (Nagyszeben)

Braşov (Brassó)

Belgrade

WALLACHIA

Bucharest

SERBIA

Silistra

Vidin

R. Danube

Varna

B L A C K

S E A

T O M A N E M P I R E

Niš

Sofia

Plovdiv

| 0 | 50 | 100 miles |
| 0 | 50 | 100 | 150 km |

Salonika (Selanik)

ANHALT
THURINGIA
SAXONY
Dresden
SILESIA
Wroclaw
(Breslau)
Kalisz

GERMAN EMPIRE

Prague
BOHEMIA

Silesia
Cracow

Český
Krumlov
(Krumau)
MORAVIA
Olomouc
(Olmütz)
Brno
(Brünn)

BAVARIA

Munich

Linz
UPPER
AUSTRIA
LOWER
AUSTRIA
Vienna

WÜRTTEMBERG

VORARLBERG
SWITZ.

Innsbruck
SALZBURG
STYRIA
Graz
Budapest

HUNG

TYROL
CARINTHIA

LOMBARDY

VENETIA

Venice
Trieste
GORIZIA
AUSTRIAN LITTORAL
CARNIOLA

Zagreb

CROATIA – SLAVONIA

EMILIA

SAN
MARINO

MARCHES

TUSCANY

KINGDOM
OF ITALY

LATIUM

ABRUZZI E
MOLISE
Rome

A D R I A T I C
Zadar
DALMATIA

S E A

BOSNIA-
HERZEGOVINA

Sarajevo

MONTENEGRO
Cetinje

Shkoder

Cisleithania – ruled from Vienna	
Transleithania – ruled from Budapest	
Bosnia-Herzegovina	

0   50   100 miles

0   50   100   150 km

THE DUAL MONARCHY

Warsaw

KHOLM

Lublin

Kielce

VOLHYNIA

Kiev

RUSSIAN

L'viv
(Lemberg)

GALICIA

EMPIRE

PODOLIA

BESSARABIA

BUKOVINA

KHERSON

Iași

Chișinău
(Kishinev)

Odessa

ARY

Cluj
(Kolozsvár)

N

Brașov
(Brassó)

ROMANIA

Belgrade

Bucharest

SERBIA

BLACK
SEA

BULGARIA

Sofia

KOSOVO

OTTOMAN EMPIRE

Edirne
(Adrinople)

SELANIK

EDIRNE

Istanbul

Salonika
(Selanik)

Bursa

Introduction

Danubia is a history of the huge swathes of Europe which accumulated in the hands of the Habsburg family. The story runs from the end of the Middle Ages to the end of the First World War, when the Habsburgs' empire fell to pieces and they fled.

Through cunning, dimness, luck and brilliance the Habsburgs had an extraordinarily long run. All empires are in some measure accidental, but theirs was particularly so, as sexual failure, madness or death in battle tipped a great pile of kingdoms, dukedoms and assorted marches and counties into their laps. They found themselves ruling territories from the North Sea to the Adriatic, from the Carpathians to Peru. They had many bases scattered across Europe, but their heartland was always the Danube, the vast river that runs through modern Upper and Lower Austria, their principal capital at Vienna, then Bratislava, where they were crowned kings of Hungary, and on to Budapest, which became one of their other great capitals.

For more than four centuries there was hardly a twist in Europe's history to which they did not contribute. For millions of modern Europeans the language they speak, the religion they practise, the appearance of their city and the boundaries of their country are disturbingly reliant on the squabbles, vagaries and afterthoughts of Habsburgs whose names are now barely remembered. They defended Central Europe against wave upon wave of Ottoman attacks. They intervened decisively against Protestantism. They came to stand – against their will – as champions of tolerance in a nineteenth-century Europe driven mad by ethnic nationalism. They developed marital or military relations with pretty much every part of Europe they did not already own. From

most European states' perspective, the family bewilderingly
swapped costumes so many times that they could appear as everything from rock-like ally to something approaching the Antichrist.
Indeed, the Habsburgs' influence has been so multifarious and
complex as to be almost beyond moral judgement, running
through the entire gamut of human behaviours available.

In the first half of the sixteenth century the family seemed to
come close – as the inheritances heaped up so crazily that designers of coats of arms could hardly keep up – to ruling the whole
of Europe, suggesting a 'Chinese' future in which the continent
would become a single unified state. As it was, the Emperor
Charles V's supremacy collapsed, under assault from innumerable
factors, his lands' accidental origins swamping him in contradictory needs and demands. In 1555, Charles was obliged much
against his will to break up his enormous inheritance, with one
half going to his son, Philip, based in his new capital of Madrid,
and the other going to his brother, Ferdinand, based in Vienna. At
this break-point I follow the story of Ferdinand's descendants,
although the Madrid relatives continue to intrude now and then
until their hideous implosion in 1700.

While writing my last book, *Germania*, I would sometimes find
myself in a sort of trance of anxiety, knowing that it was based on
a sleight of hand. With a few self-indulgent exceptions I kept its
geographical focus inside the boundaries of the current Federal
Republic of Germany. This was necessary for a coherent narrative,
but historically ridiculous. Indeed, the structure humiliatingly
mocked my main point: that 'Germany' was a very recent creation
and only a hacked-out part of the chaos of small and medium
feudal states which had covered much of Europe. These hundreds
of squabbling jurisdictions existed under the protective framework
of the Holy Roman Emperors, who ruled, with admittedly only
sputtering success, for a millennium. For the last three hundred and
fifty years of the Empire's existence, the Emperor was almost
always the senior member of the Habsburg family. He had this role
because he personally ruled immense tracts of land, indeed at dif-

ferent times owning parts or all of nineteen modern European countries.* This meant that he was unique in having a large enough personal financial and military base to be plausible as Emperor. But it also meant that he was often distracted: responsible for great blocks of territory inside the Holy Roman Empire (such as modern Austria and the Czech Republic) but also for unrelated places such as Croatia, say, and Mexico. This distraction, it can be argued, was the key motor for Europe's political history.

The Habsburg story, of Europe's most persistent and powerful dynastic family ruling the world of *Germania* from bases which were in fact well outside the modern state of Germany, was just too complex to be alluded to except in passing in the earlier book. The Habsburgs' influence across Europe was overwhelming, but often the 'great events' of the continent's history were generated as much by their uselessness or apparent prostration as by any actual family initiative. Indeed it is quite striking how baffled or inadequate many of the Emperors were, and yet an almost uncountable heap of would-be carnivorous rivals ended up in the dustbin while the Habsburgs just kept plodding along. Through unwarranted luck, short bursts of vigour and events often way outside their control they held on until their defeat by Napoleon. Moving fast, they then cunningly switched the title of Emperor so it referred to what could now be called 'the Habsburg Empire', meaning just the family's personal holdings, itself still the second largest European state after Russia. They kept going for a further, rather battered century, until final catastrophe as one of the defeated Central Powers in the First World War. The aftershocks from the in many ways accidental end of this accidental empire continue to the present. I allude to some of these in the text, but effectively the narrative ends in 1918 as the different parts of the Empire go their own ways.

---

* In alphabetical order: Austria, Belgium, Croatia, the Czech Republic, France, Germany, Hungary, Italy, Liechtenstein, Luxembourg, the Netherlands, Poland, Romania, Serbia, Slovakia, Slovenia, Spain, Switzerland, and Ukraine plus briefly the entire Spanish overseas empire. The family also came to own Portugal and its empire as well as, more permanently, Spain and its empire through Charles V's son, Philip.

This is a less sunny book than *Germania*. Visiting cities in the Rhineland, say, it is clear that however damaged they were in the twentieth century (both physically and morally) they remain great historical urban spaces filled with Germans. Their inhabitants can fully acknowledge complicity in the horrors of 1933–45 while also drawing a line connecting themselves and much older history. The great majority of Germans also escaped the impact of Soviet occupation, making their period of trauma very much shorter. The memory of the prosperity and solidity of the summer of 1914 was active for many West Germans in the late 1940s, who could go about their normal lives once more. For the inhabitants of much of the former Habsburg Empire there was no such reprieve, forced at irregular intervals during the century to endure massacres, migrations, invasions, terror and Babylonian exercises in state building and rebuilding.

Emerging from these burned-over zones in the 1990s, the descendants of the survivors had only the weakest links with the Empire whose architectural remnants still surrounded them. The narrowly thwarted plan in 2011 to demolish the last remnants of the ancient Golden Rose Synagogue in Lviv to make way for a hotel is only the most extreme instance of a numbness about the past that afflicts much of the former Empire. Scattered from the western Czech Republic to beyond the Carpathians there are towns where effectively the entire populations are post-1945 settlers. What would it take for Romanians to view abandoned German villages as part of their patrimony, or for Ukrainians to cherish former Polish churches? What a visitor can view as picturesque, a local can view with loathing or (a distinct improvement) indifference. Inevitably these tensions and discontinuities have an impact on the book's text.

The degree to which one can enjoy places that have suffered such fates is obviously a problem. But in four years of travelling around the territories of the old Empire I have never stopped feeling that I was on a mission to convey to readers why so many of these towns and cities – still in many cases hidden from English-speakers, even with the Cold War long gone – stand at the heart of Europe and the continent's experience, both for good and ill, and how fascinating they remain. By understanding something of their history before 1918 we can actively reclaim what the later totalitarian regimes wished to erase for ever: the plural, anarchic, polyglot Europe once supervised in a dizzying blend of ineptitude, viciousness and occasional benignity by the Habsburg family.

In October 2008 there was a football match in the UEFA Champions League between Chelsea FC and CFR Cluj. Chelsea fans flying into Transylvania for the game thought it would be hilarious to dress up in capes and plastic fangs and duly got off the plane lurching around, flapping their arms and putting on funny accents ('*Ach*, the cheeeldren of the night – I hear their call!' and so on). In an interview on a British radio station the next day, a memorably outraged Cluj disc jockey spluttered in perfect English (albeit – fair play – with a slightly funny accent) about how this was a national disgrace, an insult to his people, how Dracula had been the invention 'merely of some Irish novelist' and how vampirism was quite unknown in Transylvania.

All this was true enough, but the interview has hung in my mind ever since because of my own severe anxiety that I am myself merely a Chelsea fan with plastic fangs stumbling off the plane. The former Habsburg lands are places where a principal battlefield has been the interpretation of history. Indeed the very idea of the study of history has been fuelled by animosities and fantasies about ethnic, religious and class privileges. For me to enter this highly charged arena is, I am fully aware, foolish. It is very easy to be contemptuous of someone else's nationalism and unaware of one's own. The extraordinarily toxic legacy of the Empire's obsession with linguistics, archaeology, ethnography, sigillography, numismatics, cartography and so on makes me feel, in my darker moods, that the spread of these subjects and the use to which they were put was nothing but a disaster for Central Europe and that academics more than anyone else are (with help from priests) some of the greatest villains. Indeed, in comparison with academics, the politicians and military men were mere puppets, with even Hitler simply a disgusting by-product of various poisonous Viennese nationalist and scientific teachings.

The stakes have been so high because each linguistic group has obsessively picked over its past not merely out of a wish to entertain itself with fancy-that facts about ancestors, but to use it as the key weapon in establishing its ascendancy over other groups. While the Hungarians poured resources into charting their grand ancestry to somewhere out on the Asian steppe and in 1896 celebrated the thousandth anniversary of their arrival in Europe, Romanian academics in parallel scoured excavations for evidence that they were themselves the true owners of the same region, the descendants of soldiers and settlers from the Roman army (even inventing their country's name to make this point). What should have been harmless, indeed loopy, antiquarianism became instead the motive force behind terrible events, the least harmful being the abuse shouted by Romanians during anti-Hungarian rallies in the last years of the Empire, 'Go back to Asia!' Of course, the end logic of this rhetoric was to highlight those groups – Jews, Gypsies – who had no 'home', and the break-up of the Habsburg Empire into bitter nationalist mini-states in 1918 immediately created a highly threatening situation for anyone caught in the overlaps.

Parts of this book are devoted to picking over the truly horrible consequences of these nationalisms, but this does not mean I have some nostalgic wish to return to the time of the Empire. That would be meaningless. Intellectually it seems much better to acknowledge the substantial foul streak within modernity, without dreaming of a return to some aristocratic world lacking newspapers or mass literacy. After all, a vast number of these terrible ideas flowered *within* the Habsburg Empire, which can in that sense be blamed, but then so did the intellectual means to fight them (from Zionism, to anarchism, to the understanding of the unconscious).

A related purpose in writing this book was also to dramatize the sheer awfulness of living in Central Europe for some much-earlier periods, when extreme, savage violence to the point of near-total depopulation did damage of a kind not unrelated to that of the twentieth century. Such ferocity has been generally alien to the 'home' experiences of western Europeans, although they have of course themselves blithely carried out actions of comparable ferocity on other continents. To see Europe itself as an arena for slavery, punishment raids, forcible resettlement, piracy and religiously sanctioned public mutilation and execution is, to say the least, interesting. I hope I have written about it with sufficient understanding not to be offensive, but also to make it clear that such fates are *central* to Europe's story and not rooted in some mere weird 'eastern' barbarism.

In the summer of 1463 the King of Bosnia, Stephen Tomašević, was besieged by the army of the Ottoman ruler Mehmet II in the fortress of Ključ. Eventually the King surrendered under agreement of safe conduct. But once in Mehmet's hands Stephen and his entourage were killed and the surviving Bosnian nobility made into galley-slaves. The Ottoman view was that the entire Bosnian ruling class had lost its function and should be liquidated – Bosnia's new role as a small eyalet (province) in the Ottoman Empire was permanent and final. The safe conduct had been offered to a king, but now he had become a mere subject and could be disposed of at will. Indeed Bosnia, a respectable medieval kingdom, lost its independence for over five centuries. Poland was another famous example. When, in a series of negotiations of breathtaking coldness at the end of the eighteenth century, the Habsburgs, Prussians and Russians decided to split Poland between them, the intention was that this would be for ever, with the very name of Poland disappearing beneath the administrative inventions of 'West Prussia', 'Western Russia' and 'Galicia and Lodomeria'. Poland's new owners cooperated in the killing, rendition or imprisonment of anyone who threatened the new arrangement.

An intermittent theme of Central European history is this very high level of violent uncertainty, an uncertainty that could lead to an entire elite being wiped out. This has rarely been the western European or English-speakers' story. France, for example, has avoided successful invasion for most of its existence and has almost always been ruled by French people. The political decisions of

most English-speaking countries have always been taken from
positions of remarkable security. The Habsburg lands, however,
were always vulnerable on almost every frontier, with dozens of
easy and well-posted invasion routes. Allies became enemies and
a long-somnolent border zone could go critical overnight. The
Habsburgs' principal purpose was therefore military: from its origins to its collapse their empire was a machine to resist its tough
neighbours and to control its often truculent inhabitants. When not
fighting, it was preparing to fight. The idea, propagated particularly in the period just before 1914, that the Empire was somehow
backward and ineffectual in a cake-and-waltzes way was untrue.
The dynasty was never anything other than narrow-mindedly ruthless and harsh in its wish to hold itself together against all-comers.
The seemingly genial, bewhiskered old Franz Joseph's obsession
was with the Empire as a vast military organism: his life was a
series of parades, war-games, medal ceremonies and arguments
about the huge funds needed for his army. All of this would have
been familiar to his predecessors two hundred or even four hundred years earlier. A further bout of absolute insecurity was always
round the corner and the Habsburgs were endlessly monitoring
their neighbours' military preparedness and mood-swings. There
were plenty of examples of related states whose rulers had blun-
dered and then been expunged. The Habsburgs indeed themselves
frequently finessed the setbacks of others to their territorial advantage before themselves taking decisions which resulted in their
own disappearance and partition in 1918.

It is important to remember just how vague much rule over
Europe was until mass literacy, telegraphs and railways started to
tie together regions and countries. The Habsburgs loved to look at
maps, genealogies and heraldic shields, making sweeping hand
gestures over these symbolic shorthands for their ownership, but
there is little reason to believe such gestures had much substance.
Apart from a few mountain and forest communities, nobody was
left completely alone, but the sense of obligation to Vienna was
often remote and convoluted, with innumerable local, noble and
religious privileges making a mockery of modern dreams of uni-

tary efficiency. Many histories tend to present a narrative angled from the perspective of the ruler. Most dramatically this is expressed in the term 'rebellion', a word which presupposes failure (by definition: if it succeeds then it is a change of dynasty). It is too easy to see a narrative where any rebellion is an annoyance, a drain on resources, a desperate piece of backwardness, and so on. But this is to take a man wearing a crown in Vienna too seriously and I hope to make it clear just how many perfectly reasonable arguments against Habsburg rule there were. Indeed, at one point or another (and repeatedly in Hungary) virtually everybody took a turn at being 'disloyal' and this should be a valuable clue. Joseph II's war with the Turks went so badly wrong in 1788 because the Hungarian nobles would not supply him with food, because they hated him and thought he was a tiresome creep. As his vast army fell apart and he raged impotently, it is impossible from a world-historical point of view not to feel a bit sorry for him, but Europe is filled with groups of all kinds who are annoyingly insubordinate, and they should be celebrated a bit more.

One much-loved figure in so many anecdotes and novels is the Hungarian minor nobleman who lives only to drink and hunt, and refuses to open any letters or telegrams he receives, on the grounds that they are mere insolent intrusions into the life of a gentleman. The Habsburgs were always dealing with variants on such characters: defenders of feudal rights, stubborn communes, bizarre religious groups and obstreperous guildsmen. Even great aristocrats might plump for the high-risk pleasures of treason with the Turks. Generations of Viennese officials would bang their heads on their cherry-wood desktops with fury: *why* won't these people just *do* as they're *told*? But theirs was just a sickness generated by too many maps, charts and budget projections. A possible novelty of this book is that it attempts to avoid seeing Vienna as the clearing-house for all right-minded political, religious, social or strategic thinking. A Styrian farmer, Transylvanian serf or Adriatic pirate each saw Vienna in a different way, and that view was not necessarily wrong.

*

Danubia is designed to be read quite separately from *Germania*. Naturally it has to cover some of the same ground, and I deal with the overlap by using different angles and examples, but there are a number of basic definitions about how Europe functioned via the Holy Roman Empire which will need to be repeated.

There are three assurances I need to give. This is *not* a dynastic family history. You will not be obliged to read through endless marriage treaties, dusty gossip about what an archduke said to another archduke or how so-and-so never got on with her sister-in-law. This is a book about some interesting things that specific rulers did, and sometimes these undoubtedly involve marriage treaties (too often involving people called either Maria or Charles), but I try to avoid the sort of hearsay and harpsichordy, *Quality Street* royal chit-chat which has sometimes blighted consideration of the Habsburgs. I have dumped all the hand-kissing, beauty spots, heel-clicking and discreet glances over fluttered fans ('Oh, you are too forward, Count'), and I hope this will win me some gratitude.

This is also *not* a book which attempts to define specific ethnic groups by some clutch of imagined characteristics. You will not find sentences opening with assertions such as 'Like that fiery yet noble spice they tend so lovingly, known the world over as "paprika", the Hungarian people are . . .'. No specific nationality will give you the very clothes off their backs; none has natural melancholy; none is instinctively musical; no linguistic groups are implacable enemies yet also sure friends; and absolutely nobody gives herself with a self-immolating urgency rooted in her people's fatalism. This sort of rubbish has been going on for centuries – Franz Ferdinand even had a helpful list of national attributes over his desk to remind him – and it has to stop. An immediate improvement can be made to Europe's existence if we restrict qualities such as being laughter-filled, moody, built for love, quick to find fault and so on to individuals rather than entire populations, avoiding the associated ludicrous ethnic implication that whole cities must be packed with the musically gifted or valleys swift-to-anger. I started to feel vehemently about this while writing *Germania*. I listened to so many British and American friends stating as axiomatic that Germans have no sense of humour, when I had myself just come from yet another *Bierkeller* where most of the occupants were laughing so much they had turned mauve and their limbs were about to fall off; which does not, of course, mean that all Germans do in fact have a sense of humour.

And, finally, this is *not* an attempt at an exhaustive guide to Central Europe. I have restricted myself simply to writing about some of the things I personally find fascinating. There is a reasonably clear narrative, but inevitably there are huge numbers of subjects I hardly touch. There is a fair amount on music, for example, but the text reflects my love of Haydn and Wolf rather than my merely remote, ignorant admiration for Beethoven or Bruckner. This will annoy some readers and I apologize, but there seems no point in dutifully faking up topics to take up scarce space that would then threaten more interesting material with excision. Similarly, some emperors are simply more alluring than others and I have preferred to spend time on a fascinating handful rather than colour in all the duds too.

I feel quite dazed by my good fortune in being able to write this book. I have been obsessed with the cultures of Central Europe for most of my adult life, but to have a legitimate excuse to wander everywhere from Bohemia to Ukraine and read, think, talk and write about so many subjects for so long has been an absurd privilege. I very much hope that I can convey something of what I felt when at regular intervals I found myself in the magnificently restored buffet of Budapest's Eastern Station, chewing on a McChickwich and wondering what adventure would befall me next.

Place names

The naming of towns has always been a key weapon for establishing dominance over a region. The name you use for a town can
imply either that you have simply a specific ethnicity or that you
are making an aggressive or nostalgic political point. A good
modern example is the Transylvanian town of Cluj-Napoca. Cluj is
the Romanian form; Cluj-Napoca was faked up in the 1970s as
Napoca had been the name of a Roman town on the same site;
Klausenburg is how Germans refer to it; Klazin in Yiddish; Kolozsvár in Hungarian. They all have related roots but with very
different political weights. A Hungarian would say that to refer to
Kolozsvár is simply to give the name in Magyar – but a Romanian
would view this as an irredentist provocation, the rejection of rule
by Romania and a sentimental wish to return to the good old days
when it was a major Hungarian town. The Romanian is right to
bristle, but not necessarily. A similar story applies to the ancient
town of Pozsony, where the Hungarian kings used to be crowned,
known as Preßburg in German. The Czechs and Slovaks grabbed
Pozsony and in 1919 fabricated the name Bratislava, thereby
making it no longer German or Hungarian. Perhaps the worst
instance is the way that the Czech Republic is obliged to have such
an unsatisfactory name for itself because the obvious alternative,
Bohemia and Moravia, is impossibly besmirched by its Nazi usage
during the 'protectorate'.

   There is no way out of this minefield: what is now Lviv can be
Lemberg, Lemberik, Lwów, Lvov; what is now Ivano-Frankivsk can
be Stanislau, Stanisławów, Stanislavov – each of these variants provoke different forms of pain for different excluded groups. So I will
use the modern official name in each case in as bland a fashion as
possible and without implying either fondness or aversion.

   There is a lot of very unfamiliar historical geography in this
book. Units such as Carniola or Upper Lusatia existed for centuries
and need to be thought of as having a quite startling tensile
strength, with their own traditions, shields, aristocratic families

and duties towards their rulers. A famous example is the Kingdom of Galicia and Lodomeria, viewed by Poles and many others as a terrible colonial disgrace and entirely illegitimate, and yet lasting nearly a hundred and fifty years – in other words for a longer period than a united German state has existed. The mental exercise needed to think of Galicia not as a doomed and nutty fly-by-night but as a durable reality for many generations of its inhabitants is a crucial precondition to thinking about Europe's history.

Many older political entities seem small now, but most of Central Europe was made up of such units until the nineteenth century. Indeed, until the unification of Germany and Italy, somewhere like Switzerland looked fairly chunky. If Europeans in 1900 could have had a sneak preview of the continent's appearance in 2000 they would have been astonished, not just by the re-emergence of formerly independent states such as Poland and Ireland (which would have then seemed safely under the heel of superpowers), but by such fantastical new creations as Slovakia and Macedonia. These last would have had simply no meaning in 1900, one being a mere highland area of northern Hungary, the other tucked into a few folds of the Ottoman Empire. But just as striking would be the disappearance of such medieval stalwarts as the County of Görz or the Duchy of Teschen, now almost unlocatable under fresh frontiers. It is not an exercise to everyone's taste, but this book is meant to urge its readers to think about Europe as a place with strange and various borders, multiple possible outcomes and with geography and ownership up for grabs. The maps should help, but for a truly dizzying vision of how twentieth-century Central Europe might have been refixed it is worth looking at pages 444–5.

The Habsburg family

Rather than defeat the reader with a family tree which would look like an illustration of the veins and arteries of the human body drawn by a poorly informed maniac, I thought it better to start with this summary of just the heads of the family, so the sequence is clear. I give the year each ruler became Emperor and the year the ruler died. It all looks very straightforward and natural, but of course the list hides away all kinds of back-stabbing, reckless subdivision, hatred, fake piety and general failure, which can readily be relegated to the main text.

To save everyone's brains I have simplified all titles. Some fuss in this area is inevitable but I will cling under almost all circumstances to a single title for each character. To give you a little glimpse of the chaos, the unattractive Philip 'the Handsome' was Philip I of Castile, Philip II of Luxemburg, Philip III of Brabant, Philip IV of Burgundy, Philip V of Namur, Philip VI of Artois as well as assorted Is, IIs, IIIs and so on for other places. So when I just refer to Philip 'the Handsome' you should feel grateful and briefly ponder the pedantic horror-show you are spared. Perhaps the most significant omission is the important one that in their critical roles as kings of Hungary and kings of Bohemia some rulers had different numbers – so Rudolf II was Rudolf I in Hungary, and Charles VI was Charles III (or III. Károly). The style given therefore is always as Emperor, whether as Holy Roman Emperor (until 1806) or Emperor of Austria (from 1804 to 1918).

The list below shows that it is not possible to have a consistent treatment of actual names. To call Charles V Karl or Carlos would be self-defeating, as he is famous in English as Charles V. Maria Theresia is always Maria Theresa in English. For much of his reign Franz Joseph (the '-ph' rather than '-f' is in the German too) was known to English-speakers as an Anglicized Francis Joseph, but as an enemy ruler in the First World War he was Germanized back to Franz, simply because it sounded worse. The same applies to his successor, Charles I, who has always been Karl I. By using criteria remote from rationality, Karl I was beatified by the Catholic Church in 2004 and is now called the Blessed Karl of Austria, the first and – it is a fair assumption – last member of his family to be en route to sainthood.

Until 1806 'the Empire' means the vast Holy Roman Empire, of which the senior member of the Habsburg family was almost always elected Emperor. He ruled the 'Habsburg lands' or 'Habsburg possessions' personally and quite separately. Even these lands were far less coherent than they appear, with much of them in practice under the control of various aristocrats and religious enterprises and sometimes embarrassingly small bits actually 'owned' by the family. 'Rule' often meant navigating through a wilderness of privileges, favours, exemptions and ossified feudal niceties. Important parts of these personal lands were within the Holy Roman Empire, but others (such as Hungary) were not. 'Imperial troops' were therefore forces sanctioned by the vote of the Holy Roman Empire, and were not the same as the Habsburgs' own armies. For anyone reading this under the age of fifty or so, 'the Empire' and 'Imperial' will immediately summon up visions of highly organized evil from *Star Wars*. Indeed, the recent revival of interest in the history of the Holy Roman Empire might be attributed to this subconscious link. But it is important to remember whenever these terms are used that the human Empire was a few notches down from its space-based rival in efficiency, motivation and wickedness, although the two could certainly swap notes about the irritating way they both seem so prone to needless defeat.

Frederick III (1452–1493) was succeeded, after a period of joint rule, by his son, **Maximilian I** (1493–1519). He was succeeded by his grandson **Charles V** (1519–1558). Charles V decided to split his unmanageable inheritance: the Spain-based branch of the family under the leadership of his son, Philip II, went its own way while the eastern lands fell to Charles' brother, **Ferdinand I** (1558–1564). He was succeeded by his son **Maximilian II** (1564–1576), who was succeeded in turn by his son **Rudolf II** (1576–1612). After a coup Rudolf's brother **Matthias** (1612–1619) briefly became

Emperor. Neither Rudolf nor Matthias had children so the head of the family then became their cousin **Ferdinand II** (1619–1637), who was succeeded in easy stages by a straight generational dynastic run of eldest surviving sons: **Ferdinand III** (1637–1657), **Leopold I** (1657–1705) and **Joseph I** (1705–1711). Following the sudden, premature death of Joseph, his brother took over as **Charles VI** (1711–1740). Charles had no surviving male children, meaning that in the face of immense quantities of faithlessness and bloodshed, his daughter **Maria Theresa** (ruler of the Habsburg lands 1740–1780) battled to inherit a number of titles while her husband **Franz I** (1745–1765), after an embarrassing gap, became Emperor. This re-founded the dynasty as the House of Habsburg-Lorraine. Their son inherited in the normal way as **Joseph II** (1765–1790) and was succeeded by his brother, **Leopold II** (1790–1792), who was in turn succeeded by his son **Franz II** (1792–1806), who switched from being Holy Roman Emperor to Emperor of Austria, reset the numbering and started calling himself **Franz I** (1804–1835). He was succeeded by his son **Ferdinand I** (1835–1848), who was set aside in 1848 in a coup that brought to power his nephew, **Franz Joseph I** (1848–1916). After complex and famous dynastic setbacks he was succeeded by his great-nephew **Karl I** (1916–1918). Although Hungary was run until 1944 as a kingdom which claimed to be a regency on behalf of the Habsburgs, it is fair to say that when Karl stepped down in 1918 the dynasty left the stage.

CHAPTER ONE

Tombs, trees and a swamp

The southern Hungarian town of Pécs is as good a place as any to start a history of Habsburg Europe. It is hard to believe that it has ever been anything other than a genial provincial town – the unfortunate butt of wider international events, but not a place to initiate anything much. It is the last place heading south before the landscape gets terminally dusty, glum and thinly settled, so it has an oasis or frontier atmosphere and a sense that the cappuccinos are a bit hard-won. The scattering of great, much-mutilated buildings dotted about Pécs have all been repeatedly patched up in the wake of various disasters and the main square's charisma is much enhanced by the gnarled bulk of an endlessly hacked-about mosque converted unconvincingly into a church when the Turkish rulers surrendered the town's smoking ruins in 1686.

There is one quite extraordinary survival: a necropolis from when Pécs was a wine colony called Sopianae, capital of the Roman province of Pannonia Valeria. The most famous of these tombs was only uncovered in the late eighteenth century and features a set of frescos of scenes from the Bible. These were painted with the colour and sensibility of a mildly gifted nine-year-old child but rescued from inanity by the pictures' age and mournful patchiness. There are Adam and Eve, Noah and his Ark, St Peter and St Paul all somehow clinging on – bits falling off here and there – through fourteen hundred years of life underground.

When the necropolis was built in the fourth century Sopianae must have been a fairly anxious place because of the nearness of the very restive Imperial frontier. It was not a strongpoint in any

sense and if one of the Danube forts had given way then the news
would presumably have reached Sopianae via a terrified horseman
galloping only a few yards ahead of large numbers of terrifying
horsemen. The people living here were Latinized, Christian Germanic Imperial subjects and had been part of the empire for four
centuries. The very term 'wine colony' obviously sounds cheerful.
There were baths, an aqueduct, a basilica – the usual Roman fittings – and it perhaps had a jaunty *Asterix*-like atmosphere.

One element in the Pécs necropolis is gripping not because it
features pictures or any curious decoration, but because of something it lacks. One tomb, reasonably dated to about AD 400, had
been prepared for plastering, but never plastered: somebody had
gone to considerable expense to build it for a wealthy relative, but
then left it incomplete. This is just speculation, but more than plausibly the tomb was left in this state because this was the year when
Sopianae ceased to exist. Everyone involved with commissioning
or building that tomb either fled or was killed or enslaved by Hun
raiders. The next reference to the town is in a document some half
a millennium later and there is not even a single brick that can be
dated to after 400. Centuries of rain and soil accumulation buried
the tombs.

The annihilation of this part of Roman Europe is the founding
background to everything that follows. What would become the
southern zone of the Habsburg Empire was for centuries a world
without writing, without towns, with only residual, short-distance
trade, without Christianity. Some people probably always lived in
the ruins of towns because walls provided some security and shelter, but the water-systems and markets that had allowed them to
exist disappeared. There was nobody who could repair an aqueduct
once it broke so there must have been some final day when the
cisterns simply stopped filling. Ephemeral chieftains might use a
surviving chunk of a grand building as a backdrop for a semi-
realized palace, but nobody knew how to dress stone and therefore
nothing new could be built. For centuries the only towns were
wooden palisaded structures protected by a ditch. It was against
this backdrop that the notional ancestors of Central Europe's

modern nations appeared, wandering in from the east in what must have been pretty ripe-smelling military caravans.

Some clues about the fate of Europe after the Romans left can be found in Bautzen, in south-east Saxony. The town sits in gloomy woods and hills – and indeed is itself so gloomy that the great chasm that dominates it soaks up all colour, making even as lurid a bird as a jay flying into it go oddly monochrome. The chasm is created by the River Spree, a long way yet from its more famous role in Berlin. Even on a map, Bautzen looks an unlucky place – with mountain passes to the south which would tend to channel armies passing west or east into its vicinity. And indeed, in a crowded field, Bautzen must have a fair claim to be the most frequently burnt down place in the region, both on purpose and through accident.

Bautzen is interesting in all kinds of ways. It is part of the area known as Upper Lusatia, once ruled by the Habsburg Emperor (there is still a fetching image of Rudolf II decorating a watch-tower) but given to the ruler of Saxony as a thank-you during the Thirty Years War in 1635. At a jumbled linguistic crook in Central Europe's geography, Upper Lusatia was a partly Germanic, partly Slavic territory which would find itself inside the borders of modern Germany. Because of this most of Upper Lusatia's inhabitants were sheltered from the massive ethnic cleansing that turned neighbouring Czechoslovakia and Poland monoglot in 1945. This accidentally preserved the old pattern, once common across the entire region, of German-speaking town-dwellers and Slav-speaking country-dwellers, in Upper Lusatia's case a small group known as the Sorbs. So Bautzen is also Budyšin and the Spree the Sprjewja.

The town's great value is in its origins – and what it says about the origins of the whole of Central Europe. This is an issue where the stakes could not be higher. Each nationality in Central Europe defines itself by being more *echt* than any other: as having a unique claim to ownership of the land through some superior martial talent or more powerful culture or, most importantly, from having arrived in a particular valley *first*. Objectively, the carbon-dating of your language-group's European debut would seem of interest only to a handful of mouldering antiquaries. But through the labours of these fusty figures, it has become everybody's concern – and a concern that has led to countless violent deaths.

This hunt for origins became obsessive in the nineteenth century as a literate and aggressive language-nationalism came to dominate Central Europe. Town squares filled up with statues of heroic, shaggy forebears and town halls became oppressively decorated with murals of the same forebears engaged in i) frowningly breasting a hill and looking down on the promised land; ii) engaging in some ceremony with a flag or sword to found a town; and iii) successfully killing everybody who was there already. Schools rang to the sound of children reciting heroic epics. This was at the same time a great efflorescence of European culture and a disaster as the twentieth century played out these early medieval fantasies using modern weapons.

The Bautzen region is so curious because it shows what was at stake in the Dark Ages in which all these nationalities could find their roots. Archaeological studies of Lusatia show that Germanic tribes lived here, comfortably outside the reach of the Roman Empire, from about 400 BC to AD 200, but that for some six centuries after that *no humans seem to have lived there at all*. It could of course be that these were humans who lived so simply that they no longer left burials, swords, pots, fort outlines or anything – but this seems implausible. For whatever reason there seem to have been very few or no people and the default forest cover which blanketed Europe grew back over earlier settlements, leaving nothing but wolves, bison and giant oxen to roam through the picturesque fog. The situation in Lusatia was extreme, but more broadly the population of much of inland Europe does seem to have collapsed. Barbarian raiders, Huns and others, who terminated Roman towns like Pécs seem to have also killed or driven off those living in the always quite small settlements north of the frontier.

In much of Central Europe trees are now merely a pretty adjunct to human habitation, although some thick cover remains in Bohemia and Slovakia. But the ancient tree cover used to be almost total except on very high, bleak land. If humans failed to cut the trees back then they would quickly return: a small settlement that failed through a bad harvest or through a massacre would vanish, its cleared land picked apart by millions of roots. The need to clear space and fight back the trees remained a major concern well into the Middle Ages, with lords offering land to peasants at a bargain rent if mattocks were needed (to clear tree roots), with the rent shooting up once the land could at last be ploughed. Even such famously grim and empty areas as the Hungarian Great Plain were smothered in trees.

The Germanic tribes which lived in a massive swathe from the North Sea to the Balkans seem to have seized up, retreated, diminished or moved to Britain, both because of attacks by Asian nomads and as a side-effect of the failure of the Roman Empire in the fifth century, as economic links frayed and vanished. A final major horror was the arrival in the mid-sixth century of plague. We have records of its devastating impact on the major towns of the eastern Mediterranean, but it clearly must have swept through trading routes deep into areas with none of the tradition of literacy that would have allowed the victims to record their own demise. There is a parallel with North America, where many tribal groups died of European diseases years before they were even in direct contact with Europeans. I remember a tiny, mournful display in a western Canadian museum, of moccasins and beads from inland Athabascans who all seem to have died, scattered unnoticed throughout the interior valleys. It is easy to imagine something very similar in the European interior, with plague following the thin trade routes up through the Balkans and settlements being destroyed and then their very existence smudged out by the relentless trees. The ease therefore with which small groups of Slavs, Magyars and Vlachs and others infiltrated Central Europe came from its sheer emptiness.

A striking glimpse into this untamed Europe can still be found in the Gemenc Forest in southern Hungary. When most of the Danube was reshaped and made navigable and predictable in the nineteenth century, the oxbows of the Gemenc region were left, both because they are so totally intractable and so they could be used as an archducal hunting ground. Arriving there on a hot summer day, it seemed placid enough. A helpful map on a board outside the forest marked out coloured trails and was neatly decorated with drawings of the forest's massive deer plus some imperious eagles and an oddly frisking wild boar up on its hind legs like a circus poodle. This schematic and rational exposition was already under threat though because the board was itself covered in dozens of twitching, buzzing beetles – fetchingly, half ultramarine and half copper – which skittered about all over the lettering. The sunlight flaring off the beetles already made things seem a bit peculiar and threatening, but this was nothing compared to the reality of the forest. Within moments the neatly marked paths became almost overwhelmed: human order giving way to nature run mad, a foetid dementia of plant life, with hoots, squeaks and grunts filling the air and everything cloaked in stifling semi-darkness by the old trees. Within minutes I had already come across an immense, completely out-of-control pond, its surface choked in millions of seeds and with frogs mucking about on floating debris. A further pond flooded the path and only a few hundred yards in I had to turn back. This was a riotous deciduous jungle of a kind that seemed more Brazilian than Hungarian. I could suddenly see why centuries of drainage courses, weirs, mattock-wielders, grazing animals, the ceaseless, boring, human patrol-work needed to create our societies, were much more important than mere fleeting political events. In the end I walked for several miles on top of an earth dam next to the forest (the dam itself a colossal response to the oxbows' periodic convulsive floods) and was rewarded with eagles, a brass-coloured doe of alarming size, a fox skeleton and a cowherd with his cattle and cowdog – but no boars. The lack of these noble animals could not detract from the extraordinary nature of the Gemenc Forest. Here was a small indication of what most river valleys must have been like in an era of very few humans. Just as the Ganges valley, now a burnt-brown treeless plain, used to be a tiger-filled mayhem of flooded, impassable forest, so much of lowland Europe was threatening to people and unusable. Most big European animals evolved for this habitat and would disappear along with it. But it was into a very swampy, tree-clogged and unrenovated world that small bands of warriors and their families began to infiltrate in the eighth century AD.

There is a particularly hysteria-edged frieze in the Western Bohemia Museum in Plzeň by V. Saff, carved in 1900, imagining the arrival of the ancient Czechs in a forest, torturing and killing their enemies, tying them to trees, strangling them. In the usual proto-Art-Nouveau style, the sculptor follows through on an ethnographic hunch that surprising numbers of the tribal womenfolk would be in their late teens and free of clothing. The sadism of the carving is oddly reckless and preserves the nationalist mania of its period: urging the Czechs to stop sitting around reading newspapers and sipping herbal liqueurs and instead to embrace the burly virtues of their forebears. In practice we do not of course have any sense at all of what these ancient Czechs were like and Saff may not be entirely wrong about their savagery: although occasions on which women with amazing breasts swung around a severed human head by its top-knot were probably infrequent.

Romanian nationalists cleverly trumped everybody by claiming descent from the Romans, inhabitants of the old province of Dacia. This messed up all the Slav groups and the Hungarians, who had between them established a fairly clear AD 600–900 arrival date. A feature of several Romanian towns is a copy of the Roman statue of Romulus and Remus being suckled by their adopted wolf mother. This bizarre gift was handed out by Mussolini in the early 1920s to suggest none too subtly that his own new empire had a racial ally, a fellow Child of Rome. There will be plenty more of this sort of stuff as the book progresses, but I hope it is already clear to every reader just how freakish and peculiar history's uses have been in the region.

But as was the case for everybody else, it seems in fact the Romanians arrived from elsewhere – probably from the more Latinized areas south of the Danube, modern Serbia or Croatia, which would explain why so rough and marginal an area of the old Roman Empire as Dacia should have kept its Latin flavour in an otherwise drastically changed region: it didn't. This unwelcome result should make all the rival nationalist historians throw up their hands in jokey horror, call it quits and have a non-ethnically specific drink together. If the Romanians have a mystic heartland that turns out actually to belong to another country then we may as well all just go home.

To take too strong an interest in this subject is to set out on the high road to madness. The extreme mobility of all these tribes is bewildering and the almost total lack of written records for centuries does not help. The overall picture seems to be a retreat by Germanic tribes into the west and the arrival of Slavic tribes, seemingly from a start-point in what is now eastern Poland, mixed in with further post-Hun invaders from various steppe tribes, from the Avars to the Magyars. Indeed, in a despairing variant, the elites of the original Croats and Serbs may have been speaking an Iranian language, which is the point where I think anybody sensible just gives up. Arrows drawn on maps build up into an astonishing spaghetti of population movement, charted through pot-fragments, house-post remnants and casual, perhaps frivolously made-up comments written down by poorly informed monks living centuries later and far away. The net result of these migrations can clearly be seen today. The ancestors of the Czechs settled in a region protected by a crescent of mountains (the Iron Mountains and the Bohemian Forest Mountains) that happened to shield them from German and Frankish predation. Their fellow Slavs in the north and south, the Saxons and the Carantanians, were destroyed by invading Germans and the survivors converted into German-speaking Christians, bequeathing only the names Saxony and Carinthia. Further east and south the early Moravians, Slovakians, Russians, Ukrainians, Lithuanians, Bulgars, Poles, Ruthenes, Croats and Serbs spread out (and in themselves had numerous further subdivisions which have since been erased), generally under Avar overlordship.

The Avars were fast-moving Asian nomads of a kind wearyingly familiar to anyone trying to settle down and earn an honest living in Central Europe. We know almost nothing about them at all.

They hit a high point when they besieged Constantinople in 626, but they were driven off by the Byzantines and settled in a broad swath from Bohemia to Bulgaria. The Avar khaganate in many ways exemplifies why the Dark Ages are so irritating – the Avars can be seen in tiny glimpses in chronicles or in a handful of surviving, utterly context-free decorative objects and yet for two centuries they were the main overlords directing Slav settlement in Central Europe. An Avar ambassador met Charlemagne at his court on the Rhine in 790 and agreed the border between the Frankish Empire and the Avar Empire, but this was clearly just a truce and the Franks defeated the Avars in a cataclysmic battle notable for the heaps of treasure handed out to Charlemagne's friends, a substantial shift of gold from the east to the long-denuded west. There is a final reference to the Avars in a chronicle in 822 but then the name simply disappears from the record. I would love to have some sense of what that Avar ambassador speaking with Charlemagne actually looked like – we don't even know what language he would have used or how he dressed. The Avars could have as readily been from Mars – and ultimately they vanished, dissolving into the Slavic population.

By the ninth century key elements in Central Europe were now in place. The evanescent Great Moravia was a Slavic confederation which managed to be both profoundly important and frustratingly vague – it is not even clear what lands it ruled, although it is fairly certain it did include modern Moravia and Slovakia and probably a circle of lands around that core. Czech nationalists have endlessly argued over this. It lasted only a few decades, but was culturally crucial as the home first of the beautiful and strange Glagolitic script which would render SIMON, for example, as something like

$$ \text{Ⱄ Ⰻ Ⰿ Ⱁ Ⱀ} $$

(the M seems particularly lovely in its general unsustainability) and then, thanks to the tireless Byzantine missionaries Cyril and Methodius, as the home of the first Slavic script – an alphabetic decision which has ever since decisively carved out a different zone, both in itself and as a signifier for allegiance to Orthodoxy.

Indeed the missionary work of this period in shifting a large block of Europe towards Constantinople and out of Rome's reach created a fault line with implications into the present.

Each attempt to settle down and create a lasting dynastic state and even a little economic growth was thwarted by the sheer motility of these Eurasian bands. There may not have been a large European population yet (the nearest approach to a town being simply a large armed camp or a cluster of buildings around a fortress) but those that were there remained willing to travel great distances and take great risks. Two threats prevented Central European coalescence, one from the west and one from the east.

Wandering peoples

Passau, on the Bavarian–Austrian border, is a town of such absurd scenic grandeur and geophysical significance that it seems a shame to find its streets lined only with little shops selling devotional trinkets and bird-whistles – the inhabitants should be cut from some more heroic cloth. Passau's fame stems from its location on a spit of land which at its tapered point joins together two monstrous rivers, the Danube and the Inn, the former all the way from a squashy meadow in Swabia, the latter from the Alps. There is also a third river, the extremely less impressive Ilz, which dribbles down from the north – making Passau 'the city of three rivers'. The great significance of the Ilz is that it comes down from the watershed of the forests on the edge of the Bohemian Forest Mountains to the north, just as the Inn comes down from the Swiss Alps, with the Danube itself heading straight west–east along the northern side of the Alps. This combination of converging waters shows there is a gap in the mountains, and it was from here that German-speaking Europe extruded into the Slavic lands to the east.

Bavaria, of which Passau is now the easternmost point, is one of those strange semi-kingdoms that has throughout its history come close to being a real and independent state but has always been subsumed or subverted. It has some of the same advantages of countries such as England or France in having a number of thorny borders. England's sea coasts and France's sea coasts and mountains have given their rulers a militarily happy situation and it has not been an accident that both these countries have been so hard to invade. This is entirely unlike most Central European states, which have been obliged militarily to turn round and round like a dizzy dog trying to defend its drinking bowl. Bavaria had coherence because of its impenetrable southern mountains and reasonably chunky eastern ones. It emerged from the Dark Ages as a well-run, Germanic, naturally wealthy place under the rule of the Agilolfing family. In the eighth century Bavaria stretched much further east than Passau and German-speaking colonists debouched into Tirol and Salzburg.

As so often in Bavaria's history, the country's wealth and security attracted envious eyes. On the face of it a safe distance away, Charlemagne on the Lower Rhine, a Frankish chieftain, had re-established through a sheer act of the imagination a direct link between himself and the Roman Empire that had collapsed in the west over three centuries before. His ambition, his court's pomp, wealth and learning, and his military success proclaimed the end of the Dark Ages and a new direction for Europe. Instead of being a shattered jigsaw of petty chieftainships and dubious Asiatic overlords, Europe would revive as a new Roman Empire re-founded with Charlemagne as emperor. The Bavarians and the Franks had fought each other a number of times, but in an astounding decade from 785 Charlemagne completed the conquest of the Saxons in the north, deposed the long-serving ruler of Bavaria, Tassilo, in the south and then destroyed the Avar Khaganate.

The snuffing-out of the Agilolfing family in Bavaria and the absorption of the whole region into Charlemagne's empire created a fresh eastward dynamic. Massacring, Germanizing and Christianizing their way east, the Franks created new marches and duchies, pushing back the Slavs so that by the mid-ninth century something not dissimilar to the modern language map existed, with much of Austria in Germanic hands. But before the linguistic patchwork settled into place there was one more, thoroughly startling intrusion.

The Magyars were not the last of the new arrivals in an already crowded and chaotic neighbourhood, but they were certainly one of the most spectacular. Chased out of their home in the Khazar khaganate the Magyars shifted ever further west until they hurtled into Europe with their innovative cavalry skills and entirely unrelated language. They caused mayhem, defeating the Bavarian and East Frank armies sent against them and raiding deep into France and Italy before finally and decisively being stopped in their tracks by the Emperor Otto I at the Battle of the Lech in 955.

The final Magyar raids have a somewhat nostalgic air to them – as though the older warriors could not resist calls to put the old band back together again. After being chased away by Otto I they abandoned raiding western Europe but continued to carve out an ever-larger territory for themselves, reinforced by fresh arrivals from Central Asia including many of their former enemies, the enjoyably named Pechenegs.

As usual with these groups it is impossible now to unpick the true circumstances of their arrival. Everyone has an automatic picture of streams of wagons filled with seer elders, opulent wives, lisping daughters and young sons practising with wooden swords on their own tiny ponies. This is at odds with the patently rather male-only, rugby-match atmosphere of the Magyar raids themselves. We will never know, for example, what balance of the settled population managed to escape: were those unable to move fast enough killed or just enslaved? Did the Magyar men massacre the Slav and Avar men they found and take over their surviving families? Identity shifts very rapidly. In the late nineteenth century many Germans, Jews, Slovaks and others became Hungarians, changing language and religion across two generations with the same ease that other members of the same groups emigrated and became Americans. Clearly a much more local and wholly illiterate society could be blended in different combinations (particularly when imposed by terrible violence) with great speed. The chances of anybody today being a 'pure' example of any specific medieval 'race' must be close to zero, quite aside from the category being patently meaningless.

The Magyar defeat at the Lech proved absolutely decisive for the shape of Europe. The retreating Magyar army tried to attack the Bohemian Slavs but were again defeated, headed back along the Danube and then stuck there. Germans and Magyars found a demarcation line east of Vienna and the two groups clicked together like a seatbelt, separating the northern Slavs (Bohemians, Moravians, Poles) from the southern Slavs (Slovenes, Croats, Serbs), and inventing what became Austria and Hungary. And then, in a stroke of genius, the Magyar prince Géza converted to Christianity in around 972. This was a purely political gesture, but nonetheless Magyars began genuinely to convert in large numbers and therefore put themselves out of bounds for the traditional Frankish anti-pagan campaigning season. Géza's decision to plump for Rome rather than Constantinople was another of those small decisions with deep consequences, tying Hungary to the west and giving its entire culture a different shape and flavour from its eastern and southern neighbours.

The final elements in the building of Central Europe were the Bavarians, who continued to pour into the region south of Bohemia either through Passau or through the Tirol. The settlement of this area had a very American atmosphere – a constantly shifting frontier, violent setbacks, enormous riches for those with ferocity and luck. Otto I appointed Margrave Luitpold to supervise the new territory exposed by the Hungarians' defeat and a series of 'marks' or marcher, defensive states was created to organize the land and defend it. For almost two centuries this was done by the Babenberg family and others as vassals of Bavaria (and therefore at two removes from the Emperor). It was only in 1156 that the Babenbergs were made dukes (one remove from the Emperor).

The word 'Austria' is a Latinized form of 'Eastern Land'. As usual we have no clear idea how the region's population became mostly Bavarian. There were surprises for the colonists – surviving Roman Christians were found living around Salzburg, for example, and these presumably required some re-education. The flood of settlers within a couple of centuries seems to have absorbed the native population, leaving a mixed German–Hungarian border area to the east of Vienna and a mixed German–Slovenian border area in the south. The region was a classic German political patchwork and the separate territories of places such as Carinthia and Styria ('the Mark of Steyr' – the main fortress) only fell into Babenberger hands after many years. Salzburg and Passau remained separate ecclesiastical territories and there were all kinds of privileges for the great Benedictine and (later) Cistercian monasteries being founded along the Danube valley.

It is alarming to imagine just how few people there must have been: much of Central Europe hardly supported anything more than villages. But now a fresh population was being generated by southern Germany, with a great cavalcade of heavily armed chancers, psychopaths, clerics, handymen and farmers all heading through the passes. Enormous areas remained barely inhabited – a forest of unimaginable size still separated Bohemia and Austria and random outcrops of mountain made communication very tiresome. The monasteries became engines for transforming the landscape, with armies of peasants converting waste land into farm land through generations of hideous toil. Genuine towns rather than merely fortified residences became visible – the key one being Vienna, sited on the Danube at the last point where the eastern Alps still offer some protection. In 1221 it was given control of the river trade between Germans and Hungarians and became very rich.

The hawk's fortress

In 1246 after a long run of excellent luck the Babenberg dynasty at last tripped up, with Duke Frederick II's death in battle fighting the Hungarians. Very unfortunately the Emperor died in 1250 and a deeply miserable and violent era swamped much of Central Europe. Battling with the breakdown of the Austrian lands, several nobles approached Ottakar II, the King of Bohemia, to take over. An aggressive southern German ruler, Rudolf of Habsburg, was eventually elected Emperor in 1273. As had happened a number of times, the Electors had chosen someone quite weak – in Rudolf's case both through not having a large power base and through already being in his mid-fifties and therefore unlikely to do much damage. This proved to be a major miscalculation for everyone involved except Rudolf himself.

Rudolf died at Speyer and is buried in the Imperial cathedral there. I was lucky enough to arrive in Speyer late in the evening in winter and slip into the cathedral shortly before it shut. It is a staggeringly powerful, harsh and threatening building with its sheer weight of stone a perfect symbol of Imperial power. For anyone growing up in England or France and used to Gothic it is very alarming to be surrounded by Romanesque gigantism, particularly when made expressionist by malevolent pools of darkness and weird echoes from shuffling feet. At one point the place filled with a truly hair-raising, other-worldly sound – which turned out to be the susurration of hundreds of little foil candle-holders being poured into bin bags. In any event, the highlight is Rudolf's tomb figure. He looks exactly as anyone would hope the Emperor to look – austere, eagle-nosed, calm, holding his orb and sceptre, an Imperial eagle symbol on his chest and a lion at his feet. It helps that at some point he has been put upright against the wall rather than lying flat, making him look more conversational.

In many ways Rudolf I was a classic German minor ruler. He had accumulated or inherited territories dotted around Alsace, Swabia and what is now northern Switzerland (including the 'Habichtsburg', the 'hawk's fortress' that probably gave the family their name – the Swiss kicked them out of it in 1415). He proved to be a successful Emperor and took an army into Austria to expel King Ottakar. After several twists and turns Rudolf allied with the Hungarians to defeat the Bohemians and killed Ottakar at the Battle on the Marchfeld in 1278.

Rudolf then decided to resolve the Babenberger inheritance problem by simply taking most of the lands for himself in 1282 – these lands stayed in the family for the next six centuries. This began the Habsburg rise to power, but there were many cock-ups and dead-ends to follow what might have proved to be the high point in the family fortunes – assassinations, deaths in battle, splits in the inheritance. The Habsburgs rapidly came to treat their old south German lands as less important than their new Austrian holdings. They picked up Tyrol in 1363 and Trieste in 1382, so the family got a first glimpse of the sea. Before they re-secured for good the title of Emperor in 1452 the Habsburgs were certainly an interesting bunch, but not exceptional, with the rival Luxemburg family having a far larger geographical spread and prestige. It was the Luxemburg Emperor Charles IV who, as King of Bohemia, had been largely responsible for making Prague such an extraordinary place – with a grandeur of vision that the Habsburgs could not yet match.

The role of Emperor varied in importance depending on the personality of the job's holder and his luck with events. Charles IV had only become incontrovertibly emperor once his bitter rival, Louis the Bavarian, died of a seizure while out bear-hunting, which decisively shifted the luck in Charles's direction. The job was by the fifteenth century a thankless one and it had often been so too in the past. It was nonetheless key in holding together the shifting slurry of small territories which filled much of Europe, from Flanders to Vienna. These small territories were a mocking reproof to Charlemagne's original vision of a new Roman Empire. Centuries of infighting, family squabbles, natural disaster, bribes and special needs had broken up his old empire into an incoherent mass. Any part of it would have powerful independent towns, extensive monastic holdings, individual castles with zones of land around them and very occasional serious blocks of land such as Bavaria or Saxony, but even these were a mass of cracks and sub-subdivisions. The Emperor held the system together, but with hundreds of individual territories reporting to him it was from a Human Resources point of view a poor management structure. Charles IV used his power on becoming Emperor to create the Golden Bull in 1356, which pinned into place all future arrangements. Most importantly it codified the seven figures who would in future elect the Emperor and, as significantly, laid down the rule that these men's territories could not be split or alienated, giving the seven Electors solid power-bases of their own and preventing any possibility of a pretender or rival Elector messing up the election as had been the case with the shambles around his own election. The seven Electors would be the Archbishop of Cologne, the Archbishop of Mainz, the Archbishop of Trier, the Margrave of Brandenburg, the Duke of Saxony, the Count Palatine of the Rhine and the King of Bohemia. They met in Frankfurt to vote on who would be 'King of the Romans', the idea being that it was only the Pope could crown an Emperor — a distinction that would be dropped by the Habsburgs, who generally had their heir voted as King with the title of Emperor automatically being acceded to on the current holder's death.

It was definitely important to be Emperor, but it was a long way from being the incontrovertibly classy role familiar to readers of books about Ancient Rome. Every effort was made to link the job with the glory of Charlemagne, using Charlemagne's throne at Aachen (which is still there, amazingly — a very plain but venerable object) and with as many flags and trumpets as could be mustered. But none of the other leading figures at these grand ceremonies had a strong sense of being drastically inferior to the Emperor or would necessarily tremble at his displeasure.

'Look behind you!'

The long rule of the Emperor Frederick III is the point at which the Habsburg family come into focus. This is for the accidental reason that standards of painted portraiture improve in the fifteenth century so that we have a clear idea what Frederick looked like. There is a very strange and beautiful portrait of his predecessor Sigismund — the last of the Luxemburg family — wearing an out-size fur hat with the hardened yet vacant expression of someone who has spent too much time experimenting with mushrooms, say, or on the road with a band. I am not suggesting this just to be silly: his face is absolutely baffling — there are no clues as to what the painter was trying to achieve by giving him such an odd expression. The fur hat and outdoorsy complexion make him look, well, *Canadian*. Frederick's immediate predecessor, Albert II, was short-lived (he died fighting the Turks) and is known only from a portrait which could have been painted by someone at primary school, although his clothing is beautifully done. With Frederick, however, technical skill and patronage combine to produce a number of images where we have a clear sense of what he himself wanted to convey (perhaps the key point about any portrait): authority, serenity, an aura of Imperial power.

Frederick's reign, and indeed the whole of the fifteenth century, is intensely vulnerable to two problems for historians: the '*Pilgrim's Progress* Effect' and the 'Christmas Pantomime Syndrome'. The first of these views the individual monarch as a figure who needs in his lifetime to reach a specific goal – invariably the creation of a coherent state as much as possible like the modern empire or country as it would emerge in the nineteenth century. Rulers are therefore judged on the degree to which they remain on this path and are not seduced, waylaid or discouraged by other temptations, like Christian in Bunyan's allegory. In the case of England this is most painfully clear in the endless attempts to establish Henry VI as King of France – we all now know this is ridiculous and that the English should just go home; we groan at the narrative point when Joan of Arc turns up, we rally a little when she goes up in smoke. But we are over-aware that the ruler in London will never actually rule in Paris and cringe as in 1429, aged seven, Henry is crowned at Notre Dame, knowing that he is going to fritter decades in a futile bloodbath, a total distraction from England's majestic, etc. destiny.

The *Pilgrim's Progress* Effect is very powerful with Frederick III because we know that he is the true founder of a dynasty which will rule Central Europe and many other places for four centuries – and yet he himself so often does not seem to know this (as, of course, he could not). Rather than heading to the Celestial City – in other words to Vienna to create a rational and centralized administration, the heart of a great empire – Frederick meanders about helplessly, and for long periods becomes virtually inert while mayhem breaks out all around him. He founds a monastery here, repairs a castle there and intervenes half-heartedly elsewhere, and seems to wander off the True Path at the least opportunity. His enemies and friends were driven mad by his changeable nature, his lethargy and inability to do more than a very few things at once. In what must be something of a record, although he was Holy Roman Emperor, he managed to spend a somewhat insulting twenty-seven years in a row not visiting Germany at all: leagues rose and fell, towns collapsed into anarchy, technological innovations were made and castles exploded, and yet none of this seemed to impinge much on Frederick as he had another memorial designed or listened to a bit of music.

It is attractive in a way that historians have inherited the rage felt by many of Frederick's contemporaries. You do see yourself getting increasingly hoarse from shouting: 'What you are doing in *Linz* – have you *even noticed* what is happening in Nuremberg – why can't you *help* these people!' and so on. He is definitely the most annoying Holy Roman Emperor until Charles VI. But the *Pilgrim's Progress* Effect has to be resisted. The goal of a dynasty is never reached – each generation has very narrow and immediate aims and these can be undermined or enhanced through overwhelming strokes of disaster or luck far beyond its control. It is not surprising that these people spent so much time in church: the outcome of each year's events so clearly rested, whether favourable or unfavourable, on immense and unguessable currents controlled only by God. The great rivals of the Habsburg family, the Luxemburgs, had provided highly successful Emperors and, indeed, in Charles IV there is a dynastic founding figure of a complete kind. But, as it turned out, the Luxemburg dynasty, with its sprawling holdings across Central and western Europe (including the area now covered by the tiny country which – through a crazy sequence of events – still preserves their name), through bad luck simply died out. The family's end came with Ladislaus Posthumous, whose father was the Habsburg Albert II and whose mother was the only daughter of the Emperor Sigismund, the last male Luxemburg dynast. Ladislaus's strange second name enshrined his being born after his father's death. The little lad, with his distinctive golden curls, was carefully looked after by his bluff and helpful

second cousin the future Frederick III, then a Habsburg duke.
Ladislaus discovered that Frederick's hospitality in practice seemed
to revolve around not letting him talk to anyone or do anything,
and although he managed to escape, he was never more than a
pawn of various factions until his thoroughly accidental death aged
seventeen.

The other trap, Christmas Pantomime Syndrome, is more
straightforward. We all know that Central Europe is going to be
devastated by the Turks and there is a version of history where
everybody yells at the stage: 'Look behind you!' as the hero fails to
notice the monster/goblin/witch sneaking up and then disappearing each time he turns round. In fact someone might have usefully
yelled it too at little Ladislaus. As Frederick is preoccupied by yet
more petty fighting around the Swiss Confederation it is impossible not to cry out: 'Sort out your eastern border defences and
make yourself head of a serious Christian coalition with a single
purpose,' or something like that. This frustration is almost a constant in Central European history and one that has to be resisted
at every turn. When the King of France actually allies with the
Ottomans in order to stitch up the Habsburgs there is almost no
modern historical account which can stop itself from shaking its
head in incredulity. When there is a long lull in the fighting we
know that this is only because the Ottomans are having a change
of scenery and destroying their opponents in Anatolia or Persia
and that when these issues have been sorted out they will turn
their fatal attention back to the West. But, of course, there was no
means by which anything other than shreds of intelligence about
this could get back to the Habsburgs or their discordant semi-
allies. News of a massive new Turkish army might unfortunately be
received only slightly in advance of the massive new Turkish army.

The Habsburgs were in due course to become the great defenders of Europe against the Ottomans, but Frederick III seems to have
had no interest in the staggering heroics of the Siege of Belgrade
in 1456 or the attempted Turkish invasion of Italy, and carried on
just pootling around regardless. We know that the seventy-year
breathing space created by the failure of the Ottomans at Belgrade

was a mirage and that something much worse would ultimately be on its way, but nobody at the time had any means of knowing how long the breathing space would be, or indeed whether it might not simply be permanent – which it might have been.

Cultic sites

Wiener Neustadt is an extremely haggard industrial town south of Vienna, ravaged during the Second World War and rebuilt in a way that permanently enshrines a sense of exhaustion and despair. One extraordinary and painstaking reconstruction is the Military Academy, founded by Maria Theresa but built around Frederick III's castle and chapel. Wiener Neustadt was one of Frederick's several capitals as he wandered from opportunity to crisis and from crisis to opportunity and his son, the future Emperor Maximilian I, was both born and buried there, his simple tomb still in the Chapel of St George at the heart of the academy – a chapel otherwise dominated by an immense, ugly reliquary, a cuboid on stumpy legs, covered in little glass windows behind each of which is a saint's skull, with an effect more Borneo than Lower Austria.

As the Military Academy is still fully functioning, visiting it is a strange process. Instead of the usual ticket-turnstile-postcard-shop-cafe nexus, visitors have to ring a bell outside the South Gate. I stood there waiting to be buzzed in, but instead, after a long pause, there was the sound of marching boots and a cadet with a gun slung across his back unlocked the door and escorted me round. Just walking down the darkened corridor with him set my mind racing about this parallel world of order, actual skills, professionalism, of uniforms, technical training, hierarchy. We came up to a group of cadets who were on duty, all of whom radiated level-headed competence, physical fitness and pride in appearance, and lived on a different planet from the one defined by general weak tittering, the oxygen levels of which I was more used to.

As we marched (or he marched) smartly into the brilliantly

sunlit central courtyard of the academy the point of being there
came into view: the great Heraldic Wall of Frederick III, much re-
carved and renovated, but still his extraordinary personal statement
and with the same impact it must have had on its first being
unveiled. At the base of the wall there is a statue of Frederick and
then a sequence of eighty-seven coats of arms all the way up the
side of the chapel, with some of the shields representing specks on
the map, but others substantial chunks of territory. Visitors could
have been in no doubt of the crushing superiority of Frederick's
possessions. But mainly it has the air of something which he personally enjoyed. We will never know but it is easy to think of him
sitting in the courtyard, his eyes wandering over all the places he
owned.

As my escort marched me out he casually threw at another
cadet a great, medieval-looking bunch of keys which must have
weighed the same as a piece of armour. The fellow cadet caught it
in one hand without looking up. I felt a surge of panic at being
surrounded by so much tough competence and eagerly waited to
be allowed back into the world of casual ineptitude.

The other great early Habsburg cultic site is the small town of
Klosterneuburg (New Castle Monastery), just north of Vienna. For
centuries an unvarying part of the calendar was the annual pilgrimage by the senior family member to the ancient Augustinian abbey
founded by the Babenberg margrave of the region, Leopold III, to
attend services to pray for the souls of their Babenberg predecessors. It is this complex of buildings which gives the Habsburgs
their legitimacy, conferring on an extinct prior dynasty, an ugly
civil war and an Imperial land-grab all the majesty of religious
endorsement.

According to an ancient story, the deeply pious Leopold's new
bride's veil was blown away and he swore to build an abbey wherever it was found. Years later, while out hunting, he discovered the
veil on an elderberry bush and building began. This story features
in innumerable carvings and miniatures and can never surmount
the problem that a piece of cloth on a bush is hard to represent in
an engaging way, a problem generally solved by showing the extra

pointer of the Virgin Mary and tons of angels blazing away in the sky above the bush.

The abbey was apparently very beautiful, but today it is little more than a devastated carcass. The insides were given a tremendous pimping by eighteenth-century craftsmen who smothered it in stucco and paintings of acrobatic saints, before putting baroque towers on the outside. This outrage was then balanced in the nineteenth century by architects who left the inside alone, but made the outside look much more satisfactorily medieval and replaced the towers with proper Gothic ones, which of course look grindingly Sir Walter Scott and inauthentic. A final disaster came later in the nineteenth century when frescoes were put in the gaps left in the interior by the earlier baroque vandals. These were filled by scenes from the life of Jesus of hideous sweetness, with the Saviour as a sort of weedy Khalil Gibran figure.

But in the small museum in the unfinished fragment of palace that surrounds the abbey there is a single, miraculous object which brushes aside kitsch issues. This is a colossal painted panel commissioned by the canons in 1485 to mark the founder Leopold III's canonization, an image in a series of brilliantly bright roundels of all the rulers of the Babenberg family set into a great family tree. Frederick III, with his restless, anxious interest in genealogy and legitimacy, was obsessed with Leopold and it was under his reign that a standard-issue image of the new saint was invented, with an oversized beard and implausibly grand crown, often looking somewhat distracted so as to suggest holiness. And in the great painting there he is in a definitive rendering, like a proto-Father Christmas. His wife, Agnes, is in one of the side panels and is always shown as both devout and desirable. She exemplifies the usual confusion about how to deal with queens – even better exemplified by the contemporaneous tomb of Eleanor of Portugal, Frederick III's wife, tucked behind the main altar at the Neukloster in Wiener Neustadt, which features a carved statue of her as a sort of cream-of-the-crop supercatch *and* nothing less than a saint.

The Babenberg family were freebooting German fighters, working for the Duke of Bavaria as Christian forces hacked their way east, pushing back the Hungarians. The records are so poor that beyond the most basic outline almost everything they did is merely bright coloured romance. And this is exactly what the canons' painting provides – here they are praying, heading off on crusade, the victims of treachery, in a picturesquely mounted battle. The great weight of the past is brilliantly conveyed in the picture – a dynastic sequence of events stretching down through the centuries. Here is a scene of the marcher state of which they were margraves being turned into a duchy under Henry II Jasomirgott, who has made his capital at Vienna. One Babenberger died in Italy and had his corpse boiled up and his bones put in a casket and returned to Austria, another thoughtfully rendered scene. There too is the implausibly named Leopold the Virtuous – the only Babenberg to be famous in England, as the kidnapper of Richard the Lionheart, who he hated for having slighted him on the Third Crusade. In a move that defies common sense, Richard tried to get back to England overland after the crusade in disguise, crossing Austrian territory and being captured by Leopold, who insisted on an immense ransom (at least twenty tons of silver). There is hardly an old fortress wall in Austria which is not said to have been built using this money. Leopold's more lasting claim to importance was inheriting Styria (a larger block of land than the modern state, taking in much of Slovenia). He was also, and this is getting very legendary, the origin of the Babenberger flag, reputedly inspired by his white crusader surcoat getting soaked in blood, which made a nice striped pattern. This flag had minor uses under the Habsburgs (whose own colours were black and yellow) but re-emerged in 1918 as the flag of the new Republic of Austria – a piece of deep continuity which makes even something as banal as a simple flag curious and strange.

Any dynasty if you wait a sufficient number of lifetimes hits disaster and sure enough, after many adventures, here is the chaotic Frederick the Quarrelsome dying fighting the Hungarians and with no heir in 1246. The Babenbergs were finished and the Habsburgs began their clamber to greatness.

It is not difficult to see why the Habsburgs were so obsessed with Klosterneuburg. Their legitimacy was deeply bound up in the bald assertion that they were the true heirs to the Babenbergs and the elaborate ceremonies here allowed them to stare down anyone who dared even think that they were mere Swabian carpetbaggers. The Habsburgs never forgot that the basis for their greatness was this Austrian core and that Klosterneuburg was the site they had to lay claim to. Carefully maintained for centuries, the canons' painting of the Babenbergs may have the air of a giant comic book, but it sits at the cultic heart of Frederick III and his successors' view of the world. It was also oppressive: both Frederick and his son Maximilian I were mesmerized by medieval chivalry and the adventures shown in the painting had a profound resonance for them, a magical world of saintly acts and knightly derring-do in summer landscapes, a long way from their own indebtedness, depressing new guns and political scramblings.

The elected Caesars

There is a crucial preliminary which needs to be dealt with for this book to make sense: a description of the Holy Roman Empire. I apologize for this, but really there is no way round it and it is a helpful test. I could devote much of my life to thinking about the Empire but if, like many people, you rightly find the whole business boring then this section will flush out whether or not you might be more cheerily employed reading something else.

The Empire covered a vast zone of Europe and was for many centuries the key motor of the continent's history. For anyone growing up in a British, French or American framework the whole thing was an outrage – a wilderness of absurd micro-states, potty valleys run by monks and ritualistic obscurantism which made nineteenth-century German writers, who were at the heart of reconstructing its history, scarlet with shame. Indeed by the time it was wound up by Napoleon it was widely execrated, but this was of course without the knowledge of how unstable and brutal the successor states would be. The long-running prejudice against the Empire now seems odd. Its sheer longevity, and role from Charlemagne to Napoleon as the flywheel of Europe's cultural, political and cultural existence — for good and bad — makes it inadequate merely to laugh at some of its more dust-covered and sclerotic features.

As already discussed, the Empire's distant origins lay in the highly successful rule of Charlemagne, a Frankish warlord of infinite ambition who carved his way across Europe and decided that his realm was in fact the reincarnation of the long-defunct Western Roman Empire. As usual when such figures arise, packs of smiling intellectuals shimmer into view to provide the sermons and chronicles to back up such surprising claims. We can only imagine now the landscape through which Charlemagne and his shaggy henchmen rode — a landscape of very small settlements, but also of great, devastated Roman fragments, most impressively at Constantine's old western capital of Trier. The Roman palace, cathedral and fortifications there must have had some of the impact felt by H. G. Wells's traveller in *The Time Machine* as he wandered through the unguessably vast remnants of Late Human civilization in the eight-hundredth century.

Christianity provided a written, judicial and intellectual link to the Roman Empire, but the lands which Charlemagne and his successors conquered were in many cases outside the old empire and making this new construction into the successor state was much more an act of will than a genuine revival. These notional Roman origins were always a crucial element for the thousand years that the new Empire existed. It tangled the Emperor in an important relationship with the Pope, with whom he could swap honest notes about bare-faced assertions of authority based on ancient links to Rome. It also gave many Emperors an almost mystical attachment to Italy, driven in part by embarrassment at a neo-Rome being based on foggy chunks of the north rather than the region of Europe most people would — off the top of their heads — think of as Roman. The degree to which Italians themselves failed to cooperate with this vision, tending to see the Emperor as merely a rapacious and peculiar visitor from the north, formed one of several critical dynamics along the Empire's edge.

From Charlemagne's death the Empire, like all European states, suffered from a near constant, dynamic wish to fall into smaller units. This tension is extremely difficult for historians to deal with as it flushes out the basic attitude in the writer to the nature of political events: is each threat to central authority a good or a bad thing? For example, the conventional British account of France's history makes the hyper-centralized state of Louis XIV into something almost Mongol in its disgusting blank amoralism – and yet comparable accounts of Britain's own militarily fuelled centralization and ruthlessness mysteriously become a splendid tale of pluck and decency.

At the heart of the Empire was the realization that it was enormously too large and diverse to be directly ruled by a single figure. Its origins lay in Charlemagne and his successors' conquests, from their western bases heading east, north-east and south-east. It encompassed most of German-speaking Europe, plus the Low Countries, a zone of what is now northern, eastern and south-eastern France, Bohemia, Moravia, Lusatia and a chunk of northern Italy. Large and small grants of land by the Emperor endowed various of his followers with territory which they defended and consolidated both on his behalf and for their own benefit. The bigger and more obstreperous nobles might seek greater freedom from Imperial control but there was never a suggestion of actual independence. Indeed, however powerful states such as Saxony or Bavaria might have become, their rulers always kept a keen sense that their own status and security were deeply woven into the overall Imperial structure. By the time the Habsburg family permanently secured the title of Emperor it was a secular and religious post of incomparable prestige, backed up by a hieratic, ambulatory calendar of events and places: the election at Frankfurt and the Imperial gatherings at places suffused with the history of great predecessors such as Aachen, Worms, Nuremberg and Augsburg.

Through many convulsions, setbacks and total implosions, the Empire by the fifteenth century had settled into a pattern which it kept until its dissolution in 1806. Its fringes at all points of the compass generated an alarmingly high percentage of all Europe's historical 'events' and even after 1806 it was a motor for disagreement and warfare like nothing else. Too many historians have found themselves siding uneasily with the idea that the Emperor should be sympathized with when his grand plans are thwarted by pygmy localism, but perhaps this hopeless localism should be celebrated as a great gift to European culture and discourse. It is striking, for example, that the western region of the Empire was so poorly organized that it only ever had a defensive anti-French function and no ability to attack anyone at all. One western territory, Prum, had a defensive capability restricted to the spiritual force field generated by its ownership of a sandal belonging to Jesus while another, Essen (the future home of Krupp armaments), was ruled for centuries by a notably ornery and unhelpful group of aristocratic nuns.

The territory of the Empire therefore had something of the appearance of a deeply disturbing jigsaw. There were relatively large territories such as Württemberg, which looked impressive but was in practice honeycombed with local special laws and privileges that made the dukes impoverished, bitter and much laughed at. There were more substantial and coherent territories, such as Saxony, which was cursed by frequent bouts of subdivision between different heirs, with one half crumbling into tiny but wonderful fragments. There were the lands of the margraves of Brandenburg in the north-east, which had a personal link to territories in Poland that fell outside the Empire and had a profound effect when they cohered into the Prussian state.

These larger blocks catch the eye because they had real futures, but far more characteristic of the Empire were oddities such as the Palatinate, a scattering of wealthy territories across the lower middle of Germany whose rulers intervened at key points in Imperial history. They left at Heidelberg one of the quintessential Romantic landscapes, but it is now almost impossible to envisage the Palatinate as a plausible and robust political unit – indeed Heidelberg is so picturesque mainly because its principal castle is in ruins. The Palatinate is an interesting example of what makes the

Empire so confusing, with its individual units generally accretions of inherited, bought and nicked bits of land not necessarily even linked together.

Religious properties, often on land which had belonged to the Emperor but was given to the Church for specific purposes, formed an important category. So the adorable little state of Quedlinburg, ruled by nuns from good families, was endowed with enough territory to pay for its abbey and ensure a daily sequence of prayers for Henry the Fowler, a great slaughterer and forced converter of pagan Saxons in the early tenth century, who was buried there. Sometimes just as small, but far more important, were the Imperial Free Cities, lands generally focused on a single trading town, which had special privileges and were ruled by merchant oligarchies rather than a single lord. Some of these cities were consistently very important and close to the Emperor, such as Frankfurt and Nuremberg, some were quiet backwaters. Others were more remote from Imperial concerns and had extensive links with the outside world, such as the Hanseatic cities in the north, most famously Hamburg and Lübeck. Each had its own specialization, such as Lüneburg with its salt mines or Hall with its mint. Most consistently insignificant of all were the micro-territories: for example, the hundreds of bits owned by Imperial Knights, many in Swabia, and often consisting of just a tumbledown castle, a handful of vineyards and perhaps lucky access to some unfortunate river where the knight could charge a pointless toll for each trading boat rowing past.

This mass of political entities (hundreds by the later fifteenth century) was all held in place by the authority of the Emperor. As can be imagined, the very small states were frantically loyal as they needed Imperial sanction to survive at all – they tended to have elaborate shields decorating their fortress walls to show their allegiance and warn off casual predators. They supplied tiny packets of troops and often contributed to Imperial entourages in terrific costumes as well as populating many jobs within the Church. But even the larger territories believed in the Emperor, and such a system, as can be imagined, generated a staggering number of legal disputes, whether about inheritance, rights or financial and military contributions, and much of the Emperor's time was engaged in settling these disputes. This ceaseless, wearying round of hearings and travelling, which, of course, left numerous irritated or alienated losers in its wake, was central to the Empire's existence and the ability to provide justice was as important as success or failure in war in creating an Emperor's reputation. Much of the chaos of Frederick III's long reign stemmed from his losing interest in all this, and one of the reasons that the Habsburgs enjoyed their extraordinary run of success after the fifteenth century was that they felt a surprising and consistent level of inter-generational diligence (with the startling, ruinous exception of Rudolf II with his rooms full of unopened letters). They were always dealing with a stream of grumpy, trigger-happy and often quite poorly educated noblemen waving around forged 'ancient' documents of a kind familiar to the Habsburgs themselves and insisting on the application of this or that right. I do not refer much to the issue again in this book, but it should be kept in mind as an important sort of background hum at all times – an always inadequate but prestigious Imperial bureaucracy sorting through land and inheritance disputes which could take generations to resolve and which found its final expression in the great scenes of dusty paperwork in Leoš Janáček and Karel Čapek's 1926 opera, *The Makropoulos Case*, with Janáček even coming up with a beautiful, repetitive theme to represent unending Imperial legal processes.

So the Emperor needed physically to demonstrate his status by moving around his immense lands, and every town had a complex set of obligations to him, later expressed by the often very elaborate 'Imperial Halls' which survive in many ex-territories today, consisting of a lavish assembly room (swagged with toadying but chirpy murals extolling the Emperor's greatness and the extreme personal closeness to him of his host's ancestors) and an entire wing of bedrooms – sometimes only used once in a century.

Each Emperor had a power-base, which could be very important to him, even if he was often away. Much of the distinctive appearance of Prague comes from Charles IV making it both a royal (as King of Bohemia) and Imperial capital. His son Sigismund shunted around all over Europe in a long reign of baffling incoherence – if he can be said to have had a base then it was at Buda or Visegrád. But these were only ever personal choices rather than institutional ones. The south-eastern Empire is littered with building projects knocked on the head by the early Habsburgs' changes of mind or taste, or total insolvency. Maximilian I's empty tomb in Innsbruck, with his body in Wiener Neustadt and his entrails in a copper pot in Vienna, sums up the problem. As long as the Emperors were on the move then they could keep their legal, military, residential and fiscal rights going – much like a permanently turning mixer being needed to maintain wet concrete. A sustained period of inattention could make the whole thing solidify and even – as the simile is abandoned – ruin the mixer itself.

The mechanism which sat at the heart of the Empire and which made it work was the strange fact – to our ears – that the Emperor was elected. The Golden Bull stated that when the current Emperor died, the Seven Electors had to gather (either in person or through a proxy) in Frankfurt and, sitting in a specific chapel of the Imperial church of St Bartholomew, vote on the new King of the Romans. Following their choice, an immense festival filled the Römerberg in central Frankfurt, with bonfires and the usual whole roasted animals. The choice of Electors was a clever one as these could only possibly agree on someone mutually acceptable and even if one family might nobble two or even three Electors their locations in different parts of the Empire and different moral views could not be squared readily. The horse-trading and bribes could be breathtaking (although much is hidden from the historical record), but the Electors' eventual choice did have a surprising level of legitimacy, both through the crushing historical weight of precedent and because they were free to choose from a range of rich, capable and adult candidates. This avoided the nightmares of pure heredity faced by France or England, say, which would at irregular intervals wind up being ruled by children or imbeciles.

The election was hardly an opportunity for any old aspirant who felt lucky to put himself forward, though. The qualifications were formidably difficult, restricting candidature to almost nobody. This was in part because whereas the Emperors of the high Middle Ages had owned extensive lands as part of their job almost all this had by the fifteenth century been given away. The Emperor therefore needed to have access to a huge amount of money in his own right just to maintain his dignity, let alone have the potential to raise armies. In practical terms only two or three families could pass the interview. In the fourteenth and fifteenth centuries it was the Luxemburgs who were the most practical candidates as they could draw on their substantial revenues from also being kings of Bohemia, and in Sigismund's case also King of Hungary and Croatia. Attempts to make the role of Emperor hereditary within a family had seemed possible when Sigismund had succeeded his father, Charles IV, but Sigismund's failure to have a male heir and the end of the Luxemburg line meant looking elsewhere. A good candidate was a member of the Habsburg family, Duke Frederick of Inner Austria, who was elected King of the Romans in 1440 and crowned Holy Roman Emperor in 1452 after a number of local difficulties. Without intending to do so the seven Electors of 1440 had locked into the job a single family who would rule, with one short break, for three hundred and sixty-four years.

CHAPTER TWO

The heir of Hector

In the late fifteenth century Europe goes into a ferment of change
– the economy revs up, the population grows, technology is over-
hauled, new forms of artistic and intellectual life flourish. Earlier
events that appear murky and disconnected to us must have
appeared vivid and curious at the time, but now this is all verifiable
and uncontentious, simply because of a single, key invention: printing with movable type. Monarchs such as Henry VI of England or
Louis XI of France are remote and, however hard we try, not part
of our mental landscape because of the thinness of what they left
behind them – a handful of stiff portraits, a few letters and dodgy
chronicles. We would love to engage more actively with their
reigns, which were obviously but tantalizingly fascinating, but
cannot.

Maximilian I, Emperor from 1493, marks this transition exactly.
His father, Frederick III, is a baffling figure: we know what he
looked like, which is an improvement, but historians are still
obliged to cling to a handful of unreliable stories and these are so
partisan that his incompetence or cunning can in the end only be
dimly guessed at. Maximilian, however, is universally familiar, with
his beaky nose, fur cloak, Order of the Golden Fleece chain and
shoulder-length hair (one of those fashions for men which tends to
be passed over in stunned silence). He looks out from coins and
statues and paintings, but also from woodcuts, an older technology
but one now much refined, which circulated around Europe in
astonishing quantities. Maximilian was obsessed with new technology, whether this applied to fluted armour ('Maximilian' armour)
or cannon (his arsenal can still be wandered around in Innsbruck)

or – most importantly – typography. The famous 'Gothic' typeface, called Fraktur by Germans, was designed specifically for him. This typeface created a semi-separate and alienating (for non-Germans) form of book presentation which endured until Hitler banned it in 1941, aware – in an odd burst of sensitivity – that for effective communication with his new world empire Fraktur was too hard to read.

Maximilian used the new medium to pour out propaganda, both about his deeds and about himself and his family. As with everything he did, he stopped and started, changed his mind, lost interest, so there were countless unfinished projects at the time of his death – but he planned and dictated material on everything from magic to chivalry and genealogy to politics. He used to be much hated by German nationalist historians because he failed to unite Germany and dabbled and dithered in a way that undercuts any coherent, onward-and-upward narrative – but these are the very failings that now make him seem so appealing. We need no longer feel upset that he didn't create a powerful and independent German army or crush the French.

Maximilian is an unusual Habsburg in being both a convincing man of action and an intellectual. He was deeply conscious that when he took over the role of Holy Roman Emperor he would set a precedent – what if it could be permanently attached to the Habsburg family? Enormous effort went into making this feasible, much of it via print, and working with a brilliant array of great artists in all media he set out to build an image of himself that would last for ever. The Habsburgs had the most extensive terri- tories of all German rulers, but there were plenty who claimed a better ancestry or were more securely rooted in the Empire itself. A legitimate complaint about them (one that lasted until they finally stepped down) was that their interests were tangled up in the margins of the Empire – in the Low Countries, northern Italy and in the east – and that they misused Imperial funds for narrow family purposes, merely pretending to have German interests at heart. In fact it was their semi-marginality, as well as their wealth, that made the Habsburgs so desirable to many German princes –

they were rich enough not to be a burden on other territories, but they would on the whole be too busy fighting the Turks to interfere in Germany itself too much.

There are many jobs at Maximilian's court which would have appealed to me. I have never really been outdoorsy enough to make a mercenary landsknecht, although their immense two-handed swords, flowing moustaches and puffed-silk slashed sleeves take some beating. Indeed this is the last period where sheer *strength* was essential to fighting and I really shy away from this. It would be flattering to think of being one of the Emperor's humanists, musicians or artists, although a more likely post would have been as the trusted, albeit limited, figure who supervised his bowel movements. But then the 'groom of the stool' would have been a dream compared to the really horrible job of court genealogist. If ever there was a role which required fake learning and intellectual supinity it was this. Initially enormous work went into proving Maximilian's descent from Noah's family, which required some fairly seamless absurdity. Genealogies were important for the obvious reason that they implied rights and privileges stemming from historical deep background. They were also vulnerable – their circulation at foreign courts could provoke laughter from rival crawly genealogists working for other families (such as the Wittelbachs of Bavaria, who could also point to a time when they had provided an Emperor). The respect felt for a genealogy therefore was a side-effect of how, more generally, its issuer was viewed by potential rivals, but in itself it needed to be a plausible document.

When the Emperor Charles IV had come up with a genealogy for himself, he had suggested that his family were derived not only from Noah but also from Saturn, but this sort of enjoyable silliness would no longer wash in the more stringent atmosphere of the late fifteenth century. Now, after much mulling over his own lineage, Maximilian decided he was not in fact descended from Noah, but from the Trojan hero Hector. Presumably the court humanists, rather than rolling their eyes and making farting noises with their cheeks, must have smiled at the Emperor's perspicacity, bowed deeply and returned to their library to start all over again. One of

the key figures at court was noted for his rigour in creating these
family trees, but given their essentially made-up quality this was a
rigour which could only be admired so far. Hector was important
because of a series of wholly uncanonical (as in fabricated) stories
about his sons. Loosely nodding at the *Aeneid*, these proposed that
while Aeneas was founding Rome, a brother called Francio was
excitedly heading further north, with his children settling on the
River Main and building the City of the Franks, Frankfurt. This
stuff was valuable because it tried to give Germany equal prestige
to Italy, and Frankfurt a sacral value closer to that of Rome. The
family tree then descended through a series of dubious byways
down to the deeply prestigious and real Clovis, King of the Franks
and then swerved down through one of Clovis's *younger* children
(to avoid the obvious confusion that the Habsburgs would otherwise be claiming to have been kings of France, a fact that might
have been noticed elsewhere) to emerge in the relative safety of
Maximilian's direct real Swabian ancestors. Presumably feeling
pretty sullied, the humanists had now established a direct link from
Troy to Innsbruck.

It may seem odd to spend so much time describing so implausible a project, but genealogy lay at the heart of royal power.
It had been crucial to the other great Habsburg fabrication, the
fourteenth-century bundle of documents called the *Privilegium
Maius*, some signed by Julius Caesar and Nero no less, which established the inviolability of the Austrian lands and created the special
title of 'Archduke' for the Habsburg ruler, which put him on the
same level as the Electors of the Holy Roman Empire. This was
laughed at as an obvious fake at the time and much of it had been
ignored by Charles IV, but when Frederick III was made Emperor
he was able to take advantage of this to approve the *Privilegium
Maius* in effect for himself, making his lands inalienable through
the male line and allowing the wearing of a special, made-up
archduke's crown. As, from now on, the Emperor *was* a Habsburg
this comedy document stuck, and all discussion of its authenticity
was viewed as treason. So, descended from Hector and Clovis,

given the thumbs up by Roman emperors, the Habsburgs had arrived.

The great wizard

Many Habsburg rulers could be faulted for their almost aggressive hostility towards the arts and their refusal to use their unique position to create extraordinary things – Franz Joseph was notoriously depressing in this respect – but there were a number of exceptions: Charles V and Titian, Rudolf II and a whole panoply of mountebanks and oddballs, Ferdinand III and Rubens. None can really match up to Maximilian, though – his work with Dürer, Burgkmair and Altdorfer and a host of less well-known figures, as well as his support for the extraordinary music of Isaac and Senfl, makes him one of the greatest patrons. These do not seem to be merely the random sideswipes of aggrandizement either, but based around a close personal involvement, albeit one involving the same sort of untrustworthy changeability that afflicted his political zig-zagging. Some very brilliant figures spent huge amounts of their time designing for Maximilian half-finished projects for books, statues and images that were only circulated or seen, if at all, thanks to the devoted work of his grandson, Ferdinand I, many years after all those concerned had died. Almost everything that Maximilian did was hamstrung both by his own restlessness and by his frequent and unwanted experiences of the cashless economy.

As good a way as any to understand the key political events of Maximilian's life is through his own artistic vision of it. This was expressed in a number of places – not least in Altdorfer's very odd but wonderful drawings for *The History of Frederick and Maximilian*, showing the baby Maximilian astonishing the court by standing upright while having his first bath – but nowhere more vividly than in Dürer and his workshop's unmanageably enormous (twelve foot high and ten foot wide) woodcut triumphal arch. Something of a dead end as an idea, this was a highly complex set of paper sheets which could be put together like a mammoth jigsaw on a wall and which was a seething mass of allegory, decoration and

history. Its semi-portability may well have appealed to Maximilian as
his court moved around, but it will always remain unclear how such
a strange object was meant to be viewed – it is both too large to take
in and too small in its detail. Indeed, the entire *Arch of Honour* has
the air of something dreamed up by the Emperor as a reaction to
improvements in woodcut technology, and which was then sub-
contracted to Dürer's team in Nuremberg with nobody daring to
point out the borderline idiocy of the concept. In any event, a staggering amount of work went into it and the individual panels of
events from Maximilian's life are fabulous. Indeed they form a very
straightforward way of explaining why his reign was so important to
the Habsburgs' fortunes and save a lot of tedious exposition.

The first group of images in the *Arch of Honour* give the story
of Maximilian and his father's great coup in securing Burgundy for
the family. The late fifteenth century was notable among many
other things as the sole point during which the Swiss had a fundamental role in European life. The sheer obstreperousness of the
cantons allied to their military skill allowed them to carve out an
increasingly independent niche within the Empire. Their spreading
territory was partly taken from Habsburg land and one of the ways
in which the old Emperors had used to keep the Habsburgs down
was turning a blind eye to Swiss behaviour. This was highly unfortunate for the Swiss once the Habsburgs became the Emperors and
looked for revenge. In the meantime the Swiss had changed the
face of European history at the Battle of Nancy in 1477 when they
had managed to hack to bits Charles the Bold, the last (as it turned
out) of the highly successful Valois dukes of Burgundy, who ruled
a broad swath of land from the Swiss borders to Holland. The
Burgundians had created a state which, if it had stabilized, could
have formed a permanent barrier between France and Germany. It
was rich, industrious, coherent and had a great mercantile, military
and artistic tradition.

Charles the Bold had become a sort of enraged animal by the
time of his death, dreaming of creating a vast Kingdom of Lothar-
ingia and doomed to fight with great cruelty and without end
against coalitions of less-than-impressed neighbours opposed to

incoherent visions that needed their territory to be realized. His disappearance was welcomed, but it created a crisis and opportunity of a very rare kind: a large and desirable territory with no male heir. Despite being married three times Charles had only been able to have one child, Mary of Burgundy, or Mary 'the Rich' as she now became known, in a tiresome Burgundian tradition of naming ('the Good', 'the Fearless', 'the Bold') which would mercifully soon end. Mary, aged nineteen, suddenly became a figure of overwhelming importance. Louis XI seems to have uncharacteristically panicked, and instead of offering to marry his son to the heiress invaded her territory. This ungallant blunder threw her into the arms of Maximilian, at that time simply the teenage son of the Emperor Frederick III.

The marriage reshaped Europe. It gave the Habsburgs territory which now spread from the Danube to the North Sea and made them far more powerful than any other ruler, apart from the Ottoman sultan and perhaps, in some moods, the French king. It also shows the annoying nature of dynastic history – Burgundy in itself was a plausible political unit, but now it was part of a far wider, sprawling tangle of lands which would cause countless problems for everyone concerned. Mary died, crushed by her horse, less than five years after her marriage, but her decisions and those of her and Maximilian's son Philip 'the Handsome' (the last of these add-on names) would vastly aggrandize the Habsburgs in absolutely unpredictable ways.

Despite her early death, therefore, Maximilian kicks off his pictorial account of his life with an image of his and Mary's betrothal, both looking very dashing. This is the foundation of his fortune, as he takes on the legacy of the Burgundian dukes and their mystique, particularly the Order of the Golden Fleece and the musical and artistic quality that transforms the previously rather backward Austrian court. Both Philip 'the Handsome' and Philip's son Charles of Ghent (the future Charles V) would grow up in the Low Countries and this fundamentally changed the Habsburg style – indeed for many Germans their Germanness became thoroughly suspect from this point on, and their transnational quality would become a key element in their appeal and success, but not to Germans.

Of the sixteen pictures, a large group now deal with the downside of Maximilian's marriage – the long era of fighting from 1477 off-and-on to 1489 to stabilize the new inheritance, beat off rivals and tame truculent townspeople. Each image shows another blood-soaked opportunity for heroism – fighting in Utrecht, Guelders, Bruges, Liège, and a laboriously made snapshot of Maximilian posing with his dubious and intermittent ally Henry VIII of England after the Battle of the Spurs. They then show him crowned as King of the Romans at Aachen and therefore formally heir apparent to his father as Emperor (a particularly wonderful Dürer workshop woodcut with the young, beautifully dressed king surrounded by happy Electors) and marching back into Austria to retake the core lands embarrassingly snatched by the Hungarians while he was distracted in the Low Countries. There is also a picture of his worst humiliation – the Swiss War of 1499 where the traditional Swiss–Habsburg hatred found its finest expression and the Swiss gained their independence (a new concept in Europe and its novelty so confusing that it was not ratified until 1648). Other images show him being crowned in Trent by the Pope (not in Rome as, embarrassingly, the Venetians would not let him through), fighting to defend Bavaria on behalf of the Holy Roman Empire (a rare example of his actually doing his job as Emperor rather than as head of his own clan) and fighting the French in Italy.

The most important by far though are two further marriage pictures, both by Dürer himself and with a level of detail and heraldry that marks the events out as exceptional. The first shows Maximilian, weighed down by his Imperial crown, chain of the Order of the Golden Fleece and glamorous robes, looking justifiably pleased as his son Philip 'the Handsome' marries Juana, the daughter of Isabella of Castile and Ferdinand of Aragon. The second shows the 1515 Congress of Vienna and the double wedding of two of Maximilian's grandchildren, Ferdinand and Mary, to the two children of King Vladislaus of Hungary and Bohemia.

Through an unforeseeable series of disasters and chances these two weddings would shape much of the future of Europe.

Maximilian's ability to project a brilliant image of himself was most influentially achieved by Dürer's great painting and woodcut, based on a sketch of Maximilian presiding at the Diet of Augsburg and published after the Emperor's sudden death. It has enshrined the image of him as a sort of charismatic and charming wizard and has given him an unfair advantage over descendants who made the mistake of using journeyman hacks for their portraits. He was obsessed with death, carried his coffin with him wherever he travelled and even in his final illness was adding refinements to the astounding cenotaph for himself, which he had spent much of his reign designing. He seems to have been happiest in a way designing funeral monuments – the colossal marmalade marble cuboid for his father in Vienna cathedral was only completed shortly before Maximilian's own death.

This settled sense of gloom around Maximilian is of course what makes him so attractive too. Some of his court music has a burnished, sacerdotal, *capo di capi* quality which makes everything later seem either too shrill or too pompous. To be able to ask musicians to play such stuff, while idly flicking through pictures of yourself by Dürer and taking sips from a jewel-studded goblet filled with something reassuringly exclusive is a fantasy that may not appeal to everyone, but it certainly finds a mental and emotional home in my corner of south-west London.

Gnomes on horseback

On the road snaking out of the Alpine town of Bolzano there is a crag topped off by a truly perfect little castle. Bolzano was until 1918 part of the Tyrol and entirely German-speaking. As part of its loot for supporting the Triple Entente in the First World War, Italy took over the southern Tyrol and has clung to it in the face of endless appeals from Austria and intermittent terrorism from its inhabitants. It has only been in the past ten years or so that Italy has adopted a non-coercive, bilingual attitude towards one of the handful of regions in Europe where Germans were the people threatened and discriminated against. This new bilingualism has had a bizarre effect on the castle. In Italian it is called Castel Roncolo, which implies a pretty turfed courtyard with maidens in gauzy outfits skipping about to tambourines and lutes with weedy youths in coloured tights looking on. In German it is called Schloß Runkelstein, which implies a brandy-deranged old soldier-baron with a purple face and leg-iron lurching around darkened dank corridors, beating a servant to death with his crutch. Seeing the two names everywhere side by side is deeply confusing, like having one eye always out of focus.

The castle is famous both as a locus of nineteenth-century Romanticism, a cult bowed to by Franz Joseph when he rebuilt it after an embarrassing incident when Alpine road-widening resulted in one of the castle's walls falling down its crag, and for its role in fights between local noblemen and the Habsburgs in the fifteenth century. This Romantic love of the castle came partly from its being such a quintessential pile, but also because of the survival of its early fifteenth-century frescoes. Commissioned by the two brothers who originally owned Runkelstein, these frescoes somehow battled through sixteenth-, seventeenth- and eighteenth-century indifference until they landed in the safe arms of the post-Walter-Scott-neo-medieval world.

As you would expect, Maximilian appreciated the frescoes, sending an artist to the castle to restore them. His shields (Burgundy, Austria, Tyrol) are still carved over a fireplace. It is safe to say that what Maximilian liked about the frescoes was that they vividly enshrined a medieval Europe which now seemed very remote from his own mercenaries-and-gunpowder world. There is something engagingly semi-competent about the pictures and they cannot claim to be high art for a second. They are all entirely secular in their subject matter and show jousts, hunts, stars and suns, parades, men and women talking. There is a brilliantly silly sequence of events from *Tristan* with the hero killing Morald and the dragon and the voyage to Cornwall (or rather, Cornovaglia) and so on. There is also the story of the brave knight Garel, whose adventures are truncated by most of them having slid off the crag together with the wall on which they were painted in the embarrassing road-widening disaster. Most weird of all is a deeply mysterious sequence of painted triplings in the castle courtyard – the Three Ancient Heroes (Hector, Alexander and Caesar), the Three Old Testament Heroes (Joshua, David, Judas Maccabeus) and the Three Medieval Heroes (Arthur, Charlemagne, Godfrey de Bouillon). The triplings continue with Arthurian heroes, great lovers, *Nibelungenlied* heroes and end with a zany set of three male giants, three female giants and three gnomes on horseback, figures whose meaning will never be recovered. These are all painted with limited skill and are much faded, but their very survival dips us into an ancient and peculiar aesthetic based on obsessive number-patterns, attributes, virtues and morality.

Like their contemporaries, the Habsburgs saw themselves in a direct succession from these figures (the heroes more than the gnomes). As discussed earlier, Maximilian went to huge trouble to show his descent, which was both physical and spiritual. The castle embodies the cult of ancestors, courtly behaviour and knightly prowess which haunted the Habsburg court as an ideal rarely matched but nonetheless lurking always as either an aspiration or a reproach. The repulsive, incompetent grind of the Italian Wars may have been the daily reality, but there was always a place for jousting, and lordly behaviour.

To a degree now hard to imagine each Habsburg ruler viewed himself in relation both to his predecessors and his successors. His ancestors might be dead in this world, but they judged him and he would meet them when he in turn died. The elaborate family charts, trees of Jesse and sequences of coats of arms created an aura of absolute power and certainty which a successful Emperor could milk through processions, feasts, tournaments and, above all, a constant round of church services. Across the Habsburg lands there were elaborate shrines to key predecessors, such as the tomb of Ernest 'the Man of Iron', Maximilian's grandfather, at the Cistercian abbey of Rein in Styria, where monks were paid to pray *for*

ever for the ruler's soul. Equal prestige was gained from the tombs
of non-Habsburg Emperors such as Otto I at Magdeburg. This
for ever is hard for us to take, but the landscape was dotted with
chantries which did do this job for extraordinary periods of time
– the nuns who prayed for the Emperor Henry I at Quedlinburg
kept at it for nearly nine hundred years before being asked to
pack up. These heroes of the past were like a colossal battery of
prestige which the current ruler could draw on. The ancestors' continuing presence was filtered through innumerable statues, paintings,
poems and plays and the maintenance of their burial places was a
key family concern. The idea – which his subjects generally bought
into except in the face of overwhelming ineptitude – was that
when the Emperor appeared he was merely the current embodi-
ment of a great stream of grandeur stretching back to the Old
Testament, the *Aeneid*, Charlemagne, the Ottonians, the Salians
and the Babenberger and Habsburg inheritance. In a series of
ceremonies in specific great towns (Aachen, Frankfurt, Nuremberg,
Augsburg, Regensburg and others) this continuity was celebrated,
often with the attendance of the Electors, or as many of them as
were on speaking terms with the Emperor at the time, and a panoply of family members who as mothers, wives, soldiers or clerics
would have had specific forms of prestige now long forgotten but
immediately obvious and powerful at the time.

Maximilian left the greatest of these in the Court Church at
Innsbruck. In its creator's spirit of havering and lack of funds his
monument is not what it should have been. Intended as his tomb
and as a summa of Habsburg majesty, it is in fact empty, with
Maximilian winding up broke, dying and then buried at the other
end of Austria in Wiener Neustadt. Its statues forlornly stood
around for many years until his grandson Ferdinand I turned his
attention to finishing the mausoleum and creating a suitable building for it. The result is very odd as the tomb and its figures are
clearly taken from the gloomier elements in the Northern Renaissance whereas the church is Italianate and Counter-Reformation. I
was reminded of a video that used to be played at the Banqueting
House in Whitehall which told the story of Charles I's execution
outside that building in 1649 accompanied on the soundtrack by

Purcell's music for the funeral of Charles' grand-daughter Mary II in 1694; such a jump in sensibility was not unlike a documentary on World War One accompanied by 'Rock around the Clock'.

So the surroundings are all wrong in Innsbruck – but this does not matter too much as the monument itself is astounding enough. Maximilian endlessly fiddled with the design, surely one of the most fun parts of being an Emperor, and some of the giant bronze ancestor statues were cast in his lifetime with most of the remainder agreed at least as design sketches. They reflect in many ways a Burgundian aesthetic and in the history of sculpture are an odd sort of dead end, not taken up by his successors, who preferred something a bit less mad. But perhaps there was only a need to go to such lengths once. As the second Habsburg Emperor in a row Maximilian wanted to make a point about his pedigree that would reach centuries into the future and validate all his successors, trying to ensure that these too would be Habsburgs. They stand around the empty tomb like immense and alarming deactivated robots – particularly the amazing figure of Ferdinand I, the last Burgundian King of Portugal, whose lack of a surviving portrait meant that he had to be shown in a colossal suit of armour with the visor down and fantastic bronze decoration swarming over every surface.

The statues are a mixed bag. Some are fairly routine and others are perhaps the greatest of all German sculptures, including hypnotically charismatic figures of King Arthur, Duke Albrecht and King Theoderic designed by Dürer. Rudolf I, the first Habsburg Emperor, back in the thirteenth century, has the strange indignity of a prominent codpiece that visitors over the centuries have found it impossible not to touch, making the blackened bronze of his armour an unsettling contrast to the glowing orange of his cock. Various favourites are present – Ernest 'the Iron Man', his wife the Jagiellonian princess Zymburgis, who was so strong she could tear nails out of walls and straighten horseshoes, Philip 'the Handsome', Maximilian's son, who was sketched for his statue before his premature death, a rather conjectural statue of Clovis, Ferdinand of Aragon, Juana 'the Mad' – all providing back-up for Habsburg universalist claims that would come to full fruition under

Maximilian's successor, his grandson Charles V, who could draw on all these figures for sustenance.

Some of the statues have been designed to hold candles in their hands for special occasions. In a sense it is ideal that Maximilian himself, although represented by a superb kneeling statue on top of the cenotaph, has his body elsewhere as it means that these bronze ancestors (watched over too by a medley of little busts of Roman emperors, making their own nod-and-a-wink point about Maximilian's pedigree) are witnessing something more universal than simply one of their descendants. The more I look at them the more hair-raising they become, watchmen almost untouched (except in the case of Rudolf I) by five centuries of warfare, chaos and, ultimately, the end of the dynasty they were sent to protect.

Juana's children

For the generation alert by 1490 and still alive by 1530 the world would have struck them as convulsed by unparalleled, freakish change. The monarchs of the period often seem immobilized by the sheer complexity of their situation, with bold initiatives coming to nothing, inertia rewarded, and uneasy blends of the two. It is not as though Europe had previously been static, but there had been many more certainties. The Hundred Years War, most obviously, had been played out with painful predictability, with the inhabitants of Aquitaine, Normandy and Picardy barely bothering to look up as another bunch of mud-spattered characters in plate armour galloped into view. Despite some breaks, the sheer mulishness of English attempts to take over France gave a fixed character to reign after reign.

Through a queasy mix of luck and ruthlessness the Habsburg family wound up as the great beneficiaries of this process. Charles V felt that his long reign had ended in failure and he bequeathed all kinds of problems, but by the time of his resignation and retreat to an Extremaduran monastery to pray, admire the view and wistfully spin a globe of the world, his family ruled an empire of a size with no European precedent.

One good place to start explaining this rise in the family fortunes is with Maximilian staring in fascination at the unfolding situation in Spain. In Barcelona in 1493, Ferdinand and Isabella, whose marriage had combined the thrones of Castile and Aragon and whose forces had destroyed the last Muslim state in Spain the year before, stood on a set of palace steps, which are still there (perhaps one of the more thrilling and perplexing places to stand in the world). There they met and congratulated Christopher Columbus, who presented them with a selection of Caribbean exotica and unhappy Hispaniola 'Indians'. As, over the following decades, it became clear that humankind's entire mental experience was about to be hit by a flood of slavery, sugar, gold, silver, genocide, jungles, pirate ships, howler monkeys, Brazil nuts and toucans, the old Europe in which English and French knights hit each other over the head for ownership of some drizzle-washed hamlet in the Pas de Calais suddenly seemed a bit old-fashioned. The fixed-term, zero-sum atmosphere of Europe was at an end, particularly once Aztec gold and silver started arriving in uncontrollable quantities in the 1520s.

Maximilian had married his only son, Philip 'the Handsome', to Juana, the daughter of Ferdinand and Isabella, as an aspect of his policy to try to shut in France. It was never intended as a dynastic checkmate, however – Philip was made Duke of Burgundy and positioned to replace Maximilian in due course with the existing Habsburg lands and, with luck and management, as Holy Roman Emperor. But a rapid sequence of surprise deaths between 1497 and 1500 revolutionized Philip's fortunes. Castile and Aragon were still separate kingdoms and after Isabella's death in childbirth, shortly followed by the death of the male child she had given birth to, the clear heir to Castile became Juana (under laws that, unlike those followed by the Habsburgs, did not prevent female inheritance). Ferdinand looked on in horror from his own kingdom of Aragon, realizing that through this bleak sequence a Habsburg would now take not only Castile but, if he did not

himself have a son, Aragon too. The last part of Ferdinand's life
was grim. Spare a thought for the teenager Germaine de Foix, who
was rushed to Barcelona as the new wife and had to spend ten
years in the arms of the hard-breathing old dynast trying to conceive a son who could shut the Habsburgs out of Aragon. For a
few hours in May 1509 a son, Juan, existed and the entire course
of history could have been changed. Juan's survival would have
split Spain permanently between an eastern, Mediterranean kingdom based on Barcelona and a western, Atlantic kingdom based
on Toledo and Granada. But the baby died and in 1516 a despairing Ferdinand also died.

Ferdinand's only satisfaction must have been that at least by
then Philip 'the Handsome' had died too, apparently of typhoid
although there were persistent rumours that Ferdinand had poi-
soned him. Philip had been much admired as the acme of
Burgundian chivalry but, as far as we can tell, he was no great loss
as an individual or a political actor. Juana seems to have suffered
from bouts of gloomy mental incapacity of a kind that later genet-
ically leapt up and ravaged a random sequence of her descendants.
Just how unable to rule she really was is tangled up in the motives
of Philip, Ferdinand and then her own children for finding reasons
for sidelining her. As Juana 'the Mad' she stalked the first half of
the sixteenth century, refusing to part with her husband's coffin,
praying obsessively and eventually confined for decades in a convent, both the most dynastically important figure in Europe and a
melancholy cipher.

Philip and Juana had six children. Their four daughters were
variously married to kings of Portugal and France, Denmark, Hungary and Bohemia, and a further King of Portugal. One of these
daughters, Mary, had an extraordinarily varied and surprising life,
and after early Hungarian adventures became a great patron of the
arts and the regent of the Netherlands. The two sons scooped the
pool: Charles and Ferdinand.

In the gnarled, Escher-like and chaotic old prince-bishop's
palace in Trento, Buonconsiglio Castle, there is, among many
other wonders, a room with a ceiling fresco by Dosso Dossi. I

have always been frustrated by the stiff grandeur of the official paintings of Charles V, most obviously the ones by Titian which may be bravura displays but make Charles seem trapped beneath the costumes. But to my total surprise, here, commissioned by Prince-Bishop Bernardo III Clesio, are paintings of Bernardo himself – looking every inch the sort of tough, Cardinal Wolsey-style operator who had quite brief openings in his crowded calendar set aside for prayer – and of the young Charles and Ferdinand. The two young men are in beautiful armour and have been painted with astonishing informality, having just taken off their helmets, sitting on a bench with Charles caught in mid-sentence. As character portraits they seem absolutely convincing – Charles, with his cripplingly swollen jaw and his air of ill-focused and over-eager earnestness, Ferdinand more conventionally beefy and military, like a rugby player or an army commander who loves shouting. They were raised separately, Charles in Burgundy and Ferdinand in Spain, but their sometimes tense partnership shaped a large part of world history and – whether or not that was a good thing – it is extraordinarily moving to have this frescoed snapshot of the two of them in their early twenties, as yet unbattered by the implacable weight of their responsibilities.

Juana's incapacity meant that her father acted as a deeply resentful regent in the period between Philip's death and his own. The extreme difficulty after Ferdinand's funeral of having Juana sole monarch meant that in a series of broadly unconstitutional coups her son Charles arrived from his Burgundian lands and made himself not just regent but king, definitively uniting Spain in the face of widespread incredulity and resentment from its inhabitants. This meant his ownership of Aragonese territory scattered across the western Mediterranean and Italy and, of course, chunk after chunk of American coastline as each returning ship came back having found yet more. Oddly, in his uninvolving autobiography (dictated largely during an idle five days with his entourage, being rowed from Cologne to Mainz in June 1550) Charles does not even mention America, but by that time Europe's economy had already been completely reshaped by Mexican and Peruvian bullion – he probably felt it was tacky to talk about economic issues.

After three and a half years of ruling Spain and its empire (plus of course his Burgundian inheritance along France's eastern frontier and the whole of the Netherlands) Charles then had to take on (still only nineteen years old) the consequences of his grandfather Maximilian's death. In the first instance this meant inheriting all the traditional Habsburg lands in and around Austria. It then, after a series of eye-watering bribes, meant becoming Holy Roman Emperor as well. This fluky sequence of events handed power of an unexampled kind to a young, well-educated, thoughtful and diligent man. Nobody involved intended this to happen – at several points a much more modest inheritance would have been possible. The new, and only slightly older, King of France, Francis I, could only look on in stupefied anger. The England of the also very young Henry VIII appeared almost an irrelevance (which despite Henry's bullfrog-like puffing continued generally to be the case). Quite by accident almost the whole of Europe now found itself ruled by dressy young show-offs, with the last remaining Gothic smells of their predecessors suddenly gone. But if this was not enough, Charles's younger brother Ferdinand was about to get a surprise bonus.

Help from the Fuggers

This is perhaps a peculiar admission, but I have never much liked the Mediterranean and have been there rarely. It always seems a bit too out-of-doors and broad-chested for me. Just thinking of all that burning sunshine and ability to navigate in small boats makes me instinctively shrink back. I recently and reluctantly agreed to go to there on a family holiday and at once felt trapped in the sort of novel in which a young curate sits on his own in his hotel room, leafing through his fine edition of Robert Browning, while his beautiful wife hangs out with dockside minotaurs, feeling their deltoids. The novel ends in Bacchic delirium with none of the frenzied participants able to hear the reedy cries for help from the curate as – in a hopeless and ignored attempt to show his wife his prowess at swimming – he is swept out to sea by a current which, the novelist implies, was conjured up by an ancient god to expel such spindle-shanked weakness from his domain. I hasten to add that I felt this based on the unhealthy influence of British Mediterranean fiction rather than because my wife has untreatable stevedore issues.

I am really not saying that I am antagonistic to the south with any sense of pride or aggression, just to record a basic inadequacy. More often than not, particularly when in Italy, I feel irritable and unengaged and in relation to every branch of the arts am just hugely happier to be further north. This does not mean that I am idiotically against the Renaissance, but I do like it better when under more leaden skies. This recoil even affects my otherwise unbridled admiration for Henry James. If only he could have been prevented from sending his fabulous heroines to Italy and instead routed them to Prague or Budapest. The light may be less immense and golden, but they would have been pleasantly surprised by how attractive these cities are, and they probably would not have got sick.

The Habsburgs' engagement in Italy – much more substantial and long-lasting than my own – has always been viewed as awkward. By the time of Charles V they had owned the little Adriatic port of Trieste for more than a century, but it was completely hemmed in by Venetian territory, from the Terrafirma in the west and Istria and Dalmatia in the east. With the Adriatic as a Venetian preserve the Habsburgs were helpless here and Trieste only started to have real value as a side-effect of Venice's eighteenth-century decay. There was also the little territory of Görz or Gorizia to the north of Trieste, whose rulers first conceded a small portion of their lands to the Habsburgs that allowed Tyrol and Styria to be linked up and then in the will of the last, heirless, half-Magyar count the remaining territory was left to Maximilian in 1500, who promptly occupied it, much to Venetian fury. This whole area remains today a sort of linguistic mudslide, particularly once you throw in the eastern territory of Carniola (now the nucleus of

Slovenia and itself partly comprised of the Windic March, a defunct political term that sounds so lovely that it is almost as much to be regretted as the old Balkan Principality of Hum). Italian, Slovene, German, Friulian, Ladin and Croatian have always competed in highly unstable ways, but for much of Habsburg history Venetian power meant that this area was an agreeable dead end, a territorial appendix that provided some manpower and some revenue and some very beautiful little towns.

The line of the Alps meant that the Venetians blocked the eastern end of Italy, the French blocked the west except through the vulnerable County of Burgundy and much of the rest was taken up by contemptuous, crazily anti-Habsburg and self-sufficient Swiss. Once they had defeated Maximilian in 1499 the Swiss lived in a strange legal limbo, with the surrounding states effectively pretending they were not there. In practical terms the only way the Habsburgs could get into Italy was in their role as Holy Roman Emperor, using the Brenner Pass and down through the Imperial territories of Brixen and Trento, the former mainly German-speaking, the latter Italian. It still required transit through a small area of Venetian territory, but this was unproblematic: if the Empire was at war with Venice too then it could trample regardless.

So the Habsburg interest in Italy was always a very uneasy one. It had powerful if somewhat notional origins in the link between the Emperor and the Pope, plus the niggling sense that a revival of the Roman Empire which did not include Italy was a bit odd. As it turned out Frederick III was the last Emperor to be crowned in Rome by the Pope, with Maximilian agreeing with the Pope that he should simply be considered Holy Roman Emperor without the ceremony and Charles V crowned at Bologna in an atmosphere of some acrimony as his troops had recently sacked Rome. After that there were sometimes distant and sometimes close links with the Pope, but there was no attempt to make the Holy element in the Empire's name reliant on a specific blessing.

The Italian Wars which traditionally marked the end of the Renaissance and ushered in generations of helpless misery for Italy were a classic example of the mix-up in Habsburg interests. Maximilian's personal links to Milan (he was married to the duke's daughter) made him concerned as head of the Habsburg monarchy, but also with the hope (unrealized for a further three centuries) of destroying Venice.

The sense that this period sees all the pieces being thrown into the air perhaps kicks off with the unpleasant Pope Innocent VIII's proposal in 1489 to the young French king Charles VIII that he would be sure of a warm welcome if he tried to invade and take over Naples. This initiated a devastating sequence of events that ruined perhaps the most economically dynamic area of Europe to no great purpose beyond ushering in centuries of chaotic and inconclusive foreign meddling. The tin ear for power politics exhibited by a sequence of Popes worsened the mess, but by the time of the Sack of Rome in 1527 the Vatican had long lost control of the proceedings, and a key contributor to the Reformation was less papal demands for money to rebuild St Peter's and more a sense that the leader of the Universal Church had been reduced to a failed and eccentric power-monger.

The arrival of a huge, artillery-toting French army in the peninsula was like the introduction of a fresh predator into some biogeographically sheltered island – its inhabitants had created a series of city states of great complexity, beauty and belligerence but they were militarily governed by codes and values which could not compete with this horde. Historical events can often seem completely pointless, and there can be few better examples in the period than the Italian Wars. In a strategy of shocking dimness the French barrelled through the northern and central Italian states, ending up at the bottom of the peninsula and seemingly without realizing that this meant they were now trapped there by all the vengeful territory they had just laid waste.

The many different actors in Italy formed and re-formed a series of highly unstable alliances. The League of Venice was created by the Pope to expel the French and included Maximilian – this was the first of many leagues which were such a feature of European states whether fighting each other or the Ottomans. It fulfilled its purpose and the bankrupt Charles VIII retreated back to France where he accidentally banged his head while playing

tennis and died, but having established a French role in Italy, as
well as an undying Habsburg enmity that stretched with small
gaps until the end of the Napoleonic Wars. The dismaying contest
carried on, with successful interventions tending to automatically
generate fresh coalitions to take on the new winner. Maximilian
did not shine in all this, a nadir being his attempt to take the Venetian city of Padua (in a short-lived alliance with France). His army
lumbered along from Trento, many troops deserted from lack of
pay and he was defeated by a scratch group of Venetian troops
who had survived an earlier battle. Maximilian's retreat was an
unedifying spectacle, but it was part of a general melee of uselessness which has caused historians to tear their hair out with
frustration at the ferocious yet absurd events they are obliged to
recount. Troops deserted, Swiss mercenaries arrived, decided they
didn't fancy the situation and left again, monarchs staked their
entire reputations in hysteria-ridden, chivalric band-of-brothers
ceremonies but then wandered off again once their reputations
began to tarnish.

A new generation of protagonists, Francis I of France and
Charles V, renewed Italy's disasters in 1521. It is fair to say that
Francis hated Charles. A series of outrageous bribes, funded by the
Fugger family in Augsburg, had allowed Charles to become Holy
Roman Emperor despite Francis's best efforts to make himself
Maximilian's successor. We will never know the private arguments
among the Electors – Maximilian may have been an appealing
figure and a great and imaginative intellectual patron, but his rule
had hardly been a success for the Empire even if it was a few
notches up from the chaos of his father's reign. There was certainly
a case that the Habsburgs had tried and failed, but an at-heart
German-speaking empire stomaching a French leader was even at
this point a bit implausible and while Charles was young and
untried this was also true of Francis. It could be that the vast bribes
were not needed, although such figures as the Prince-Archbishop
of Cologne must have received them with smiles – but in fact this
proved to be the last real chance to wrest the job away from the
Habsburg family until the mid-eighteenth century, as the chaotic

and ad hoc arrangements which had prevailed were now superseded by Charles V's long-term planning.

In Italy one of the most spectacular instances of the France–
Habsburg rivalry was resolved in 1525 at the epochal Battle of
Pavia. It was then that Charles' extraordinary status as inheritor
of both Spain and the Habsburg lands and the Empire came into
play, with both sides amassing huge forces. Many thousands of men
in wildly varied uniforms and weapons – and with equally varied
levels of commitment – marched and countermarched and in a
cataclysmic encounter Francis' army was utterly defeated by the
Imperial–Spanish force, with Francis suffering the humiliation,
extremely rare among monarchs, of being personally captured.

This was the early high point of Charles's career, an event
immortalized in the slightly non-instantaneous media of tapestries
and oil paintings, generally of questionable accuracy, which flashed
– or lumbered – the message of Habsburg victory across Europe.
Its longer-term impact was muted though by the Pope's anxiety
that he had encouraged a monster he could no longer control. The
Pope therefore conjured up a fresh anti-Charles alliance, the
League of Cognac, which looked like pure quality on paper –
France, Venice, Florence and others all joining together with a
cynicism which even the most hard-bitten mercenary should have
blushed at – but which rapidly collapsed, resulting in Charles'
unpaid troops running amok in Rome, killing thousands of troops
and citizens. It was a benchmark low in Papal–Imperial relations
and ended the Roman Renaissance.

Much of Italy had been destroyed and its wealth drained off.
By various criteria it did not really recover until the twentieth century, and outside Naples and the north-west it became a byword
for backwardness and failure, split between a shifting cast of parti-
tionary powers. This disaster was in many ways mere collateral
damage from Franco-Imperial rivalry and an inability to dig out
from under this galvanized Italian nationalists in the nineteenth century just as much as the parallel later story of German humiliation
and failure in the Thirty Years War did for their northern colleagues. But events in Italy now appear very low-key and low-risk.

Charles V had – as so often –concentrated his energies in the wrong place. There were only two adversaries who really mattered: Martin Luther and Suleiman the Magnificent.

The disaster

In this period, pitched battles in which one side feared it would lose were very rare. Except in an ambush, battles rarely happened except when both commanders were confident. But the speed with which one side is suddenly proven wrong in their calculations must be terrifying. Years of tournaments, musters, borrowing to buy weapons, the inter-generational transfers of fighting skills, arguments over dinner about formations, commanders, the value of heavy artillery over light artillery and then, suddenly, one last inspirational harangue and it is all put to the test. A major battle was an unusual event and rulers could feel crushed beneath the weight of historical expectation with everybody hauled back and forth between the sense of their acute danger and the opportunity for the great heroic act.

The marshy plain south of Mohács in southern Hungary is a perfect example of why visiting battlefields is a waste of time. Some twentieth-century monuments there tell you nothing, but it is unclear what one could expect to find here, or indeed on any battlefield. It would be a peculiar mind that could accurately imagine the twenty-five thousand Hungarian troops' catastrophic interaction with fifty-five thousand Ottoman ones on the afternoon of 29 August 1526 as they moved across the fields and woods, particularly as we have little accurate information about any aspect of the battle beyond its disastrous outcome. Much of the Hungarian nobility was killed in the fighting and most of those who survived were captured and executed. The king, Lajos II, fled the field and was either killed or drowned, the subject of numerous later Hungarian paintings, generally showing a poignantly futile figure in brilliant armour and ostrich feathers being hauled from a stream. In the somnolent nearby town of Mohács there is an excellent modern sculpture of the unfortunate monarch, his face creased with suffering, his body consisting only of elaborate decorative armour – the only oddity being that Lajos is shown as worn and grizzled rather than what he really was, a neurotic, uncertain and twerpy twenty-year-old. As had so often been Ottoman practice against earlier opponents, the aim of winning the battle was not to discuss a treaty or extract ransoms but to eradicate the existing ruling order and start afresh.

This catastrophe ended the old Hungarian kingdom, and the rage and distress discussions of the battle have always caused come not least from a sense that it was absolutely avoidable. We see the battle as an overwhelming defeat for Christendom which buried swathes of the Balkans under Turkish rule for centuries, but for contemporaries it cannot have seemed like that for a moment. Indeed, the run-up to Mohács is a near perfect example of how unuseful the term 'Europe' is as a collective description, with almost every court at odds with every other. The only hope in facing the Ottomans lay in unified action, but this never happened. Throughout the long emergency there were gaps in the fighting, but these were generally caused by rebellions in other parts of the Ottoman Empire. As the sultan's troops went off to Egypt or Persia, everyone in Europe seems to have relaxed, clapped their hands to get the court musicians on their little balcony to start playing again and then sat for yet another technically accomplished royal portrait (Lajos nonetheless looking a berk in every single one). For at least a generation it had been clear that the Turks were on the move. A brilliant holding action by the key eastern ally, Ştepan the Great of Moldavia, had bought time, but Ştepan found himself as much threatened by Poles and Hungarians as by the Turks. He eventually concluded that the best advice he could give his descendants was to cut a deal with the more reliable Turks, a deal finalized in 1512. Moldavia therefore became an Ottoman vassal state and the Christian west waved goodbye to what had been a friendly bulwark just through sheer stupidity. Throughout these years the steady chewing sound of Ottoman forces working their way through the map of Europe could be heard – Venice forced out of her Aegean islands, Montenegro surrendering in 1499, Rhodes giving out after a heroic siege in 1522 . . . But the response was confused and helpless and had little sense of urgency, with events in Italy and elsewhere seeming more compelling.

Hungary spectacularly tore itself into bits, convulsed with hatred between the monarchy and many nobles and between the nobles and their peasants. There are too many depressing indications of decline to enumerate them in full, but as usual at times of great stress rival groups stepped forward with ideas for national renewal incompatible with one another. One was the creation of the *Tripartitum*, a disastrous document that equated the Hungarian nation simply with the Hungarian nobility. This was a by-product of disaffection between monarch and nobles, claiming an absolute authenticity for the Hungarians as against their, admittedly often dubious, foreign monarchs. But the result was in the very long term legally to alienate huge numbers of poorer Hungarians as well as – less surprisingly – the mass of non-Hungarian peasants. Given the ruins into which Hungary was about to fall, the *Tripartitum* was blindly clung to by surviving, traumatized noble families and became a sort of poisonous mantra for the True Way which would warp the brains of the ruling class until that class's destruction in the twentieth century. This sense of fear and distrust that undermined Hungary showed through most horribly in the wake of the Archbishop of Esztergom's seemingly sensible plan to launch a crusade against the Turks in 1514. This promptly got completely out of control, with over forty thousand peasants and minor nobles rallying and given weapons under the leadership of the charismatic Szekely soldier György Dózsa. The more substantial aristocracy stayed away from the crusade and this so enraged the soldiers that they devastated the countryside, massacring every real and imagined opponent in their path before being exterminated by a professional army from eastern Hungary. The aftermath is hardly believable, with the captured Dózsa strapped naked before a huge crowd onto a red-hot 'throne' and then mockingly made king with a red-hot crown. His key surviving lieutenants were forced to eat roasted strips of his flesh before being themselves executed. This was a society literally devouring itself without needing any help from the notionally Satanic and uncivilized Ottomans.

The fall of Belgrade in 1521 made a mockery of the young Lajos's regime. The citadel which an earlier generation had so magnificently defended became — partly through bickering and treachery between its defending commanders – a key Ottoman redoubt for nearly three hundred years, with its entire Christian population shipped off to Istanbul as slaves. The devastation caused by Dózsa's war, fear and dislike of the court and simple lack of resources made it impossible for Hungary to defend itself. The court did its bit by setting out to alienate every conceivable source of help, spurning Ottoman proposals for a truce, and potential Polish and Venetian alliances. On top of this the court accused the Fuggers of embezzling from the mines it controlled in Hungary, thereby also alienating perhaps Europe's most powerful family and much of the Holy Roman Empire with it.

Lajos strutted about at the centre of events, but was too inexperienced and unimpressive to gain any real loyalty. He was the king not just of Hungary but also Croatia and the Bohemian lands – Bohemia itself, Moravia, Silesia and Lusatia. Feuding and chaos meant that while he was notionally one of the most powerful men in Europe, he was in practice a short-lived pawn of his two great neighbours, Charles V's brother Archduke Ferdinand and Suleiman the Magnificent. Ferdinand and Suleiman's long reigns would define the future of Central Europe and carve out political units and structures of great durability. Ferdinand acted as his brother's deputy in the east, but Charles was so frequently absorbed in fighting in other parts of the Empire that Ferdinand, with his compact but relatively small Austrian and Tyrolean territories, had to deal on his own with the wave upon wave of catastrophes that threatened to swamp Europe. Both Charles and Suleiman had more sprawling, sumptuous and world-historical sorts of reigns, but it was Ferdinand who had the task of creating the Habsburg monarchy in the form in which it persisted to 1918, eventually himself becoming Emperor.

Maximilian's brilliantly engineered family compact of 1515 meant that in the event of Lajos having no heir his kingdoms would switch to Habsburg rule. The court at Buda was in any event suffused with Habsburg influence because Lajos's wife Mary was Ferdinand's sister and Ferdinand was married to Lajos's sister, Anna. Indeed, a core grounds for dissention among the Hungarian nobles was that they had their own proud anti-Habsburg tradition, most brutally expressed when their King Matthias Corvinus had marched his army into Vienna as recently as 1485, one of Frederick III's many less good moments.

Ferdinand fulfils in Hungarian demonology the role of both saviour and scavenger on national disaster. Events moved with hideous speed after Mohács, with this fundamental breach opening up a seemingly unstoppable western and north-western campaign area for the Ottomans. In 1527, Suleiman's army besieged Vienna, retreated and then returned again in 1529 to finish the task. It was this campaign which initiated the first of the great, self-immolating acts of sacrifice which were all that Hungarians could take away from their general disaster – the siege of Kőszeg.

Driving through the dozy Hobbitons on the hilly borders between the Austrian Burgenland and far western Hungary, it is very hard to imagine that this backwater among backwaters could have been chosen as 1529's focus of destiny. The doziness is now much enhanced by the woodlands which so thickly flourish as part of the principal Cold War border and indeed the trees seem to cut off the area like the spell in *Sleeping Beauty*. But it is also a great linguistic border, bitterly fought over in the earlier twentieth century, so perhaps the placing of Kőszeg is not quite accidental. In any event an enormous Ottoman army stopped there to dispose of its small fortress before moving on to Vienna. The fortress, manned by some seven hundred Hungarian-Croatian troops with no artillery, managed to hold off repeated assaults. The Ottomans were always at a disadvantage because of their short campaigning season, much of it spent getting from Istanbul to, say, Kőszeg and the rest spent getting back before the weather deteriorated dangerously, and the delay at Kőszeg proved fatal. The exact details of the siege are mysterious, and wandering around the little reconstructed fort now it seems completely impossible that it really proved difficult to raze. The Ottoman commanders were so embarrassed by their situation that they exaggerated the size of the garrison and claimed the fort was on a steep hill, making it hard to assault, as opposed to being on a flat piece of land just a bit down from the car park. The deaths of many defenders set a benchmark for ever more extreme sieges, most spectacularly at Eger (1552) and Szigetvár (1566), the defence of the latter being so fervent, reckless and prolonged that Suleiman the magnificent actually *died* of a seizure, presumably brought on by sheer exasperation that another campaigning season lay in tatters thanks to a Hungarian refusal to be reasonable. Instead of surrendering, the last surviving elements in the garrison, under their magnificent Hungarian-Croat commander Zrínyi, charged out to their deaths, taking as many Turkish soldiers with them as they could, an event immortalized in any number of poems, novels and histories and by perhaps the most magnificent of all the great historicist paintings in Hungary's National Gallery, Johann Peter Krafft's *Zrínyi's Last Charge* – a brilliantly coloured cataclysm with fiendish, orc-like Turks cringeing, gawping and tumbling to their deaths before the sheer tangerine-and-scarlet beauty of Zrínyi's costume.

For every heroic stand there were dozens of now-forgotten disasters, as Ottoman troops spread out across Hungary and destroyed it. But the Turks, within their new and extensive lands, remained boxed in by the Adriatic to the south-west and by a thickening chain of Habsburg forts and obstacles that protected the area behind Buda (taken by the Ottomans in 1541) and stabilized the frontier. In the midst of these catastrophes perhaps the only beneficiary was Ferdinand, who stepped into the vacated shoes of Lajos, and changed overnight from a major prince along the lines of the dukes of Bavaria to unquestionably the greatest ruler in Central Europe. The kingdoms he now ruled were all elective monarchies, but it was under these emergency conditions not difficult to persuade the panicked, surviving electoral diets.

After many reverses, betrayals and plots, the Peace of Edirne in 1547 formally split Hungary into three sections. The largest, encompassing the Great Plain, the Hungarian Danube and Croatia, became a full part of the Ottoman Empire. Transylvania became a vassal state, much like Moldavia or the cunning Dalmatian entrepôt of Ragusa/Dubrovnik, and the heart of a subservient but nonetheless vigorous Hungarian area of rule. For many Hungarian nobles Transylvania had clear continuity as the surviving piece of Lajos's kingdom, the rest reduced to alien Habsburg colonial rule. The remaining pieces, including most importantly the Hungarian coronation site of Pozsony (later Bratislava), and comprising very roughly what is now Slovakia and western Hungary, became a new element in the Habsburg monarchy: Royal Hungary. For those living in this rump remnant, it was comparable to an Englishman suddenly finding himself confined to Kent and Sussex and ruled by a Frenchman. As usual such analogies do not work, as the comparison could be both better and worse, but this remnant became the nucleus for the reconquest of Hungary, which would take many reigns. In return for control of it, Ferdinand (initially on behalf of Charles) agreed to pay an annual tribute to the Ottomans of thirty thousand gold florins. This was worth it. Ferdinand could not beat the Ottomans but he could try to pay them off and in the meantime establish the defences which would mark out the new, shockingly mutilated Hungarian borders, borders which continued to impact on the life of Central Europe until the break-up of Yugoslavia in the 1990s and perhaps beyond.

Ferdinand can be thought of as the key ideologue of Habsburg rule. Charles had in one of his frequent acts of intelligent improvisation made him his deputy in the traditional eastern Habsburg lands – initially for the merely expedient reason that Ferdinand needed ownership of a block of territory to give him sufficient status to marry into the Hungarian/Bohemian royal family, as arranged by Maximilian when Ferdinand and Anna were children. Ferdinand sorted out the defence of his massively increased dominions against the Ottomans and had with Anna a tremendous number of children who were dispersed across the whole of Europe, creating a dynastic bedrock. Charles V's role as sort of

Habsburg super-chief turned out to be a temporary one, as Ferdinand's growing seniority, aggression and importance made it ever more likely that Charles would be obliged to split his empire in half – with his only son taking over the Spanish and Burgundian elements and Ferdinand keeping the traditional hereditary lands and his two new kingdoms. But this – as with so much Habsburg history at the time – required a lot of luck and many other outcomes always stayed possible, not the least being the total collapse of the eastern territories to Ottoman depredation.

Charles eventually conceded that Ferdinand would inherit not only the eastern territories but also the role of Emperor. This was both at Ferdinand's insistence and through the logic that the links between the largely German-speaking Empire and Vienna were more obvious than those with Spain. One of the fun bits of mumbo-jumbo now carried out by Ferdinand was the announcement of the 'inalienable heirlooms'. These are now in the Imperial Treasury in Vienna, fittingly in the section of the Hofburg built by Ferdinand and which still proclaims his name and titles in its marvellous gateway. The two 'inalienable heirlooms' were a giant narwhal tusk and an elaborate agate bowl. Ferdinand was anxious that these be 'inalienable' as so many members of the family had a poor record when it came to pawning stuff. These objects therefore had a special status – held by the entire family across all future generations in a way that put them beyond the reach of any specific member. The tusk was a simple piece of necromancy, something that would have been recognized as workaday and unremarkable to some laughing Inuit, turned by distance and ignorance into a unicorn horn giving great potency and virtue to its owner. The agate bowl was far more interesting – this was believed to be the Holy Grail, not least because the letters XRISTO appeared to shimmer inside its translucent stone in certain light conditions (and seemingly only visible to certain individuals). It was in fact made during the reign of Constantine the Great, in the fourth century, and had almost certainly reached Europe as a result of the disgraceful events of the Fourth Crusade – but both tusk and bowl show the strangely hieratic and spooky nature of Habsburg imperial power, with Ferdinand now a fine successor to his grandfather Maximilian.

The Treasury is filled with such cultic objects. That they are viewable today behind glass to anyone with a ticket is, of course, a spectacular collapse in their aura. They would have been shown only to favoured individuals on key occasions, together with such later additions as a colossal emerald from South America carved into a rather tacky green goblet. The physical ownership of such things had a power which no longer has an equivalent. It was on a par with a sense that the Emperor had a more direct relationship with God than others, that he was almost more than human. The Habsburgs could manage this trick better than everyone else because from Ferdinand onward they successfully entangled their own importance as kings and dukes of many territories with the separate cultic power of the Imperial regalia.

During the life of the Empire the coronation regalia were kept in Nuremberg but they are now in the Vienna Treasury, stolen by the Habsburgs at the dissolution of the Empire during the Napoleonic Wars. These objects, which added to their sacral power by being mostly hidden away, sit at the heart of the Habsburg legend and, even in the cold neutrality of a modern museum, are awe-inspiring. For example, a gold scabbard made in Italy in the 1080s for the coronation of the Emperor Henry IV and decorated with images of his predecessors back to Charlemagne. Or a pair of red samite gloves covered in jewels made for the Emperor Frederick II in 1220. Or – my favourite – the scarcely credibly beautiful Imperial mantle decorated with stylized gold camels, a palm tree and Arabic script made by Islamic artists in Sicily for King Roger II of Sicily in the 1130s. This marvel is celebrated now as one of the greatest examples of medieval Sicily's multicultural tangle (the culture immortalized in Szymanowski's delirious 1926 opera *King Roger*). But – as with the historical and zoological confusions over the Holy Grail and the unicorn horn – at the time the mantle was believed to be a battle trophy of Charlemagne's, won in a campaign against the Moors. This is why Charlemagne is shown wearing the mantle in Dürer's wonderful imaginary portrait. In reality it is safe to assume it became associated with the Emperor's coronation quite straightforwardly in the era of Frederick II, whose mother was Roger II's daughter. It is a tribute to the somewhat wonky and chaotic nature of these notionally immemorial and top-of-the-line ceremonies that even such basic information at some point got lost.

Rather liberatingly I think I do not have to mention ever again Habsburg ceremonial and cultic issues. To us the Habsburg rulers – many quite mediocre or merely dutiful – can seem as specialized and helpless as koala bears and their claims to grandeur and the highest place in Europe an obvious try-on. But while they were always hated and schemed against they hardly ever lost their very powerful force-field. Once they successfully established themselves under Charles V and Ferdinand I they remained somehow exceptional. This was achieved through practical measures (bribes, threats, soldiers, presents, marriages) but also through the creation of this formidable magic circle, which each generation reinforced through manipulation of special objects, events and ceremonies. The genius lay in corralling together both the great family symbols (the walls of shields in Innsbruck and Wiener Neustadt, the various tombs, the Babenberger family tree at Klosterneuburg, the 'inalienable heirlooms') and the Imperial symbols. Ferdinand for most of his life was overshadowed by his elder brother and was only actually Emperor for eight years, but the solidity of Habsburg succession in their core lands stayed in place into the twentieth century and Ferdinand effectively ensured that this bizarre, unfolding drama was played out from Vienna, the focus of resistance to the Ottomans. He may have misunderstood the origins or purpose of the symbols he surrounded himself with and given too much credit to a wacky-looking sea-mammal's tooth, but his power was real enough and quite immune to the smirks of twenty-first-century literalists.

CHAPTER THREE

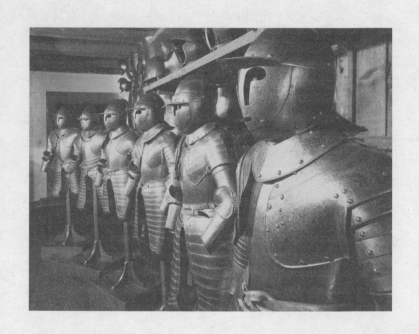

'Mille regretz'

It is frustratingly unclear how much Charles V enjoyed his decades as Emperor. He seems never to have let his Imperial mask drop and this public impassivity became the model for later members of his family. His court wandered from place to place, and although raised in the Low Countries and often surrounded by soldiers, advisers and musicians from around Flanders, Charles in the end became a sort of adopted Spaniard, revelling in the rich, Stygian, formal court style which was to become the essence of Habsburg rule when his son, Philip II, made Madrid the unified country's capital. In European history Charles can only really be compared to Napoleon and Hitler in his grip on the continent – but he never seems to have revelled in such a role and, as it came to him through the deft machinations of his grandfather rather than through conquest, his efforts to defend it have an air of weary dutifulness rather than megalomania. Maximilian had dreamed of so many combinations – at one point pondering whether he should have a shot at making himself Pope as well – but always suffered from an appealing inability to follow through on anything except his board-game-like marriage alliances. Charles inherited a genuinely vast and unprecedented sprawl of territories from Maximilian, but no serious effort was made to give them any unity. He scurried from place to place, swapping around hats, crowns, necklaces and special cloaks. He was always reading up constitutions and mottos and being drilled on the membership and peccadillos of dozens of prickly aristocracies and urban oligarchies in different bits of Europe. At every turn he had to face rebellious townsfolk, Ottoman pirates, annoying Protestants, double-dealing German princelings and problematic family members.

Charles's frequent illnesses, his inability to eat in public (because of his enormous jaw) and his personal, very knowledgeable enthusiasm for gloomy music suggest a long-wished-for private existence, perhaps as the abbot of some deeply refined and closeted monastic order – a wish he was able to grant himself after his resignation. His favourite song seems to have been 'Mille Regretz', described in his lifetime as 'the Song of the Emperor' ('So great is my suffering and painful woe / That my days will soon be ended'), which about summed it up. Charles always lived under the shadow of his mother's mental illness – but a quick look at his in-box would have given quite enough of a basis in itself for lapses, silences and indecisions. Another favourite was the tune 'Belle qui tiens ma vie', a much more cheerful, albeit wistful, piece which must be (and I will be immediately contradicted here by dozens of more knowledgeable readers) one of the earliest of all European melodies still familiar and widely recognized.

We will never know, during one of the key crisis points of his reign, when in 1521 he was face to face with Martin Luther at the Diet of Worms, whether he was thinking more about the perils of heresy or about the almost unimaginable great shiploads of Mexican treasure which had arrived for him in Brussels. His need to be stiff-necked and decisive year in, year out (and at Worms he was still only twenty-one years old), created a great, chiselled facade and a form of kingship which his successors copied, whether or not that facade hid an intellectual ferment akin to Charles's or mere vacuity. Charles's enterprises sprawled crazily in every conceivable direction, with his 1535 invasion of Tunis being funded by tons of gold extorted from the Great Inca. He presided over a staggering increase in the range and experience of Europe – a process by which blamelessly downtrodden Castilian peasants and Flemish bureaucrats found themselves shipped off to the New World and pushed into behaviours, foods and sights for which there were no precedents. The creation of the Viceroyalty of New Spain and the Viceroyalty of Peru under Charles (their flag the Cross of Burgundy) made existing European political arrangements something of a joke, with the area taken up by Henry VIII's England tuckable into a small part of Central America. Francis I has always been much condemned for his Christianity-betraying alliance with the Ottomans, but really what choice did he have in the face of this haughty, unbeatable champion of an unstoppable family? Things were even worse than his contemporaries knew. In Regensburg to attend a meeting of the Imperial diet, Charles slept with the daughter of a local burgher. The result, a bastard son who grew up to become Don John of Austria, commanded the fleet that destroyed the Ottoman navy at the Battle of Lepanto, long after Charles's death. So even in his down time he was shaping the world's history.

But Charles seems to have quite rapidly realized that there was no future for all this pan-European excitement, shedding and sub-contracting whatever he could. As on other occasions, the secret mechanisms that lurk in Europe's political structure ensured that enemies of a universal monarchy generated like antibodies. The history of Protestantism simply *cannot* be disentangled from Charles's own prominence and power. He faced off against Luther at Worms and made his great speech: 'What is true and a great shame and offence to Us is that a single monk, going against God, mistaken in his opinion, which is against what all of Christendom has held for over a thousand years to the present, wishes to pervert Us.' Charles was acting here both as a true son of the Church and as a figure whose resources already threatened to destroy all dissent.

How better to resist such a man than by embracing Protestantism? The decision by Charles at Worms to spurn Luther clearly saved the Pope from potential Armageddon, but it also created a situation where religious dissent could also mean dissent from Habsburg rule. Distracted on a thousand fronts, by the time Charles took clear military action against the Protestant threat in the brief Schmalkaldic War twenty-five years later it was all too late and despite his victory Europe was awash with anti-Catholic forces. Even the famous portrait Charles commissioned from Titian to mark his triumph, in plumes and full armour on what must be one of the greatest of all ramping steeds in Western art, is a study in failure. Charles's small, grey-bearded head looks unconvincing, as though, like those painted boards at the seaside, he has popped it through the hole and is unaware whether he is being portrayed as a Catholic Champion or in a comic red-striped one-piece bathing costume. Sadder still, Charles had in fact been too ill even to mount a horse during the battle and had been carried in a litter – so Titian's incomparable vision would have been known to everyone at the time as a bought polite lie.

'The strangest thing that ever happened'

The sheer speed of the Reformation seems almost as alarming now as it did then. In 1517 the unknown Martin Luther was nailing up his Theses in a Saxon university town, by the 1520s there were mass conversions as far south as Slovenia and by the 1530s the charming polymath Johannes Honterus was instilling the Word in the far south-east of Transylvania, the 'infection' already some seven hundred and fifty miles from its source. This religious cataclysm flowed at its heart from a collapse of authority. The actual details of what the new religion would involve were acrimoniously thrashed out over the following century, but for Central Europe there was a sudden change not unlike that of 1918 or the end of the Cold War in 1989, with a broad coalescence around the idea that the status quo no longer made sense. To many people with many motives the Pope became almost overnight a fat, sinister brute, the figure in a thousand woodcuts, covered in rich vestments and jewels being chased down into Hell.

As the entire structure of obedience caved in, some secular rulers could not believe their luck as the dazzling array of properties and treasures under Rome's protection looked vulnerable. All over Europe, most famously in England, figures in power just helped themselves. None of this came from a crisis in faith itself – Europe had experienced a huge burst of rebuilding and decorating churches just before Wittenberg (after all, the crisis was caused in part by the Pope's wish to raise cash to rebuild St Peter's), including hundreds of the sensational just-pre-Reformation painted altarpieces that now fill Central European art galleries. But faith took a new direction, with ferocious arguments within an ever larger number of camps, including an intellectually recovered and aggressive Catholic one.

Within the Habsburg framework there was never a real chance that the Reformation would be accepted – the apex of power was so entangled in Rome's sanction that it was inconceivable that Charles V could change his allegiance. But for many powerful aristocrats the situation was different, with an unstable blend of personal devotion and greed giving an irresistible momentum to fresh arrangements. Not entirely unlike the Communist revolutions of 1917–19, there was a sense of being part of a wave of the future. With both Protestants and Catholics proclaiming a universal truth, the success of the former dismayed and demoralized the latter, and it was a shock from which Protestantism never recovered that its new and universal truth was ignored in places such as Spain and Italy, embraced confusedly in England and in the end scornfully rejected by both the Habsburgs and the kings of France. As the New Jerusalem stubbornly failed to turn up, Protestant doctrine became so self-contradictory that an enormous intellectual and spiritual space opened up – spotted by the reforming Council of Trento (Trent) – for a successful Catholic fight-back.

Charles and Ferdinand were now stirring up great fear and anxiety. Composite ownership of territory had always been a commonplace, but Maximilian I's scheming had created a family network of extraordinary power and with fluky extras he cannot have guessed at. It had been routine for royal families to criss-cross Europe and generate curious combinations, claims and possibilities. Lajos II of Hungary had parents born in Poland and France and Charles V himself united all kinds of strange pan-European flavours. But the Habsburgs seem at this point on their way to being the genuine heirs of the Roman Empire, with other surviving monarchies reduced to subservience or (like the once great thrones of Hungary and Bohemia) total absorption.

There was a great gap between the grandeur of Charles's polit-ical inheritance and the misery of his personal one. It seems to have been his great-grandmother, the Masovian Piast princess Cymburgis, who introduced the terrible Habsburg jaw which afflicted Charles and so many of his descendants. The men could try to hide it with extravagant beards, but the women in portrait after portrait appear to have a sort of awful pink shoe attached to their lower faces. He also seems to have been crushed by the same melancholy that ravaged both his mother's and his grandfather's sides of the family and which would again emerge among his descendants, most famously in his great-nephew (and grandson!) Rudolf II.

Europe was now raddled with Protestantism and this split in Christianity became linked to one's attitude to Habsburg hegem-ony. But it was not simply a question of two religious sides. At the Peace of Augsburg in 1555 that followed Charles' crushing of the Lutheran princes, it was at last decided that each territory in the Empire would have its own religious practices and that they would be those of its ruler. This was already inadequate since both sides chose to pretend that Calvinism did not exist, a serious prob-lem as this austere form of Protestantism was becoming all the rage and would reshape countries as far apart as Scotland and Transyl-vania. It also fudged the problem of Catholic religious territories. In a jaw-dropping coup back in 1525 the Grand Master of the Teutonic Knights, the Hohenzollern Prince Albert of Prussia, had spent long hours talking with Luther and searching his soul before coming up with the idea that God had told him to become Lutheran and make the monastic territories he had been elected to rule on the Baltic into his family's private hereditary possession. This sort of outrage, where a great crusading Catholic bastion could simply be pocketed by a cheeky individual, set other rulers across Europe stroking their beards. Henry VIII, for example, real-ized that if he made a leap like Albert's he could cash in his old wife, get a delightful new one *and* grab all his kingdom's monastic property for himself: to break with the Pope certainly seemed something worth thinking about.

The Peace of Augsburg therefore tried to hammer into place a deal which benefited many individual, current rulers; but what level of Protestant abuse, sincere or cynical, would provoke a violent Catholic response? Charles and Ferdinand's successors, Maximilian II and Rudolf II, were both, in the manner of the period, live-and-let-live on religious issues and in that sense the Peace was a success, but religion, inheritance and personality were all tangled up in ways that under the right circumstances could prove catastrophic. From Charles's point of view the Peace was a failure – there was probably nothing he could have done to arrest Protestantism's progress, but he was definitely too late by 1555. His private agonies, exhaustion and premature ageing had little impact on his opponents, all of whom could only see the sheer power of the Habsburg family. Even notional Catholic allies among the German princes turned on him. One last curious inheritance gambit went wrong. In yet another total surprise the fifteen-year-old Edward VI of England suddenly died and his much older sister, the very Catholic Mary I, became queen. Charles arranged for her to marry his son Philip. Philip's role in England was carefully hedged about but it is generally forgotten in a frenzy of English nationalist huffing that he was at the time called the King of England and features equally with Mary on the coinage. Nothing was fully settled but Charles mulled over the idea that if Philip and Mary had a son he would inherit England and Burgundy, creating a formidable, coherent and curious new state – but also making England permanently into a Catholic Habsburg province. This chilling what-if came to nothing: Mary was already very old to have a first child, seems to have suffered from a phantom pregnancy which if real could have had the most astounding consequences, and died after only five years on the throne, taking a possible Habsburg England with her. Phew.

Charles saw only disasters around him after the Peace and, shattered and sick, took the unprecedented step of actually resigning. The Pope thought this 'the strangest thing that ever happened'. The whole point of hereditary office was that the decline and death of the ruler was a central part of the pattern – to bail out in favour of others made no sense. Charles is usually seen as rather noble and impressive, standing there in Brussels, surrounded by sobbing noblemen, making his great act of renunciation. But it could be argued that this just showed his startling family arrogance – thinking about both his predecessors and his successors, Charles seems genuinely to have seen himself as a mere link in a great Habsburg chain. Rather than dying in office surrounded by the usual hypocrites and impatient whispering, how much more imposing to hand out his offices in person. The process took a satisfying eleven months to complete as, in a series of grand pronouncements, he gave Burgundy to Philip in October 1555, Spain to Philip in January the following year (plus of course the Americas), the Franche-Comté (the confusing, separate 'County of Burgundy' as opposed to the Duchy) to Philip in April and the job of Holy Roman Emperor to Ferdinand (who already owned the Habsburg hereditary lands as well as being King of Bohemia and King of Hungary) in September.

As with many other Habsburg subdivisions there always lay open the chance that the two parts of the family might reunite at some future date. It was extremely unclear which of them should be seen as the senior branch: the Holy Roman Emperor trumps everyone, but it was impossible not to notice what was happening in Spain, now united fully and with a proper resident monarch at last, who in 1581 tacked on Portugal and its own American and Asian empires just for good measure. Both branches of the Habsburgs behaved as though they were senior, and this was a key factor in keeping them apart. Philip II in Madrid was undoubtedly the wealthiest and most powerful man in Europe. Spain's culture had a decisive influence – the rich, sombre gloominess of its court totally shaped Vienna's atmosphere into the eighteenth century, and Vienna had in turn little impact on Madrid. Maximilian II lived at the Spanish court for years before he became Emperor and his son and successor Rudolf II was raised there. There was a sense in which the Austrian lands were a bit of a backwater – a dreary fighting frontier not comparable to the greatness of the Spanish Empire. The key moment was Ferdinand's death, after only a short reign. Charles's deal had been that Philip would take over, but Ferdinand instead insisted on keeping with his direct line. It is hard to imagine the Electors accepting a Spaniard as Emperor, particularly one so very powerful and Catholic. So it could be that Ferdinand's move to have himself replaced with his son, who would become Maximilian II, was necessary to the Habsburgs holding on to the office at all. This in some measure estranged the families, but it did not prevent them marrying each other in a notably creepy way. It became part of their arrogance that nobody else was good enough. So Maximilian II married Philip II's sister Maria (so that makes them first cousins) and later Philip II married Anna, one of Maximilian's children (that makes him her uncle!). Mercifully there then followed a group of bachelor or outlying Emperors, but the two branches were back intermarrying by the 1630s with catastrophic genetic results, birth problems and big jaws scattered everywhere.

With a strong sense of regret, the scene now shifts from the incense-laden grandeur of the Spanish court – a separate story with its own trajectory, featuring silver mines, chocolate, and electric eels – to the snowbound, fortified, inland territories which Ferdinand's descendants ruled into the twentieth century.

The armour of heroes

In one of the saddest events of 1665, a ship heading along the Danube to Vienna foundered and sank, taking with it the entire music library of the Habsburg court at Innsbruck. The dissolution into the murky water of many thousands of irreplaceable handwritten sheets of music was the final act winding up the Tyrolean Habsburg family. The exact nature of this catastrophe is unknown but Innsbruck had been as important a musical centre as Salzburg or Vienna and attracted generations of brilliant Italian players and composers. One of these was Giovanni Pandolfi, who we only know about at all because he happened to publish two sets of

violin sonatas which had a substantial impact on composers such as Purcell and Bach (indeed, Purcell stole one of his
most beautiful tunes from Pandolfi). The sonatas' publication in
Innsbruck in 1660, dedicated to the reigning archduke and archduchess, is the only information we have. Pandolfi may have been
the elderly and prolific composer of many great masses and an
unparalleled sequence of works for all the major instruments, and
single-handedly made seventeenth-century opera a whole lot more
interesting than it turned out to be. Or he may have been a pettish,
violent and gruesome child prodigy who turned out a handful of
sonatas before his disgusted guardians quietly sold him off to a
man scouting around for reliable galley-rowers. We will never
know – whatever was on that ship is lost.

The sonatas themselves conjure up a magical, deeply refined
world. They are dedicated to key Italian musicians at the court:
violinists, castrati and the great Antonio Cesti, whose work
obsessed the Emperor Leopold I in the following decade. But as
usual they show the stark limits to what music can tell us – we
have literally no knowledge at all about the composer, his intentions in the sonatas and what his relationships were with any of
the dedicatees.

His patron, Archduke Ferdinand Karl, was by any measure a
deeply unpleasant absolutist, who even in his great portrait by
Frans Luycz – a mass of delirious scarlet cloth and brocade and
perhaps the most beautifully designed boots in European history
– sneers at posterity. It was Ferdinand Karl's sudden early death,
followed by his younger brother's equally early death three years
later, which ended the dynasty. The latter, Sigismund Franz, who
had been Bishop of Trent, with all speed chucked in the ecclesiastical jobs, set himself up in Innsbruck and got married so as to sire
a son. But it was too late: he died only twelve days after the marriage ceremony. Innsbruck itself now became a mere provincial
outpost of Vienna – hence the unhappy decision to try to relocate
its musical archives – now a cultural backwater after a long golden
period that stretched at least from Maximilian I's great funerary
statue array to Ferdinand Karl's composers.

The Innsbruck court was the heart of the Habsburg territories entangled in the Alps south of Bavaria, at that time ruling both Tyrol and the zany smorgasbord of Further Austria. Much of the Habsburg inheritance had a superficial coherence (proper kingdoms, directly ruled duchies next to each other), which makes it quite different from the rest of the Holy Roman Empire. But as someone who has spent too much time wandering around such political absurdities as Schaumburg-Lippe or Hohenlohe-Weikersheim it is with a little cry of happy recognition that I recognize the friendly oddness of Further Austria. On a map the Tyrol itself seems compact enough and has a sort of plausibility, but in practice it was a demented mass of particularisms, parcels of Alpine valleys seasonally cut off from one another, self-reliant and with very specific ideas about outsiders. It is symptomatic of the Tyrol that the celebrated Copper Age human 'Ötzi' should have had his mummified corpse dug out of the ice there – both because of Ötzi's air of rather priggish, rugged self-reliance (his furs, his bag of healing herbs) and because he had an arrow stuck in his back.

If the map of Tyrol could be coloured in by some measure of 'usefulness' then it would appear, instead of as a compact block, as a series of small strands and spills hedged in by ferocious mountains, enjoyable as a whole only to late-nineteenth-century railway builders of the kind who relished expensive challenges. This patchiness continued in the rest of Further Austria, to scattered, tiny territories between Augsburg and Strasbourg and intermittently around the Danube and on to Lake Constance without any rhyme or reason. These were picked up by Habsburg ancestors after the original south German 'Big Bang' that fragmented Swabia after the extinction of the Hohenstaufen dynasty in 1268. Even the most detailed historical maps lose patience in trying to convey the mass of 'forest towns', strong-points, religious foundations and pointless villages that made up Further Austria. The small populations of the region meant that at various levels it just did not matter very much. As this was the Habsburgs' original home (even if chunks had been bitten off by the Swiss) its awkwardness was not allowed to stand in the way of its defence. In many ways it was the existence of

such arbitrary chunks as the Sundgau (a very ancient family possession – part of Alsace) that made the Habsburgs into a western
European power, building in a core Habsburg–French animosity.
But perhaps the key point of this book is to shelter the reader
from topics such as 'the strategic value of the Sundgau', although,
naturally, they do have their own fascination.

Just to polish off Further Austria for ever, various blocks would
be given to the Spanish Habsburgs as bribes for not pursuing their
own claim to Vienna's territories and to allow the Spanish to communicate with the Low Countries. As a result the Sundgau was
almost eradicated by criss-crossing Imperial, Swedish and French
troops during the Thirty Years War and the unpopulated ruins sold
to the French in 1648, with the money paying for Archduke Ferdinand Karl's penchant for Italian music. Most of the Sundgau and
other scraps were later handed over to the Duke of Baden and King
of Württemberg by Napoleon, and at the Congress of Vienna the
Austrians decided they needed these rulers' good will and would
not ask for Further Austria to be handed back. The one exception
was the small chunk of land at the end of Lake Constance – the
Vorarlberg – with its main town of Bregenz, which stayed on as a
western extension of the Tyrol. This region made no further contribution to world history, except for an ungrateful and thwarted bid
at the end of the First World War to detach itself from Austria and
become part of Switzerland. I promise to never ever raise the issue
of the outlying territories of Further Austria again.

The oddness of these lands and the challenges they posed to
their rulers cannot detract from the importance of Innsbruck itself,
which is both hedged round by daunting geographical obstacles,
and the key to the great trading route from Bavaria to Italy. Indeed,
as the city controlling access to the Brenner Pass, it was one of
those chokepoints at which European culture was most fluid and
creative – the German-speaking Ferdinand Karl had followed his
father's example by marrying a member of the Medici family and
the German–Italian blend of Innsbruck is exactly what would be
expected. In my own small way I felt this, having travelled there
after a few days of sitting in the sunny world of Gorizia and the

Trentino eating risotto and delicious tomato salads. To mark the crossing of such an exciting cultural watershed I ordered a 'Tyrolean farmer's omelette' which proved to be of an enormity and fattiness that would strike dead – mottled, puce and bolt-upright in his tractor cabin – any farmer stupid enough to make it his lunchtime choice.

Discussion of the Tyrol Habsburgs has to go somewhere in a single section and it is here rather than later because Innsbruck's real claim on everyone's time is the great Archduke Ferdinand II of Tyrol, who ruled from 1564 to his death in 1595. The separate Tyrolean line came and went and at various points was absorbed back under direct control in Vienna. Indeed Ferdinand himself married a very beautiful commoner whose sons were not allowed to inherit, and a late second marriage only produced daughters, so his own death ended this one patch of Tyrolean independence. Ferdinand had been given the job after an adventurous youth fighting the Turks and helping his father, the Emperor Ferdinand I (there are too many Ferdinands). At the Emperor's death, he made Ferdinand ruler of the Tyrol and Further Austria, while his elder brother, Maximilian, ruling from Vienna, became Emperor Maximilian II. Ferdinand set out to do something remarkable at Innsbruck and it is a shame that the city today is so far off the cultural trail rather than just on the skiing trail, as Ferdinand's home, Schloss Ambras, is such a marvel, one of the few places where it is possible to get an almost unalloyed sense of walking about in a Renaissance patron's mind.

Because Ferdinand had no successor his collections were much messed about, with his nephew the Emperor Rudolf II taking for his own collection some of the choicest armour and curiosities, these first going to Prague and then on to Vienna under Rudolf's successors (and with some heading to Stockholm thanks to marauding Swedish troops in the Thirty Years War). Flood, fire and insects have disposed of some of the remainder, with some further bad input from the catastrophic sunken boat full of music. But Ambras has also preserved a lot and the courtyards and halls still feel convincingly Ferdinandine.

The collections include the earliest painting of Dracula and a huge sequence of Habsburg family portraits where the dreadful chin can be followed down the generations. A mass of peculiar objects from various sources recreate an approximation of Ferdinand's cabinet of curiosities, including two perfect memento mori – an archer skeleton carved from pearwood by Hans Leinberger, commissioned by Ferdinand's great-great-grandfather Maximilian I, and a little carved skeleton in a frame, his hand resting on his chin in a mock philosophical pose which you can only see properly by looking up close, when you see *your own face* reflected in the mirror behind him. I have always loved this sort of slightly goth-metal object, but on my last trip to Ambras realized I was getting old enough for memento mori to have a bit too much bite and found myself more dismissive and impatient of them than before. Like wedding or graduation photos they sit there patiently over the years, waiting to have their full impact.

An important piece of family history is told in an oddly naive narrative painting of young Ferdinand being sent by his father all the way to Brussels to plead with his uncle Charles V not to resign. The mission was of course a failure, but worth it for this picture, with its little image of a house through the window of which you can see the poorly Charles, and over there is a ruffed Ferdinand on his big journey. The whole thing seems to cry out for simple captioning in big letters. I also cannot prevent myself from mentioning the extraordinary portraits of Petrus Gonzalez and his family, natives of Tenerife who were cursed by a total covering of thick hair and who adorned a number of courts, from Paris to Brussels to Parma, spending much of their time with Ferdinand's aunt Margaret. The sheer, irreducible strangeness of their genetic condition (now called 'Ambras syndrome') is perfectly preserved in these paintings, the family members looking dignified but uncanny in their elegant court clothing.

At the core of Ferdinand's collection were stories of heroism – bravery in battle, chivalric courtesy and flamboyant generosity. He paid out huge sums, called in favours from across Europe, inherited earlier collections and was given the most extraordinary presents by other rulers to allow him to fulfil this obsession. The collection is now a fraction of what it was, but still remarkable – a sequence of elaborate armours worn by the greatest paragons of the age: the fire-blackened armour of the Marquess of Mantua, who expelled the horrible Charles VIII from Italy at the Battle of Fornovo; the armour of the Count Palatine of the Rhine, commander of the German cavalry at the relief of the Siege of Vienna in 1529; the armour of Ferdinand's key aide during the 1556 Turkish campaign; the armour of the young and glamorous Archduke Matthias, decades before he became the petulant, elderly Emperor of the Thirty Years War. It would all be better with the lighting a bit lower, indeed ideally viewed with a flaming torch, but even so these elaborate and beautiful armours, like historical exoskeletons, keep their resonance. For Ferdinand these were the armours of a Golden Age around which exemplary stories could be told. There is also a mass of tournament equipment, Ottoman weapons, 'Turkish' masks worn in chivalric melees and the colossal armour of Bartlmä Bon, the giant who accompanied him (to sensational effect) at the great 1560 tournament at Vienna. Ferdinand seems to have been racked by a form of obsessive military melancholy, of great deeds and companionship, a soldierly equivalent of the sort of weepiness that hits rugby players in middle age.

This tone lurks everywhere. There is a huge painting of the admirals at the Battle of Lepanto in 1571, the greatest event in Ferdinand's lifetime, when the forces of the Holy League destroyed the Ottoman fleet and ended the Turks' psychological death-grip. There, against a suitable backdrop of sinking and burning Turkish galleys, are the heroes of Christian Europe – Ferdinand's bastard uncle Don John, Marcantonio Colonna and Sebastiano Veniero, all with an air of trying not to smirk with pride. As with the armour it remains very easy to see Ferdinand talking through the details of the victory for the *n*th time to his latest visitors.

It could be that Ferdinand was in fact a dreadful man, but whenever I am at Schloss Ambras it seems clear that he was one of the Habsburgs who make the family worthwhile, who more than balance all the pious timeservers who congest the family tree – a figure up there with Maximilian I. His willingness to agree to disinherit his successors so that he could marry a commoner also gives him an immediate chic. It is appropriate therefore that he is buried in an upstairs chapel of the Hofkirche, which his father, Emperor Ferdinand I, had built to house Maximilian's cenotaph. Alexander Colyn, a Flemish sculptor, carved the reliefs of battles and marriages (designed by Dürer generations before) which cover the cenotaph's sides, but also Ferdinand of Tyrol's first wife's tomb, and then Archduke Ferdinand's own. As a final odd but happy touch a step juts out of the chapel wall and a full suit of Ferdinand's own armour kneels to a statue of the Virgin Mary on the altar. This stylized piece of Renaissance mystical courtesy feels eerie and immediate, as though Innsbruck was still successfully signalling to us the strange ideas of the past.

Europe under siege

The frontier zone that marked the border between the Habsburg lands and the Ottoman Empire was a shifting, frightening reality from the fifteenth century to the end of the eighteenth. A straggling line from the Adriatic to the Carpathians, prone to violent bends westward in the face of Turkish attacks, dominated the lives of countless families who, simply to survive, organized themselves around permanent war-readiness. However distracted the Emperor might be by concerns in the Low Countries or Tunisia or Germany, a permanent war council, based at Graz, tried in his absence and quite often failed to regulate this huge region. After the disaster at Mohács the Turks often ravaged areas of what became known as the Military Frontier and made some further gains but the zone broadly held.

The sheer awfulness of front-line life is preserved in a remarkable wall-painting on the outside of the cathedral in the Styrian city of Graz. The year 1480 had been so grim that it was felt appropriate to pay the painter Thomas of Villach to commemorate the survivors' awareness of their debt to God for watching over them (although, as with plague monuments, there is mixed in an inevitable air of reproach about just how attentive God was being in practical terms). Although much faded it is still possible to see a heavenly host hovering above Graz, as plague, Turkish raiders and harvest failure hideously combine to carry off a large part of the population. The famine was caused by a plague of locusts, appearing in the picture particularly horrible as they are the size of crows (a not unreasonable distortion by the painter as they would be invisible at their true size). Plague victims are shown being put in their coffins and 1480 was a not untypical example of these devastating, random blows that might in a few weeks kill a quarter of a town's entire population, a level of natural catastrophe for which we now simply have no comparison.

The third element in Graz's 1480 martyrdom is a Turkish raid, and little figures are shown in a slave-pen prior to being strung together in lines and led back into Ottoman territory, the fate of hundreds of thousands of Germans, Croats and Hungarians. The penalties of defeat were therefore extraordinarily high in Central Europe. For troops fighting, say, across Italy the general penalty for losing was to be offered a place in the winner's army; with some infrequent exceptions, civilians on the losing side tended to be left alone or made to pay an exorbitant tax. On the Frontier to lose meant to become a slave. Most of Graz's fortifications have been taken down but for centuries it bristled with ever more elaborate walls, towers, water obstacles and artillery platforms. It was the central place from which troops, supplies, money and orders were sent out to the zigzag of smaller forts to the south and east and its successful defence was crucial if the Habsburg southern flank was to hold. It remains, despite the loss of much of its military kit, a startling place, its defensive origins clearly still seen in the colossal central rock on which the castle used to stand.

A frequent subject of conversation in families across the region must have been the quiet suggestion that it might make sense to move somewhere a bit nicer and the Graz authorities constantly had to battle to keep an adequate population in place. This was done by lavishing the most remarkable privileges on those who could be persuaded to move there, with land, money and prestige in return for a high level of military readiness. Many refugees from Ottoman-held Serbia and Bosnia moved, sometimes in large groups, over to the Habsburg side, the origins of the very mixed cultures of areas such as Slavonia which were to be so brutally unmixed in 1992. Systems of scouts, watchers, spies, couriers and alarm towers formed the Frontier's nerve-ends, but a large Turkish raiding party could move at the same speed as the news of its arrival and could smudge out whole communities in a couple of hours. The only defences were walls sufficiently thick and well-manned and provisioned to hold up the raiders until help arrived, with the usual nightmare, carefully exploited by the Turks, of having somehow to keep up a state of readiness over the course of decades of quiet (and therefore, in practice, often letting readiness slip), waiting for that fatal attack.

A completely extraordinary survival is the Armoury in Graz. This truly disturbing sequence of rooms consists of thousands upon thousands of weapons, hung in row upon row. Most of the weapons have no decorative features at all and they fall into a quite different category from the aristocratic showpieces surviving in museums. A pistol covered in pretty silver chasing is a pleasure to look at, but the Arsenal weapons are simply there to kill people – sickeningly utilitarian spears piled up in uncountable numbers; those disgusting spiked frames known as 'Spanish riders' designed to cripple horses; shelf after shelf of robot-like grey metal breast-plates; an infinity of muskets. The older and simpler equipment, which runs every imaginable sadistic variation on sharpened edges and points, is the more sinister as its power to do terrible things is undimmed after four or five centuries. I can think of nowhere else which gives anywhere close to so vivid a sense of the workaday business of fighting – of the frightening emergencies that would have activated this great mass of equipment.

This standardized turning-out of just-good-enough basic equipment for militia use was quite separate from the elaborate weapons and armour carried by commanders and their retinues. These men were a mix of local families and adventurers who would come from all over Europe, sometimes taking a turn in defending the East to gain prestige or as part of a crusading vow. It was rare for any serious fighting man not to turn up here at some point in his career and the structures of the Empire encouraged this. In the Vienna Armour and Weapons Museum there is a spectacular portrait of the landsknecht Konrad von Boyneburg, painted in old age in the 1560s. He is wearing the most beautiful decorative armour and – in a heroic coup – the museum shows this actual armour next to the picture. Konrad knocked about everywhere, working for Charles V on the whole, and he looks like a perfect Christian knight, except for the tiny giveaway details of the commander's batons scattered about proudly at his feet to indicate his campaigns. These have written on them the places he fought in: southern Germany, northern Italy and – most completely disgracefully – Rome, where he was a key figure in the city's sack in 1527, a shameful event which he seems pleased enough by. But Konrad boasts too of having fought in Hungary, the northern part of the Frontier, and he was one of many highly mobile, brilliantly equipped freebooters and scoundrels crucial to the world of raids and counter-raids that formed Christendom's first line of defence.

The pirates' nest

The brutal glamour of figures like Konrad formed a very different world from the woollier and more remote regions of the Frontier. The most famous holders of the far southern flank, in the murky network of Dalmatian islands and fortresses – with names like Bag, Klis and Krk – were the immortal Christian irregulars known as the Uskoks of Senj. The authorities in Graz were rarely able to impose any real authority on Senj and luckless Habsburg envoys would sometimes be sent down there to be either disregarded or murdered. The Uskoks used the maze of channels and bays to harass Ottoman shipping and occasionally raid the mainland. It was a very peculiar, hothouse society of fervent Catholicism entangled in flagrant piracy. Papal delegates had to deal with thorny issues here, such as the rights and wrongs of taking a battle-axe into church, of priests blessing Uskok ships and weapons – even instances of priests actually taking part in raids. There was also the exquisite problem presented by the tithe, the tax which paid for the churches, being paid out as a percentage of *stolen* goods, the goods often being taken after the summary execution of a luckless ship's crew. The showy Uskok habit of using their victims' blood to flavour their bread was another talking point.

As favoured children of the Church then, doing God's work, the Uskoks were definitely falling into an 'at risk' category. Because so many reports were written about them to Rome by badly shaken official visitors throughout the sixteenth century, we accidentally have really good evidence for one isolated area of the Military Frontier. Most striking is the way the reports show the extreme malleability of ethnic tagging, with Italians and Bosnians rapidly becoming Croats in name and language once they settled into the society of Senj. This suggests in microcosm how in a preliterate society the markers that became sacred to later nationalists were in practice almost without meaning – what you spoke, what you called yourself and where you went to church were shaped by what happened to be nearby rather than by genetic coding. For centuries Dalmatia was celebrated for such mobility, but in the twentieth century this became unacceptable to at least five different kinds of nationalism with tragic results.

Both Christians and Ottomans resorted to extreme levels of cruelty of a Grand Guignol kind. The bags full of Turkish noses sent by the Uskoks from Senj to Charles V in 1532 may have been one of those gifts more fun to send than to receive, but for much of the century it was in effect these bags that made it clear how useful the Uskoks were. Their sheer excessive savagery allowed them, from Graz's point of view, to act in a semi-deniable way, a tendency exacerbated by Graz's lack of money or supplies, which meant that they had no leverage anyway with Senj. Unfortunately, Uskok proclamations about destroying the commerce of the Muslim infidel in the name of Jesus tended to provoke hollow mirth in the Venetian Republic. The Uskoks – like reformed alco-

holics brought face to face with row upon row of brightly coloured
liqueur miniatures – were simply unable to avoid helping themselves to passing Venetian Christian ships. When the Habsburgs
and Venetians were hostile to each other this was not a problem.
Graz found itself having to make weak excuses along the – embarrassingly not inaccurate – lines that they could not control the
Uskoks anyway. As Senj was simply a pirates' nest there was
another acute issue: that regular Habsburg ports further up the
Adriatic, such as Rijeka, made a great deal of money from fencing
excess Uskok goods, whatever the source. An entire stolen cargo of
ostrich feathers, for example, caused mayhem as it made its way up
the Adriatic from Senj – which had little use for ostrich feathers
– to Istria, where Habsburg merchants sold them on to the highly
specialized group in Venice who dealt in ostrich feathers, presumably the same people who had first ordered them, or indeed owned
the original ship whose crew had been butchered by the Uskoks. It
is easy to imagine grave and richly dressed Venetian patricians
banging their fists on pearl-inlay tables. After ever more unmanageable outrages the Uskoks were finally shut down in 1618 by
joint Venetian and Habsburg action and the era of lolling, panta-
looned figures, battle-axes in church and funny-tasting bread was
at an end. Resettled in family groups along the rest of the Military
Frontier, the Uskoks of Senj became a folkloric memory.

The sheer, long-term violence of the Military Frontier is astoni-
ishing. The Uskoks pinned down its furthest southern point, but
irregularly, along swathes of modern Croatia and western Hungary,
spasms of extraordinary ferocity laid waste to regions which,
while always quite tough places to live, had before the disaster
of Mohács been good farmland, with the usual accompaniment of
small castles, mills and monasteries. The inhabitants were faced
with impossible problems of loyalty. A powerful strand within the
Hungarian lands found itself terrified of Muslim rule but also
dubious about Habsburg legitimacy (a dubiety fuelled heavily by
Rudolf II's incompetence) and driven mad by the collapse of any
hope for a normal existence. It is not surprising that a chiliastic
dementia took root, with even basic civilization breaking down in

the 1570s in the face of the fearsome reign of the 'Black Man of Debrecen' and desperate armed bands laying waste to Croatia and Slavonia. These were countered by bouts of Habsburg ferocity that through pouring in German mercenaries – who had also been defenders of Senj – gradually brought the region back under control. After decades of 'peace' – meaning that armed slave-raiding by Tatar bands was acceptable, but nothing by more formal armies – Rudolf II and his allies in 1593 initiated what became known as 'the Long War', a wearying grind that embittered and disappointed everyone involved. The fighting scarred and blackened the entire landscape, leaving large areas of Hungary and Croatia with no remaining populations. A further layer of horror came from a rebellion by Hungarian aristocrats against Habsburg rule, provoked both by a dourly unintelligent policy of re-Catholicizing Royal Hungary and by a continuing feeling that the Habsburgs were simply not legitimate – that they had stolen the Hungarian crown. This resulted in a further round of frenzied violence, famous for the role of Hungarian irregulars known as Hajduks. After a peace treaty was signed, the Hajduks were brought under control and became another important element in the Habsburg armies, on the Military Frontier and elsewhere, coming gradually to mean in very general terms a swaggering, semi-detached and picturesquely clothed irregular of an Uskok kind.

It could be argued that until the Ottomans were finally pushed back in the late seventeenth century the frontier never really stabilized. Graz relied on militia (increasingly useless), aristocratic followers, mercenaries, temporary European crusade tourists, smaller Imperial states whose rulers sought to find favour or who just loved fighting and a complex mix of military settlers. Long periods of formal peace between the two sides never prevented large-scale raids and one of the many functions of the monasteries that dot Carinthia and Slovenia was to take in thousands of trau-matized refugees that might follow a successful Ottoman incursion. From their principal bases at Sarajevo, Belgrade and Buda, none of which was seriously threatened by the Habsburgs until the late seventeenth century, the Ottomans funnelled countless prisoners into the slave-markets. In scenes more familiar to us in descriptions of West Indian slave auctions, Serb or German men would be stripped naked and whipped across Belgrade's main square to demonstrate their fitness to potential buyers.

We know much less about the impact of comparable Habsburg raids into Ottoman territory as they did not attract the same outraged pamphlet literature, but the two sides formed mirror images of one another and the obsessive depravity of the Uskoks and Hajduks was let loose on the Ottoman regions of northern Serbia and southern Hungary. A landscape today associated with endless corn and sunflowers and dusty little villages soon ceased to have any viable population. Until the end of the eighteenth century, this zone, with its malarial marshes, enveloping new forest cover and great packs of wolves, became a nightmarish part of Europe into which whole armies could march and become sick, starving, lost and demoralized with terrifying speed.

Perhaps the final heroes of the Military Frontier were the Pandurs, a fighting force of shakoed raiders under the charismatic, albeit psychopathic, leadership of Baron Franz von der Trenck. Trenck brought together a group of mainly Croat fighting men in the 1730s, and used them to fight everyone faintly inimical to Habsburg authority, whether Turkish or Prussian. The Pandurs became famous more perhaps for their picturesque and motley uniforms than their actual exploits, tapping into old Uskok or Hajduk nostalgia as a last hurrah for irregular fighters in a now boringly regimented world. To this day an infinity of cheap prints of Pandurs smoking pipes or wearing hats at rakish angles takes up valuable space on the walls of provincial museums and fly-blown hotels across the old Habsburg lands.

Trenck ended his short, violent, wandering life locked in the Špilberk fortress in Brno, a thoroughly disgraced figure. However, he has enjoyed a long and peculiar afterlife as the prime exhibit in the freakish vault of the Capuchin monastery in the town. This odd place contains the mummified corpses of monks, laid out in rows, their heads resting on bricks, dressed in their habits and holding crucifixes, the whole place having the air of a deeply unsuccessful hospital. But before visitors get to the severe example of the monks, there is a very ornate open-topped coffin with Trenck in it. With his hell-raising reputation, Trenck could not be a more exemplary figure to see reduced to a blackened mummy, naked except for a modesty loin-flap, and lying on a 'bed' with ruffled fancy sheets of a griminess perhaps more nauseating than the corpse itself. The rest of the vault contains a selection of mummified judges, architects and generals including one Baron Filiberti still looking dashing in his cavalry boots. Trenck was always there just as a raree show as his body was brought to the vault only in 1872, long after the crypt had been closed to fresher residents. There is an excellent pre-First World War photo of monks solemnly taking off the glass lid of Trenck's coffin so that some extra-special visitors can take a closer look, an option now luckily no longer available.

Trenck's remains put us, in a distant, shrivelled way, in touch with the final gasp of the Military Frontier – a place that had rewarded violence, luck and recklessness for some three centuries and which now became merely historical. For Croatians, Albanians and Serbs particularly it would in due course become a model for their proto-nationalisms, even if this needed a highly selective reading, pretending that there was no German or Hungarian element. It encouraged a devil-may-care, big-moustached, big-shirted Romanticism which for much of the region's later history was pleasantly at odds with the stolid, farming reality of most of the old Military Frontier – a dullness perked up by ballads about the quintessential Uskok Ivo Senjanin and the Hajduk Mijat Tomić, hammer of the Turks. These figures have enjoyed a fresh life in post-Communist Central Europe where both scholarly and popular enthusiasm for these totemic fighters has taken root, and statues, often with a strongly heavy-metal flavour, scatter town squares and parks wherever there was notable Christian–Muslim fighting. Indeed, the Capuchin vault in Brno was crowded with heavy metal fans looking at the grisly selections and this seemed to me a charming, if nutty, example of cultural history's wending ways. In the summer of 2010 I was spending a happy few days in

Cluj and was almost dazed at my good fortune at having just missed Iron Maiden playing there at the central arena on their head-bursting, Earth-girdling 'Final Frontier' tour. It is not perhaps something that can withstand even the most cursory scepticism, but I feel it might just be possible to create a richly textured explanation for continuing Central European devotion to such leather-clad British dinosaurs as Iron Maiden via the shared Hajduk heritage across the region. Or not.

A real bear-moat

Sometimes my endless travelling around on trains can be rewarded in a way that makes up for all the indignities, smells and boredom. A good instance was taking one south from České Budějovice, through torpid countryside, often on a single track and that track nearly engulfed by trees. At one stop there appeared to be no settlement of any kind, as though the tiny train was halting simply in memory of an earlier village – which is not impossible in such a vexed, resettled part of Bohemia. The train finally reached a little wooden station and I walked down a nondescript street, struggling with a bag which was to be the bane of the rest of a long trip as it held not just a toothbrush and clothes, but an immensely heavy illustrated history of the Škoda works which I had just bought with feelings of great (and correct) excitement but without thinking through the weight implications. In any event, panting and gasping and increasingly unkeen on Czech industrialization, I came to a small park: and to one of central Europe's great sights – a huge cleft filled by the crowded red roofs of the town of Český Krumlov: a switchback bend in the lacquer-black Vltava River and a glowering cliff on which is heaped a castle complex of ineffable charisma.

On the whole castles tend to have more impact in the imagination than in real life. Kafka's castle or Sleeping Beauty's or Gormenghast are all in their different ways far more extensive and spooky and to be savoured in a way unrelated to disadvantaged

actual buildings, where the walls are never quite sheer enough or
the car park is too prominent. Český Krumlov is an exception,
mostly because once you are down inside the town the castle walls
loom so high over it and seem so organically linked into the
huge, sheer cliffs above the river that there is no question as to its
absolute, almost sneering authority. It is topped off by a bulky
yet pretty watchtower, conjured up from sgraffito, colonnades, pink
paint and gold bobbles, which soars above the already unfeasibly
high-up battlements.

There is also, it turns out, a real bear-moat. I excitedly texted
my family, who replied asking for clarification: was this a moat
with bears *in* or a moat to keep bears *out*. I could see where the
confusion had arisen, although a few moments' thought would
show that bears could be kept out just by a door with a little latch
as this would in itself trump bear intelligence, but still: the fact of
a genuine bear-moat does take a while to sink in. The drawbridge
used to be put up each night, making the bears in the moat the
first line of defence: albeit a possibly flawed one as they could be
neutralized with a drugged honey sandwich. Sadly the bears have
been put in a standard zoo environment with healthful rocks, a
tree-trunk and a little pond to pace listlessly around – but in the
past bear-moat bears would have enjoyed more baroque surroundings. There is a delirious seventeenth-century picture of the Elector
of Saxony's bear-moat, where the bears clamber onto trees with
high platforms and a pretty fountain. Presumably there must
always have been a tension between bears as a decorative element
and all the lumps of shit, mange and half-eaten food which had to
be rapidly whisked away to maintain a picturesque effect.

Understandably bear-moats are now very rare as there is little
call for them – one has been re-established at Franz Ferdinand's
old castle at Konopiště but there is just a single bear and its deter-
rent role is compromised by its being penned in a small corner of
a moat now mainly devoted to a witless archery feature. Even the
famous Bear Pits of Bern are now empty, with the final, elderly
bear killed in 2009. The Český Krumlov bears are peculiar because
they genuinely date to the sixteenth century, when the Rožmberk

family did a deal with the infinitely rich and greedy Orsini family, who in return for some money allowed the Rožmberks to pretend to be their relatives. To mark this absurd deal, the Rožmberks put bears in their castle moat because of *orso* being Italian for bear. Presumably a Rožmberk would gesture casually from the wall and wait for his guest to say: 'Why on earth do you have bears in your moat?' before pointing out the pretty pun and its apposite nature. The bears have therefore been listlessly pacing back and forth for some five centuries, having long outlived the Rožmberks themselves, who died out four centuries ago, a last, extraordinarily tenacious survival of an infantile branding exercise.

The Rožmberks were one of the greatest of all Bohemian aristocratic families and did not need to pay for an Orsini endorsement. Their last leader, Vilém of Rožmberk, worked for Ferdinand I, Maximilian II and Rudolf II and was a diplomat, adviser and the most senior ceremonial figure in Bohemia. He was a great polymath, collector and obsessive alchemist and built a state-of-the-art laboratory in his castle at Třeboň. He also built the vast carp ponds which still dot southern Bohemia and are drained annually for the fish which so many Czech families eat at Christmas rather than turkey, and the very idea of which just seems upsetting.

Despite marrying four times Vilém had no children and rooms remain decorated with charming but despairing illustrations of childlessness or the wish for children taken from the Old Testament. His younger brother, Petr Vok, was already old when he took over after a lifetime of extravagance. He was obliged to sell the castle to Rudolf II and then in a final act of courtly self-sacrifice used all his remaining money to pay off a mercenary army that had invaded Prague (as part of Rudolf's quarrel with his brothers) before dying in 1611.

I would hate to appear to be working for the Czech tourist board, but the pleasures of Český Krumlov really are almost too great. It is still not really part of anyone's consciousness even though it has been easy to visit since 1989. The whole area of southern Bohemia was thinly settled and mainly German-speaking – Egon Schiele's mother came from the town and he lived there for a time, creating some of his most wonderful pictures. Like many Bohemian castles, Český Krumlov was expropriated for use by the Nazis and then fell into disrepair. The ravages of the 1945 expulsion of German-speakers added to the feeling of it dropping off the map. In the Cold War the town was the front line, with a deserted zone to the south between itself and Austria. Part of me would be happy to live here – although this is a doubtful and promiscuous favour I feel like extending to at least two dozen other former Habsburg towns.

CHAPTER FOUR

The other Europe » Bezoars and nightclub hostesses »
Hunting with cheetahs » The seven fortresses

The other Europe

The reality of Ottoman rule over a huge swathe of central and south-eastern Europe remains at the heart of the Habsburg experience, but also more broadly as an awkward and confusing issue for all European history. If the sixteenth and seventeenth centuries are supposed to represent the triumphant expansion of Europe, with great areas of North and South America cleared providentially for Christian enjoyment, then why in Europe itself is there a similar experience being inflicted on Europeans themselves? Slave-raiding, frontier warfare and terror tactics of a kind used by the Spanish Habsburgs in Mexico and Peru were themselves inflicted on the Austrian Habsburgs as they battled for four centuries to deal with an Ottoman enemy which, until the later seventeenth century, seemed unbeatable, and which was only finally expelled from Europe just before the First World War.

After the destruction of Hungary and some final mopping-up operations in Bosnia, there was a great surge of settlement and rebuilding by the Ottomans across their new lands. Sarajevo had been founded in the mid-fifteenth century and Belgrade (or the *Dar al-Harb*: the House of War) had effectively been re-founded after its capture from the Habsburgs in 1522 following the entire population being sent to Istanbul as slaves. The Military Frontier really did shut off the two parts of Europe from each other and there were brutally enforced rules by both sides against trade with one another — the tiny but curious exception being the Ragusan Republic (Dubrovnik), kept by the Ottomans in much the same way as Communist China permitted Hong Kong, as a readily controllable and dependent window on the West.

Since the nineteenth century, nationalist historians have stared into this closed system trying to perceive the fates of their proto-countrymen under Ottoman rule. As late as the terrible Bosnian War of the early 1990s, these topics had a sickening relevance as Bosnian Muslims were accused of being Ottoman quislings, not real Europeans and so on. In nationalist terms the stakes have therefore always been very high. The gradual liberation of these areas by Habsburg forces (often working with Imperial or Polish allies) was meant to rescue from bondage populations who would spring back upright and be much as before – but in practice not only were these peoples quite different from their pre-conquest forebears, but these forebears had themselves only carried the faintest resemblance to what these nationalist historians imagined.

The initial conquest was extraordinarily brutal. The heroic last stands of Magyar garrisons ended with localized forms of Arma-geddon. So many noblemen were killed at the Battle of Mohács in 1526 that there was administrative chaos even without the mass appropriations and ravaging of land: towns effectively disappeared, the process of food distribution caved in. The Great Hungarian Plain has never really recovered from this period – decades of fighting and raiding chased off almost the entire population, its elaborate irrigation systems were destroyed and it became a semi-desert. The plain's wearying flatness may be natural, but its catastrophic emptiness was man-made in the sixteenth century. Populations moved to fill some of the spaces created by the Otto-mans, but the incessant fighting, insecurity and bouts of plague never made this very attractive. It is not as though these lands ever enjoyed some prelapsarian golden age, but their particularly shock-ing harshness became normal in this period.

The Ottomans had no problem with Christian subjects and there were only intermittent attempts to convert anyone to Islam. For reasons which will never be fully understood there were none-theless substantial conversions by the Albanians and Bosnians in the late seventeenth century. In the wake of Habsburg battlefield setbacks some two hundred thousand Orthodox Serbs moved north into Hungary, leaving empty lands filled by new Albanian emigrants, thereby creating the Kosovo issue which has dogged post-Cold War Europe – but these were only two of many confusing shifts, as Romanians headed north into Transylvania and north-west into the Banat; Bulgarians and Albanians moved west and east respectively; and Jews, Vlachs and Gypsies migrated, split and changed identity in often barely recorded ways. Attempts to impose order and after-the-fact nationalist tidiness on these groups have generated first a highly tendentious historiography and then, in the historians' wake, massacres and deportations of staggering viciousness and futility. This unmanageable confusion is perhaps summed up by Buda, which by the seventeenth century was, far from being the unsinkable bastion of Magyardom, a predominantly Serb-speaking Bosnian Muslim town, leavened by a few Jewish and Armenian merchants. Beyond Slav converts across the Balkans there were also many genuine, new Muslim settlers, some from as far away as Turkmenistan, who generally formed elite groups across the region. Disentangling these from converts has proven impossible – particularly as settlement was never permanent and ambitious Muslims growing up in rural Hungary might well move on to the great Ottoman centres in Edirne, Istanbul and Bursa. Military service also shifted groups – so that, for instance, in 1723 some five thousand Bosnians marched off to fight in the war with Persia, of whom only five hundred came back. Many of these presumably died in battle, but there is no reason not to think that others simply settled elsewhere in the Ottoman domains.

One revolting claim that bobbed up during the implosion of Yugoslavia was that the Balkans were riven by 'ancient hatreds', implying something almost biological and permanent about fighting in the Balkans, with the corollary that there was no point engaging with such irrational bandits. The centuries of Ottoman rule of course show no such pattern at all, as virtually *every* party involved was a powerless and much discriminated-against group, viewed with an even-handed contempt by Muslims. The central core of the regime was a road system that headed west, linking Istanbul to Edirne to Plovdiv to Sofia to Niš to Belgrade to Buda. Christians, in return for specific but not glowingly generous privileges, had to maintain this road and its key spurs, not with trade in mind, but for the swift movement of troops and messengers. An elaborate system of legal disability much more familiar to the inhabitants of Europe's overseas colonial empires was practised on Ottoman Christians. They could not bring law suits against Muslims or act as witnesses, they could not ride or fish or hunt or race, they had to wear specific clothing, live in specific parts of town, and – the classic colonial under-pinning – always show sufficient 'respect' to Muslims. Particular Christian groups tended to be given hereditary tasks in a way that makes the Ottoman Europe sound rather attractive in a Legoland sort of way. So Doğancis raised hunting falcons, Bulgarian Voynuks raised horses for the Imperial palace, Derbencis guarded mountain passes and bridges, and so on – all with very carefully laid down clothing requirements and tax privileges. Most prominent in western European minds were the Martolos, who manned the anti-Habsburg frontiers often purely in return for plunder and who ran, among other things, immensely byzantine ransom systems whereby hostages would be sold to their families on the Habsburg side or sold as slaves if a deal could not be reached.

A further element in the border defenders were the Morlachs, a group hotly contested by various nationalists, otherwise described as Vlachs. They seem originally to have been pastoralists, surviving the Slav invasions of the Dark Ages as shepherds in the higher hills, and maintaining their Latin-influenced language, which clearly related them in some direct or indirect way to the Romanians further east. This fairly straightforward explanation has not prevented their origins being turned into an ethnographic rough-house of predictable dottiness, with one Romanian theory being that their dark skin showed they were descended from Roman legionaries from Morocco, settled in Illyria in the ancient days. As the Vlachs never had reason to write down their language they readily assumed whichever ethnicity was dominant in any town they settled in, with many becoming Serbs – a particularly clear-cut instance of how religion and language as markers of immemorial identity are more or less useless.

Long-distance trade across Ottoman Europe tended to be in the hands of specific groups that had privileges in particular territories or commodities: Greeks, Serbs, Jews, Armenians and Ragusans all acted as middlemen. The Ottomans were particularly favourable to Jews for the uninspiring reason that they had no external sponsor and were therefore quite helpless in the face of whatever demands might be made of them. The Orthodox Christians were allowed to worship, but their churches had to be smaller and lower than mosques and have no towers. Most Orthodox leaders were under the thumb of the Ottomans in Constantinople and could not therefore imagine a context for independence, but in 1691 the Serbs managed to persuade the Emperor Leopold I to give them a church headquarters in Slavonia (the lovely town of Sremski Karlovci) which through many twists and turns was to give them a focus with important future implications. It is reckoned that during the course of Ottoman rule in the Balkans some two hundred thousand Christian children were taken from their parents and sent to Constantinople to be raised as Muslims and work in the administration and army there, a considerable privilege by some definitions, but not brilliant by others.

Behind the Military Frontier this Ottoman world had settled down by the later sixteenth century into an effective, well-run and civilized sphere. The distinctive landscape of mosque, madrasa, caravanserai, coffee-house, public bath, hospital, fountain and market dotted innumerable small towns, maintained in many cases by the *vakifs*, the charitable Islamic foundations run by important citizens. Small elements from these can still be seen in scattered, dusty and battered buildings or in mosques converted to use as churches. In Szigetvár, site of one of the great immolatory encounters between Hungarians and Ottomans, there are still occasional scraps of Muslim buildings – a house that once formed part of a caravanserai, a Roman Catholic church with some very slight indications of its former role as a mosque, another church where the font is an old Turkish wash-basin.

This world was far from static, but it seems to have had its great period in the seventeenth century and then fallen into increasing disrepair, with towns such as Belgrade and Skopje undergoing catastrophic population losses from military strain and from an inability to renew Muslim populations hammered by plague. The revival of Persia meant that the key traditional eastern source of settlers for the Ottoman domains was shut off and there were simply more attractive parts than the northern Balkans to settle anyway. It was also clear that as the Habsburgs were breaking through into this parallel Europe, the Ottomans failed to react to the sort of freewheeling trading environments ever more rife in the West. These decorative arrangements of yellow tunics with red hats, the neat division of towns by occupation and religion just did not work any more. Once the Ottoman armies gave way in the face of the vast, annihilatory campaigns in the north-west at the end of the seventeenth century, the lands they were defending turned out to offer little but desolation and malarial marshes. Everywhere, the Muslim population gradually drifted down and what had once been almost entirely Islamic towns, such as Banja Luka, had large Christian majorities by 1800 or so.

This was a very complete world while it lasted and innumerable engravings of these Ottoman towns show an alternative and alluring reality – of minarets, turbaned officials and camels filling Belgrade or Sarajevo or Pećs. Pećs is even now still surrounded by the descendants of the fig trees planted by the Ottomans. Some changes are relatively recent. Budapest has become much less Turkish through two huge changes in the late nineteenth and early twentieth centuries: the switch from a cuisine based on mutton to one based on beef – chewing through the huge new Hungarian herds of cattle – and the spread of the espresso machine, which did so much to push to one side Turkish-style coffee. Perhaps the only major remaining Ottoman legacy is the bathhouse.

One of the many torments of the Bosnian War was seeing this Ottoman heritage blown to pieces in a deliberate and self-conscious element in the conflict, driven by mystical and corrupted historians, whether it was the destruction of the bridge at Mostar or the targeting of the Orient Institute in Sarajevo. These were attempts to deny the legitimacy of Muslims as European citizens at all, when of course they are ancient European citizens, drawing on a great, refined and beautiful culture which ruled much of south-east Europe for far longer than any of its successor states.

Bezoars and nightclub hostesses

Tucked into a corner of the Natural History Museum in Vienna is a small glass jar containing a basilisk preserved in spirits. It is of course a fake, created by some specialist figure in a far-away sea-port buying a ray from a fisherman and cutting, folding and sewing it to make legs, wings and horns. Its teetering plausibility comes from the much abused creature's underside having holes that seem somewhat like a pair of eyes, with its strange smiling mouth arranged below them. It looks just hopeless, and yet hundreds of miles inland, perhaps seen through murkier glass, it might have seemed a *slightly* curious object and perhaps the merchants who dealt in basilisks – a small and evasive group unlikely to have even met up for an annual Christmas lunch – shared information on particularly credulous customers or trainee alchemists looking to add a little tone to their labs.

Vienna and Prague are almost as far inland as it is possible to get in Europe and perhaps it is not surprising that the court of Rudolf II, located initially in the one city and then in the other, became the greatest locus for strangeness and magic in the later sixteenth century. Some of this reputation is undeserved, a nineteenth-century confection looking back wistfully on the last time that a city had been great. One of its classic showpiece narratives, Rabbi Loew's clay monster, the Golem, seems only to have been invented in the 1840s, sadly, and indeed much of Loew's long and brilliant career was spent outside Prague. There were many courts dotted about Europe with similar obsessions, but somehow all the wizardly and alchemical preoccupations of the period have long been imaginatively delegated to Rudolf's Prague.

The bottled basilisk shows, in perhaps its most acute form, the difficulty of making sense of the era. Any attempt to grapple with the scientific and magical preoccupations of the court founder on

the Further Reading problem. Given that even the most simple
alchemical issue makes no sense to us, we can only hope to understand it by reading books from the tradition that led to the belief
that, say, powdered gems were a legitimate medicine. But as soon
as you start on the Further Reading it is clear that these intellectual
streams are themselves so rich, various and contradictory that
they can offer no help: that you are simply wading deeper and
deeper into what seems to be ever worse nonsense. What are we to
make of the *Steganographica* of Trithemius, Ficino's translation of
the *Hermetica*, Hermes Trismegistus's *Emerald Tablet*, Paracelsus's
Archidoxa, or the sickening *Picatrix,* a compendium of Persian and
Arabic spells viewed for many years as too dangerous to transfer
from manuscript to printed form? We have little information on
who read what or how widely they were circulated, and have to
cling instead to specific endorsements or denigrations of these
books preserved in other writings, in a context where most key
discussions would have been oral. There is also the impossible
problem of having somehow to come up with an intellectual recovery point before 1600, when a more densely plausible modern
science starts to accrete.

We simply do not have the intellectual equipment to spot when
contemporaries themselves started to scoff at Pseudo-Balinus's
Secret of Creation. Presumably there were always those who thought
basilisks were rubbish and who heard reliably that unicorn horns
came from narwhals. Dürer was sketching a walrus brought in
by Dutch fishermen in 1521 and Arctic fishing trips were now
common, so the word on the street about unicorn issues must have
been increasingly adverse. Horns and tinkered-with fish are at least
solid objects, but we despair in the face of trying to chart the rise
and fall of belief in hidden arcana. A final disaster stems from our
now having the ability to create a plausible pattern across Prague,
as though viewed from high in the air, where we can simultane-
ously see all the different lines of alchemical enquiry – whereas, at
the time, speculations within the Jewish Town or the Jesuit observ-
atories or within the Castle would have been carried out in almost
complete ignorance of each another. And even within these sepa-

rate worlds there were backbiting, grandstanding and intellectual nervous breakdowns, with even figures as distinguished as Tycho Brahe and Johannes Kepler at each other's throats. It is a shame that we cannot get closer to the sheer chaos of Prague in this period, its streets thick with mountebanks, zanies, mercenaries from the Turkish wars, religious fanatics of every stripe, zoo-keepers, exotically dressed ambassadors and even the occasional serious scientist.

At the heart of it all sat the peculiar Emperor. His father, the amiable crypto-Protestant Maximilian II, was buried in Prague and Rudolf decided early in his own reign to move the court perma-nently there, partly because it was safer from Turkish attack than Vienna, partly because the Bohemian nobles had urged that he should, and partly because he could do whatever he liked. Rudolf does not seem to have been an appealing figure by most criteria – secretive, changeable, swinging between bouts of Imperial activism and total lethargy. He shared with his English contemporary, Eliza-beth I, the peculiar problem of having no clear-cut successor – he never married but, unhelpfully, had several bastard children so *could* potentially have procreated to Habsburg ends. His five broth-ers also failed to have legitimate children, so Rudolf was in the unattractive situation of being hemmed in by a sterile generation of irritable siblings who could die in any sequence, with one or more potentially becoming Emperor. This was a particularly dire issue as after 1600 or so Rudolf withdrew from serious decision-making, with the unique result that Habsburg solidarity totally broke down. But this only happened because Rudolf was so useless as Emperor, disappearing for months and simply unable to carry out normal business. Compared to the ferocious Catholic activism of his suc-cessors he can now seem amiable, but in a world split between Christian and Muslim and between Catholic and Protestant it is an unfortunate example of where being reasonable and laid back seems to create not tolerance but merely deferred viciousness.

As he left no account himself and those near him wrote frus-tratingly little we can only project our own likes and dislikes on

Rudolf's private mental world. In many ways he seems to have been one of the most fortunate men who ever lived, taking more advantage than anyone else of the golden age of exploration and excitement that reached its apogee in the later sixteenth century. He was a lot richer and more focused than Elizabeth I, a lot less desiccated and pious than Philip II and lived longer and more agreeably than the chaotic French kings of the period. The inspiration for his collections came from the intellectual atmosphere of the time, but had specific roots too. Growing up at Philip's court in Madrid he would have had the great luck to have been able to spend as much time as he wished staring at the pride of Philip's collection, Hieronymus Bosch's *The Garden of Earthly Delights*, a sort of vade mecum of Rudolf's later interests. And en route from Madrid to Prague he had stopped off in Innsbruck and stayed with his uncle Ferdinand of Tyrol and so would have enjoyed the sensational guided tour available there. Once he had settled in Prague Castle, word went out that he was interested in effectively *anything* strange or unusual and entire businesses sprung up just to furnish him with fancies that might please him. These decades were host to a riotous sprawl of fresh information, sourced from the very smallest (with the invention of the microscope) to the largest (with the invention of the telescope). This new knowledge involved the reordering of most of the world's men, creatures and plants, with tomatoes, potatoes, sunflowers and corncobs stumbling ashore and taking their first steps in what would prove their all-conquering invasion of Europe. It was an era as happy speculating on the nature of a supernova (a term derived from Tycho Brahe's work, with the quintessential supernova observed and argued over in Prague in 1604) as on the nature of a naked flame.

There seems to have been no limit to Rudolf's curiosity. At some point it must have toppled into a mere mania for heaping up room after room of Stuff, but until his final decade there is a clear sense of someone who must have grinned with excitement at the opportunities available to him. The great banking family, the Fuggers, had a busy warehouse in Antwerp lined with cages to deal with the exotic creatures brought in by enterprising Dutch

ships, and soon Prague Castle was full of extraordinary exotica –
macaws, lories, lovebirds and cockatoos all shivering away in their
bleak new homeland. Rudolf had a dodo, birds of paradise and a
cassowary. This last had gone through endless adventures, starting
off as a diplomatic gift for the ruler of Java from an unknown king
or vassal even further east and in turn given to a Dutch sea-captain.
This enormous, violent and rather made-up-looking bird caused a
sensation when it landed and Rudolf eventually secured it for
himself, with its own specially decorated house. Two traumatized
ostriches made the journey from Africa to Venice and then up
through the Brenner Pass to Innsbruck and then, ultimately, to
Prague. None of these creatures, unsurprisingly, lasted long.

There was an unedifying and futile quarrel with Philip II that
lasted decades to get hold of an Indian rhinoceros that had landed
in Lisbon. The rhino wound up being sent by Philip on a prolonged tour of Castile together with an elephant to show his
subjects something of the power and majesty of the Spanish
Habsburgs (a relatively rare surviving clue to the sorts of processions, displays and special events thick with symbolism that must
have been part of the everyday business of projecting royal might).
Eventually, when the rhino died, a deal was done to let Rudolf get
hold of its hide, but given that nobody knew how to cure rhino
hide it unsurprisingly and spectacularly rotted to pieces and the
only bits that reached Prague for Rudolf's pleasure were the horn
and a few bones.

It is a measure of the problems of Rudolf's reign that we are
happy thinking of him, ruffed and in black, in some semi-darkened
room slowly turning in his hand a bezoar (an animal gallstone
meant to be a poison antidote), but cannot see him as the aggressive, fussy and well-organized collector he must in fact have
been, constantly badgering, articulating and making demands.
How could someone who seems introvert to the point of stasis
have been such a great organizer of things and people? What drove
him on? Perhaps at heart he had a perturbing, deeply hidden sense
of humour, revelling in a very odd, secret way in unlimited power.
This can be the only explanation for his having a lion and a tiger

which wandered around Prague Castle more or less as they wished. For years these menaces were both a matchless representation of royal power and, presumably, a cause for innumerable scullions, vintners and linkboys going about their tasks in the gloom of the Castle corridors, trying to hold a silver drinks tray level while their legs went bandy with terror. Indeed surviving account books are dotted with references to compensation paid to surviving family members or to mutilated attack-survivors.

Allied to Rudolf's obsession with living things – which were soon, on their deaths, converted into dried-out members of the cabinet of curiosities – was an all-encompassing mania for the decorative and the curious. The shorthand for Rudolf's reign has always been the bizarre paintings of Arcimboldo, with the Emperor's portrait a complex assemblage of fruit and vegetables (his nose a pear, his throat two courgettes and a turnip), but this Milanese oddball was in fact inherited from Maximilian II, for whom he produced some of his greatest work and who had become merely formulaic by Rudolf's reign. The real tragedy is that we can never recover Arcimboldo's almost certainly brilliant contribution as a decorator for parties and banquets – Maximilian had revelled in elaborate entertainments on classical themes. Perhaps these ephemera were his greatest works? More generally, it is galling that we have inherited only the sorts of objects (such as easily rolled-up paintings on canvas) readily taken by the generations of looters who dismantled Rudolf's collections after his death, but not the things which at the time would have been most miraculous and all-encompassing – like rooms filled with dazzling painted decoration and matchingly uniformed servants, or connecting corridors down which you might have to walk past a tiger.

Setting aside Arcimboldo, Rudolf's needs were tended to by dozens of peculiar geniuses. He had calligraphers, etchers, costume-designers, zoo-keepers, goldsmiths, print-makers. He had Bartholomeus Spranger (from Antwerp – another figure he inherited from his father) to paint some of the most aggressively pornographic paintings of the late sixteenth century, now livening up a back corridor of the Kunsthistorisches Museum in Vienna.

These are based naturally on 'classical themes' and include his celebrated Minerva, whose steel-fur-weapon outfit and posture would cause issues even for the most niche contemporary members-only club. There is also a Spranger painting in Prague Castle of Christ wearing a flimsy mantle and in the same sort of nightclub hostess pose as Minerva, his foot on a glass sphere with a human skull inside it and a flush-faced angel grabbing in an appreciative way one of his nude buttocks. Some very odd things were going on.

Rudolf seems to have been obsessed with glyptics, the art of carving on precious stones. This is perhaps the quintessential private artistic obsession, immune to modern museum display as it only really works through someone holding the tiny object in their hand and turning it in the light. He poured money into accumulating jewels – his agents fanned out across Europe and beyond to intercept and divert the flow of diamonds, pearls and sapphires to Prague, with the sapphires coming from as far away as Kashmir. The spectacular Crown of Rudolf II seems never to have been designed to be worn, but again simply to be handled by its owner. It was designed by Jan Vermeyen (also from Antwerp), who was brought to Prague to create this remarkably untacky (by crown standards) and beautiful object with the golden panels of its mitre celebrating the key regal events in Rudolf's life: coronation as Holy Roman Emperor in Regensburg, marching through Pressburg (Bratislava) as King of Hungary and through Prague as King of Bohemia. The last panel shows him as victor over the Turks which, unfortunately, was not true and the real root of his reign's disaster.

Among his great ancestors there had been men, most notably Maximilian I and Charles V, who had combined vigorous military, procreational and artistic policies. Rudolf managed only the last of these. The time he spent chatting to John Dee about his magic mirror made from Aztec obsidian should probably have been spent more wisely. His role as Holy Roman Emperor lapsed almost completely. His tolerance of – or more probably indifference to – religious issues meant that as his reign progressed the Catholic position in Bohemia caved in; it was perhaps nine-tenths Protestant by 1600. Rudolf's failure to marry gave the latter part of his reign an air of ruinous stasis, even setting aside his own personal inactivity, with the future religious direction of the Habsburg lands depending on the views of his successor. This meant an extraordinary array of religious belief blossomed in Prague. Tolerance also made it a great shelter for wizards of a kind who were simply killed by the ruler of any surrounding state they were rash enough to wander into – the exotic fraud Marko Bragadino's luck ran out when he was beheaded in Munich in 1591, dressed in a suit decorated with fool's gold.

Rudolf's one major foreign-policy initiative was a disaster. In 1591 the Ottoman frontier became vigorously active once more with the fall of the key Hungarian fortresses of Komárom, on the Danube, and Győr, seventy-five miles from Vienna. A significant but highly misleading raid at Sisak in 1593, principally involving Croatian troops, resulted in an Ottoman defeat and the first hint that the implacable enemy might in fact be placable. Determined to recover from this humiliation, Sultan Murad III declared war on Rudolf and initiated a wearying and horrible conflict that lasted for thirteen years. The initial coalition (brought together by the Pope rather than the Emperor) was formidable, with troops arriving from all over Europe as well as alliances with the eastern tier of principalities – Moldavia, Wallachia and Transylvania – which now turned on their Ottoman protectors. Remarkably little is written about this war, but it was perhaps one of the most important fought in Central Europe, a training school for the Thirty Years War for an entire generation and one of the main reasons that the region became so depopulated, with city after city and surrounding countryside left empty after ceaseless terror-raiding and mutual ferocity. So complete was this depopulation that it reshaped the ethnic map, as new linguistic groups moved into areas left empty by the extermination of their predecessors.

The Long War was a hideous, endless grind. There was one major battle, at Mezőkeresztes in 1596, the largest since Mohács, and the Christian forces came painfully close to winning before losing discipline, falling to looting and then being cut to bits. Some hundred and fifty thousand troops seem to have been present and casualties on both sides were enormous – but the Ottomans had a much larger army and this proved decisive. Mutual massacres, sieges and the usual mass deaths by disease sapped both sides but the fighting went on interminably. Rudolf was notionally in charge but never went to the front, with members of his family, most notably his brother Maximilian, doing the heavy, if inept, work. From a Habsburg or Christian point of view the Long War was a disaster and its prosecution shameful, but there was a separate story, not clear at the time, of matching Ottoman desperation. It is not unreasonable to say that the fighting burned out the Ottomans, with the febrile hysteria in Constantinople that greeted the news of the narrow victory at Mezőkeresztes symptomatic of an empire no longer the confident wonder of the world it had been under Suleiman. Army after expensive army trudged from Constantinople to the Hungarian frontier, but with no longer anything much to show for it. The 1606 Peace of Zsitvatorok ended the wretched conflict, signed by Murad's successor Ahmed and Rudolf's younger brother Archduke Matthias. It recognized minor changes in the frontier, but the Ottomans kept everything that was important. The bitter Habsburg signatories were not to know that the Ottoman threat (aside from the desperate throw of the Siege of Vienna seventy-seven years later) had hit its peak.

Hunting with cheetahs

The Star Hunting Lodge, in what is now a suburb of Prague, was built by Rudolf II's uncle, the man who became the great Castle Ambras collector Ferdinand of Tyrol. When still a teenager he was appointed Governor of Bohemia by his father, the Emperor Ferdinand I, and he needed a rural base. There is even his sketch showing how he wanted it to look: a ground plan of a six-pointed star, probably based on a building he had seen in Rome. The lodge survived the most extraordinary rigours over five centuries and is still surrounded by a park used by generations of invaders – Swedish, Prussian, French, German and Soviet. As a fancy command post many an invader has found it impossible to resist setting up there – but in some odd way it must be cursed, as every single one has left. The lodge has been a gunpowder magazine and the park used both for Wehrmacht vehicle repair and for herds of cattle to feed Soviet troops. The Lodge roof has been stripped of its copper by mercenaries during the Thirty Years War, given a baroque cupola (now removed), neglected and abused. Its heyday was the latter half of the sixteenth century, when Ferdinand and his older brother the Emperor Maximilian II and then Rudolf used it for hunting and entertainments. In a completely extraordinary scene, Rudolf once hunted deer around the park with cheetahs – an image almost infantily exotic – as he and his followers orchestrated this no doubt mutually baffling encounter between fearsome, if chilly, African megafauna and some appalled Bohemian ungulates.

The Star Lodge's mystery and absolute oddness lies in its six-pointed structure. It is as though it has battled through every vicissitude for many hundreds of years just so that at last its design can make sense when looked at on Google Earth. Originally the surrounding parkland was arranged in screens of vegetation in the same star shape, which must have made the building more conventionally decorative, but now in isolation, at the end of a long alley, it has the air of something that has been donated by a civilization from another planet. It seems to have no link to any architectural period and provides none of the interaction with the viewer that normal buildings have. It is almost as though it neither absorbs nor reflects light, the star's arms angling sun and shadow in ways unrelated to normal physical experience. It is uncanny, and a perfect instance of the world of the sixteenth century, more potent than any cabinet of curiosities: an exercise in mathematics drifting through history.

I wanted to see it because I had read about the cheetah hunt. This hunt was both a classic Rudolfine conceit and at the heart of the mystery of Rudolf. Did he *often* go hunting with cheetahs? Was this a one-off after which he lost interest, decided to focus instead on perusing sketches of the Bohemian forests, and left the unfortunate cheetah whippers-in undisturbed with their restive and hungry charges? How is it possible to reconcile Rudolf's introversion with something so exuberant? Clearly as his reign progressed Rudolf tended less towards cheetahs and more towards gem-stones and small, immaculate drawings. As the unanswered business heaped up and the Empire juddered to a halt, with the Turkish war going on for year after year like some grinding constant in a science-fiction novel, the exuberance around the Star Lodge became a very distant memory. Rudolf would be seen by nobody for weeks and the entire structure of both the Empire and the Habsburg lands began to cave in.

The Habsburgs' astonishing longevity stemmed above all from the ability of the senior male to produce heirs and avoid going mad. A successor and a reasonable level of bureaucratic and kingly ability in a world based around heredity and hierarchy meant that, with a couple of spectacular wobbles, they were able to keep going without the British or Spanish habit of the principal stem simply running out. There were many reasons for hating the Habsburgs or being bored by them, but the family itself gave very few chances for its enemies to bring it down on dynastic or competence grounds – the children arrived, the wearying court protocol kept trundling on. The senior Habsburgs also stuck together. Behind every ruler there were a group of relatives whose importance we can now only guess at in most cases – dowagers, sisters, brothers who, whatever their private vexations, defaulted to a blank family solidarity.

Rudolf's collapse created a huge crisis, and one which broke that solidarity. With no heirs apparent and even the alchemists left twiddling their thumbs, Rudolf's personal terrors and melancholy meant that Central Europe was under threat. By the end of the century Maximilian II and Maria of Spain's once prize-winning phalanx of nine Habsburg children was not what it had been. Maria had gone back to Spain (glad to live in a land without any heretics) and two of the children were in the Spanish Habsburg orbit (one as a governor of the Netherlands, another as a nun). Four of the remainder had died, leaving only Rudolf, Matthias and Maximilian. Both Matthias and Maximilian had led lives of action, the

former fighting the Turks in the Long War and the latter trying
and failing to become King of Poland and serving as Grand Master
of the Teutonic Knights. The situation was poisonous both because
Rudolf disliked his surviving brothers and because they were all
close in age and none had children. This meant that while Matthias
was the heir, he was also old and a stop-gap and hardly worth
investing the energy in sorting out the bribes, robes and jewellery
for everyone to anoint him to his different jobs on Rudolf's death.
So just below the immediate successor were a variety of predators
– most alarmingly Philip III of Spain, who could claim the whole
lot through being the son of one of Maximilian II's daughters,
or Ferdinand, the ruler in Graz, whose father was another of
Maximilian's offspring.

This uncertainty became tangled in vicious, gloomy religious
issues. Maximilian II, like many of his courtiers in each of his
kingdoms, had been prey to ill-defined Protestant sympathies.
Following from his father's short reign, Rudolf found himself
ruling over lands in which so many leading families in Bohemia,
Austria and Hungary had become Protestant that his own more
orthodox Catholic leanings were irrelevant. In many areas there
was now a clear majority of non-Catholics, whether old Utraquists
or Lutherans or Calvinists. Both Rudolf and Matthias understood
that messing with the Peace of Augsburg, however distasteful Protestantism might be, was simply too dangerous. The latter half of
the sixteenth century became a tense but intellectually respectable
exercise in semi-tolerance. This was not the case for the post-Rudolf
generation, with both Philip III and Ferdinand seeing Protestants
simply as inspired by the Devil. For many people across the
Habsburg lands the succession was therefore extremely worrying,
with both of the most obvious successors liking to occupy themselves with expelling, killing and disinheriting Protestants.

We can always rely on Bartholemeus Spranger to paint something odd for every occasion and he certainly does not disappoint
after the Peace of Zsitvatorok brought the Long War to an end
in 1606. The final phase of the war was a hideous bloodbath, as

rebellious Hungarians supported by the Ottomans fought against Habsburg forces, with the entire conflict taking on an ever more messianic Protestant versus Catholic fervour. Overruled by Matthias, who concluded the Peace, Rudolf commissioned Spranger to create an allegory of his own unhappiness. On a huge canvas, Spranger painted perhaps the most amazingly desirable figure of Victory ever. She is trampling on a prostrate Turk who is either dead or simply dazed and gawping because of the bits of Victory he can see from his vantage point. But Victory's lissom feet unfortunately balance only on unstable blocks of stone and the Imperial eagle with sceptre and orb squats sadly on the ground next to the lucky Turk rather than soaring up into the air, as is more traditional. Such a direct and personal piece of work is an extraordinary survival – there is no doubt that Spranger was following very precise instructions from Rudolf. Instead of the usual, vacant suck-up allegories, here is one designed to make a very clear point: that the defining Central European event of Rudolf's reign had ended in massacres, compromises and failure, and in his own authority ignored.

The rest of Rudolf's reign was a desperately sad diminuendo. Matthias's cynicism allowed him to work with the Protestants in ways that Rudolf could not. He recognized religious freedom in Transylvania and the rest of Habsburg-ruled Hungary and during the final years of Rudolf's life (he died in 1612) edged him out of each of his titles. The deals done with each part of the Habsburg patrimony meant that in return for Protestant support Matthias got each job. We would of course see this as being positive, but the reality was feverish, vicious and chaotic. 1611 was the nadir. The peculiarly belligerent and quarrelsome Archduke Leopold, Bishop of Passau (and younger brother of Archduke Ferdinand in Graz) came to Rudolf's aid. An engraving in the Prague City Museum shows the Catholic Passauer mercenaries running amok in the Lesser Town, with smoke pouring from the houses, corpses everywhere and house-to-house gun-fights. In a perfect example of the use of the Charles Bridge, the heavy fortifications at its eastern end prevented the Passauers from getting into the Old Town and eventually they were bribed to leave. Meanwhile Protestants lashed out in the Old Town, with Franciscan monks at Our Lady of the Snow hacked to death or gunned down from the roof and with attacks on the Jewish Town. The Thirty Years War would not start for another seven years, but all the ingredients were already there. At the end of 1611, Matthias, frantic to have an heir, at last married, although in his mid-fifties, a luckless first cousin. Rudolf died a few days later and was buried alongside his parents and grandparents in the Habsburg tombs in St Vitus's Cathedral, the last Habsburg ruler, as it turned out, to be buried in Prague or use it as his capital.

It seems a shame to end on such a glum note. In one of the most imaginative meditations on Rudolf II, in 1922, Karel Čapek wrote the play *The Makropoulos Case*, quickly turned into a strange and marvellous opera by Janáček. The story revolves around Dr Makropoulos, one of the mountebanks and oddities at Rudolf's court, who invents a potion that gives its user eternal life. He offers the potion to Rudolf, but he fears it is a poison and orders Makropoulos to try it first on his own daughter. In a typically ingenious Čapek twist this, of course, does not help Rudolf at all. The drink may not be a poison, but its potency can only be proven long after Rudolf has himself died anyway of natural causes. He is doomed never to know if the potion is real, or just another of his alchemists' failed fakes. The play/opera is set in Čapek's modern Czechoslovakia, with a beautiful woman arriving in Prague who seems to know a remarkable amount about the city's past centuries . . .

The seven fortresses

One of the world's most introvert, besieged landscapes, south-east Transylvania is like a physical expression of mental breakdown. It bristles with bastions, walls, watchtowers and crumbling gateways – and these are a mere fraction of what was once there, left as picturesque reminders of a stiflingly militarized and suspicious past. It is beautiful but it is not happy.

Where you lived in the Empire was always sifted by language and religion. The glowering old German merchant city of Kronstadt (now Braşov), wedged between two mountains, still keeps some of the old security paraphernalia along its northern boundary, which kept Romanians outside the walls. The rhythm of life was set by systems of passes and privileges as heavily armed convoys of goods (cloth, weapons, cereals) moved from strongpoint to strongpoint. Braşov was the last one before the Carpathians and the Ottoman territories beyond, from which – at enormous risk and in intervals between wars – huge fortunes could be made selling exotic northern goods to Constantinople.

Transylvania was under Hungarian rule for centuries and sometimes close to being an independent state, but it generally fell resentfully into the orbit of either Vienna or Constantinople. From the Middle Ages to the end of the eighteenth century, it was a society based around defensive war, using the natural fortress of the mountains to the south and east, with Braşov in the crook where the ranges joined. The Transylvanians never solved the problem which always dogged such crenellated, reveted defensive measures – that it was not economically possible to have troops standing on hundreds of miles of platforms perhaps for *decades* between attacks. The attacker always had the advantage, being able to pick his moment and location, leaving most of the defenders helplessly in the wrong place. The principal nightmare for the region was the Tatars – either fighting on their own account or as direct allies of the Ottoman Empire, latterly through the Khanate of Crimea. Clouds of these steppe horsemen, lightly armed and focused on human and non-human loot rather than holding territory, could arrive at any moment. Even when there was notional peace between Transylvania and its eastern neighbours, the raiders tended to pay no attention.

As with much of the frontier, the population was at irregular intervals eradicated. A successful Tatar raid (successful from the Tatar point of view) resulted in the killing of everybody who would not be of use as a slave. Into the late eighteenth century, Habsburg-sponsored colonization projects could go absolutely wrong as a change in military fortunes would expose an entire population to catastrophe – with areas such as what is now south-west Romania (the Banat) first filling with new German farmers and then being completely ravaged. From the twelfth century onwards the only way to start afresh was to offer extraordinary privileges to a new and hopeful group – generally from sufficiently far away that they might not have a clear grasp of what they were letting themselves in for. The 'Saxons' were only in part from Saxony – indeed many seem to have come from as far away as Flanders – but in return for a range of incentives they were given land for their own towns. This was the origin of the 'Seven Fortresses', Siebenbürgen being the German name for the region still (Transylvania is a Latinized version of the Magyar Erdély: beyond the woods). Some of these seven towns thrived, others did not, but they included the two famous lynchpins of German life, Schässburg and Hermannstadt (now Sighişoara and Sibiu) and the mixed Hungarian–German town of Kolozsvár or Klausenburg (now Cluj-Napoca). Schässburg's straightforwardly military origins are shown in its Latin name, Castrum Sex, Encampment Number Six. The settlers brought with them German town-law codes – Schässburg's and Klausenburg's the 'South German Law', and Hermannstadt's from Iglau (Jihlava) in Bohemia, with specific norms, laws and responsibilities shaping them in much the same way that new towns were laid down across the American West in the nineteenth century, but without the open, lung-clearing and optimistic aspect.

This promotion of new settlers was not restricted to Transylvania. Repeated depopulation meant that the medieval kings of Bohemia, Poland and Hungary and their Habsburg descendants were obliged to offer special privileges, leaving much of the running of each town to its inhabitants in return for specific defensive duties and fixed annual sums. This resulted in a great fan of German towns across the Baltic, Poland and the Habsburg lands and created a new landscape. Some of these were specifically mining colonies, such as Kuttenberg/Kutná Hora in Bohemia or the Zips/Spiš towns in what is now Slovakia. This Germanness extended to surprising places such as Kraków (Krakau), which developed under Magdeburg Law from 1257 and which only lost its German character in the later Middle Ages.

It is, of course, almost impossible not to think of these Germans in terrible 1940s terms, with 'Krakau' as capital of the Nazi General-Government. Of all Central European subjects it is perhaps the most difficult on which to exercise intellectual discipline. But a huge effort has to be made to think of these Germans simply as 'people who happened to speak German' and unlinked to later nationalism. They could have arrived from anywhere in the Holy Roman Empire from Ypres to Steyr, bringing with them all kinds of political, social and linguistic ideas from wildly different regions. It was only in their new towns that they became 'Saxon' and therefore self-consciously German rather than just Bavarian, Hamburger or Holsteiner. In Transylvania the Saxons only lost the last of their special privileges in the mid-nineteenth century – an astonishing run for a clannish, excluding and oligarchic way of life now quite baffling and alien to us.

This strange Saxon atmosphere is still most clearly visible in their fortified villages. The bigger places are marvellous, but Sibiu and Braşov are now unquestionably Romanian towns with a lot of effort put into their becoming thriving and modern, however dotted with Saxon survivals. By contrast the intense conservatism of the Saxon villages has pickled them in about 1650 or so. Many of their defensive structures survived for at least a century after technological changes made them useless against even the smallest raiding party, and then for at least three centuries during which the threat had in fact disappeared. The villages are melancholy places. After seven centuries of Saxon life, most survivors left for Germany from 1990 after years of Romanian collectivization and discrimination. Many villages have now mostly empty houses, groups of transient Roma and no imaginable future, despite extensive renovation work. But they are very beautiful and extremely strange.

A famous example is Deutschweißkirch (Viscri) near Sighişoara. (Incidentally, that last sentence shows the almost impossible problem of naming in this region: Viscri is its correct modern Romanian name, but in the context of its Saxon past Deutschweißkirch is also right – but as is the Hungarian Szászfehéregyháza.) The village gives a startling glimpse of the isolation and self-sufficiency of much of Central European life, away from the handful of properly maintained roads, and even today only reachable from one side down a long dirt track. Two rows of low, chunky houses face each other across a strip of land. This central strip, long converted in most places to a proper road, is visible still in many late-nineteenth-century photos of Habsburg villages: a messy communal zone for geese, chickens, ducks and fruit trees, and perfect for riding through on a horse. Every house was a miniature factory for turning out clothing, bedding and food: inescapable, intricate monotony pegging every week of the year to specific tasks and functions. Extremely precise instructions were laid down as to who did what and when, with almost every job being genuinely essential to the security and indeed survival of the village, which would have been absolutely cut off from the outside world for months each winter. Indeed, wandering around Viscri, there is an odd feeling of being directly in touch with the forms of human behaviour which shaped most history until very recently: ruthlessly enforced conformity, the centrality of the Church, literacy as a specific skill needed by a handful of people but irrelevant to the rest – and more broadly the apportioning of tasks across the village, often to specific families, each one essential to the whole. Also, strikingly, the great importance of women in a huge range of roles – a division of labour which valued pickling as much as scything or stitching as much as setting snares. Each day would spring into existence with everyone carrying out their appointed business: feeding animals, mending clothes, preserving cherries, checking the hay. Except at very specific times the work was not intensive and it could often be sociable, but it was relentless and narrow, punctuated only by the major personal and religious commemorations, which themselves created huge demands on all the village's inhabitants. If everyone capably contributed their element then the village survived, but there was only a limited margin of error. It all sounds dreadful, and it is hardly surprising that as their way of life diverged ever more crazily from the rest of Europe during the twentieth century, the Saxons all headed off to a better life in Stuttgart.

The more time I spent in Viscri, the more it seemed to suggest interesting things: a context for suspicion of strangers, the importance of Jews and Roma as the itinerant links that tied the country together, and the significance of that quintessential folktale moment, the arrival of the tinker's cart with its manufactured, brightly coloured materials which could make young male or female villagers dream of a life beyond their one muddy street. These outsiders could bring scissors, dyes, salt, but also plague, which could, with one unlucky visit, kill almost everyone within a week. Above all what is so chilling about these villages is their insecurity: that far more even than plague, it was images of lawless bands, whether Magyar rebels, undisciplined Imperial troops or, most of all, Tatar raiders that filled villagers' heads as they spent their long, cold, relentless and weary winter months endlessly pickling footstools and adzing geese, or whatever.

This insecurity is famously expressed in the Saxons' fortified churches. These are addictively fascinating and it would be possible to spend many happy weeks wandering from village to village comparing watchtowers, portcullises and escarpments. The churches are somehow both plain and practical and strange works of art. Sometimes, as in the great church at Biertan (Birthälm), they have burst free of their origins and become quite grandiose − but most, such as Viscri and Prejmer (Tartlau), keep a white-washed simplicity which is deeply appealing. The dramatic heart of the Saxon experience is the seating arrangement. Prejmer preserves this perfectly. The entire village would attend service each Sunday, with the women obliged by their elaborate skirts to sit on long backless benches in the middle and the men ranged around the edge of the nave so that if the alarm bell was rung they could more quickly grab their weapons and run to their battle stations.

I climbed up into the top of Viscri church tower ('You can visit nothing like this anywhere else in Europe'; 'Oh, why's that?'; 'Because it is so incredibly dangerous'), a wilderness of yawing

planks, spindly ladders and missing but important-seeming structural elements. It is an odd but fascinating feeling to be standing in
a space that exactly dramatized the battle between height and distance that dominated all pre-telegraph combat. Church towers
have always had crucial defensive roles, but the toytown element in
Viscri makes it more personal and imaginable. The view of the surrounding country makes the critical calculation clear: how each
extra foot of height in the tower would buy a view of some hundred and twenty-five further feet of distance from the town. The
sentry's vigilance would therefore be matched against the speed at
which a party of horsemen could rush the village before the inhabitants got to the safety of the fortified church. In the larger towns,
such as Braşov, in times of tension any groups of horsemen
approaching the city gates, unannounced or undismounted, would
be shot down, but this was a luxury for well-appointed big places
with actual garrisons, rather than resource-poor villages, whose
defenders were simply farmers taking a turn on the walls. The plan
was never to defeat attackers, but to hold them up long enough to
make it not worth their while. Slave-raiders had no interest in
Viscri per se and if checked would simply head off to find a less
well-defended place to attack. A proper army would not want to
be distracted or pinned down by besieging such minor obstacles,
even for the time it took to bring up the artillery. So the defences
were in some measure a bluff, albeit a bluff which if called would
result in a defence to the last villager, as the stakes were understood to be the highest. Until the very end of Habsburg–Ottoman
fighting in the 1790s it was understood that defeat meant invariably the murder of the wounded and enslavement of the rest, an
entirely different war code to that in western Europe.

Despite their still formidable carapaces today quite a bit has
been taken down: the extreme conservatism of the villagers has at
least conceded that moats, rows of anti-horse stakes and outer
defensive walls should probably be dismantled. The fantasy church
at Prejmer, brilliantly restored, is still entered through a thirty-
metre fortified gallery with portcullis, leading to the massively
thick walls and towers protecting the main enclosure. These walls

are dotted with slots for crossbows and would have had various fighting platforms built around them. The real miracle of Prejmer is the inside of the walls, which still has the emergency dwellings for each household in galleried rows – tiny rooms, each with its number matching that of the house back in the village. Other rooms would have been filled with supplies to withstand a siege, everything from hams to crossbow quarrels. And in the centre of the fort is an exceptionally beautiful and simple church, built on a Greek cross pattern, and with a usefully high tower.

The oppressive mournfulness of these villages is inescapable: it would be impossible to view them as *fun* specifically. But the simplicity of the walls and towers of Cincşor (Kleinschenk) or Homorod (Hammeroden) seems (to this male anyway) a fulfilment of a most basic child's fantasy of being able to walk around in a life-sized version of a toy fortress (or of being shrunk to fit inside the toy).

CHAPTER FIVE

A surprise visit from a flying hut

The elderly Matthias became Emperor at last in 1612, but, in a marvellously awful fashion (having at last outlived his brother Rudolf and wrested from him the job he had craved for so long), he was now face to face with the mockery of all his once-vaunting ambition. The court atmosphere must have been even worse than in the closing years of Rudolf. The increasingly decrepit Matthias, with no children, and his even more elderly adviser Cardinal Klesl were besieged by a whirl of much younger figures, chatting, praying, conspiring and occasionally looking in to see if he had died yet. In a frantic attempt to leave an heir, Matthias had married the unfortunate, much younger Tyrolean Habsburg Anna, but she died childless shortly before Matthias himself, making the final weeks of his reign possibly the Habsburg nadir. The impatient younger court around Ferdinand of Styria was a clear example of generational change. The mix of cynicism, accommodation, fervour, experimentation and mysticism which had dominated Habsburg thinking through the reigns of Maximilian, Rudolph and Matthias was now discarded. The new tone was one of disgust at what Ferdinand saw as the backsliding weakness and confusion that had led Europe into a heretical morass.

Ferdinand as ruler of southern Austria had already cut a hideous swathe through a region then riddled with Protestantism. His minions left a landscape of blown-up churches and pyres of burnt books, with the corpses of Protestants dug up from their graveyards and scattered across roads and draped over fences. From his base in Graz, Ferdinand imposed a ferocious orthodoxy, still captured in a remarkably chilling portrait now in Schloss Eggenberg,

home of one of his most dankly creepy lieutenants. Here the pale-
eyed, impassive young ruler is shown, sword and crucifix in hand,
crushing heresy under foot, flanked by the approving figures of
Minerva and Father Time (not usually central to Christological
ideas) and bathed in glory. Ferdinand therefore had form, even
before it became clear he would inherit the Habsburg lands and
potentially become Emperor. The smaller Austrian territories he
already ruled – Styria, Carniola and Carinthia – were by now effectively 'clean'. To the Protestants who formed a substantial majority
in many areas of Austria and Bohemia, this man, educated by
Jesuits, a passionate and unyielding Catholic, was a mortal danger.

A fair measure of Ferdinand's problematic nature can be understood from his having gone on the pilgrimage to the church at
Loreto. This crazy shrine was meant to mark the point where the
hut in which the Virgin Mary had once lived came to rest after it
whirled up into the air and, after several bounces, landed in Italy,
having successfully escaped the Muslims who had invaded the
Holy Land. As a rule of thumb, if you do not find the story of
the Holy House completely absurd then you have failed some basic
test, Catholic or not. Ferdinand believed in it fervently. He and his
gruesomely pious companions seemed to egg each other on – both
his surviving siblings and his equally unattractive Bavarian relatives
favouring showy excesses of personal spirituality.

In so many ways Europe seems to have settled into a harsh,
wretched period even before war broke out. It is as though an era
of intellectual and cultural excitement had burnt itself out, with the
Protestant ideas that had so fascinated the previous century hard-
ening into sour orthodoxies. The assumption that Protestantism
was the wave of the future had proved untrue, with much of
Europe still Catholic. In part Protestant success had been caused by
Catholic disarray. Protestants had imagined their religious vision
had a self-evident truth which would sweep everything before it,
that Catholicism had become a mummified shell to be kicked in.
Given that both sides were dealing in absolutes – the nature of
salvation, man's duty to God, authority and obedience – the stakes
were inconceivably high. Effectively, by the early seventeenth

century the Protestants had shot their bolt, with many powerful, highly intelligent and motivated rulers simply unconvinced
by their claims, and indeed both contemptuous of and angered by
them.

In this exhausted and static world Ferdinand was new, vigorous
and crushingly self-confident. Having first secured the Bohemian
throne, he made a secret deal with the Spanish Habsburgs: they
would give their blessing to his becoming Emperor after Matthias's
death, in return for crucial scraps of western Habsburg territory
along the fault line between France and Germany. This would
revive the 'Spanish Road', the supply route which would allow
endless troops to be securely funnelled north from Spanish-held
Italy up to the rebellious provinces of the Netherlands. All Ferdinand's arrangements can be seen in a religious-political light. The
secret treaty secured Ferdinand's throne – with his track-record of
anti-Protestant unpleasantness – and released the forces of Spain
on a similar track to dispose of their own heretic rebels. Now the
arteries of Europe could flow freely again, expelling the Protestant
poison. All the new regime had to do was wait for Matthias to die.

After years of tolerance under Rudolf, the Protestants were
therefore right to be alarmed – a coordinated Habsburg attack
across the continent seemed to be threatened. For the Bohemian
Protestants, staring at Ferdinand's devastation of southern Austria,
it was clear what would be in store. As soon as he was their king
he insisted on specific Catholic rights and there was no reason to
imagine he would not go for broke once he became Emperor. It
was in this context that the summer of 1618 saw the Defenestra-
tion of Prague, with Catholic councillors sent by Ferdinand flung
out of a window of Prague Castle by enraged Protestant nobles,
surviving only because their fall was broken by angels rushing to
their aid (at least, according to Catholic accounts) or because they
landed in a dung heap (the post-match analysis preferred by Protestants). Egged on by the Dutch, the Bohemians then deposed
Ferdinand as their king and asked the young Frederick, Elector of
the Palatinate, to become the new ruler of independent, and no
longer Habsburg Bohemia.

There is something frustratingly useless about this rebellion. Under Rudolf and Matthias the general decay and drift made the Bohemians feel far more secure than they really were. They had a deeply rooted non-Catholic tradition and in the Utraquists something close to a national Church, one with Protestant roots long predating Luther and with services in Czech. But although most Bohemians were non-Catholic they were split in all kinds of ways. Each Protestant group saw little reason to help the others and many were disgusted by their new king who, as a Calvinist, alienated many who should have been close supporters, particularly when his retinue started smashing idolatrous statues and shrines in a way specifically enraging to the Bohemian mainstream. It must have been clear to the Bohemians that breaking from the Habsburgs (who had ruled them for a century) and the Empire (whose constitution they were messing up completely) could not be achieved without some titanic struggle, yet little had been done to secure sufficient allies. After hearing even more masses than usual and private conversations with his Jesuit friends, Ferdinand opted unsurprisingly for war. Matthias died in March 1619, Ferdinand was crowned Emperor in Frankfurt in September and his rival Frederick was crowned as the usurper King of Bohemia in Prague in November.

The Bohemian rebels' position was extremely poor – even major Protestant states such as Saxony were outraged at the illegality of their actions and supported the Emperor. There is a sad contemporary cartoon showing the two-tailed heraldic Bohemian Lion trapped in a thicket of thorns. Along comes the new king Frederick, clad in terrific clothes and a stylish hat, to release the Lion, pull out the thorns and nurse it back to health. This wishful Protestant fantasy almost comes across as mere sarcasm as the Lion was going to need a great deal more protection than that provided by a fop from the Palatinate. Even England & Scotland, where Frederick's father-in-law, the weird James I & VI, ruled were nervous and unsympathetic about his rash decision to go to Prague. The Dutch were constrained from providing much military assistance by their continuing truce with the Spanish. The following year, at the painfully lopsided Battle of the White Mountain, the Bohemian army was destroyed and Bohemia disappeared under the same bleak, ferocious rule Ferdinand had imposed in Styria.

The mainly Czech-speaking upper class were forced to convert or go into exile. In horrifying scenes, Prague's Old Town Square was the site of mass executions of leading rebels, any dying exhortations or yells of defiance drowned out by massed drummers. Many German-speaking associates of Ferdinand were given large estates and quite rapidly Czech became the language of the countryside and the dispossessed. The whole kingdom made a model of conformity – a dream of successful ideological erasure that later rulers marvelled at. The German-speaking Catholic carpetbaggers who swept in grabbing all the castles were never able to extinguish Czech, but they came close. Of course, there were many much older German communities scattered across Bohemia, but it was after the Battle of the White Mountain that German became the language of bureaucracy and command, seemingly as terminally as in Austria or Bavaria. A great medieval kingdom was stubbed out and reduced to a mere province – a source of revenue and troops, but with Prague an ever more insignificant and rustic place, with Rudolf II, hunting with his cheetahs and chatting with necromancers, a very distant memory. The entire Catholic package was Chinooked in, not least lowering into place a Holy Hut of Loreto – with one for Brno too – which still wackily dominates the area behind the Castle's aristocratic quarter today.

One remarkable reminder of this period remains inside St Vitus's Cathedral in Prague. Despite the battering of sieges, invasions and waves of neo-Czech fervour, two massive wooden panels can still be seen flanking the altar, preserving the new regime's view of Frederick's brief reign. One of the panels is interesting but routine, showing the Calvinists in Frederick's entourage demolishing sacred images inside the cathedral. But this is nothing compared to the same carver's astonishing panorama of the whole of Prague: a bristling mass of glowering, contemptuous church towers looking down on a tiny, almost invisible procession of mere men and carts on the Charles Bridge: Frederick and his regime fleeing the city

with their finery and loot, never to return. Prague is shown as a
once more pure and healthy organism, free of the human fleas
who so pitifully tried to challenge the True Church. The effect is
genuinely frightening – as haughty and crushing as anything
twentieth-century dictatorships could come up with and a perfect
example of victor's art.

The reasons why the Thirty Years War was so catastrophic can
be seen in its origins. Once the Bohemians had been disposed of,
a band of European rulers from Spain to Transylvania, goaded by
motives holy, cunning or idiotic, saw good reasons to fight, golden
if will-o'-the-wisp opportunities, political principles worth standing up for. In this churn of ambition and fear, the question of
whether Ferdinand II was a sort of proto-Hitler can never be
resolved. For some later German nationalists he was bravely trying
to tie together the German lands – a giant brought down by
pygmies, and by the perfidy of France. For Catholics he was the
man who stopped the rot – remade Austria and Bohemia as pure
countries – a giant brought down . . . etc. For Protestants he was
a dangerous, vicious zealot, blinkered and beyond reason. The
modern era's lack of enthusiasm for a Europe either under German
military rule or forcibly placed under uniform Catholicism tends to
tip the argument today in favour of the Protestant view.

The extent of Ferdinand's war aims was never clear as he was
obliged to fight such a range of opponents. For a while he was able
to dispose of them with the ease of a marksman shooting plastic
ducks at a fairground. For the loss of Alsace (to the Spanish) and
the two Lusatias (a thank-you present to Saxony for joining in the
invasion of Bohemia) he secured the rest of the Habsburg inheritance and regalvanized the role of Emperor in a way not imagined
since the time of Charles V. Under Rudolf II the Empire had fallen
into almost total disarray except as a context for channelling troops
into the Turkish war, but Ferdinand was working in a broad, pan-
European context, using his Habsburg resources to back up his
wish to subjugate anyone who resisted his absolutist and Catholic
policies. All his initial enemies were defeated: a Protestant Danish
attempt to hold him back ended in complete disaster and the

Emperor's principal warlord, Generalissimo Albrecht von Wallen-stein, conjured up armies on a scale not seen in Europe since the Roman Empire. With his Jesuit friends baying and convulsing with excitement, builders and decorators starting on a great wave of Catholic building and rebuilding, Ferdinand understandably – but fatally – overreached himself. In 1629 he recklessly announced an Edict of Restitution which transferred a vast mass of property and territory from the Protestants back to the Catholics. Using a start point of 1555 to establish religious' ownership, this visionary scheme alienated all but the most zealous or supine. Many Protes-tant rulers had grabbed territories from the Catholics since 1555 and major cities such as Bremen and Magdeburg were at stake. Allies or neutrals were appalled at Ferdinand's hubris – but also by a clear sense that this was only an instalment: that the nature of his faith meant that even the 1555 benchmark would be sooner or later superseded by a wish to take back *all* land in the Empire. And then, responding to cries of help from the Protestants, in the following year Gustavus Adolphus and his Swedish army arrived in northern Germany to change Europe's history.

'His divine name will be inscribed in the stars'

The Thirty Years War threw up some strange heroes and villains, generally transient, but who caught the contemporary imagination and have been transmitted down to us as vague echoes of the excited news-sheets and sermons of the time. One of these is Beth-len Gábor, the Calvinist ruler of Transylvania who is probably unique in being enshrined in British histories with his name in the correct Hungarian sequence (surname first, Christian name second) – but out of sheer ignorance rather than sensitivity. This is the only time that Transylvania really impinged on Britain's consciousness – the heroic prince's attempts to destroy the Habsburgs in the early stages of the war were used by Puritans to contrast with the supine policy of James I. Bethlen's principality formed one of the two surviving Christian-held remnants of the old Kingdom of Hungary,

carved out of the disaster of the Ottoman invasion a century
before. Both parts had 'East Germany' problems in being viewed
by the rival half as illegitimate and quisling. Royal Hungary was
under Habsburg rule while Transylvania was a semi-independent
Ottoman vassal state. The rest of Hungary was simply carved into
Turkish eyalets with no special status. Bethlen Gábor's Hungarians
saw themselves as the final, unextinguished bastion of Magyardom,
whereas Royal Hungary was a mere haggard adjunct to Habsburg
pretensions. Some aristocrats in Royal Hungary rather agreed
with the Transylvanians, but others – a sufficient number – were
relieved to be under Habsburg protection and saw Transylvania as
semi-orientalized, disloyal and religiously funambulesque. These
divergent regimes protected many Hungarians from the Habsburgs'
Catholic uniformism – and by the time Transylvania ultimately fell
into Habsburg hands at the end of the seventeenth century it was
far too late to give it the treatment that had been meted out to the
Czechs. Bethlen and his predecessors carved out for themselves
an autonomy from the Turks sufficient to make them rulers of an at
least semi-independent Hungarian state, although one that always
operated in the knowledge that it could be annihilated by Constantinople if it stepped too far out of line.

Transylvania was remarkably tolerant. The princes themselves
favoured Calvinism and supported the Calvinist power-house town
of Debrecen, paying for religious students to stay in other friendly
European states. The crazy-paving linguistic and religious structure
of Transylvania made tolerance a necessity as the alternative would
have been civil war. This tolerance was not extended to the Orthodox Romanians, who were generally serfs, but it became a defining
element in the Transylvanian state, which allowed it to contrast
itself with the ferocious homogenization imposed by Ferdinand II.

As usual religion and politics are so intricately tangled that it is
impossible to assign clear-cut motives to anybody. Religion was
so important and the stakes of personal salvation so high that a
merely cynical reading of belief is on the whole implausible. But
the Calvinism of Transylvania's rulers became a crucial, perhaps
unintended, element in Hungarian resistance to Habsburg rule.

Indeed, it could be argued that it was the shelter provided by the Ottomans for Hungarian Calvinism at this time that kept Hungary alive as an idea and prevented the whole lot from succumbing to an *Invasion of the Body Snatchers*-style fate as pliant Austrian Catholic peasants. The implosion of the independent principality later in the seventeenth century did not change this: as long as the Habsburgs defined themselves by their Catholicism (which they always did now, despite occasional gestures), the plurality of Transylvania remained as an alternative model and core of Hungarian self-belief. The anti-Habsburg rebel Imre Thököly would be happy to fight alongside Turkish troops against the Habsburgs in defence of Transylvanian Hungarian independence and in the generation after that Francis II Rákóczi, from another proud Habsburg-loathing family, allied himself with both the Ottomans and the French. Both men died in Turkish exile, but their examples would powerfully feed later nationalist ideology.

The region has been rolled so flat by centuries of violence and looting that traces of Bethlen Gábor are scarce, with one wonderful exception. Transylvania is crisply delineated by its surrounding mountains, but there is a region to the west and north-west that was known in this period as Partium and ruled by the princes of Transylvania – an arc of land from Carpathian Ruthenia (now in Ukraine), consisting of cities such as Debrecen and Arad, down to dusty bits-and-bobs in south-western Romania. One of Bethlen Gábor's most important strongholds was the city of Oradea. Like many of the major towns, it is home to a citadel – a monstrous walled pentangle which dominates the southern half. In burning summer sun, the citadel has an appealingly Indian atmosphere, its crumbling battlements implying the death of all human vanity as effectively as the walls of Tughlaqabad, say, but minus the cobras. As always at such sites the crows are an immense help (in this case jackdaws) without whose desolate, clanging *chuks* the spell of ruin would be much less potent. The Citadel was the site of the original treaty between the Habsburgs and the princes of Transylvania splitting Hungary and of several valiant sieges, with the scars of repairs after Turkish and rebel attacks still visible. On one bastion there is a small surviving plaque. Somewhat mutilated, it still reads:

GABOR OF PANNONIA, DESCENDANT OF HERCULES, BUILT
OUT OF LOVE FOR HIS COUNTRY THESE WALLS OF A
GIGANTIC STRENGTH, WHICH WOULD REVERSE EVEN THE
FATE OF THE GREAT MYTHOLOGICAL WARS: TROY, THE
TARPEIAN ROCK, BABYLON. HEAVEN ECHOES HIS MERITS, HIS
DIVINE NAME WILL BE INSCRIBED IN THE STARS.

Of course it is very easy to see this as loopy Ozymandias-style
presumption and foolishness, but surely it is far better simply to
revel in these magnificent words, somehow preserved since the
1620s?

Bethlen came close to defeating the Habsburgs, his army on
three occasions crashing into their lands and at one point reaching
the gates of Vienna. Transylvania's role was characteristic of the
reasons the Thirty Years War became so horrendously destructive
and unstoppable. Not unlike the First World War it more or less
accidentally pitted against one another rival forces whose alliances
were fatally complementary. The absolute disarray of the Emperor's
initial situation appeared to give what proved a chimerical sense of
limitless possibility to his enemies. As happy predators swept in
(including Bethlen) they were in turn defeated, but the Emperor
lacked the power to go after them and finish them off. Bethlen
was able to intervene at will, not least because a direct Habsburg
invasion of Transylvania could have triggered a response from its
Ottoman overlords. This would not have been brilliant for Ferdinand's plans – indeed one of the oddities of the Thirty Years War
is that the accident of the Ottomans' distraction in this period
prevented them from taking advantage of what was probably their
best shot at finishing the Habsburgs off.*

Over the course of the war most European countries thought
they saw an opening for personal gain and joined in, but they had
a disastrous tendency to take turns and then be defeated in turn, or
run into a stalemate. But, at last, after so many humiliations, occu-

---

* The Venetian Republic also held back, surprisingly – very much a case of the
doge that did not bark in the night.

pations and setbacks, Gustavus Adolphus and his army transformed the anti-Ferdinand forces. A pan-European victory for Ferdinand II now became impossible. In a few months the Swedes did so much damage to the Imperial forces that even Gustavus's death in battle in 1632 could not change the situation – and what became a rapidly deepening French involvement was way beyond Ferdinand's strength, even when he was allied to Spain. But Habsburg resources remained sufficiently powerful that a defeat serious enough to knock Ferdinand out of the war was also implausible. The sheer complexity of the war drove it forward, with individual countries making peace terms only to be replaced by others. Semi-independent mercenary armies ravaged the countryside and the Swedes moved from Protestant heroes to violent and extortionist menace.

Death in Eger

If Bethlen Gábor and Gustavus Adolphus are two of the most enduring Protestant heroes, then perhaps the greatest villain (aside from the Jesuit-fuddled Ferdinand himself) must be 'the Generalissimo', Wallenstein. A turncoat minor Bohemian nobleman, Wallenstein benefited hugely from Ferdinand's confiscation of rebel territory, great chunks of which he gave to Wallenstein partly as thanks, but also as a sub-contracting arrangement by which he was authorized to raise ever vaster armies on a scale far beyond the reach of Vienna itself. Funded by 'contributions' (in other words, protection money against the threat of having your town destroyed), these forces marched and counter-marched across Central Europe, powerful enough to prevent anti-Habsburg forces from winning but, even as they ballooned out of control, not strong enough to land a winning punch either.

A very long way to the west of Bethlen's Oradea lies the Czech town of Cheb, formerly called Eger. This is an extremely interesting if dispiriting place, very much in the front line for everything that went wrong in the first half of the twentieth century. For many years though it was famous for one major event enshrined in its town museum. Hardly able to control my excitement, I tried to stay focused and walk around the museum in the right order, starting in Room One with actually rather absorbing displays of ancient Obotrite storage vessels, bracelets and the rest. But staring at a black and white photo of some people excavating a pot I could stand it no longer and bounded up the stairs two at a time to get to the museum's real point: the bedchamber in which Wallenstein was assassinated! Naturally this has been completely reconstructed and with magnificent stylishness – wood panels, a big bed and a halberd (of a kind perhaps used by one of the killers) hanging from wires in the middle of the room, threatening a similarly hanging nightgown (to represent the Generalissimo).

Given his importance to Ferdinand, Wallenstein's relations with the Emperor seem to have been fairly distant and unsympathetic. In 1633 there were growing fears that with his vast resources, wealth and troops he might break free from Vienna's control and seize control of the Holy Roman Empire himself. His motives remain oddly opaque and for such an important figure it is frustrating how little we know about him. It could be that he was just a rather uninteresting military man with a lot of cash. He was certainly rescued and given a major wash-and-brush-up by Schiller in his great trilogy of plays from 1799, where he becomes a complex, flawed, astrologically obsessed figure betrayed by mediocrities. In any event, Ferdinand and his advisers, in the general gloom and paranoia of the period, after some fifteen years of fighting, came to believe perhaps correctly that Wallenstein was planning to betray his notional masters. A conspiracy was hatched and a group of Scottish and Irish soldiers massacred Wallenstein and his supporters in Cheb in a scene dramatized in a thousand cheap woodcuts.

The murder room's lack of authenticity doesn't stop it being a treat – and in an amazing and totally unexpected bonus the museum also has one of Wallenstein's horses stuffed. I am a big fan of Gustavus Adolphus's stuffed horse in Ingolstadt (taken as a trophy after the Catholic inhabitants shot it from under him during his unsuccessful siege of the town), which I had previously thought must be the oldest preserved animal in the world. But it looks as though Wallenstein's wins by a nose. Sadly it is in rather too good a state of repair, whereas Gustavus's has charismatic patches all over it and what must be wine stains from feasts at which it was once used as a centrepiece. I feel something of the same sense of suspicion in fact around Wallenstein's horse as I do about the famous Brno crocodile, which hangs in the Old Town Hall, a gift to the Emperor Matthias from the Turks, but one which has an unavoidable air of careful Victorian taxidermy. The crazy mess of the Ingolstadt horse seems much more authentic and enjoyable – although the motives behind actually faking elements in a Wallenstein horse (or indeed a Matthias crocodile) seem hard to fathom.

Ferdinand II died in 1637 and his son Ferdinand III supervised the further eleven years of the conflict, much of it a weary, futile, nightmarish shambles as anarchic military forces sought out undamaged areas to loot. The latter phases of the war are chiefly famous for a general uh-oh feeling across Europe that the France of Richelieu and Mazarin had become enormously powerful again, having been internationally a negligible force for generations. So a war fought in part to hold back what had appeared an unstoppable Catholic Habsburg revanche had – in the traditional European manner – simply resulted in helping along the career of a new bugbear.

When the Peace of Westphalia was signed in 1648 almost all the leaders who had begun the war were dead, except for the gruesome old Catholic zealot Maximilian of Bavaria, who kept gloomily praying away for a further three years. Nobody really knows how many people were killed, but a reasonable guess would be eight million, making it in relation to population quite as horrifying as the wars of the twentieth century. Many regions were so devastated that they only really recovered with the spread of industrialization over two hundred years later. The fighting had burned out the religious impulse that had begun it. Ferdinand II seems genuinely to have believed (as did many of his Protestant opponents) that the war was related in some way to the end of the world, and that what was at stake was religious salvation itself.

Such an idea was almost immediately undermined by other factors, from personal loyalty (Protestants nonetheless supporting the Emperor) to realpolitik (Catholic France supporting the Protestants). By the time it ended the Habsburgs had indeed successfully cleansed most of their direct dominions – Austria and Bohemia had been substantially Protestant and would from now on be famously not Protestant. But for the wider Holy Roman Empire the project failed and Europe remained politically and religiously hostile but exhausted.

In the wooded hills above Prague are the remains of several exhibits from a late-nineteenth-century festival. My favourite is a Hall of Mirrors. With the mirrors still kept in place by lovely woodwork and with its air of genteel entertainment it almost perfectly preserves that late-Habsburg atmosphere dear to so many novels and films. It is difficult wandering through the Hall of Mirrors not to feel as though I should be wearing a swallow-tail coat and perhaps a monocle. At its heart lies one of those completely random things beloved of the period – an enormous painting of the defence of the Charles Bridge in 1648, dramatically showing the students and Jesuits fighting back against vicious Swedish mercenaries. It is almost comically uninvolving and leaden and it is hard to imagine it ever provoked gasps even from an original audience whose bar was probably set a lot lower than those of us raised on *Titanic 3D*. The diorama atmosphere is helped by a woeful little cannon and a few bits of armour strewn in front of the painting. The battle it commemorates was one of the last actions of the war as the Swedes, having ransacked the castle (and taken back to Stockholm a lot of loot from Rudolf's era, including his best Arcimboldos), tried to break into the Old Town. The solidity of the defence showed how much Prague had changed during the war. From being the core of Protestant resistance, drawing on its deep-seated Hussite roots, it had become a docile Catholic town, filled with monasteries, rededicated and rebuilt churches and numerous German-speaking newcomers. The Swedes who would have been embraced in 1619 with grateful tears were now shut out. It was two centuries before Czech nationalists began to rediscover this older, dissenting past and built an entire ideology around it. But for now much of Central Europe had been successfully religiously cleansed and the Habsburgs were back in the saddle.

Burial rites and fox-clubbing

In the later stages of the Thirty Years War the dynasty finally and conclusively settled in Vienna. Exhausted by seemingly endless fighting, on the verge of bankruptcy, Ferdinand III sat in his austere, bad-news Viennese court and somehow ended up staying. Prague, in many ways a more imposing city and with plenty of office space honeycombing the Castle Hill, was too tainted, both with Rudolf's weirdness and as a former nest of heresy. There never seem to have been any discussions about moving to somewhere more Imperial and less Habsburg – one of the obvious German cities such as Regensburg or Nuremburg or Frankfurt. The shift from Prague to Vienna, some two hundred miles further south-east, meant the archducal family lands were what really mattered and gave the Habsburgs a decisively eastern focus. Since France was for almost two centuries their principal enemy, it also provided an enormous defensive glacis of territory which was to be repeatedly helpful, but it also put them alarmingly near the Ottoman border. The constant wanderings of the earlier court, where Frederick III or Maximilian I and their locustine merrie band would turn up, filled with hungry kettle-drummers and mounted-archer bodyguards, looking for hospitality from some despairing local grandee, were long gone. A town that Ferdinand I and Maximilian II had used on a somewhat provisional, emergency basis now became the permanent court.

The shift to Vienna was reflected in all kinds of cultic ways. Indeed, one of Matthias's few permanent acts of value was to marry the deeply religious and very much younger Anna of Tyrol (daughter of the enchanting Ferdinand II of Tyrol). She died young and left in her will provision for a church of the Capuchins, a

famously ascetic monastic order who had come to the Empire
during Rudolf II's reign and whose leader, the later canonized Law-
rence of Brindisi, had acted as Imperial Chaplain during the Long
War. The Capuchin church was built on New Market Square, and
there the monks would look after her and her husband's tombs.
Building was delayed by the Thirty Years War, but completed in
1632. Ungratefully, Ferdinand II had himself buried in his beloved
Graz, but as a further indication that Vienna was stabilizing as the
genuine capital Ferdinand III and almost all his successors were in
due course carried unresisting into the Capuchin Crypt.

Their bodies were buried in the Crypt; their hearts were buried
in the Augustinian Church next to the Hofburg Palace; their intes-
tines were pickled in copper canisters under St Stephen's Cathedral
(with little labels on: *Leopold I, Joseph I*, etc. – it seems a shame not
to be able to pick a canister and give it a shake to see what sort of
sound it makes). With these gestures the Habsburgs definitively
staked out Vienna as their dynastic ground. Indeed, much of the
city centre is a sequence of mystical spaces for the Habsburg
family: the Stephansplatz, the Graben, Am Hof, the courtyards of
the Hofburg and all the connecting routes were for centuries part
of the intricate clockwork of court ritual.

The Habsburg public calendar became ever more crazily packed
as the seventeenth century progressed, with the canopies, incense
and choristers dusted off at the drop of a hat. There were annual
processions to mark victory over the Turks, victory over the
French, a lucky escape by Leopold I from a lightning bolt, and at
the Holy Trinity Pillar in the Graben every October to commemorate the end of the great 1679 plague. In the later eighteenth
century Maria Theresa and then Joseph II swept a lot of this stuff
away, but right to the First World War there was still a sort of
zodiac chart of absurdity by which Franz Joseph measured out his
sacerdotal duties.

It is generally reckoned that the Habsburg court was not much
fun. Most gallingly it had very much less money than its seventeenth-century French rival, where state-of-the-art palaces would
fill up with perfumed courtiers lightly tapping their gloved fingers

together in appreciation of all the coloured fountains, special drinks, peacock-strewn parterres and mirrored halls being laid on for them. Indeed, the relentless Habsburg emphasis on prayer could have just been filling up some of the moneyless stretches of time. It certainly made a different aesthetic, with the Hofburg as a whole always having the air of cheerless functionality it keeps today. A further startling difference with France was the general lack of mistresses – the severe morality of the court was often genuine, and there was much less of the gossip or factionalism that made Versailles so distinctive. Instead, the Habsburgs had a far less threatening but baffling enthusiasm for court dwarves, a form of chic imported like so much else from Spain. These men (with names like 'Baron Klein') were unthreatening confidants, jesters and factotums, their size making clear their distance from the real world of high-rank noblemen. Indeed the dwarves must have been among the few who could kick back and relax at court, with most of its other members mere parts in a grinding machinery of precedence, cap-doffing, bows, curtsies and stylized movements fetishizingly borrowed from Madrid.

Emperors could be in danger of becoming trapped in this machinery. From an anally retentive chamberlain's point of view the court performed like some brocade-trimmed orrery, with the annual sequences of religious festivals evenly rotating round and intersecting with the daily sequences of meals, prayers, audiences and council meetings. If the Emperor were to just sit there like Father Christmas this would be fatal, and the unaccountable gesture (a sudden demand for music, an act of spectacular and spontaneous generosity, a decision to go riding in the Prater) was critical both to keeping everyone sane and to illustrating the Emperor's ungovernable nature. When Joseph I spent the equivalent of the entire year's food and banquet budget at the Hofburg on a diamond he fancied, this may have caused seizures among his staff, but it was part of a long tradition of the Emperor showing through his actions how little he cared for bourgeois plodding. This sort of financial recklessness was shared with an aristocracy similarly addicted to grand gesture and conspicuous display.

A huge amount of card-playing and dice games filled up the court's time. This kept everyone happy by creating patches of the day (like listening to opera) during which the Emperor did not need to talk to anyone. Surrounded by odd-looking ambassadors, professional toadies and drunken former military heroes day in day out, the Emperor was constantly obliged to find reasons for *not* engaging, *not* promising anything to yet another of an effectively infinite supply of supplicants. A sudden decision for war could have simply been provoked by a wish for something to break the monotony – and indeed one of the key ways in which a court *failed* to be a clockwork mechanism was its periodic emptying out for major campaigns and emergencies, the great tests of the cohesion, fellowship and trust that could be developed by a successful ruler.

Enormous stretches of time, when there was no piquet and no fighting, were spent hunting. The Habsburgs were enthusiastic about some odd forms – the annual use of falcons at Schloss Laxenburg to kill herons is perhaps the oddest. Herons in flight always have an air of a spindly, poorly constructed balsawood model covered in feathers and it seems an at best tepid achievement to bring them down with a sinister, compact fist-of-fury sort of bird like a falcon. It is hard too to see the pleasure in having beaters chase dozens of deer into pools of deep water and then take them out with crossbows, or in tossing foxes in blankets before clubbing them to death (Leopold I used to enjoy this particularly, aided by his game-for-a-laugh dwarfs). Presumably these forms of the hunt were meant to show aristocratic mastery over the largest forms of life, but also not risk the Emperor with personal embarrassment. So the heron is the largest bird, but if shot in a normal way with a gun would presumably go all over the place like some exploding spindly chair and the Emperor's hunt would appear mean rather than masterful; a proper, uncontrolled deer-hunt is simply far too dangerous and is in any event not something that can be watched by spectators, so the deer need to be brought to the Emperor; foxes are too nimble to kill in an honourable way so they need to be stunned and rolled up in a blanket. So the Emperor was obliged in everything he did to take actions which appeared masterful and yet, in practice, were not. But perhaps this was the supreme form of masterfulness: did anyone at court, for example, *dare* think it ridiculous when Leopold tossed a fox in a blanket? Presumably not. The more we read about the past the more completely odd it appears.

The devil-doll

In scattered pockets in the southern Tyrol lie the territories of the old Imperial bishopric based around the town of Brixen, now called Bressanone, a German-speaking part of Italy. Brixen formed, with its southern neighbour Trento, the 'plug' that secured the Brenner Pass for the Emperor. For those who enjoy such things, the Brixen diocesan museum is an absolute classic of its kind, crammed with tortured, worm-eaten wooden panels of biblical suffering of a kind churned out by the region's sculptors and painters for centuries. Its unique, and indeed demented, claim on everyone's time however is its extensive and elaborate sequence of crib scenes, little panoramas crammed with tiny people and commissioned by the bishops in the late eighteenth and early nineteenth centuries. 'Crib' generally just implies Baby Jesus, and there are many renderings of him, but the sculptors in wood and wax soon tired of such simplicities and branched out into areas of ever greater mania. There is one amazing ensemble of Herod, with the face of a gold-painted monkey, laughing dementedly as his chariot is escorted by demons (with spitted babies on their spears) into the Mouth of Hell. There is a bizarre scene of Jesus helping his father to cut up timber, with some angels assisting – not a scene I remember from the Bible. And, even more apocryphally, a masterpiece Flight into Egypt, an event which conventionally has all the interest and excitement of a long family car journey on a motorway, but which is spectacularly bought to life here by showing the Holy Family on a rickety bridge with their donkey, crossing the Valley of Wild Beasts, with dozens of little model lions, tigers and porcupines (oddly) waiting below to eat them if they fall off. This is a fate fended off by a hit-squad of angels wielding swords of flame to secure the area – another scene I *really* cannot remember from the Bible.

Chuckling at the wilder shores of popular Catholicism and taking in yet another room crowded with saints and martyrs, suddenly the mood went all wrong as I found myself face to face with something truly horrible: a small carving from about 1495 of the child martyr-saint Simon of Trento. Most of these devil-dolls have long been chucked away or boxed up and the Vatican itself finally disowned him in the 1960s, but here was a brilliantly extreme rendering of what was once a ubiquitous image. Early in the reign of Maximilian I the sensational discovery was made in Trento, apparently in the cellar of a Jewish family, of the body of a missing two-year-old boy. The story got around that the Jews had killed him and had used his blood to mix into their matzo bread. The little statue shows the child covered in dozens of knife nicks with blood dripping from them and holding up a sign showing the pincers, augers and so on used by the Jews. The result of the discovery was a spasm of violent hysteria which resulted in eight Jewish men being executed and a ninth committing suicide in prison (three of Simon's assailants are shown as tiny figures beneath his feet). The entire Jewish community was then arrested and a further fifteen Jews burned at the stake.

The devotional cult of Simon of Trento spread rapidly, with altars and churches and shrines in his name scattered everywhere. The notorious Old Bridge Tower in Frankfurt was decorated into the nineteenth century not only with its horrendous portrayal of the 'Jewish Pig' but also with an image of Simon's corpse and the instruments of his death. This cult proved unstoppable, with dozens of miracles assigned to Simon's intercession, and it popularized anti-Semitic fantasies which bubbled up at seemingly random intervals across the Empire.

The real reasons for the blood libel turning up in Trento in 1495 can never be recovered, but it was an important example of the often unstable and vicious links between popular Catholicism and anti-Semitism which littered Habsburg history (and which would also, of course, implicate Protestants). There is no correct place in this book for a discussion of the Jews of the Empire, but here is as good a one as any. By the seventeenth century the events in Trento may have seemed a long time ago, but they existed too in a sort of permanent present, folded into a Counter-Reformation iconography which created a Manichaean opposition between Christian and Jew, but which nonetheless could not hide the enduring, long-standing nature of an oddly stable relationship.

Under the intolerable shadow of the 1940s it is extremely hard but necessary to reimagine a world of sometimes violent and yet *not* genocidal oppression. In his general ban on all forms of religion in the Empire except Catholicism, even Ferdinand II made an exception for Judaism. The Jewish communities were as ancient as, often far more ancient than, any other settler group in Central Europe, and they held a place of confused respect because of their crucial role in the Christian story. Jews could not be understood simply as heretics if they shared the religion of Jesus himself and they fell into a quite separate category from simple evil-doers such as Muslims. But this category was nonetheless not an enviable one, with Jewish 'stubbornness' and engagement in businesses forbidden to Christians (such as money-lending) making their presence inter-mittently unacceptable and with the threat of massacre or expulsion always waiting in the wings.

From the point of view of Jews themselves this 'stubbornness' was at the very heart of their identity, since their European diaspora in the centuries after the destruction of the Temple by the Emperor Titus. This exodus gave them a separate narrative of great power – of an endless, generationally renewed act to maintain themselves in a hostile, cold and forbidding environment. For Christians much of the Old Testament provided simply a pictur-esque and enthralling sequence of dramas suitable for wall decorations and engravings. It was understood that the Old Testa-ment was crammed with clues that, in an immense effort of futile scholarship, were made anticipations of the New Testament. For the Jews the same material, grotesquely abused and misunderstood by Christians, was an endlessly rich source of reassurance and chal-lenge, a constant reminder of the need for constancy in exile and the keeping of the laws maintained at such cost by their ancestors. This oddly shared inheritance, however much mutually denied and contested, is of course one of the defining and most powerful and creative threads in European history. But except for short periods (under Rudolf II in Prague, most obviously, but even then for in many ways trivial and freaky reasons) there was almost no dialogue. The Jews could draw on a rich range of louche and brutal stereotypes from across the Hebrew Bible who could easily be seen as prefiguring of the richly clad and mounted European princes who either threatened or patronized them. In theory a densely nuanced alternative history of the Habsburgs could be reconstructed through Jewish eyes, except for the basic problem that the events we consider 'history' were viewed by them as irrelevant, the 'abomination of the land', a mere backdrop of meaningless European savagery against which their real life could be carried out.

The story of Simon of Trento is merely one incident, albeit a particularly disgusting one, in a centuries-long argument within Christianity about what to do with Judaism. The Habsburgs had special tribunals to look after issues of financial or administrative concern: these dealt variously with mines, vineyards, forests, rivers, soldiers and Jews. So just as colonies of German miners in northern Hungary reported in directly to the Emperor, so did they. This protection was real and meant that except at times of civil collapse it was rare for Jews to suffer genuine violence. But it was also far from benign, with often crushing levels of taxation and impoverishment in return for being otherwise left alone. The sheer restrictiveness under which Jews operated is very hard to conceive, but was much less extreme than it appears to us, as for centuries everyone lived within a highly constrained society with many duties and few privileges. But as these 'feudal' shackles fell off and gentiles and landlords and guilds lost their power, the disabilities of the Jews became ever starker, with eighteenth- and nineteenth-century Emperors twisting themselves in knots over how to deal with them legally.

What is striking throughout the arguments about the right place for Jews in society is that the Jews themselves were never consulted. The Emperor and his advisers, generally key Catholic notables, were driven by an odd mixture of piety and efficiency, but almost never by curiosity. The actual needs of Jews were not relevant to their decisions. There was a scholastic strand which valued the Jews almost as living fossils. This saw them not just as the much-debased inheritors of Old Testament traditions but also as intermediaries with ancient Egyptian magic, through the Kabbala and, even more bizarrely, as the unwitting descendants of the 'Land of Cham' with access to the secrets hidden within the still-undecoded world of hieroglyphics. These very odd forms of esoteric study bothered few people, but it did mean that there was an active academic curiosity which could border almost on respect within Catholic university circles, and which again made Judaism quite different from any other religion. The other powerful strand within Christianity was a sense that certain actions might result in the final removal of this anomaly scattered across the Empire, through some dazzling act which would at last convert the Jews. In the fervent and peculiar world of Ferdinand II there were attempts to force Jews to listen to sermons, grand gestures such as the establishment of a privileged new ghetto on the opposite bank of the Danube from Vienna, offers of money.

Each of these actions simply fed into the Jews' own worst fears and a rich parallel argument developed over what level of cooperation was permissible under Torah and to what extent any leeway at all was going to simply spring the trap which would result in a Jew ceasing to be a Jew. These anxieties expressed themselves in countless ways. For example, Habsburg moves to make Jews write accounts in German not Yiddish were motivated by a genuine wish for greater accountability, but they forced Jews to learn German – which could easily be seen as the high road to a disastrous and shameful assimilation. Each of the stages by which legal disabilities were lessened triggered both creative and sterile fights within each Jewish community as to what would or would not be appropriate as a compromise with the Christian authorities. Each Habsburg dispensation was seen as bountiful, but also – by both sides – as cunning. Perhaps this would be the gesture that at last would

persuade the Jews to convert? Some dispensations were provoked
by the wish for greater efficiency but they were never provoked by
an active concern for the actual welfare of Jewish subjects. With
the First Partition of Poland in 1772, the Habsburgs found themselves with three times as many Jewish subjects and a new era
arrived but, however rational and even secular, it was not one from
which the disgusting little figure of Simon of Trento ever entirely
disappeared.

How to build the Tower of Babel

At the end of the Thirty Years War the papacy's authority lay in
ruins. The Pope's bull attacking the Treaty of Westphalia's religious
toleration clauses was simply ignored and he was increasingly
viewed as just the inept ruler of a backward Italian state. The
anomaly of the Pope's still being an elected and generally quite
elderly figure also caused problems – in the seventeenth century
the papacy appeared almost a revolving door for semi-cadavers,
with twelve popes in the saddle as against only five Emperors.
These men avoided the low comedy of corruption, stabbings and
poison enjoyed by their predecessors and were in some cases intelligent and thoughtful figures, but they seldom had much control
over events and the world twisted and turned in ways which they
were unable to catch up with.

   None of this is to deny the spectacular vibrancy and aggression
of Catholicism itself in the century and a half between the Treaty
of Westphalia and the French Revolution, but this was achieved
with the Pope's acquiescence rather than through his leadership.
Above all, this was the great era of the Society of Jesus. This
extraordinary organization has left its stamp all over the Habsburg
Empire, and the Jesuits' distinctive flat-fronted churches and bulky
colleges still dot the landscape. A perfect example is in the central
Bohemian town of Kutná Hora, left a haggard ruin by the Thirty
Years War but put back on its feet as a stronghold of Catholicism
with a glowering set of Jesuit buildings at its heart, decorated with

the inevitable statues of martyred saints. Each of these colleges was, as one Jesuit perfectly put it, 'a Trojan horse filled with soldiers from heaven'. Brilliantly educated, self-confident, conniving, the Jesuits dominated teaching across Catholic Europe and specialized in all sorts of town-square spectaculars with fluttering banners, marching and self-examination, sifting the population for conformity and obedience.

Originating in the first shock of the Reformation, the Jesuits fanned out across the globe, converting and studying, ensuring that much of Christianity's presence would be Catholic rather than Protestant. This global mission put the Jesuits under an intolerable amount of torque, as the world they did so much to analyse and explain, particularly India and China, raised a host of ever more awkward questions about the exclusive claims of Christianity. This would turn into a more general problem for Western religion by the later eighteenth century, with the researches of the Jesuits contributing so much to their own diminution. In the meantime the Jesuits ruled the roost and nowhere more so than in the Habsburg lands.

The Jesuits' mode of operation is now very hard to sympathize with. One confusion comes from the sense that if some of these highly intelligent men were gathered around a table and we could listen in, almost everything they said would appear to be nonsense – by which I don't mean a cheap jibe against religion, but their entire understanding of society, science, education: everything would appear to us questionable or odd. They did not have the sort of Gestapo function of the Inquisition, and indeed always kept a distance from that bizarre body, the Society having suffered from investigation itself in its early days. But they did have a deep contempt for other Christian variants, let alone other religions, and pursued ruthlessly any form of intellectual backsliding – generally through teaching and exhortation rather than the rack and thumbscrew. Their churches, often the greatest examples of baroque decoration, may seem to us headache-inducing explosions of gold paint and cherubs, but this Jesuit feeling of emotional excess was all in the service of teaching, and needed the images of exemplary lives and events that littered the ceilings and side-chapels. Above all, they had the Virgin Mary, a figure of extraordinary power whose cult could not really be countered by Protestants, who were left looking rather male and wooden.

The Jesuits' sheer oddness and distance from us is summed up in the career of the great Athanasius Kircher, a German who died in 1680 having spent his adult life as a Jesuit, mostly living in Rome under the protection of the Pope and with the Emperors Ferdinand III and Leopold I as the sponsors of his publications. It would be possible to spend a profitable lifetime just delving around in Kircher's work. A polymath of scarcely credible range, a prolific author and owner of a museum in Rome, Kircher managed in modern scientific terms to be wrong about almost every subject he turned his attention to. Through the many engravings he commissioned to accompany his work, however, he conjured into being a whole world, plausible and peculiar and with its own value system, which allows us to see something of a Jesuit world-view. As an opener Kircher wrote a series of poems and acclamations to Ferdinand III in forty-seven different languages, including one notionally in Egyptian hieroglyphs (Ferdinand is 'the Austrian Osiris . . . the Austrian Momphta, etc') and prettily laid out on an engraved obelisk, with the hieroglyphs all completely wrong. He was obsessed with labyrinths, mirrors, volcanoes (he was one of the first men to descend into the crater of Vesuvius), magnets (the frontispiece of his book *Magnets* features the arms of the Holy Roman Emperor, but with metal crowns and sceptres hanging together, magnetized, from the claws of the double-headed eagle), music amplification and freaks of nature. He drew on the Jesuits' international network for images of Egypt, of Mexican temples, of Chinese wonders.

In some of this it is possible to see exciting glimpses into scientific method, with Kircher's magnificent curiosity trumping any attempt at derision. He is also one of the key figures in imagining the ancient world, with superb renderings of the Colossus of Rhodes, the Hanging Gardens of Babylon and the rest. But at the heart of his research lay a demented enthusiasm for the literal nature of the Bible. In one of his greatest and most futile images, he showed how the Ark's interior could be subdivided to find space

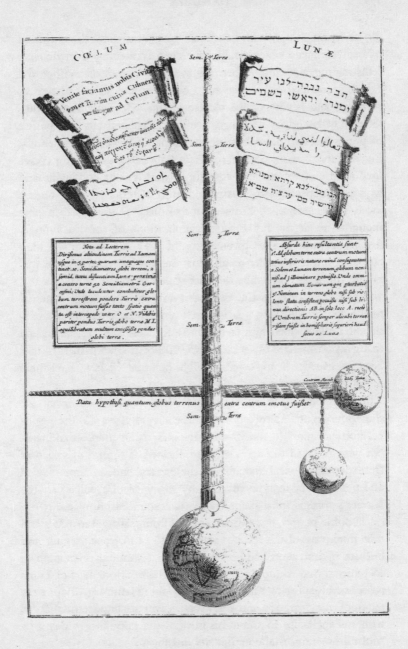

for all living things, with conditions much eased by the exclusion of many animals which could have been created by post-diluvian cross-mating: e.g. giraffes because they are a cross of panther and camel, armadillos of tortoise and hedgehog and so on. The sheer craziness and beauty of the picture of the Ark, with its countless little animals and its seemingly sensibly calculated jars and barrels of provisions, is one of the highlights of the seventeenth century. But it is in his work on the Tower of Babel that everything comes to a head and we are left wondering what is a practical joke and what is just spectacularly misapplied effort. Kircher commissioned a lovely illustration of the Tower but then became immersed in zany thoughts about the full practical implications of the frustratingly fleeting mention of the Tower in the Bible. He assumed it was built by Nimrod (on no evidence) and that the Tower's reaching 'heaven' meant 'the moon'. He then did some calculations to prove that this was never practical, as the Earth did not contain enough material for bricks to build such a structure. Even if it *were* technically possible to build such a tower (see p. 175), Kircher carefully established that it would need 374,731,250,000,000 bricks, with such further headaches as the horses needing eight hundred years to haul them up to the top even at a gallop.

Before being lost in such marvellous material for ever, we should move on. As the eighteenth century progressed, the Jesuits became ever more hemmed-in by enemies. Their intellectual methods were reduced to tatters by the influence of figures as varied as Descartes and Pascal and just as the papacy had become viewed as an unacceptable type of rival by many secular rulers, so the Society's transnational nature made it ever more anomalous. In a catastrophic period, it was first expelled from Portugal in 1759 and then from most of the rest of Europe by 1773. A great, curious and brilliant organization had come to an end, its muted re-creation in 1814 rendering it into a far more normal and minor part of European society. The Jesuit role within the Habsburg Empire as religious shock-troops and intellectuals was so important that, as with so much else in Central Europe, we are looking today at a landscape with crucial components missing.

CHAPTER SIX

Genetic terrors » The struggle for mastery in Europe »

A new frontier » *Zeremonialprotokoll* »

Bad news if you are a cockatrice » Private pleasures

Genetic terrors

In December 1666 in Vienna in the main courtyard of the Hofburg an attempt was made to crunch together all the grandeur, solemnity and extravagance available to human ingenuity to mark the marriage of the young Emperor Leopold I and the Spanish infanta, Margarita Teresa. We have pictures of the event and some of the music has been preserved and recorded, most strikingly Schmelzer's thunderous *Cavalry Ballet*, heaped with trumpets, bombastic in a good way. The music accompanied hundreds of men pulling carts with the usual woebegone giant carvings of allegorical figures, a float featuring a mock-up of a battleship and tons of horsemen in elaborate costume. Flares, explosions, kettledrums – and as the finale the young Emperor himself stormed forward on horseback, followed by over a hundred musicians blaring and pounding away, to greet his Spanish bride.

The sense of fear and anxiety in the courtyard on that day is completely lost to us, merely reading about these events centuries later. We after all know the vast pattern of historical, political, personal and geographical events that will play out from this meeting of Leopold and Margarita Teresa. But the nature of what followed was of course absolutely unknown to the struggling crowds of grandees, musicians, symbolic statues and brightly decorated horses in the Hofburg.

As good a starting point as any for understanding this ceremony would be Rubens' commission to paint the meeting of the two branches of the Habsburg family before the decisive Imperial victory at Nördlingen in 1634. The foreground and sky stiff with allegorical figures, the son of the Emperor Ferdinand II and the son of King Philip III eagerly shake hands, their joint forces about to crush their Protestant enemies. The painting dates from the same year as Velásquez's even more majestic *The Surrender of Breda*, celebrating one of the greatest triumphs of the Spanish Habsburgs in the war with the Netherlands. Both these paintings have an unintended *vanitas* quality, cruelly freezing in time what seemed a high-water mark for Habsburg fortunes in the Thirty Years War. It all ended up as so much dust – with the dismantling of Ferdinand II's dreams of a universal Catholic empire and Breda's absorption into the independent Dutch state. But, putting aside these setbacks, Rubens' painting shows both branches of the Habsburg family in good shape: rulers of most of Europe, confident and glamorous. A little over thirty years later both branches had been overtaken by genetic disaster and were threatened with extinction: what was being played out in the Hofburg courtyard in 1666 was potentially the last gasp of a catastrophically inbred and unlucky family.

Leopold was the last survivor of an extraordinary massacre of Austrian Habsburgs. His father, Ferdinand III, married three times; his first two wives were killed by childbirth and three daughters and three sons died as babies. This was a horrible sequence of events, but in 1654 there were still seven males, some of them seemingly in good order. But Leopold (who had been in training for a blameless career in the Church) witnessed the sudden deaths of his elder brother Ferdinand (the heir), his father Ferdinand (the emperor), his uncle Leopold Wilhelm (the military commander and great patron of the arts – key originator of the Kunsthistorisches Museum) and his younger brother Karl Joseph (aged fourteen). In a further twist the brothers Ferdinand Karl and Sigismund Franz had, as described earlier, died in their thirties, both sonless, ending with shocking speed the Tyrolean branch of the family. The long-term importance of the Tyrolean disaster was that Leopold now took over all their territories and these became fully integrated under Vienna's rule until 1918, but in the short term it eradicated the only other source of male 'supply'.

Margarita Teresa, Leopold's Spanish bride, came from a similar family disaster. Her father, Philip IV, had six daughters with his first wife with only one surviving infancy and one son, who died in his teens of smallpox. His second marriage (this is where things get very odd) was to his niece Mariana, Ferdinand III's daughter. In a development that would not surprise modern biologists, of their five children only two survived: Margarita Teresa herself and her younger brother, the overwhelmingly handicapped Charles.

So at the Hofburg, Europe was face to face with the Habsburg family's last chance: a marriage between the two final fully functional members, albeit with Margarita (in the same style as her mother) being Leopold's niece. Leopold was no oil painting and she was little better. Both inherited the distorted Habsburg face – the tiny Leopold's jaw so distended that his mouth would fill with water if it rained. If they could have a son then (assuming the sickly little Charles died) that boy might recreate the huge empire of Charles V, inheriting both Vienna's and Madrid's realms. But if they failed then the Habsburg family would vanish and this – much crisper and shorter – book would end in the next few pages. If Leopold had swept into the Hofburg celebration on his horse and had fatally fallen off then the entire course of European history would have flowed into a fresh channel.

But Leopold lived, his strangely shaped head familiar in profile on innumerable coins over nearly half a century. Despite his awkward habit of fleeing at key moments in his reign, he has a fair claim to be the most successful of all the Austrian Habsburgs and he did indeed have the male children to succeed him; but not with Margarita Teresa. She has become immeasurably famous – far more widely recognized than her husband – as the little five-year-old girl at the centre of Velázquez's *Las Meninas*, a painting only known at the time to those who could enter a specific room in Madrid's royal palaces, but which to us must have a fair claim to be one of the greatest paintings ever made: the – presumably unintentional – shadowed swansong of the Spanish Habsburgs.

As the wife of Leopold (who she correctly but very peculiarly called 'Uncle' throughout their marriage), Margarita Teresa suffered the same unavoidable curse as her relatives. At this point in the family's history each confinement must have been treated with far more terror than hope. She suffered many miscarriages, and gave birth to two sons who died at or shortly after birth, to a daughter who survived and then a further daughter who was born by caesarean section after Margarita Teresa herself had died, aged twenty-one, and who then also died. The surviving daughter, Maria Antonia, lived long enough to marry the Elector of Bavaria and herself have two sons who died at birth before dying aged twenty-three shortly after giving birth to Joseph Ferdinand. This boy, as the only great-grandson of Philip IV, would have become King of Spain but he foiled the plans of Europe by dying aged six.

This truly awful sequence of events was the reality which is so often hidden by the self-confident sequence of official portraits of men with wigs, armour, swords and horses that fills the conventional European history of the period. A parallel but unbearable history could be written of the human byways and culs-de-sac, pain and humiliation that lay behind this facade. A book could be written which told the Habsburg story just from the point of view of the disregarded queen mothers, the terrified wives, the daughters used as trans-national pawns, the widows and daughters who vanish from history as they are put into convents or into little-frequented palace wings: all those moments of bored irritation when the child being born proved to be merely female and the grand witnesses to the mother's agonizing labour hurriedly dispersed. But there is also the story of the devastating sequence of dead children. Even in an era of high infant mortality there were clearly special factors around Habsburg inbreeding that made things far worse. The worst focal point for all this is the 'Children's Columbarium' in the Imperial Crypt, put together in the 1960s in a cold fit of tidiness to corral into one place eleven prematurely dead sons and daughters of Ferdinand III and Leopold I.

In the Kunsthistorisches Museum there is a marvellous portrait by Jan Thomas van Ieperin of Margarita Teresa in fancy dress in a sylvan setting, shortly after her marriage, her warped face smiling from under an enormous white-and-orange feathered crown and in a dress of matchless charisma. She shared her uncle-husband's enthusiasm for music and masques and they seem to have been a

cheerful couple during their short marriage, but the forces bear-
ing down on her – familial, sexual, genetic – were really beyond
human capacity.

The struggle for mastery in Europe

A very slow train trundles through southern Hungary and northern
Serbia (the old Hungarian county of Bács-Bodrog). The flat, bleak
landscape becomes hypnotic – hours go by with eyes jumping at
anything like a house, or a clump of trees. Occasional very small
towns, storks and buzzards perk things up and there is, of course,
the usual cowardice of doing this sort of trip in the summer, when
it is at least a plausible region to be, rather than in the winter
months when it is one of those places like Nebraska which are
only tolerable if you are inured to them from birth. Its big fields
and oppressively broad skies make it seem, like so many places in
the former Empire, 'remote' – but there is the usual problem with
the term in that it begs the follow-up, 'remote from where?' In the
later seventeenth century this was part of a huge, thinly populated
area that was briefly very busy, with fantastically dressed soldiers in
their many thousands struggling across bogs, always on the verge
of running out of food and leaving a trail of small, ruined settlements behind them. Colossal armed clashes (Harsány 1687,
Slankamen 1691, Zenta 1697, Petrovaradin 1716) featured combined forces far larger than the population of Vienna. These were
wars which were won as much by disease levels and supply chains
as military valour. For a generation, this was the most exciting,
frightening and mythic region in Europe. Hundreds of thousands
of soldiers died here before the entire zone reverted to being the
backwater's backwater.

For much of the seventeenth century the border between the
Habsburgs and the Ottomans had been relatively quiet – relatively in
the sense that large-scale raiding did happen (baking in a level of
violence which we would consider scarcely credible) but it was not
by the standards *of the time* serious. Between the disappointments

of the end of the Long War under Rudolf and Matthias and the
eruption of the 1680s everyone had plenty to do (e.g. the Thirty
Years War) but little of it involved direct Christian–Muslim hostili-
ties. A short, curious war in 1664 broke out over Transylvania
(which just about held onto its unstable semi-vassal status). This
war had little practical result as both sides had other preoccupations which brought it to an end, but it was striking from the
Habsburgs' side because at St Gotthard, east of Graz, they actually
defeated an invading Turkish army – the first serious indicator in a
century and a half of fighting that Ottoman fighting power might
at last be depleting. The Habsburgs also constructed a worthwhile
alliance system, with troops from all over Europe (even France),
and a serious sense within the Empire and elsewhere that holding
back the Turks was a shared venture. The end of the war was a
humiliating one, with Leopold paying tribute and the Ottomans
keeping Transylvania. But it was an interesting precedent.

The problem that the Habsburgs faced both now and during
the forthcoming Great Turkish War was how to deal in practical
terms with a thinly populated area four times the size of their
hereditary Austrian holdings. Once a few obviously headline-
grabbing things had been achieved (the taking of a handful of
specific fortresses, such as Belgrade or Buda), there could never be
agreement as to just how much fighting was needed to ensure the
Turks no longer menaced Europe – this was simply too existential
a question. It would be another two centuries before the idea of
taking Constantinople itself became plausible. The great advantage
the Habsburg and later 'Holy League' armies had in the fighting
was a relatively short supply chain – but as they moved forward
this stretched and the Turks moved closer to their own forward
base. Each advance merely generated a fresh security problem,
another line of fortresses to man. It is fair to say as a summary that
the Habsburgs never had any serious plans for Constantinople,
whereas the Ottomans had plenty for Vienna.

The nearly twenty years of Habsburg–Ottoman peace after
St Gotthard were filled by heavy fighting in Poland which, under
its charismatic Grand Hetman Jan Sobieski, also managed to fend

off the Ottoman assaults. By the time Sobieski was elected king he was a European hero who seemed to have ended a horrific era of evisceration for Poland. He mulled over his options and had elaborate plans to absorb Transylvania into Poland, or perhaps to ally with the Turks against the Habsburgs. Fortunately for everyone he decided instead to become the saviour of Christendom.

The monstrous Ottoman invasion army which Sobieski's spies reported as assembling outside Constantinople in the summer of 1682 could have been heading for Poland again – security in these cases seems to have been extraordinarily tight, with most of the Ottoman commanders themselves totally in the dark. Sobieski and Leopold agreed a pact to send troops to defend the other, depending on the army's movements. As it proved, the Ottomans were concerned by the heavy skirmishing between Habsburg and Transylvanian forces: if they could not protect their vassal then Ottoman prestige could only wither further. So the army marched to Belgrade and then straight into Austria, ignoring the usual fortresses designed to hold it up. Light Tatar forces caused chaos across Lower Austria, killing and burning so widely that after the campaign much of the area had to be resettled almost from scratch. No real figures exist but a rough guess would be that a hundred thousand people were killed or taken off as slaves. Disastrously the alarm systems – signal guns and beacon chains – had fallen into disrepair and there had been no local warning: how can you keep a system of watchers going over entire generations on the off-chance? At one chilling moment, the Imperial commander, Charles of Lorraine, was with his army just west of Bratislava when he saw ahead a great cloud of red dust. This proved to be the approaching Ottoman army of perhaps a hundred and fifty thousand men. And then behind he could look back and see, between him and Vienna, the smoke of innumerable fires from Tatar burned towns.

Leopold has been much laughed at for the way that he scarpered to Passau, but his core skills were music appreciation and paying for masses to be sung. He had been raised for the priesthood, was tiny, and never claimed to know much about guns. He had only two very young sons (from a third marriage) and no living brothers or uncles, so if Vienna had fallen he could have been executed by the Ottomans like the King of Bosnia or died in battle like the King of Hungary, and his dynasty would have ended. The little chapel to the Virgin Mary, thanking her that things worked out, which he and his wife put up in the hills above Passau, is still there and a well-judged humble gesture.

The defence of Vienna was in the hands of a garrison who had the advantage of recently completed defensive walls and a fanatical attitude that envisaged building-to-building fighting if the Turks broke through. For Charles of Lorraine the key concern was to keep his army intact until it could be added to on a large enough scale to try to break the siege. Three increasingly desperate months in, Charles's plans came to fruition. In an orgy of military swagger with few equals in European history a group of substantial royal egos came together on the summit of the Kahlenberg, a hill north of the city. A monument to mark the meeting's bicentenary records how King Jan III Sobieski, Duke Charles V of Lorraine, Elector Johann Georg III of Saxony, Elector Maximilian II Emanuel of Bavaria, Prince George Frederick of Waldeck, Margrave Louis William of Baden and (evasively) 'the troops of Leopold I' met. This extraordinary multi-national force was a triumph for Habsburg diplomacy and an intelligent use of the Holy Roman Empire. After a special mass the forces poured down the Kahlenberg in what is generally reckoned to be the largest cavalry charge in world history, and, in one of those rare absolutely decisive battles, destroyed the Turkish army.

In Charles of Lorraine's army was the annoyingly young officer Eugene of Savoy. He would turn out to be not only the hammer of all the Emperor's other enemies, but would, as he was swiftly promoted, cause untold damage to the Ottoman forces. It is striking that despite the crushing of the original siege army, the Ottomans were still able to mobilize a vast stream of replacements and the following decades probably marked Europe's heaviest level of militarization to that date. In a sequence of sieges and battles of overwhelming brutality these Ottoman relief armies were destroyed one by one and Central Europe fell into Habsburg hands. The ethnic balance of the region was completely changed. Muslims who had lived there for many generations fled with the retreating fragments of their armies; massacres cleared out whole towns; mosques were destroyed. Buda, substantially Muslim and Jewish, became a Christian city, in a series of barely recorded horrors. As Hungary fell, a great upwelling of excitement hit the nobility who (to their later regret) voted to make the Hungarian crown heredi-tary in the Habsburg family, ending (theoretically) a huge area of uncertainty. In one of Eugene's greatest set-pieces, the Battle of Zenta in 1697, some thirty thousand Ottoman troops were killed or drowned and Eugene could begin to enjoy himself by doing things like building the Belvedere Palace back in Vienna.

In the southern outskirts of the attractive Serbian town of Sremski Karlovci (Karlowitz) there is a strange little chapel built to commemorate the 1699 Treaty of Karlowitz. It is meant to imitate the Turkish campaign tent in which the 'Holy League' and Otto-man negotiations (under British and Dutch mediation) took place, with the lead roof entertainingly shaped to seem to be falling in folds. The building has four doors to match the original tent, which was designed so that the four groups could walk in simulta-neously, thereby giving nobody precedence. Inside (for the first time) a round table was used to prevent there being any chance of a negotiator looking dominant – a curious breakthrough in diplo-matic practice. These in themselves were astonishing concessions by the Ottomans, who were not used to viewing their enemies as other than helpless supplicants, but from a European point of view it also acknowledged the Ottomans as a legitimate European great power. The treaty transformed the map – not just with the Habsburg acquisition of Hungary and Slavonia, but also the Vene-tians getting the Peloponnese and Dalmatia and Poland recovering Podolia, a region it had lost in Sobieski's earlier war with the Otto-mans. The treaty was a disaster for the Ottomans, and the little dignity the negotiators retained was from their successful insistence on the documents being signed at 11.45 on 26 January 1699, fol-lowing instructions from a court astrologer. As the town of Sremski

Karlovci has spread out, the little chapel is surrounded now by new houses and looks very odd, with the building's general air of goofiness played up by its workaday context. Further north, on a great bend in the Danube, is a far more imposing monument to the era.

An early eighteenth-century map shows just how awful the region must have been to operate in. The lack of features, the sheer relentless flat marshiness north of the river, meant there was no point that could be defended and a trapped army could starve to death or be wracked by malaria with little intervention needed from the enemy. The sheer, wild ungovernability of the Danube can even now still be seen in the chillingly alien bogs visible from the Sremski Karlovci bus – an unpassable mess of water, mud and thick reeds, itself a relatively tiny residue of what dominated the area before nineteenth-century drainage and canalization. The map shows a tiny area of higher ground on the north bank marked 'Serbian town' (Rätzen-Stadt), and a separate south-bank sliver marked 'Village of the Croats' and another 'Village of the Swabians' (i.e. Germans) – but it is easy to see that these populations must have been in the low hundreds. The truly boggling feature of the area is Petrovaradin, the vast bulk of the only serious Danube rock outcrop before you get to Belgrade. This outcrop, which had for so long been well inside Ottoman territory, now became the front line and the Habsburgs spent the next eighty years turning it into a fortress of extraordinary size and complexity.

Walking over the bridge from Novi Sad (the charismatic and very much larger successor of the old Rätzen-Stadt) I realized that (perhaps rather pathetically) I had been waiting for this moment for some years, ever since I had first heard of the place. The fortress complex seemed a perfect example of the sort of giant feature which, like so many townscapes or paintings, cannot be reproduced in any adequate way and which can only be experienced face to face. Initially, it has to be said that Petrovaradin was a bit disappointing, with the brick bastions looking rather like Claes-Oldenburg-style wedges of cake. But then you noticed that the very thin line of colour along the top was in fact people looking over the fortifications and the tiny, moving blocks of colour catching the sunlight were cars at the rock's base, and the complex suddenly appeared very disturbing (but, of course, also exhilarating) and almost non-human in scale.

The approach to the fortress is via a dusty, neglected little town, up some stairs by the church and then through a long, steep tunnel carved into the rock. A big puzzle was the sheer numbers of children making the same journey with me – and as more and more squeaking tinies threatened to choke the tunnel I was briefly impressed at the idea that so many Serbian schoolchildren should take an interest in Habsburg defensive architecture. This perception was, alas, rapidly proved wrong. Quite by accident my visit coincided with the extraordinarily frenzied world of the Baby Exit Festival. This is a children's version of the very adult annual summer Exit rock festival held in the fortress (where, enjoyably, the Scottish group Franz Ferdinand played some years back). Baby Exit[*] is a sight to behold, with virtually every child in northern Serbia screaming and hula-hooping, surrounded by gigantic plastic inflated models of cheese tethered there by the sponsors. The children pour over the fortifications in an irresistible torrent, clearing gallons of face paint, grosses of kazoos, stickers, pencils, funny hats. Van after van of juice boxes, popcorn and sausages ground slowly up the narrow road to the top of the fortress, disgorged their cargoes and went back for more. A single, terrified donkey seemed in danger of being patted to death. A folk-dance competition of near murderous seriousness dominated the proceedings, complete with the sort of blank-faced, bayingly competitive parents familiar to my corner of south-west London, albeit more in a children's football than a polka context. A haggard accordion player wiped his forehead, waiting for the last-minute sweaty pep-talk to finish for each little squad of bonneted and blousoned hopefuls. The whole festival was completely charming and it was such a relief to find that Petrovaradin had at last, after so many years, found a sensible purpose.

---

[*]   The somewhat unfortunate name is originally in English and is not a silly translation.

The fortress itself endlessly and as it turned out pointlessly pro-
liferated throughout the eighteenth century in preparation for a
Turkish attack. In one of Prince Eugene's masterpieces, a Turkish
army of perhaps a hundred and fifty thousand men was completely
thwarted – unable to break into the fortress and encircled. This
defeat then opened up the Banat to Habsburg conquest. Petrovaradin itself seems to have become a hobby for generations of military
engineers. There are mile upon mile of tunnels, in sections separated by blocks and twisted passageways. The fiendish idea was
arrived at that each military section commander would simply not
know how to get into the next bit, so even if caught and tortured
he could not tell the Turks how to proceed further into the fortress's bowels. This kind of sick military ingenuity never came to
anything: the dream of thousands upon thousands of Ottoman
troops being soaked into the fortress like water into a sponge, of
whole armies vanishing, locked inside, and being massacred at
leisure, came to nothing, with the front line moving far away. It
was held by Hungarian troops during the 1848–49 War of Independence. They kept themselves entertained, while defying all
attempts by the Habsburgs to root them out, by using their heavy
cannon to gradually destroy most of Novi Sad on the far bank,
which must have provoked some bitter laughter from the Viennese
military authorities after they had spent all that money on fortress
upgrades. It was also a prison and at the beginning of the First
World War the young Tito, then just Sergeant Broz, was briefly
imprisoned there.

On his release Tito rejoined the Habsburg army and fought
against the Russians on the eastern front, which brings us to
the obvious problem the Habsburgs faced even back during the
heroic years of Prince Eugene. As the prince's forces stormed into
the Balkans, an immediate question arose: just how weak did the
Habsburgs really want the Ottomans to be? As great swathes of
Central Europe became organized as new territories, as Transylvania became ruled from Vienna, as thousands of colonists came
from all over Europe to areas whose populations had been erased
in the fighting or fled, the Russians stepped forward. As Orthodox

co-religionists and as Slavs, could a case be made for the Russians having a special mission to protect the native peoples of the region from the Catholic, German-Hungarian hordes now threatening their lands? As post-Sobieski Poland and the Ottoman Empire became weaker, what would an appropriate division between Habsburgs and Romanovs be? As usual with military strategic issues no sooner is the 'to do' list complete then you get handed another one: all that trouble to dispose of the Turks merely to find yourself threatened by a new neighbour. For the next two centuries (ending with the erasure by the Russians of the Austro-Hungarian army) this would be the single most important issue for the Habsburgs. But mercifully it does not loom large at all for the happy characters at Baby Exit.

A new frontier

In a moment of really shameful childishness, I once found myself on Castle Hill in Budapest about equidistant between the Hungarian National Gallery and the Museum of Military History – two institutions which in their different ways are so stimulating that they put everything else in the shade. Like the fabled donkey that starved between two equally delicious bales of hay, I stood there frozen and incapable. A new temporary exhibition at the Museum of Military History on the Ottoman–Magyar military relationship promised to be a happy wilderness of hedging, blurring and tiptoeing about. But in the end the National Gallery had to win – I could not let another hour go by without seeing again that most sprawling and heady of late-nineteenth-century blowout paintings, Gyula Benczúr's *The Recapture of Buda Castle*.

This demented canvas shows the moment when, after a siege of startling cruelty and destructiveness, the 'Holy League' commanders led by Charles of Lorraine stand in the shattered ruins of Buda Castle, its grand and honourable Ottoman commander Abdul Pasha dead on his back, his snowy beard providing a pleasing contrast to the skin of the African archer's corpse he is lying on. A herald blows a trumpet, a monk looks piercingly at a crucifix, troopers cheer and surviving exotics are led off into captivity. After a hundred and forty-three years Buda is once more a Hungarian city and the Ottoman past lies dead on the ground.

The end of Ottoman rule in Central Europe raised immensely difficult questions about whether or not these new conquests were a reintegration of lost lands that had in the past been undoubtedly part of 'the West' or whether these were lands irredeemably tainted by 'Easternness'. The old Habsburg core, running from Lake Constance in the west to the Military Frontier in the east, was some three hundred miles across. The addition in a generation of the old Ottoman territories more than doubled the monarchy's width, taking it to only a hundred and fifty miles from the Black Sea. The monarchy which had once been unmistakably Alpine, German and Italianate was now very different. Most 'eastern' of all was that the new territories were religiously pluralistic and in that sense liberal, with Lutheran Saxons, Jewish Jews, Calvinist Hungarians and Orthodox Serbs and Romanians. This picture would have been even more complicated if so many Muslims had not fled the advance of the 'Holy League', seeking safety in Bosnia and Thrace.

The triumph of the West therefore perversely released a huge wave of Catholic intolerance on these religiously patchwork territories. This renewed religious intolerance had begun even before the Siege of Vienna with increasing discrimination against Protestants in Royal Hungary – leading, in a spectacular piece of cruel lunacy, to hundreds of Protestant pastors being sold to Naples as galley-slaves. This unusual transfer of skills may have resulted for a short while in some agreeable devotional hymns wafting across the Mediterranean, but was a public-relations disaster. There was also the unwelcome suggestion that the Habsburgs had no specific right to the new territories, as it had been a pan-European alliance that had cleared out the Turks. A series of ferocious uprisings contested their claim – three waves of 'Kuruc' rebellions (between 1672 and 1711) devastated an already haggard region, with a particularly disastrous impact on the previously intact area of Upper Hungary (Slovakia). These were serious rebellions with major goals, supported and interfered with by a range of outsiders, from Poland to

France to the Ottomans who wished to use the Kurucs to damage Leopold I. Outside interference gave the Kuruc rebels more weight and power, but was fatal to their chances of success. The Habsburgs would never allow the new territories to fall outside their orbit. The Kurucs could inflict local setbacks on Habsburg forces, but were reliant for eventual success on a crushing defeat by either the French or the Ottomans of a kind which would make an independent Hungarian buffer-state part of a resulting peace treaty. As so often was the case with Hungary, external powers in the end were not particularly fussed about this issue and the circumstances for Kuruc success never emerged.

The initial rebellion was an uncoordinated gesture of despair, mainly by Protestants, at Habsburg encroachment on their civic and religious practices. This event will always be remembered by those of us who collect funnily named Habsburg military leaders for the role of the inglorious General Paris von Spankau. This was followed by a second rebellion under Imre Thököly, which became fatally reliant on Ottoman backing and was a minor casualty of the Ottoman catastrophe at the Siege of Vienna. The third, under the leadership of Ferenc II Rákóczi, appeared close to success, occupying much of Hungary and seeming to be on the verge of international recognition, but in a classic instance of the Hungarian problem, its territory was only held because most of the Habsburg army was otherwise engaged. The overwhelming Anglo-Habsburg victory over the French at the Battle of Blenheim both devastated Rákóczi's main sponsor and allowed Habsburg troops to stream back eastward and defeat him at the thoroughly lopsided Battle of Trencsén. Rákóczi spent the rest of his long life abroad, another common Hungarian rebel topos, latterly under Ottoman protection as leader of a Hungarian exile colony in Tekirdağ on the Sea of Marmara.

Each rebellion was damaged by the fatal quietism of so much of the Hungarian nobility. No matter how severe the emergency the nation always refused to do as it was told and never rose up as it was supposed to. In part this was a genuine backwoods nuttiness, a refusal to engage even with the next valley. In part it was fear of a popular uprising in a society which in many places had Magyar-speaking landowners with potentially very unreliable Slovak, Romanian, Serb or Ruthene peasants, who might very well be in favour of a Habsburg rescue from local oppression. There was also a religious split – did the Kurucs really support religious freedom or were they in practice anti-Catholic, in which case would Hungarian Catholics by definition have to support the Habsburgs?

The rebellions did just enough to ensure that the Habsburgs would always treat Hungary as a separate state – but in every other way were a disaster, leaving huge areas as a wilderness of burned-out estates, castles and towns, with many dispossessed families and a depopulation as bad as in the areas fought over with the Ottomans. They offered too the first taste of post-liberation ethnic tension, as many Serbs chose to rally to the Habsburgs rather than the rebels, making it clear that an external ruler could, through careful distribution of favours and punishments, keep in play antagonisms that made successful uprisings impossible. This became one of the chief pleasures of various regents and governors over the coming two centuries. Many Hungarian noblemen who survived the purges and religious discrimination that followed the wars became deeply ambivalent about the idea of national independence: with the departure of the Ottomans there were simply too many non-Hungarians around to guarantee that the future would be theirs.

This uncertainty was much enhanced by the mass migrations that ran alongside the rebellions and which changed the landscape drastically. Just how terrible the situation was in the new territories during the early eighteenth century was captured in a series of letters by Lady Mary Wortley Montagu as she travelled southeast from Vienna en route to her husband's diplomatic posting in Istanbul. She describes the region as 'for the most part desert and uncultivated, laid waste by the long war between the Turk and the Emperor, and the more cruel civil war occasioned by the barbarous persecution of the Protestant religion by the Emperor Leopold'. The towns she passed through were ruins, the fields uncultivated, the woods filled with wolves; a major battlefield from twenty years before was still strewn with the skeletons of men, horses and camels.

It was this unpropitious environment which now became the focus for as major a movement of Europeans as the contemporaneous ones by settlers into the Thirteen Colonies. The Hungarians themselves moved south-east, repopulating large areas of what would become modern Hungary, alongside many Slovaks who moved into the regions north and east of Buda. Romanians headed west, into Partium and the Banat – in such numbers that they would be able to make a sketchy case for absorbing much of this land into Romania after the First World War. As significant was the mass migration of Serbs north, to avoid continuing life under Ottoman rule, who eventually settled in the region of southern Hungary now called the Voivodina, home of the Petrovaradin fortress.

Each of the great rebellions against the Habsburgs has been burnt into the Hungarian national consciousness, the landscape dotted with statues of Thököly and Rákóczi, poems, novels, paintings. But most of these events happened outside modern Hungary – the sieges and battles almost all took place in what are now Slovakia, Romania and Ukraine and in a completely unrecognizable political landscape. The hope for the Hungarian nobility as the Ottoman period came to an end was that they would get their old kingdom back, but the settlement made by the Emperor Ferdinand I after the death of King Louis II at the Battle of Mohács in 1526 rather surprisingly still held, with even the long semi-independence of Transylvania (Rákóczi proved to be its last prince) now abruptly ended. The new borders established under Habsburg rule seemed to guarantee a Hungarian sphere, but this turned out to be based on the transnational power project of Vienna and have little to do with Buda. The fantasy that this enormous new land was in fact 'Hungary' would be cruelly exposed within moments of the last Habsburg Emperor resigning in 1918.

Zeremonialprotokoll

In many ways the enormously long reign of Leopold I was the acme of the Habsburg experience – lots going on, exciting geopolitical changes, good music. Leopold was one of the very few of his family who managed to get the yin and yang of his duties about right – balancing his role as Emperor and his role as ruler of the Habsburg lands. This distinction, between Reich and Österreich, was often forgotten, not least by the Emperors themselves. Leopold's predecessors, Ferdinand II and to a lesser degree Ferdinand III, had tried to use Imperial forces – meaning the troops they could call on across the Empire – to pursue a narrowly Catholic goal, which ended in what was effectively a giant civil war within the Empire. Ferdinand II's attempts to beat his subjects into submission showed the stark limits of his power. Ferdinand's principal goal was to destroy Protestantism, but to achieve this he had to hammer all his notional Imperial subjects into accepting his authority in a way that had never been true in the past, and it did not work. Even Charles V had been reduced to blowing up whole sections of cities in the Low Countries trying to get them to do as they were told. The pettifogging and obscurantism of the Empire, with its stubborn micro-states and interminable, dust-covered legal cases, was designed to keep the forms of the Empire in place (to prevent little states being swallowed by bigger neighbours) and to keep the Emperor at bay except when needed. Its efficiency was not brilliant, but this is our own perceptual difficulty rather than that of the time.

Historians and economists impatient with the Empire assume that if only innovation x or reform y had been carried out then a greater financial rationality would have emerged, but it is unclear that anybody at the time was much interested. Of course all rulers wanted more money, but their attitude towards it seems quite astonishingly chaotic, with sudden decisions to build yet another monster baroque church or give a courtier a new house far more central to ideas of how a sovereign should behave than grindy book-keeping.

Leopold I's Imperial and Habsburg roles fitted like a glove, and he sometimes seems invisible at the heart of the great, cold circuit of his ritual calendar and its obsessive *Zeremonialprotokoll*, as chamberlains herded around aristocrats, ambassadors, visiting soldiers, confessors and the minor members of the royal family so that they all stood or sat or kneeled in the right places and nobody felt slighted. There were some sixty grand religious ceremonies played out annually, and major events such as Christmas, Easter, Pentecost and the annual Feast of the Order of the Golden Fleece at which the Emperor had to eat in public. He had to be seen, he had to exchange a few words with the noblemen who expected this (with immediate gossip if he appeared to slight someone), he had to talk to petitioners. It must have been a very peculiar life, and perhaps the bouts of hunting and even declaring war were just attempts to shake off the humdrum aspects of being in charge and being obliged to make small talk. Margarita Teresa pointed out that things like card-games, concerts and operas were excellent ways of avoiding speaking to anyone and she filled up as much time as possible with them.

This sense of tedium, of endless bowing and scraping, of ritual hand-kissing, of special clothes for court, of pretty compliments, was in practice interrupted the whole time, but these and the endless masses were the backdrop against which the Emperor took his decisions. He met his council, his key generals, his confessor (a crucial but now wholly mysterious figure), members of his family, but all the time the final say on any important subject lay with him alone. He sat at the hub of this highly complex but thoroughly wobbly wheel while large stretches of Europe waited. I would have myself plumped for a masterful inactivity, with plenty of leisure time set aside for music, mistresses, big jewels, a private library with a very comfortable chair and lots of talented painters to chat to about the iconography to be used for triumphant ceiling-paintings featuring me. Some of this worthwhile programme

would undoubtedly have appealed to Leopold, but his key decisions were taken for him: by his belligerent neighbours to the east
(the Ottomans) and to the west (the French).

The twin threats Leopold faced allowed him to make brilliant
use of Imperial resources to block both Louis XIV and the Turks.
He was an effective member of the great coalition including
England, Spain and the Netherlands that was able to contain Louis
during the Nine Years War. Leopold brought on board the band-
of-brothers military element that had successfully defeated the
Turks at the Battle of Vienna and its follow-ups, swung this to the
west to wreck Louis, and then shifted it back east to do further
damage to the Ottoman Empire. In fact, racking my brain, this is
one of the *very* few cases where the Empire–Habsburg linkage
across Europe worked fairly well, albeit as part of a much bigger
coalition. Leopold was effective at using his Imperial position to
horse-trade and took two decisions crucial to the future of Europe.
The first was to allow Friedrich Wilhelm I, the Elector of Brandenburg, in return for support in fighting Louis, to become a king.
This was a startling change – the only people called king in the
Empire were all Habsburgs (two of the Emperor's titles: King of
Bohemia and German King; the other owned by his heir: King
of the Romans), otherwise it was all a rubble of princes, knights,
burgraves and what not. Friedrich Wilhelm may have been called
by the strange title of 'King *in* Prussia' (it was changed to *of* after
the whole of Polish Prussia fell into his hands), but it still provided
a unique status and glamour for the family who would become the
Habsburgs' nemesis. Almost as significantly Leopold agreed to
make the north-west German ruler Ernst August, who fought in the
Turkish wars, an Elector. This was a momentous change and one
much resented by other rulers in the Empire, who only agreed to
verify it after Ernst August's death. But his son and successor
Georg I Ludwig, Elector of Hannover, also became George I of
Great Britain in 1714 and this surprising twist gave Britain a major
voice in the Empire, albeit an Empire that was rapidly decompos-
ing. It also further solidified the somewhat abusive but nonetheless

crucial relationship between London and Vienna, which I will come back to in a little while.

Bad news if you are a cockatrice

Putti have a peculiar and confused lineage. They have been around since Renaissance artists copied classical originals and are often mixed up with Cupid, an altogether more sexual, fateful figure, and barely related in practice to these small, tumbling babies with wings. They zoom about looking vaguely serious in religious paintings, and throw flowers, fall off clouds and perform other light duties in hundreds of painted ceilings featuring rulers and ancient gods. They can look wistfully appealing (most famously in Raphael's *Sistine Madonna* in Dresden) but generally they just add lightness, charm and variety to what might otherwise be somewhat plodding canvases. They seem to have more or less disappeared around the time of Napoleon and this is probably something else he can be blamed for.

I was thinking in a slight state of panic about *putti* because they feature so oddly in the weighty Marian column in the square called Am Hof in Vienna. It was originally erected by Ferdinand III to thank the Virgin Mary for her intercession in preventing the Swedes from breaking into Vienna during the Thirty Years War. It is a very strange monument and still the focus of pilgrimage and special masses. Pope Benedict XVI gave prayers next to it in 2007 to mark its three hundred and sixtieth anniversary, exclaiming to a huge crowd: 'How many persons, over the years, have stood before this column and lifted their gaze to Mary in prayer!' This is a very moving idea and it is easy to imagine many moments, both national and personal, where this might have happened. The Marian column has been through a lot but has come out the other side of the most extraordinary political convulsions unscathed, unlike the matching one in Prague, which a gleeful crowd heaved over and smashed in 1919 as soon as Czechoslovakia got its independence.

The Prague crowd had perfectly good motives for toppling the column, but the strongest one was the Marian column's extremely nasty imagery. In Vienna, Mary herself on top seems harmless enough, but she has her foot on a writhing dragon (with a beautiful jet of gold flame coming from his mouth) which she is presumably treading flat, like it is a giant squeaky toy. The *putti* are around the base and something seems to have gone very wrong. Far from welcoming a saint into heaven or flinging garlands about they seem to have emerged from some sort of experimental farm. These *putti*, despite keeping their chubby little cheeks and dimpled arms, have been put into heavy murmillo-style armour and given hacking swords with which they dispose of various disgusting, squirmy creatures such as cockatrices. It becomes clear that when the pope said that the column was raised by Ferdinand III 'in thanksgiving for the liberation of Vienna at a time of great danger' he was referring not just to Swedes but to the contagion they brought with them – Protestantism.

Each special-forces *putto* is dispatching Error with its little sword just as Mary herself, in an unusually active move for her, is crushing the dragon of Heresy. So much explicitly anti-Protestant material has been destroyed or quietly put away that it is strange coming face to face with it here, but there is another column surviving and just as bad in Munich. The idea that Protestantism can be represented by a wriggling freak with a cock's head and two scaly legs is not ideal, nor is an ideology which ropes in *putti* to do its dirty work. There is too the delusive sense that this was a problem that could be fixed by a sword blow – if brought to life the *puttis'* falling swords would have ended the Protestant threat a split-second after the statues had been carved, whereas in practice the Habsburgs hacked and hacked at heretics for hundreds of years before at last giving up. The Prague column had stood near the marvellous memorial to Jan Hus, unveiled in 1915 and one of the great symbols of a Czech nationhood snuffed out by Ferdinand II. When the crowd pulled down their Marian column it was both an anti-Habsburg act and a futile gesture against the outcome of the Thirty Years War.

There seems to have been a general rush of enthusiasm for showy but oddly abstract public monuments under Ferdinand III and Leopold I. The Empire is still littered with Plague columns and it is a minor pleasure of wandering from place to place to see if the Plague column is still around, with a perfunctory but charming one in Graz and an extraordinary one in Olomouc which has the air of a baroque design for a surface-to-air missile. The status of these columns is always a bit unclear. They marked thanks to the Holy Trinity for ending a specific plague. As he ignominiously fled Vienna in 1679 Leopold I promised to build a column and this amazing welter of clouds and saints now fills up the middle of the Graben, its impact somewhat reduced by the hordes of mimes and human statues dotted around it. But, given that the plague was going to end anyway, it seems a bit sarcastic to put up such an elaborate object just because it stopped after only a quarter of the population had been killed. It would surely have been preferable to have put one up because a town was miraculously spared – although that would not have washed I suppose with nearby towns ravaged by sickness. In any event they are very peculiar objects and in many cases have survived just through accident of location and durability, their original function of course long gone. During one of the Silesian Wars the Prussians besieged Olomouc and some cannonballs crashed into the Plague column. The horrified inhabitants sent out a delegation pleading with the Prussians to redirect their fire away from it. This they agreed to do, presumably resulting in random, pointless deaths and homes and shops being destroyed, whereas previously the only casualties were chunks being knocked out of gnarled and over-expressive statues of saints, plus the odd *putto*.

Private pleasures

One question that must bug anyone entangled in Habsburg issues is the question of pleasure. If you have effectively infinite money and nobody to tell you what to do, is that fun? Generally these are walls we cannot look over. The sheer oddness for the Emperor of having public and private roles almost perfectly overlaying each other is beyond imagining. He lived out most of the day in symbolic duties both secular and religious and was circled by men whose sole task it was to make sure he was wearing the right diadem, pendant or decorative cape. He had an acute personal awareness of precedence and the degree to which a simple exchange of words in public with a given individual would be viewed as a sign of potentially life-changing honour. And finally, of course, there is the alarming idea that it is only his own death that releases him from this jewel-encrusted treadmill, a death at which you only get one shot, but which must also be symbolically 'good' (surrounded by family, confessing at the right moment, holding a crucifix). On the face of it this would all have been fairly grim, particularly when a pile of bitter, costive relatives is thrown in, plus the grand old Habsburg tradition of having at irregular intervals to listen to really terrible military news from some out-of-breath messenger.

Perhaps the real reason for valuing some of the Habsburg family was as commissioners of beautiful things. The great collectors have left a boggling legacy. It is the most obvious source of enjoyment to us today and these things must have been enjoyed by their initiators in a way or degree closed to others. Areas of expertise such as the collecting of small, fine objects – coins, jewels, intaglios, seals – are by definition based around holding them in the hand. At one point I carried out a rather abortive few afternoons of research into Habsburg coins and medals (there is not really all that much to say about them, it turns out) and the whole business of little wooden trays, tiny handwritten labels and special thin white gloves was such fun. Of course, part of that fun is merely snobbish and self-grooming, but the better part is the solitary contemplation of something designed to be angled to the light, slowly turned and hefted. The strange *weight* of a small gold disc (particularly to someone used only to handling chocolate gold coins) is in itself alarming, as though some rule of gravity has been contravened. Coins too are startling because from the late fifteenth century onwards the image of the ruler is really expected to be realistic. A coin's role is to be circulatory: a travelling assertion throughout his domains of the monarch's power and legitimacy. So the exact face of the Emperor, familiar to those bowing and scraping to him on his throne in Vienna, ripples out to the woolliest bits of the Tyrol. On fine-art gold coins and medals issued as rewards or to mark Imperial successions, victories or marriages, their artwork transmitted these events to specific families and high-end individuals, who would in turn show them to favoured visitors to their castles or palaces, making these too a strikingly direct enforcement of Imperial rule. Holding such discs at the right angle (in special gloves!) it is almost a miracle to see with no loss across the centuries the tiny details of hair, jewellery and ruffs on the spectacular, late-sixteenth-century coins made for Archduke Albert (son of Maximilian II) and his wife, the Infanta Isabella (daughter of Philip II), during their rule over the Spanish Netherlands, all their haughty glamour preserved, whereas all their palaces, music, values and political power have otherwise utterly dissipated. And, at the opposite end metallurgically speaking, a worn and battered cheap coin of Maximilian I still preserves the distinctive hair and nose in a jauntily charismatic way half a millennium after his death. Because coins had to be realistic, they are also the one place where you are most likely to encounter Habsburg ugliness. Cursed by inheriting the Roman coin tradition of the head and shoulders profile shot, the coins catch the almost frighteningly swollen jaw in a way that is otherwise fixed up with angles, lighting, beard and moustache in the more familiar paintings. Leopold I's long reign and the military victories of his reign meant numerous Caesar-style appearances on all kinds of coins, medals and decorative schemes where his dignity is undercut by his unhappy profile.

These coins were collected avidly by many of the Habsburgs and they must have created a powerful sense of private communication with their ancestors, and have been an enjoyable pastime. To spend an idle morning messing about with small drawers of medals commissioned by your predecessors and handed on to you must have been both a form of extraordinary intimate connoisseurship and a history lesson, one seen through the prism of how well or badly your own reign was going. With each of the Habsburgs, one of the great comforts must have been the degree to which even if things were hitting some fresh nadir there was always a precedent – gazing at the seemingly commanding profiles of Rudolf II and Matthias – for things being worse.

Museums are obliged to denature and make dreary the impulse which led to an object's original creation. Serried rows of coins are like Panini football stickers in a more ponderous form. But as objects to be handled they tell an extraordinary story, from the most over-the-top gold monster to a clipped, almost featureless little square of rough metal used as emergency currency in the Siege of Vienna.

Coins were for obvious reasons a famous form of intimate Imperial collecting, but the Emperors would have been surrounded by a mass of fine objects, prints, miniatures, table-settings and so on, all needing to be both the best in Europe but also up-to-date and reflecting the latest taste. Again, this is an area that is so difficult to access. We cannot know the gusts of fashion-panic on news that some other court has been showing off an elaborate new silver-and-coral banqueting centrepiece just in from Florence, or the word on the street that there is a new portraitist who makes everyone else look positively medieval. Some Emperors clearly just delegated such things to courtiers or relatives who understood them and contented themselves with praying, hunting and procreating, but the cusp between public display and private taste was always a curious one. Rudolf II by any measure was the most extreme example of an Emperor who used his public role for his private pleasure. His dodo was both his own obsession and a means by which he could show his realm's grandeur by securing a creature all the way from the Indian Ocean for his own chilly palace (its much diminished remains are now in the Strahov Monastery in Prague). Much of his collection was clearly and greedily (if not crazily) for himself. The thousands of objects heaped in room after room at some point must run out of control and become

an external clue to a brain also run out of control, but before it
went wrong – and perhaps even towards the end in specific, quiet
spaces – Rudolf must surely have taken huge pleasure in what he
had. So a cassowary or a lump of fossilized wood was both something for the Emperor to rub his hands over and a more public
indicator of power (even if only at the level of hearing dismal
squawks from the cassowary enclosure).

Rudolf's very broad collecting mania made him one of the first
Europeans to be genuinely European, with interests that extended
from Italian gem-makers to Dutch painters. In a sense his own
mind was the first continent-wide museum. His obsession with
Dürer, a very old-fashioned part of an extinct tradition, led him,
after endless and costly negotiations, to buy the extraordinary *Feast
of the Rosary*, a painting commissioned for the altar of the German
traders' church in Venice. The Dürer, following Rudolf's direct
instructions, had to be carried by four extremely strong men from
Venice to Prague over the Brenner Pass, ensuring that the picture
remained upright and was not rested on the snow. How wonderful
it would be if we knew what they talked about on their strange
journey.

Rudolf must have taken an active, private delight in this picture.
Could the highlight of his reign have been the opportunity over
many days simply to sit in front of it? In the following centuries,
this dream-like picture suffered many vicissitudes and was much
battered. Appropriately it has now come to rest in the National
Gallery in Prague. And there, still, in the painting that Rudolf
spent so much time with, is the Emperor Maximilian I kneeling
before the Virgin, who has put a crown of roses on his head, surrounded by a crowd of now anonymous German grandees and
soldiers and with Dürer standing in the background (looking as
usual just like Rick Wakeman – how did people understand Dürer's
strange hair and beard in the centuries before prog rock?).

As with Rudolf himself, it is very hard to write about this intimate world without wallowing for paragraph after paragraph in
what he enjoyed, so I will not even mention the *Mira Calligraphiae
Monumenta* – a collection of miraculous pages of calligraphy by

Ferdinand I's Imperial secretary which Rudolf commissioned Joris
Hoefnagel to decorate with paintings of tiny creatures, fruit and
flowers. These were of such vividness and beauty that it makes
everything else seem a bit grey – a definitive blackberry, slug,
peach or blossom, but each painted in a format only accessible to
the individual holding that small sheet (i.e. the Emperor), an utterly
private and surely unbeatable pastime. It is perhaps one of the most
startling aspects of the Internet that for the first time it is possible
to regain some of that same sense of intimate, hop-from-branch-to-
branch joy that had previously been available only to a
black-eye-bagged reclusive in Prague Castle.

Perhaps the other major and mysterious aspect of private artistic
pleasure was music. There was a whole world of public music – fan-
fares, marches, mass settings, associated with the different Imperial
and archducal offices – and these were regularly updated, with the
result that earlier generations of music tended to just moulder in
cupboards. Since the 1970s musicologists have dug out much of the
surviving material so that it can be heard again. It is a shame that
the almost apostolic succession of musical greatness is so relentlessly established, as there are so many wonders that fell out of
circulation for the simplest reasons of function and fashion. For the
Habsburgs a crucial event was when in the 1590s the young future
Ferdinand II at his court in Graz began to collect together the Italian musicians and singers (many Venetian) who would do for the
Counter-Reformation in sound what Ferdinand planned architects
should do in white stucco and gold paint. He took them with him
to Vienna when he became Emperor in 1619 and – in the usual
non-paradox – there is no link that can be made between the
horrors of his reign and the excellence of its soundtrack.

The tradition continued down through the reigns of Ferdinand III, Leopold I and Joseph I. Figures such as Giovanni Friuli,
Antonio Bertali and Massimiliano Neri (a favourite of Ferdinand III,
who ennobled him) should be familiar to everyone – varied, grand,
poignant, more than capable of coming up to the awkward challenge of the sort of all-engulfing blow-out needed for a coronation.
I mention them here because alongside their official duties they

also provided all kinds of small-scale and occasional music just for the immediate family circle. All these Emperors seem to have been very musically alert and these private forms of music-making must have been for Rudolf's successors the aural equivalent of buying a cassowary.

This enthusiasm was so great that – in a move that would baffle, say, most of the British royal family – the Emperors themselves became composers, perhaps as intimate a form of deeply interior enjoyment as handling medals or sheets of calligraphy. Even more surprising, much of what they wrote is extremely good, if rather hard to listen to objectively. Ferdinand III's hymn 'Jesus, sower of human salvation' is a floating, elegant thing of beauty* and Joseph I's 'Queen of Heaven' would win any devotional Marian cantata competition even if the piece's author had his name blanked out. There is a problem with knowing how much of this excellence stems from toadying by people like Bertali helping out with the actual notes. There is also a problem with so much seventeenth-century music working within such tight, Sudoku-like compositional rules that perhaps anyone could have a go and come up with a nice result. But even so, for Emperors who could have just filled their time slurping from ostrich-egg goblets or killing herons, it is striking that their leisure should have been filled with the infinitely unfolding, almost alchemical world of instruments and annotation.

Leopold I was undoubtedly the most obsessive and talented musician and in the pluses and minuses of his reign it is possible to balance his fleeing the Siege of Vienna by throwing into the scales his sacred music and *Sonata piena* for brass and strings. He was perhaps unique too in being able to write a requiem for his first wife, Margarita Teresa, after her early death – an appropriate final flourish, in memory of someone who in her short lifetime provoked much remarkable art.

---

*   Even Ferdinand's death was musically good news, provoking Schmelzer's matchless *Lament on the Death of Ferdinand III* with its atmosphere of a ghostly, just deserted ballroom.

So alongside the public life of the Emperor there was a private or at least intimate one, one which has in many ways survived very effectively. We ought to care about the wearying progress of the Long War, but Rudolf now conjures up for us a far more intense interest in the manias which were meant to be a mere subset or by-product of his main task in life. We can be shaky about the details of the interminable struggles between Leopold I with the French, while valuing far more his role in nurturing the rich musical life in Vienna, with astonishing consequences in the century after his death.

CHAPTER SEVEN

Jesus vs. Neptune

Leopold's greatest obsession was probably with the music of the Tuscan monk Antonio Cesti, whose brilliance as a singer, instrumentalist and composer made him bounce back and forth between the sacred and profane during his short but travel-packed life. He worked at the court of the unpleasant Ferdinand Karl in Innsbruck, but on the latter's totally unlamented death moved to Vienna and produced a series of grand operas in the 1660s for the young Leopold, most famously *The Golden Apple* for Margarita Teresa's seventeenth birthday (a special present from 'uncle'), to which Leopold himself contributed several genuinely beautiful arias. This opera must have been something to see, so scenically unwieldy that it took two days to put on, but with spectacles of flames, thunderclaps, flying dragons and shipwrecks of a dangerousness and scale that we are sadly sheltered from today. Cesti's peculiar status, a Franciscan monk writing operas about the ancient gods, is a good example of an important but very baffling aspect of court life across Europe, certainly from the fifteenth century and in many ways not really expiring fully until the nineteenth century. How was it possible to square a triumphant, militant and no-nonsense Holy Trinity with all these palaces being cluttered up with people like Jupiter? The soprano allegorical figure who warbles the prologue to Cesti's interminable opera *The Disgraces of Love* is aware of this problem and makes clear that Faith has 'crushed beneath her feet' the false gods of ancient paganism. She then makes way for wave after wave of static dialogue between Cupid, Venus, Vulcan and their friends of a kind that must have made members of the original audience privately pray for the evening to be brought to a halt by an Ottoman invasion.

Everywhere in the Habsburg lands the classical gods and their helpers have almost as secure a presence as their modern, jealous and notionally monotheistic replacement, God. They writhe in fountains, hold up doorways, festoon ceilings. As someone who grew up with the simple and exciting tales of Greek and Roman heroes it became a chief pleasure for me to see how town after town, from Trentino to Transylvania, had its own suite of classical decorations. More often than not there would be a central market square featuring a little, pallid and agonized Jesus glaring from his cross at a colossal fountain of imported white stone filled with a lolling, hirsute and heavy-loined Neptune romping with a selection of nude water-nymphs (various Habsburg rivers embracing the ocean, apparently).

One argument for the coexistence of the two religions is that the earlier is mere decoration – it is there to provide the sort of sexual or royal panorama missing from the New Testament. The inspiration of Rome was central to Charlemagne's insistence that Europe was its true inheritor and the ancient gods were in practice religiously neutral. This has to an important extent to be true: nobody at all was actually worshipping Jupiter and his friends. It was no threat to the Church that the secular and religious ruling classes were so steeped in the classical world and read and recited Latin so broadly that its gods and heroes were as vivid as the mass itself.

I had been despairing of getting my great seventeenth-century hero, the painter Claude Lorrain, into this book as his long career of painting matchless landscapes filled with classical (and occasional Christian) figures was carried out with no involvement from the Habsburgs. But much to my happiness it turns out he made a series of prints to celebrate the lavish festivities in Rome which marked Ferdinand III's election as King of the Romans at the end of 1636, so I can just wedge him in. Ferdinand was crowned with little time to spare, as his father, Ferdinand II, died only a few weeks later, allowing him to progress easily to the role of Emperor. In the interim the Spanish ambassador decided to put on an extraordinarily lavish celebratory display in Rome, where Claude lived (and whose key patrons for his classical scenes were in the papal bureaucracy). This was at the high point of Austrian–Spanish friendship, in the wake of young Ferdinand and his Spanish cousin Ferdinand[*] destroying the Protestant army at Nördlingen (the scene immortalized by Rubens) with its aftermath offering a chimerical chance that the Thirty Years War might be at an end. As the war was fought in the name of Catholicism, Rome was a place where Ferdinand's succession would be importantly celebrated and the Spanish ambassador was the man to do this. He arranged a series of completely boggling displays (of a kind which would be familiar in the next generation to the audience for Cesti's operas) and commissioned Claude to create his equally masterful prints to celebrate his own cleverness. The objects assembled in the principal squares of Rome could not have been more explicit about the link between the classical world and the present. In the area now dominated by the Spanish Steps there was a twelve-metre-high statue of Neptune with sea monsters and a Habsburg eagle, floating on an artificial sea filled with artificial fish. Nearby was a smaller but bulkier square castle with a Habsburg eagle on top and allegories of the four continents at its corners. In what must have been a ridiculously enjoyable scene, once it got dark the whole lot blew up in a massive sequence of fireworks, the square tower first exploding to reveal a smaller round tower underneath, and then the round tower itself exploding to reveal a statue of Ferdinand on horseback, which then trundled across the square and into the Spanish ambassador's palace thanks to (frustratingly imprecise) *occulte macchine*, 'secret machines'. This last scene must have been happily redolent of the immortal *Horror Hotel* ghost-train ride on Brighton Pier.

These events were recorded by Claude in his almost miraculous prints, conveying the explosions, crumpling stage-sets and general grandeur and silliness with uncanny plausibility. Each European dynasty had its own interest in classical imagery, but in the Roman festival the link is very clear: that despite being based in Prague

---

* Luckily the air clears of confusing Ferdinands very shortly.

and Vienna for many years, the Habsburg family remained true to
the original fib of Charlemagne, that they ruled an empire that had
its legitimacy from ancient Rome, and that being King of the
Romans and Holy Roman Emperor, despite the awkwardness of
not directly ruling Rome, was part of their job description. Classical imagery therefore could not have been more appropriate, once
shorn carefully of any actual religious value.

Classical subjects also allowed an easy and obvious route into
pornography, with many of Rudolf II's pictures of 'The Loves of
Jupiter' clearly for private use. But there is definitely something odd
about the way that the greatest painter of the Counter-Reformation,
Rubens, widely used by various Habsburgs, seemed to be able to
turn his hand with equal ease from images of saints racked with
suffering being welcomed into Heaven by God the Father to big,
nude Dutch girls pretending to be the Three Graces. But then, his
career disguises the whole, otherwise grim, era of Ferdinand II and
III by its sheer outrageousness, his paintings in the Kunsthistorisches Museum creating a sort of blast zone around them where
everything else hung nearby seems plodding and drained of colour.

The Emperors tended to see themselves as Jupiter. Their double-headed eagle symbol, on endless flags, allegories and walls
across the Holy Roman Empire, could be seen as the Roman eagle
(a claim of descent it shared with the similar Russian eagle) and
Jupiter in the form of an eagle. The Habsburgs owned it as Emperors, but they brazenly pinched it after Napoleon (another eagle)
destroyed the Holy Roman Empire and they managed to get the
eagle to set up shop in Vienna as simply their personal symbol.
This eagle hovers over everything from prints of victorious
Habsburg battlefields to witless fireworks displays in Rome. It was
one of those intangible yet powerful indicators of legitimacy which
are hard mentally or emotionally to recapture once a dynasty has
collapsed, the potency of the two being so closely intertwined. In
one of the very stylish gestures which Charles V could pull off, he
once spent some time in Genoa, carrying out his official business
in the Palazzo Andrea Doria beneath the freshly painted (and
astounding) ceiling frescoes by Perino del Vaga. These showed

Jupiter defeating with effortless authority the rebellious Titans, who are scattered, naked and cringing, at the bottom of the picture while a phalanx of haughty gods look on. Charles could not have found a more devastating vision of his own role or of the clods who dared to take him on.

Jupiter keeps bobbing up, but with surprising frequency the Emperor preferred to be seen as Hercules. I should say in brackets here that I have always loved Hercules, and his Labours have haunted my imagination from a young age. My only anxiety was the one that I felt too about Theseus, that at some level he rather humourlessly cleared Greece of some enjoyable creatures and people. These heroes may be making Greece safe for civilization, but as they wander about there is a price to pay: Procrustes with his bed at least had a sense of humour, and the killing of the Giant Crommyonian Sow was a straight loss. Being such a parodically English middle-class child I had a big book of Greek myths and became so obsessed with the Twelve Labours of Hercules that they became a sort of Stations of the Cross for me – an immutable sequence of story-telling excellence. Even most of a lifetime later, excitedly looking at yet another Habsburg palace ceiling featuring a giant painting of the labours, I would find myself bristling whenever I saw a labour that was non-canonical and it was only when doing a final round of research for this book that I finally realized why there were several versions. In retrospect it is obvious: no painter could possibly paint for his patron, on some colossal ceiling under which dances, banquets and flower-strewn betrothals would be held, Hercules battling to clear up hundreds of tons of cattle excrement from King Augeas's stables. There is really no way of doing it: a small pile simply would not be heroic – Hercules would look like a farmer doing a little light composting – whereas a mountain of steaming brown so big as to be worth diverting a river to clean up, spread across half the ceiling, would make for a very unpleasant visual experience.

The Liechtenstein garden palace in the suburbs of Vienna has one of the greatest of all Hercules ceilings, painted by Andrea Pozzo in 1707. This extravaganza deals with the labours in one

corner, with such magnificent creatures as the Lernean Hydra and
Nemian Lion reduced to looking like funny stuffed toys. This
enthusiasm for being identified with Hercules is in some ways
peculiar: it could at least be argued that, unlike Jupiter's, his tasks,
given his superpowers, were a bit one-sided and easy – even, to
take the argument to its extreme, that Hercules was a bit thick. His
enemies do not seem to have ever stood the slightest chance and,
wandering the countryside, tearing a lion's head apart or feeding
the creepy Diomedes to his anthropophagous horses, Hercules
seems engaged more in the nature of routine, if showy, police work
than anything more exalted.

But in my enthusiasm for the labours, I had not noticed Hercules' role as son of Jupiter, law-giver, hero, defender of Olympus,
all of which fitted in much better with the Habsburg world-view
than his role as pest-controller. The glowering bronze bust of
Rudolf II by Adriaen de Vries shows him wearing Hercules' lion-
skin, as Defender of Christendom against the Turk (savagery,
non-civilization), an implausible pose for a man famous mostly for
pottering around his seashell collections and chatting with mountebanks. The labours in this context become a kind of pictorial
shorthand in the Habsburg lands, showing the range of punishments and foresight available to such great rulers. This is definitely
the message of Ferdinand II of Tyrol's Spanish Hall at Innsbruck.
There, paintings of ancient members of the Habsburg family, the
current family, and Hercules' battles are intertwined, using an
'alternative' labour of his killing Antaeus to avoid a picture of him
washing away heaps of excrement. Effectively the pictures are
saying: we will crush you, cut off your heads, drag you out of Hell
or feed you to your own horses if you dare to defy us.

At the heart of Habsburg interest in Hercules lay one of the
labours most usually forgotten about – the mysterious expedition
to cross via Libya to the far west of the Mediterranean, defeat the
multi-headed Geryon and his ugly friends (a dog and an odd-
looking herdsman) before rounding up his cattle and bringing the
herd back to civilization. This was the furthest point of the labours
and the story became tangled up with the Pillars of Hercules, in

some traditions seen as the point where he pushed the two shores of the Mediterranean apart to form the Straits of Gibraltar. In another tradition Hercules actually builds two enormous pillars to mark the end of the Mediterranean. This in turn tangled him in the story of the founding of Cadiz by the Phoenicians and a strange mishmash of associations which meant that Charles V took Hercules as his personal symbol, expressed in a design of two pillars. The pillars at the Strait were supposed to have carved on them *Non plus ultra* ('Nothing beyond this'). So Charles took as his motto *Plus ultra* (in effect 'Go further') to boast that his subjects had passed the Straits and conquered the New World. In other words he had exceeded Hercules and laid claim to be the law-giver not just of Europe but of perhaps the whole planet. These formed part of the heraldic battery that so spooked his opponents and added to the sense of limitless Habsburg power.

Very oddly *Plus ultra* remains the national motto of Spain, featuring on the royal coat of arms when, perhaps, some adjustment should have been made for changed circumstances long ago. Most sad are the symbols on the ceiling of Klosterneuburg in the huge stump of Charles VI's partially built palace outside Vienna, abandoned on Charles' death in 1740. As a teenager he had hopes of being King of Spain and nearly inherited much of his earlier namesake's empire, so he revived the Pillars of Hercules as his own personal symbol. By the time Klosterneuburg was being built this dream had long been swept away by a tidal wave of military and diplomatic humiliation and the pillars must have seemed intolerably sarcastic. Indeed if Charles had decided to have a great Hercules ceiling fresco painted then I fear the brown would have just uncontrollably heaped up.

The first will

A thought-experiment – and a very unenjoyable one – I have been trying lately is to imagine what might have happened in the mind of the Emperor Charles VI as he woke up each morning. This may just be a sign of the madness which is creeping in while trying to keep this book under control, but it is really worth pursuing. All hereditary rulers face the same blood-freezing problem: of being inescapably and for every moment of each day both the key political actor and the symbolic heart of a vast sequence of ritual – personal, religious, dynastic – by which that political role is made valid. This implacable orrery only ceases to function at the ruler's death – and only then in the sense that the ruler himself is no longer able to appreciate the actions of the thousands of individuals who are engaging in a further series of actions, like singing in a sad way, or burying his body, heart and guts in three different Vienna locations. Of all the Emperors, Charles VI must have suffered from the most cruel hypnopompic shudders – teetering on the verge of consciousness with yesterday's cock-ups waving at him again and the coming day's cruelly guessable. Did sleep provide any real respite – were the Emperor's dreams different from our own? It is probably fair to assume a separate but related world of courtly functions unfolding inside the unconscious – perhaps, in Charles VI's case, a world in which he is a much-loved figure, a successful warlord with numerous male heirs, a witty man with a full treasure chest. But now the servants and courtiers approach the enormous, canopied bed once more, the dream stops, the day begins.

For potential biographers, Charles has always been a sort of giant tar-baby with the Order of the Golden Fleece around its neck: they have all run off after other less depressing subjects with less complicated and gruelling reigns. We therefore know relatively little about him and he looms very small in the public imagination compared to his father Leopold or his daughter Maria Theresa. And yet, as long as some of the numbing detail is missed out, his life, almost entirely lived stretched out on a rack of fiascos, is a remarkable one.

Charles's existence was spent trapped in the orbits created by two failed wills, each of overwhelming importance for the entire future of Europe. His inability to impose himself on either document doomed him. The first of these wills was one issued by King

Carlos II, the last Spanish Habsburg. This figure, both terrifying and pitiable, was the final survivor of genetic experiments engaged in by generations of Habsburgs marrying each other, so that Carlos II's mother was also his cousin (I think) or, taking his mother as the main line, his father was also his uncle. The unfolding disaster of the Spanish royal family was caught in a series of brilliant snapshot portraits by Velázquez, showing the once dashing and masterful-looking Philip IV getting older and older and ever more haggard. Philip had to face the death of nine children by two marriages, leaving two daughters and the severely handicapped infant Carlos. The two daughters married Louis XIV and Leopold I. The former, Maria Theresa, had two offspring who died as children, but crucially also had one son who survived – Louis. The latter, Margarita Theresa, as we saw earlier, married her uncle Leopold. Predictable genetic disaster sprung from this, as she died at the age of twenty-one having had four children, three of whom (including both her two sons) were by then already dead. Leopold's brief second marriage, to a more distant relative, resulted in two children dead and the mother also dead aged only twenty-two. These horrors at last convinced the Habsburgs to marry 'out' next and Leopold married a devout princess from far-off Düsseldorf and a notably fertile family. She had a long life and successfully restocked the dynasty.

But Leopold's own dynastic move was too late for the Spanish Habsburgs. Carlos II, who could hardly speak, could not eat solid food, was generally carried around and who was unable to even try procreating with either of his two unfortunate spouses, marked the end of the line. His achievement was simply to stay alive. What was assumed would prove a brief and sorry interlude when it began in 1665 proved to be a wearying thirty-five-year reign marked by gloom, hysteria, decay and frantic exorcisms in the hope of curing the king. Carlos's only substantive action was the irregular announcement of yet another new will. These documents were ignored by his gleeful royal neighbours, aware that the largest conceivable land grab was at hand. Plotters and emissaries – in the enormous wigs and buckles favoured by the period – stalked across Europe, cooking up all sorts of plans. These plans are complex, but worth following as none were *less* likely than the final outcome and each would have created a quite dazingly different world for us today. As early as 1668 the young Louis XIV and young Leopold I had realized that without an agreement war on a cosmic scale could result. The two monarchs had married the two surviving sisters of Carlos II just to keep their hand in, and in conditions of the strictest secrecy agreed that on Carlos's surely imminent death Leopold would receive Spain, America and northern Italy and Louis the Spanish Netherlands, Franche-Comté, Navarre, southern Italy and the Spanish bases in north Africa. The plan was both an interesting measure of how relatively unimportant America was still felt to be at this point and a mad vision of a future that never happened. This was quite possibly a future in which Paris and Vienna were so much more powerful that Britain could never have prospered as it did in the gaps and failures in the two empires' security arrangements. In a further twist, in 1670, with Leopold still without a male heir, Louis did another secret deal, this time with the Elector of Bavaria, the entertainingly named Ferdinand Maria (apparently a sensible boy's name in Catholic countries). Recognizing the coming extinction of both branches of the Habsburg family, this deal allowed Louis to take the entire Spanish Empire in return for helping Ferdinand Maria to take the Habsburg lands after Leopold's death while also keeping Bavaria – the nightmare reverse of the usual Habsburg dream of adding Bavaria to their own domains. This scenario was only chased away by Leopold's finally having a son and heir, Joseph, in 1678.

Louis and Leopold got older and older, still waiting for Carlos to die, and by the 1690s an entirely different solution had been reached, with the Spanish throne going by a neat and clever compromise to Joseph Ferdinand, a grandson of Philip IV via Leopold's daughter. But we need to move on quickly before wearying genealogical tables are dragged out to establish why on earth that would be the case, as it just does not matter: Joseph Ferdinand suddenly and highly unfortunately died in 1699, predeceasing Carlos II himself by nearly two years – a gap just long enough for the now elderly, jaded and exhausted Louis and Leopold to initiate what proved to be the War of the Spanish Succession, the most brutal and wide-ranging conflict experienced by Europe since the Thirty Years War. Leopold's army came close to disaster but in 1704, at the great Anglo-Habsburg triumph of the Battle of Blenheim, the allied French and Bavarian armies were devastated and the Habsburg lands secured from invasion.

In parallel with events in Bavaria, the original purpose of the war was being grimly played out in Spain. Charles, Leopold I's younger son, who began this section, was the Habsburg candidate for the Spanish throne in opposition to Louis's new candidate, his grandson Philippe of Anjou. Louis, in a spirit of haggard recklessness, announced that Philippe would in due course inherit *everything* and therefore become the ruler of a new globe-girdling Franco-Spanish superpower. Leopold more frugally announced that he wished Charles only have the current Spanish domains (which meant he would be supported militarily by a badly frightened Britain, Holland and Portugal) – even though this was a lie and a secret plan (again) was hatched which would mean that if either Charles or his elder brother, Joseph, were to die without a son the other branch would get the whole lot, creating an Austro-Spanish superpower, a further souped-up version of Charles V's old empire.

Charles, aged eighteen and now rebranded as Carlos III, arrived in Lisbon in 1705, at the head of an Anglo-Imperial-Portuguese army. Philippe of Anjou, backed by France and rebranded Felipe V, faced him. What followed was a catastrophe for Spain as both sides drew on local loyalties to create a civil and regional war that completed Spain's collapse as a great power – as the fighting continued, the prize got ever smaller. Britain happily pocketed Gibraltar in what was to prove a permanent piece of opportunism. The war in Spain resulted in both France and the Empire pouring in resources, latterly at the instigation of Charles's elder brother Joseph I, who had succeeded as Emperor on the death of Leopold in 1705. At its height there were over fifteen thousand Imperial troops in Spain. Fighting in different forms and on various excuses devastated much of Europe. Charles was boosted by his marriage in Barcelona to the tough Elisabeth Christine of Braunschweig-Wolfenbüttel, a Protestant who had converted to Catholicism, and been pushed on Charles by her formidable grandfather Duke Anton Ulrich, who readers of *Germania* may remember for his enthusiasm for paintings of nude women dying under oddly orgasmic circumstances.

With the ebb and flow of his military fortunes, Charles had the exquisite humiliation of marching triumphantly into Madrid twice (once in 1706, and again in 1710), the second time presumably having to listen to somewhat ragged and ironic cheering from the crowds. But then, in another completely surprising twist, the Emperor Joseph I, after only a six-year reign, suddenly died of smallpox – and Charles jumped on a ship to make himself Emperor in the place of his sonless brother. Elisabeth Christine was left behind in Barcelona to rule Charles's collapsing patrimony as now only the Catalans and a mixed bag of anti-French loyalists kept faith with his claim, and the rest of Spain was made to fall in line behind Philippe. In 1714 agreement was finally reached over a reasonable split of the Spanish Empire which would not create a single superpower, with Philippe cutting himself off from succession to the French throne and Charles gaining the Spanish Netherlands, Milan, Naples and a sprinkling of smaller pieces of Italy.

But as Emperor, Charles VI stubbornly refused to give up his claim to be also Carlos III. Vienna filled with Spanish refugees and Charles dressed in gloomy black and red, praying ostentatiously at all hours of the day in the Spanish manner. The only good thing to come out of his experiences was the re-establishment of the Spanish Riding School in Vienna in a lovely new building. But religiose maundering was the order of the day: the French ambassador worked out irritably that in the eight days between Palm Sunday and Easter Monday he had been obliged to spend over a hundred hours in church with the Emperor. Perhaps it was only prayer that allowed Charles to function at all – a clear space in which substantial choirs and his ballooning court could all join together to extol his greatness and call on God to protect him. As his disastrous reign unfolded, Charles must have wished to spend an ever-larger portion of his life either in the midst of mass, or asleep.

Devotional interiors

Some years ago I went to a choral concert in Chicago in which a friend was one of the singers. The music was much enhanced by the venue: a startlingly harsh, sombre Catholic neo-Gothic church – nothing but whitewash, chairs, a small font and a simple altar. Tactlessly enthusing afterwards more about the beautiful building than the singing, I was told that in fact the church had only just been given a severe makeover and that it was completely unrecognizable to its parishioners. For many years the church interior had been famously dominated by two immense macramé and cloth panel hangings, put up in the early 1970s, high on the left and right sides of the nave, and depicting Jesus with his disciples as fishers of men. This awoke all kinds of ghastly memories for me, having myself gone to a Catholic primary school and attended mass for years in a church built in the 1970s with an excessive fondness for macramé. I also had clear memories of doing paper collages of the 'Fishers of Men', a topic chosen in a daft subordination of content to form because it was easy to make nice effects with fish-shapes and the patterns of the fishing-net. In retrospect of course the topic has a vaguely hippy quality appropriate to the era.

In any event, the enormous Chicago panels started to go wrong quite quickly, as damp made them balloon and sag. Jesus and his friends were apparently never very clearly defined even at the best of times, but the internal catastrophe straining the materials reduced them to spade beards, a blessing hand and a chaos of fisherfolk-style clothing elements – plus of course the readily identifiable catch and netting. Each service became a nightmare as these things generated ever odder smells and yawed and spasmed, and

– in hot weather – huge communities of centipedes, silverfish and other vermin raced about under the unsavoury, crusted surfaces. It is possible that my informant was exaggerating slightly, but his interesting point was that the congregation, the priests and the macramé artist had invested heavily in these monsters and for many years, despite their disruptive and ultimately even dangerous and frightening role in the mass, the hangings stayed. In the end some off-duty firemen were asked to come in and in full protective gear, wielding hooked poles and industrial shears, carved the hangings into chunks, hauled them into the yard and burned them. In scenes seared into the memories of all who saw them, the huge pile of parti-coloured macramé started off by emitting a layer of disturbingly low-lying, viscous smoke, causing everyone to get way back before suddenly the whole lot – emitting well-nigh intolerable squeals – went up like a bombed fuel-dump, jetting freakish carmine and ochre flames into the sky.

The reason I mention this at best tangential story is that it has always raised in my mind interesting thoughts about the nature of change in religious settings – the tension between a church building's authority being based around a sense of its unchanging, indomitable sanctity and the need, keenly felt at particular times and in specific cultures, to radically overhaul and renew. This is a particular problem for Catholicism, which invests so heavily in images, while at the other end of the spectrum Protestantism in some flavours can be close to indifferent, with churches merely seen as roofs under which to pray. For the latter the issues were resolved in the sixteenth century by wave upon wave of the most savage iconoclasm – an iconoclasm which in countries such as Scotland and Switzerland led to the smashing or burning of almost all art produced up to that point. Once this clearing out was achieved the question of the design of the church's interior by definition rather fell into abeyance. But for Catholics the nature of church decoration, when to change it and how to use it, lies at the heart of worship, and wandering around Austria it is an issue which cannot be shaken off.

A beautiful, if lurid, example is the Piarist church that looms above the Danube town of Krems. The Piarists (or, in full, the Order of Poor Clerics Regular of the Mother of God of the Pious Schools, understandably shortened) are one of the great Catholic monastic teaching orders, lying at the heart of the Counter-Reformation and an element in the renewal that has little resonance to anyone raised in a Protestant country, but which has shaped much of the rest of Europe. This church at Krems bristles with teaching tools. The outside is devoted to ancient, naive sculptures of key events from Jesus's life, with statues and painted backdrops (including a particularly charismatic fantasy of the Jerusalem town-scape) so that anybody walking past the church would receive an automatic lesson in the key points. But it is the interior that is amazing. Every surface – every wall, ledge, pinnacle and window – is a mass of instructive biblical or martyrological anecdote. It must have been pure pleasure to give sermons here, pointing with a vehement finger at one of the many extraordinary images and engaging the congregation with tales of extreme moral choice, heroism, resignation and courage.

My own children went to a genial Anglican Sunday school where they mostly learned about things like 'sharing' or, in an admittedly uncharacteristic nadir, mulled over the meaning of the Marriage at Cana by playing musical bumps (because you have a party at weddings). How different to be a charity-foundation Kremser child in the seventeenth century! This was a world in which the fates of the good thief and the bad thief flanking Christ at the crucifixion became central and personal challenges, where each martyr's steadfastness under torment became a focus for personal meditation as intense as that felt by Buddhists for a specific bodhisattva. Here is St Roch with his pustulant leg and strange dog; an oddly insouciant St Sebastian; St Donatus holding an appallingly realistic human heart squeezed in his hand (or perhaps a bunch of grapes – it's a bit dark in here); St Elizabeth of Thuringia, a princess who worked herself to death helping the sick and the poor. Here too are the towering figures of the Counter-Reformation, who devoted everything to God and transformed Catholicism: St Ignatius of Loyola, St Aloysius Gonzaga and St

Francis Xavier of the Jesuits, whose exemplary and tortured lives would have been known inside out by generation after generation of Piarist-taught children. There is also an oil painting of a girl with a sword sticking into her chest which I have been completely unable to place, but presumably she must have viewed this by some obscure measure as a positive experience.

A side altar features a painting of St Joseph Calasanz himself, the founder of the Piarists, surrounded by grateful children and smiled down on by the Virgin Mary. Children educated by the Piarists included figures such as Mozart, Goya, Schubert, Haydn, Hugo and Mendel so, in ways quite hard to recover, such teaching lies at the very heart of European culture. What struck me at the Krems church is that many of the sculptures and paintings are major works of art (mixed in with some dreadful tat), but, as so often in Catholic contexts, there is an active discouragement from viewing them aesthetically – they are simply meditational and teaching tools, well made only to ensure that they are more effective. While staying in Krems I found myself heading to this church a lot – it seemed a particularly striking demonstration of the weak, partial nature of Weberian Protestant history and it really bugged me. Here was an entire world of teaching, prayer and ideology of a kind which had produced extraordinary results, but within a framework which eluded me and which required forms of belief I was incapable of.

This Piarist church could not be a more swarming instance of these surges of religious confidence and change that mark sacred buildings across Europe. Only a very specific sequence of events can allow a medieval building such as this was to have been so drastically hacked about, not only with the addition of all those side chapels and statues, but with the delicate, narrow-windowed east end being swamped in the eighteenth century by a colossal, lurid, pink, scarlet and gold altarpiece festooned in angels and crowns and saints, like some Car of Jaggernath with the wheels off. But almost as interesting is that the convulsion which allowed these changes was never followed up by any further change beyond electrical wiring. We will never know what exactly was destroyed to make way for the Counter-Reformation fittings. Presumably some of it was rescued for other chapels and religious interiors and some went up in smoke like the Chicago macramé – but what we are left with today is the point at which each church decided to stick rather than twist, a high-water mark of confidence which has never been approached since.

This issue haunts the valley of the Danube around Vienna which forms a very self-consciously planned sacred landscape, dotted with abbeys of great size and grandeur and generally finding their final shape in the frenzy of building that marked Joseph I's and Charles VI's reigns. The region must have once been packed with the sound of hammering, the clopping of hooves from the horses pulling huge carts filled with gold-leafed cherubs and marble columns and teams of first-responder fresco-experts from the four corners of the monarchy. As usual the building work tangled up money, history, faith and aesthetics in a highly complex cat's cradle, with backbiting, politics and genuine inspiration shaping each site. The immediate occasion for this rebuilding was the end of the 1683 Turkish emergency, the need to repair battle damage (as at the Tatar-wrecked Abbey of Melk), the wish to give thanks for deliverance and a willingness to spend eye-watering sums of money for the glory of the Habsburg regime. Some of these projects came a-cropper. Charles's Herculean plans for Klosterneuburg stopped with his death, leaving the chronically under-realized stump still there today. Others (such as at Göttweig) ran out of money embarrassingly early, starting off well with an enormous, triumphant Imperial staircase (up which Napoleon once rode his horse in a fit of sheer exuberance), but then flanked by a perfectly ordinary set of rooms of a kind familiar from business conference centres. But the astounding, more fully realized set-pieces at St Florian, Kremsmünster, Altenburg and Melk freeze in time a particular aesthetic, a deliriously rich and showy celebration of monasticism just at the point when many people began to wonder, first, why exactly monks needed quite such gorgeous surroundings – and, more broadly, why have monks?

Charles VI might have been a dreary and unpleasant man, but he is aesthetically the most interesting of the Habsburgs by miles. A striking patron of major buildings, he encouraged a form of 'representation' which has not really been seen since. Later libraries or churches or palaces may be more practical, but each seems a diminution of what was confected across the Habsburg lands in the early eighteenth century. If you want to represent the control, ownership and mastery of books, then the Court Library in Vienna or the monastic library at Melk are two of the world's greatest buildings. If you want to represent the control, ownership and mastery of horses, then the Spanish Riding School in Vienna has the same status. And if you want to represent the control, ownership and mastery of religion, then this applies too to the abbeys and monastic Imperial halls and Imperial staircases of Charles's reign, as well as his wonderful church in Vienna, the Karlskirche. The group of architects, sculptors, masons, decorators and painters who did the heavy lifting for these projects created elaborate and all-consuming works of art of a kind which subsequent generations had simply had no interest in repeating. The projects have a fervour and almost pantomime quality quite out of place in all subsequent Habsburg courts (which tended to be austere, often to the point of mediocrity). Later rulers and builders may have found the demented waves of gold leaf that fill Melk abbey either exhilarating or disgusting, but never an aesthetic to engage with seriously in a spirit of actual prayer (churches) or learning (libraries).

Almost all this construction was achieved during a single, long lifetime, with St Florian and Kremsmünster under way in the 1680s and places like Göttweig grinding to a halt in the 1730s. Like all major innovative movements it is startling how rapidly it goes from a peak of glory into softness and decline. The inventiveness that could handle heaped angels, balconies, elaborate organs and drastically foreshortened painted renderings of saints' lives in the 1710s soon came to grief. St Florian's abbey church is possibly the most magical of these buildings – prayerful and imperial, monastic and aristocratic, with its Brobdignagian columns and strangely erotic angels holding aspects of St Florian's martyrdom:

Florian's Roman *fasces* and soldier's sword, and the millwheel tied round his neck before he was thrown into the River Inn for refusing to pray to pagan gods. (Incidentally, St Florian cheers up churches all over the Empire as the patron saint of firefighters, with a sword or lance in one hand and – an area of happy interpretive licence for sculptors – a little bucket of water in the other, which he is tipping over some flaming building.) St Florian commands absolute respect and its aim is to strike the visitor artistically and religiously to the ground – you feel stunned somewhat in the manner of Saul, but with less lasting effect.

By stark contrast, by the time you climb, panting, up the forest trail to Göttweig, it is clear that decay has set in. The Abbey Church is no less grand than St Florian, and equally engaging, until it becomes clear that the painters have reached an unacceptable level of silliness: a painting of Babel which makes it look like a high-end holiday-camp, another of the Last Supper which has the air of a gala meal among friends. The last straw is a picture of the touching little scene in the gospel where Mary Magdalene in her panic assumes that a figure she sees by Christ's empty tomb must be a gardener, before realizing that he is in fact the risen Christ. Here is Mary, and here is Jesus, but he is wearing a floppy hat and carrying a spade, neither of which features in the Bible. He is actually *disguised* as a gardener, a very different, eccentric move perhaps reflecting the mental confusion attending resurrection. Admittedly other painters do similarly silly things with this rarely used scene, but it was the point for me, having spent a week drenched in this stuff, that the dream came to an end. The Göttweig pictures were merely ridiculous (if of course very enjoyable) and, shortly before Charles VI's death, the whole tradition had caved in. A cult of ever more elaboration, decorative daring and symbolic obscurantism had come to a perhaps merciful halt, setting aside the dazzling (if non-Habsburg) aftershock of Tiepolo.

The sheer size and grandeur of places such as Melk, a monastery notionally devoted to private prayer and the teaching work of a small group of celibates, makes its inhabitants mere collateral damage from its main purpose: to celebrate the triumph of the

Habsburgs and of Austria over the forces of both Protestantism and
Islam. Any journey across the old Austrian heartlands would now
be marked by rebuilt, often onion-domed, parish churches, inter-
spersed with the massively overhauled abbey complexes. Because
much of this stretch of the Danube valley remains a rural backwater – its only resource seemingly the production of apricot
liqueur – little has changed today. There is almost no large-scale
architecture of a later date to look at, and it is fair to say that with
the end of this frenzied round of rebuilding there is a cooling-off
of ambition and confidence, both within the Habsburg family itself
and within a Catholicism which was as the eighteenth century
progressed once more put under siege.

The second will

An attractive place with a grim history, the Polish town of Cieszyn
was once one of the duchies of Silesia – a large region stretching
north of Bohemia composed of small duchies under separate members of the Piast family. Many of these dukes came to hold their
land from the King of Bohemia so after the 1526 catastrophe at
the Battle of Mohács they owed allegiance to the Habsburg family.
Over the following century the dukes' families died out and one by
one the territories reverted to direct Habsburg rule. Some chunks
went elsewhere – Crossen to Brandenburg (later Prussia) and Zator
and Auschwitz were linked to the Polish crown. The region was
historically a tangle of Poles, Germans and Czechs and its fate in
the twentieth century was a terrible one.

The town of Cieszyn (known as Teschen in German) was the
site of a brief but vicious war between Poland and Czechoslovakia
in 1919 which partitioned the town along its river. This was one
of thousands of injustices of the period but a particularly harsh
one, with the bridges across the river choked with barbed wire and
relatives who had happened to live in different parts of the town
cut off from one another for a generation, often not allowed even
to communicate by post. In the centre of the town today a shop

displays a very beautiful Austro-Hungarian map from about 1910 showing the town whole, bound together across the river at its heart by an elaborate figure-of-eight of tramways. The splitting of the town for those living in it must have been something akin to having a stroke. A little-remembered aspect of the Munich Agreement was Poland's absorption of the whole of Cieszyn as part of the general tearing-apart of Czechoslovakia, the possession of which was enjoyed for less than a year before Poland was in turn invaded and the area became part of Germany. The old border was then re-established in 1945. It is a very peculiar feeling today to walk between the Czech Republic and Poland over a river border that once generated such hatred and misery but which is now utterly harmless. The harmlessness has been achieved though through ethnic cleansing, with Cieszyn now an entirely Polish-speaking town and Český Těšín Czech.

. There is a lot to say about Cieszyn but here I must confine myself to mentioning the remarkable museum, now called the Museum of Cieszyn Silesia and housed in a late-eighteenth-century mansion in the middle of town. The core of the collection was established by a local Jesuit in 1802 and is one of the oldest Central European public museums. The entire building is completely fascinating. Some of the rooms have kept their decorations from when it was a nobleman's house. There are wacky, naive frescoes on very loosely 'Ancient World' themes, including a notably loopy Egyptian Room, with sphinxes and a rough shot at hieroglyphs. In what I hope will be permanently kept as a reminder of past wretchedness, the Roman-themed Ballroom is severely damaged, with large chunks of the decoration missing – the result of a Hitler Youth party in 1942 at which a fire got out of control. This is not the only shock in the museum. Much of the original collection has been kept in a sequence of beautiful cabinets and more vividly than anywhere else in the former Habsburg lands it gives a sense of the last non-scientific period of collecting, the absolute end of the Rudolfine tradition before it all became more systematic and rational. So here, for example, is a whale's penis (an alarming object), the jaw of a young mammoth, an ammonite, a hopeless

attempt to make a unicorn by tacking a narwhal horn onto a
horse's head, the shoes of a geisha. This is all fun – but in one of
the cases there is what seems to be a strange, umber-coloured rec-
tangle of paper. I battle for a moment with the Polish caption: it
says 'a piece of Turkish skin'.

The process by which the Ottomans went from being the terror
of Christendom to a strange absence (or merely a sick curio) was
long drawn out. After the battles that cleared Hungary they were
routinely seen as in decline, and yet they continued to rule a huge
block of Europe for over two more centuries. Vienna would never
be threatened again but the Ottomans had a powerful defensive
capacity and were, of course, themselves European. A huge number
of the troops defending Oriental despotism were themselves Greek
or Serb, Albanian or Bulgarian and ethnically identical to many of
their Habsburg opposite numbers. Whether being ordered about
by some Rhineland German general in a big wig or a beylerbey in
a turban, those actually fighting were in many cases the same.
Ottomans could pretty much wave at Catholics across the Straits of
Otranto and the rich tangle of areas such as Bosnia was as much a
pluralist glory of European civilization as was Transylvania. And
yet it was essential to the whole Habsburg project that somehow
the Ottomans were infinitely remote and alien (you would not
see 'a piece of Austrian skin' in a museum). This was notable in
the early 1990s during the break-up of Yugoslavia, when the EU
behaved as though these notional 'ancient Balkan hatreds' were
bubbling up somewhere almost on Mars, when the serious fighting
was only a short boat-trip from Italy or a gentle morning drive
from Austria. This sense of the Ottomans as being alien was always
of course very powerful in Central Europe, but what was new after
the Battle of Vienna was that at last they could also be seen as
beatable and wretched. In Jan III Sobieski's superb tomb in the
Wawel Cathedral he is shown carved in all his glory below a pile
of guns and battle-flags, while below these huddle chained and
fearful Turks, their moustaches drooping helplessly and – a very
odd touch – with their teeth broken, as though Jan had actually
beaten them up.

A similar and contemporaneous tone is set in the grand ceiling painting of the Abbey of St Florian, where the Emperor Charles VI is in all his glory and with similar chained and fearful Turks cowering at his feet. As so often in Charles's life he wished to be painted as a victor, but all the images of him as a new Caesar, as a dashing young prince on a cavalry horse, and so on, all came back to mock him, like some awful dream where all you can hear are unexplained and coldly derisive giggling sounds.

Despite being ejected from Spain after the War of the Spanish Succession, Charles seemed to have good prospects once he got back to Vienna and accustomed himself to his surprise new role as Emperor. The settlement that ended the war was on the face of it attractive. Charles added to the Habsburg Empire a remarkable spread of fresh territory, from the old Spanish Netherlands, to Milan, Naples and a selection of small Italian bits and pieces. In a further triumph, a war with the Turks commemorated at St Florian heaped the Empire with further lands, including the great prize of Belgrade and stretching down into what is now south-western Romania ('Little Wallachia') – a region which today dozes in total obscurity, but which, if it had remained in Habsburg hands, would have had a drastic impact on how nationalism developed in the Balkans. The Habsburg crusade against the severely weakened Ottomans gave glimpses of future glory: a potential, vastly enlarged empire stretching perhaps to the Black Sea and the Aegean, and perhaps even to Constantinople itself. Sculptors specializing in statues of chained and turbanned captives sharpened their chisels.

This seeming triumph for Charles sadly petered out in multiple humiliations. The new Austrian Netherlands was peculiarly hedged around with disaster, geographically entangled in the independent territory of Liège and glowered at by powerful neighbours. This region had once driven the Spanish Habsburgs mad and virtually bankrupted them, and now this cursed inheritance was transferred to the Austrian branch. It was also galling to Charles to know that the British only favoured his rule there because they knew it would be weak and ineffective – their only concern for the area since the time of the Armada. The sheer absurdity of trying to defend what would become roughly Belgium, a defence only possible in alliance either with Britain/Holland or France, meant that the Habsburgs were always trying to swap it for somewhere else (generally Bavaria), an attitude which did little to foster local self-esteem or pro-Habsburg sentiment. These new territories, with decent sea coasts, meant that Charles had to become involved with naval issues – a real first for a previously near landlocked power, and not a happy adaptation. A major initiative, the Imperial and Royal Company of the Indies, based in Ostend, was the principal effort to make the Austrian Netherlands a paying concern. It started out well, began trading with India and China and had two small bases in the Bay of Bengal. The Company even planned to take over the Nicobar Islands, which implies a very odd parallel universe in which the Bay of Bengal becomes synonymous with raw, freebooting Habsburg colonial power and Vienna fills up with nabobs and curries. This was not to be, however, as Britain simply insisted the whole thing be shut down, permanently putting an end to the sound of Flemish in the Asian Torrid Zone.

Ownership of Naples and the rest of southern Italy turned out to be just as bad. In a further trade Charles had cashed in Sardinia, an island with a small population that produced only a sort of fish sauce, for what looked to be the much more worthwhile Sicily. This whole southern Italian expansion could all have been a great boon – perversely Naples was now the largest Habsburg city. The ongoing influence of southern Italy on the cultural life of Central Europe continued to be all-consuming, musically and visually, but actual ownership was a nightmare. It was a truculent place and impossible to defend; most of the revenue raised from the area went on the costs of the troops stationed there, which must have made everything feel rather bitterly futile. In just one humiliation tucked away in a heap of them, Charles could not even reinforce these troops without asking for a lift from the Royal Navy. He built a small Habsburg navy but unfortunately the only role of small navies is to be sunk by bigger ones; it was never used and eventually rotted at anchor. As it was, during the War of the Polish

Succession, Charles was obliged to hand over southern Italy, getting the tiny and very landlocked Duchy of Parma instead, probably to his relief. This entire war was a disaster for Charles, who was savaged on all sides with his British and Dutch allies remaining neutral. To try to regain some credit and somewhat in the spirit of the Habsburgs 'putting together the old band', he launched yet another war against the Ottoman Empire. This seemed an easy option as the Turks were already fighting the Russians. It became another total shambles, with the Battle of Banja Luka and, even more so, the Battle of Grocka devastating the Habsburg armies. The only good news was that at least Prince Eugene had died the year before this fiasco unfolded and so was spared knowing that his life's work had been made such a monkey of. Belgrade, Little Wallachia and other hard-won prizes gained by the previous generation were handed back to the Ottomans and a fresh wave of Serbian refugees and embittered German colonial farming families headed north and helped repopulate southern Hungary instead.

Charles VI's court then was one where bad news arrived at regular intervals. As bad in its way was the ghost that hung over everything: that of Charles's elder brother, the short-lived Emperor Joseph I. Joseph in his short reign was a startling and inspiring figure – hard-drinking, reckless, adoring warfare, sexually chaotic: it is hard to imagine a less Habsburg Habsburg. He didn't even have the giant chin. While he had been impatiently waiting for his father Leopold I to get out of his way, Joseph had developed a clear, very German ideology and saw his role as Emperor as central. Once Emperor, and when not grabbing desirable noblewomen or firing guns, Joseph was also disposing of the gloomy and obsessive credulity of the old court and hacking at the sclerotic and weary calendar of religious observances. A Jesuit, appalled that Joseph had given a prominent position to a Protestant, dressed up as a ghost and lurched into the Emperor's bedroom urging him to dismiss the heretic. Joseph simply called his servants and had the Jesuit thrown out of the window. This curious story reflects well on the new atmosphere at court, but also reflects terribly on the Jesuits, that one-time intellectual power-house now reduced to camping it up in sheets and grease-paint.

Joseph both came to the throne and died with the War of the
Spanish Succession still going on, but his short reign was vigorous,
stylish and successful with the devastating victories pouring in
from his commander Prince Eugene more than outweighing rebellions in Hungary. Charles, by contrast, stomped back into Vienna
as an embarrassing failure and having been away during the six
years of reform under his brother. The shocked and confused court
started off with him on the wrong foot and, as Charles never even
tried the other foot, the tone of his reign never really changed. It
is hard not to feel a bit sorry for him. His chief and permanent
torment was to be surrounded by huge numbers of often resentful
and privately derisive women. These included his wife, two dowa-
ger empresses (the wives of Leopold I – i.e., Charles's mother
– and Joseph I), several sisters and two nieces. Of course, not all of
these were at home all the time, but the tone of the court was
definitely wall-to-wall female with Charles as the single, unlovely
male. This need not have been a problem, except for the obvious
one – that the Habsburg titles could only pass through the male
line. The title of Emperor was elective, so this was not a problem
– except that the Electors would not elect a landless woman. This
was the point at which the Habsburgs were condemned by their
own ridiculous fourteenth-century forgeries signed by Julius Caesar
which had almost incidentally specified descent through the male
line. The lack of men had worried Leopold I, who had first
arranged that in the event of Joseph and Charles dying, descent
would be through Joseph's elder daughter. But how anyone would
agree to this remained unclear.

The chief aim of the Habsburg monarchy during the weary
twenty-nine years of Charles VI's rule was to persuade Europe's
rulers to sign the document which would permit female inheritance. Known as the Pragmatic Sanction, it was perhaps the most
useless document ever dreamed up. Charles's representatives fanned
out to all the courts they could think of and in return for bribes,
threats, concessions and pleading got *some* signatures. But these
signatures were all given by figures putting on their most lizard-
like and blank expressions. As everybody knew, the only guarantee

came from Charles being alive. The moment he died everyone would crack their knuckles, rub their hands together and see what they could most readily pick from the wreckage. There were two moments of excitement, when Charles and his wife had in quick succession two children – but these were also daughters. In a moment of characteristic idiocy, he then changed the terms of the Sanction: instead of descent running through Joseph's daughters, this was now switched to his own elder daughter. As can be imagined, the atmosphere between members of the Imperial family now turned icy. Apparently, whenever petitioners requested something of Charles he would only ever reply in a brief, incoherent mumble and it is easy to see why. And in a further, absolutely baffling failure, as his daughter Maria Theresa grew up he did nothing to train her in her future duties – he hardly talked to her, did not include her in any of his roles at court and left her absolutely unprepared for her position. His mulish obsession with the Sanction became a vindication of his own, otherwise wretched record, but in his attitude towards Maria Theresa he showed that he did not really believe that she should inherit either.

All this gaucherie made Charles's rule the least successful in the entire Habsburg experience. He even managed to alienate himself from the affairs of the Empire, again a startling contrast to his predecessor, focusing almost exclusively on Habsburg family concerns. As it turned out, Joseph I's reign was the last point at which the Empire really functioned properly and for the rest of the eighteenth century, before its final destruction, it was in many ways robust, culturally brilliant and admirable, but this had little to do with the last Emperors. It must be the case that if Joseph had not got smallpox the shape of Europe would have been very different – although not, of course, necessarily better. As it was, a large part of Europe floundered under the last male Habsburg, who finally came to an unlamented end gorging on mushrooms in oil.

As usual, political and dynastic tone has very little to do with artistic tone. This was the era of great architects – Prandtauer, Hildebrandt, Fischer von Erlach, father and son; great painters – Rottmayr, Gran and Troger, who between them made Austrian

ceiling frescoes into wonderlands; and heroic sculptors including
Matielli and Moll. Balthasar Moll was originally employed as a
talented maker of public entertainments – floats, zany sledges and
so on – but then used his Disney-like talents to make Charles VI
and his wife Elisabeth Christine into the absolute star turns once
they were down in the Imperial Vault. Posthumous fame is not
ideal, but all the gloom and failure of the reign itself can be swept
away by these two great decorated bronze caskets. Elisabeth Christine's is decorated with the heads of mourning women with their
faces smothered by veils, an effect in bronze which is both violent
and erotic in a way not generally looked for by people visiting
crypts. And even these masterpieces are trumped by Charles's
matching figures: bronze skulls wearing the crown of the Holy
Roman Empire. It is perhaps the different, implicit textures in these
sculptures – gold, jewels, bone, hair, damask, skin – all reduced to
tarnished bronze that makes them so extraordinary. They seem
to sum up, and then tip over the edge, a whole Late Baroque
atmosphere.

Above the great Imperial staircase at Göttweig Abbey, Troger
made one last giant fresco of Charles right at the end of his reign.
Gods, *putti* and the Arts lounge about on clouds in a brilliant sky,
Error is, as usual, chased away and Charles is Apollo, rushed across
the sky by champing white horses seemingly carved from marsh-
mallow, in a great gold chariot with sun-rays bursting behind his
head. It is both a masterpiece and a sorry spectacle. The sullen
Turkish captives from the St Florian ceiling fresco have been tact-
fully taken away given how that didn't work out, and Charles
himself is shown in what seems a deliberately ludicrous light –
half-nude, wearing a sort of toga but also a wig and with his
haggard face a congested puce colour. He looks like someone
living in a very expensive, but also very oddly run care home. And
that is probably where we should leave him.

Zips and Piasts

The upper geographical edge of the Habsburg territories holds a number of politico-geographic oddities of a kind that could easily swamp this book, and should in a fit of self-discipline be corralled together. Compared to much of the rest of the Holy Roman Empire, the monarchy's own territories tended to consist of reasonably compact units and there is little to match the sheer pleasure of the little Wettin and Reuss states of Thuringia, say, where each valley had its own colourful ruler. The nearest approximations are on this upper edge. One total weirdness is the Zips (Szepes) region – now part of Slovakia, but for centuries a string of mostly German mining settlements under Hungarian rule. I kept planning to visit it, but was prevented for one petty reason or another. I eventually realized it would be a literal-minded and rather sad thing to go to the towns, as it could only be a disappointment compared to the sort of cheerful-blacksmith, birds-whistling-in-the-forest, *Snow White* atmosphere they increasingly had in my mind. For very short-term gain the Emperor Sigismund, abusing his title as King of Hungary, had mortgaged them in 1412 to the King of Poland in return for seven tonnes of silver (an interesting indication of the resources then available in Poland) to allow him to fight some futile war with Venice. The money had long been spent and there was never any serious prospect of paying back this immense sum. So quite unintentionally the Zipsers found themselves under Polish rule for some three hundred and sixty years, entire populations effectively the equivalent of some unredeemed old clock on a high shelf in a pawnbroker's. Maria Theresa eventually marched in without bothering with repayments and three years later her rule was confirmed in the First Partition of Poland and the Zips towns became part of the Kingdom of Hungary again, maintaining their somnolent oddness in the face of all subsequent change, until, as 'Carpathian Germans', the Zipsers fled or were expelled in 1945.

As peculiar was the territory west and north-west of the Zips: the ancient amalgam of Silesia. I pride myself on having an unlimited enthusiasm for this sort of political rubble, but even I blanch at the ins and outs of the Piast dukes and their tiny territories. The whole lot were shovelled together and handed by the Polish king Casimir the Great to the Bohemian king John the Blind as an intelligent bribe to stop John's insistent claim to own the Polish crown himself. So in 1335 at the Treaty of Trentschin these splintered pieces became part of Bohemia, with a single hold-out in the appealingly named Bolko the Small, ruler of Schweidnitz, who carried on until his death in 1368 (you can begin to see the bog of information into which one can sink). For Casimir this was a small decision (Poland was enormous and had any amount of land to play with – and indeed his successors would pick up the Zips!), but it alienated a block of Polish land for some six centuries, with the region's complete return only in 1945. For John the Blind, with his much smaller lands, it was a sizeable chunk – roughly the same size as Bohemia itself and with a wealthy population. John, despite his blindness, went for chivalric reasons to fight at the French court where he was killed in the crushing English victory at Crécy with his personal motto ('Ich dien') being picked up by the Prince of Wales, who has used it ever since.

In any event, like the rest of the Bohemian crownlands the Silesian territory was collected by the Habsburgs after the death of Lajos II and it became a useful, productive element in the monarchy for more than two centuries. Their rule was protected by their very solid legal claim, but also by the weakness of the other rulers flanking Silesia – this weakness indeed being a key reason for Habsburg strength in more cases than the monarchy itself would like to have imagined. The Polish kings were too preoccupied both by the Ottoman Empire and the increasing menace from Russia to be concerned about Silesia; and the Brandenburg rulers to the north were a classic Holy Roman Empire joke-shop outfit: easily the most financially feeble and geographically incoherent of the Electors. In the later seventeenth century the Brandenburg situation began to change with alarming speed. The Electors were an odd bunch but their territories (added to by guile, luck and marriage) grew in a curious echo of the Habsburgs' own good fortune many years before. They gained the title of 'King in Prussia' from the elderly Leopold I and, as Charles VI floundered around trying to get the rulers of Europe to support his daughter's accession, there was one of those traditional discussions by which intellectuals in the service of power disgrace themselves, in this case digging out weird old Prussian documents to show the possible illegality of Habsburg rule over Silesia. As soon as he heard the news of Charles's death, the very young new Prussian king, Frederick II, saw that here was a chance to grab a major piece of land. This decision was to shape a generation.

Silesia in the right hands was extraordinarily valuable – in the Habsburgs' it allowed them to threaten Brandenburg; in Brandenburgs' it made the Habsburg lands vulnerable; in either case it separated Saxony from Poland and fatally weakened that relationship. It undoubtedly had a large and economically worthwhile population, but given how many thousands of lives were lost struggling for it and the wider wars which drew in almost every country in Europe, Silesia became ever more of an abstraction. In the nineteenth century its value as an industrial zone was considerable, but it was rapidly overtaken by the Ruhr, and its eventual reabsorption into Poland in 1945 was accompanied by much suffering but little international interest. Just looking at it on a map Silesia has a fuzzy inability to cohere under whichever rule: it is a between-land and has suffered accordingly. But in 1740 it was the true centre of Europe and for the young Frederick II and the even younger Maria Theresa it was a fight to the death.

CHAPTER EIGHT

The great crisis » Austria wears trousers » The Gloriette »
The war on Christmas cribs » Illustrious corpses »
Carving up the world

The Polish Plumb-Cake.

Russia

Germany

France

Prussia

J. Lodge sculp.

Thy Kingdom Stanislus, is now at stake.
To four such stomachs, tis a mere plumb-cake.

The great crisis

I once read a truly harrowing account by marine scientists of an attack by a pod of some thirty killer whales on a blue whale. The attackers repeatedly smashed into the sides of the whale, twisting off great lumps of blubber to get at its internal organs. The whale swam grimly along, gradually falling apart like a cheap home-assembly sofa-bed, with stuff trailing everywhere and randomly exposed angled bits of rib. Reading this really made me feel that, having given up whaling, humans should now start intervening actively to make the oceans less awful – perhaps by dropping enormous blocks of buoyed-up, nutritious tofu as an alternative for the killer whales to enjoy. Oh no – you think – he is typing rubbish about tofu to put off confirmation of the awful truth: that he is about to foist on us the feared Habsburg monarchy sea-mammal analogy. Maria Theresa's lands are that krill-loving but increasingly incoherent behemoth and people like Frederick the Great and the Prince-Elector Charles Albert are toothed whales. Such an assumption would be unfair – I had a different, more geo-political analogy in mind which is a bit more thoughtful. What seems so nightmarish to me about the blue whale's plight is that he has nowhere to go: he shares the medium inhabited by his attackers. Once wounded, he cannot dive, he cannot hide and can only plough along, hoping his attackers get full and pack it in. This variant sea-mammal analogy does seem marginally worth-while as it shows how Habsburg strategy had to be entirely different from that of many other countries. Britain's and the United States' entire histories are based around their ability to opt in or out of conflict – their isolation making them near invulnerable.

France and Spain also have a mixture of sea-coast and mountains that make them fiendishly hard to attack: nobody successfully invaded France between the early medieval period and the end of Napoleon's empire. The Habsburg territories, however, *like the blue whale* (I'll now drop this) have only a single element in which to operate – in their case: land. As an accidental and tacked-together cluster of hereditary possessions sprawled across Europe the potential vulnerabilities are almost infinite and the neighbours unavoidable. Britain's only consistent interests have been to keep the European coast opposite Kent and Essex weak or friendly and allow nobody to invade Ireland – beyond this Britain could dip in and out of continental affairs as it wished. The Habsburgs never had such a pick-and-mix option.

1740 was a supreme challenge for the Habsburgs, but it was also something they were used to. Being surrounded by numerous, changeable kings and dukes seems like an unworkably vulnerable and head-spinning nightmare to us, but for them it was normal. I really am trying not to load up this book with too many battles and readers may not be aware just how much I am sheltering them from. In any event there is a tedium about eighteenth-century fighting which makes it hard to engage with. There is a British narrative which is upbeat because, with a few setbacks, Britain wins, but it wins in ways which are broadly unavailable to mainland Europe itself, helped by the way their allies the Prussians or Russians in the end were not very interested in who ruled Bengal or some Caribbean island. Even the French and Dutch when under pressure had to choose the security of their own borders over anything more exotic. Only the Spanish cared as passionately as the British about colonial issues – but even they valued them because they provide much of the revenue which allowed them to pursue their ruinous policies within Europe, policies which reduced Spain by the end of the eighteenth century to a burnt-out shell.

It takes a curious effort then, from a narrowly British perspective, to understand the degree to which Europe's concerns were different. The Habsburgs were vulnerable to invasion from almost every angle. And even the destruction of one opponent would reveal another behind it: most famously, the more they weakened the Poles and Ottomans, the closer they got to the Russians.

Britain was often a valued Habsburg ally and source of money, but it was also a mischievous outsider whose obsession with what it saw as the 'balance of power' tended to mean a manipulation of short-term allies to ensure a Europe mutually weakened in ways which allowed Britain to get on with its own imperial projects undisturbed by any would-be European hegemon. So the rather exciting British story in the eighteenth century tends to be contrasted with the sheer, stultifying inconclusiveness of European fighting – an inconclusiveness that Britain itself encouraged. The Habsburgs were always deeply aware of this and resentful of their reliance on Britain, which they knew was at most levels simply using them – if Maria Theresa's war effort had collapsed, the British would have happily moved on to some other ally who could help them take on France. Indeed, after the eight grinding years of the War of the Austrian Succession, the British did not even bother to tell Maria Theresa that they had come to terms. Meanwhile the Habsburgs still lived in their very different natural environment, with a constantly changing constellation of enemies, friends, threats and opportunities; with the same rhythm imposed by mountain passes, fortresses, winter, summer, money, provisions and the distance an army can march in a day.

The military intricacies of the War of the Austrian Succession are famously soporific. A quick glance at one of those monuments favoured in the eighteenth century, of heaped military trophies looked down upon by the uncaring figures of Time and Fame, gives much the same effect as slogging through hundreds of pages about glum sieges with people marching about in wigs. Of course, just writing this makes me feel ashamed as I am fascinated by it and have a dark side that cannot be happier than reading a crazily detailed account of the Siege of Bergen-op-Zoom. European cities were all still a great mass of fortifications, with the working and shopping areas crowded inside walls, and towers that were a

constant focus of expensive fixing and upgrading, quite probably
to no avail. Not least through the genius of the French commander
Maurice de Saxe (as his name suggests a Saxon in fact, a bastard
child of Augustus the Strong), city after city found its elaborate
defences ruined by artillery and trenches. This direct and specific
sense of panic in the war makes it gripping. Prague, for example,
after being left alone and sinking gradually into the provincial
marginality that has preserved so many of its great buildings,
found itself occupied first by Franco-Bavarian troops and then by
Prussians. The usual city-dwellers' terrors emerged – not just violence, rape and looting, but the more insidious problem of whether
or not to cooperate with the invaders. The Franco-Bavarians were
there because the Bavarian ruler had made himself King of Bohemia. Should the inhabitants of Prague be loyal to Vienna or to
Munich? Once all the invaders were cleared out, Maria Theresa
was ferocious in her reaction – expelling the entire, ancient Jewish
community, confiscating properties and humiliating and ruining
anyone she felt had been even slightly disloyal. It is this sort of
terrible, specific grief and turmoil that should somehow sit at the
heart of thinking about eighteenth-century warfare, but it inevitably gets swamped by the sheer strategic complexity of the larger
picture, with its dreary emphasis on armies marching and counter-
marching, with one side or the other taking turns to be shot up.

The drama of 1740 came from the rapid realization that
Charles VI's endless efforts to get signatures on the Pragmatic
Sanction were all for nothing. Across Europe rulers got down to
the serious business of working out how to defraud Maria Theresa
of her inheritance. 1740 saw a major change in the European cast
list, with Frederick William of Prussia and the Empress Anna of
Russia dying. This led to a curious fluidity and sense of possibilities, fuelled too by France appearing to be in one of its brief
ineffective and non-hegemonic moods.

Maria Theresa faced a nightmare on almost every frontier, the
only good news being that at least the Ottomans were quiet. In
Italy she faced the machinations of the peculiarly single-minded
and obtuse Elizabeth Farnese, the Spanish queen who was deter-

mined to get her sons Italian possessions to rule. She had already
settled one in Naples (as a result of the Parma swap with Charles
VI) and now wanted to get Parma back for the other. Bewildering,
heroic and baffling battles followed from this determination, with
the potential excitement of Maria Theresa's expulsion from the
whole of her northern Italian lands. With the invaluable help of the
now hard-to-visualize but stubborn Duchy of Savoy, Maria Theresa
ended up holding on to the parts of Italy squeezed between Savoy
and Venice, but giving up Parma to Elizabeth Farnese's son Felipe,
who had unedifyingly been carried around in the baggage of various armies for much of the conflict before at last getting his rather
small prize.

It is impossible to exaggerate just how little Maria Theresa
understood her position initially and how much she was betrayed
by the feebleness and deceit of those around her. From a standing
start, though, she learned at a tremendous pace and the vacillating
cipher of 1740 rapidly became formidable. She may in later life
have appeared a bit of a *mouton sublime* in her portraits, but this is
totally misleading. Despite bouts of despair in her battle to defend
her family inheritance, she seemed to have an extraordinary ability
to be refuelled by her outrage at the knaves who, with their usual
fake legal pronouncements, were coming up with reasons for
snatching her lands. The newly crowned Frederick II of Prussia
never bothered to take seriously the rubbish his lawyers had come
up with to justify his 'ancient right' to Silesia. In a lightning campaign he snatched almost the entire province and grimly held on
to it in three wars with Maria Theresa, separated by intervals that
allowed her to trounce her other enemies. His ability to humiliate
Austrian armies rapidly became legendary, his risk-taking and
bravura making him seem almost a demonic figure to Vienna. All
efforts to get Silesia back proved to be futile (including a Third
Silesian War of 1756–63, a subset of the far, far wider Seven Years
War) and eventually treaties recognized the loss of everything
except some southern fragments which ended up as the tiny region
called Austrian Silesia. Just to round off this part of the world, the
Duchy of Auschwitz, to the north of Teschen, was owned by Maria

Theresa separately, snatched from the Polish crown in 1772. It is hard to work out what impact the loss of Silesia had on the Habsburgs. Perhaps the oddest counterfactual would be to think what would have happened if Maria Theresa had won (and it was only Frederick's peculiar genius that prevented this – and one lucky bullet or a fall from a horse could have changed everything), and this concerns 1918. When the Empire broke apart at the end of the First World War, a substantial German-speaking state could have been made from Silesia–Moravia–Austria (the main towns of Moravia, Brno and Olomouc were still substantially German) and all subsequent human history perhaps have been different. But then so many things would also have been different that perhaps such speculation is just too tiresome.

The Habsburgs could lose Silesia and bits of Italy without fatal damage (indeed, losing bits of Italy was to become as regular a feature for them as Christmas), but the mortal threat came from Charles Albert, the Elector of Bavaria. As a woman, Maria Theresa legally could not become Emperor. She conceded this and worked on the assumption that her husband, Franz, should take the job. Unfortunately, as a Habsburg only by marriage, he had in himself none of the qualifications, being merely a jobbing princeling who had already knocked about Europe trying his hand at running a number of small territories. The disappointment here is that the contest was such a battle of mediocrities. Charles Albert seems to have disappointed everyone he met, while Franz was clearly charming (his portraits radiate a chump-like sympathy), but mainly of value as a collector of minerals and delightful *objets* and father of Maria Theresa's innumerable children, rather than a political actor in his own right.

Charles Albert, as a member of the ancient Wittelsbach family, saw the Habsburgs as mere late-medieval carpetbaggers, and with substantial and mischievous French help was able to get elected Emperor, as Charles VII, thereby ending the unbroken sequence of Habsburgs since Frederick III. Even more catastrophically he marched into Maria Theresa's lands claiming them also as his own. This was a highly unfortunate result of Charles VI's decision to ignore the daughters of his older brother, Joseph I. He established the Pragmatic Sanction through his own daughter, Maria Theresa. Charles Albert, who was married to one of Joseph I's daughters, could rightfully point out that she had the better claim. All the bickering and iciness of Charles VI's court now came to fruition (if iciness can fruit) with Maria Amalia taking revenge on behalf of her sisters.

With an invaluable French army at his side Charles Albert marched east, and threatened an absolutely different European future. His success would have made his joint capitals of Munich, Prague, Vienna and Buda into an almost unrelated power configuration, closely allied to the French and probably more than enough to have changed the course of all subsequent wars, cultural movements and so on. His army charged through Upper Austria, conquering Linz, and marching on to St Pölten – still, to this very day, one of Central Europe's least interesting towns – and paused and then panicked. If he had headed straight to Vienna he could perhaps have destroyed Maria Theresa's claims, with many key figures changing sides to (in effect) the other female branch of the family. Instead, worried that Vienna was too strongly defended, that it was late in the campaigning season and that he was a long way from his base, he headed back to Bohemia, took Prague, and was acclaimed and crowned there as king. As King of Bohemia he had an extra vote for himself in the Imperial election, but this was not enough to get him the far bigger prize of subsuming Central Europe into Bavaria. From then on nothing went right – Maria Theresa counterattacked, threw him out of Prague, invaded Bavaria and occupied Munich. The short remainder of Charles Albert's life was a sort of nightmare of humiliation as he huddled in Frankfurt, with the by-now purely symbolic value of being Emperor starkly clear. The Habsburg hold on the title could be enforced by their own troops and money and the Electors had over the years, sometimes only grudgingly, admitted that this was the case. The last glory days of being Emperor, under Leopold I and Joseph I, had allowed the two roles of Emperor and Habsburg ruler to be attractively mixed in a way that demanded intermittent but genuine fealty. Charles Albert had neither the resources nor the prestige and his taking the job had the hideous effect (hideous particularly for him) of making it clear that being Emperor was a bit pointless. He had some attractive coins made, briefly returned to Munich and then died. The suitably chastened Electors replaced him with Maria Theresa's husband, as Franz I. He was entirely happy to treat the job as an honorific one, sitting in a pavilion at Schönbrunn sipping hot chocolate and admiring his giraffes. Europe's grandest title was grand no longer.

The final theatre of fighting (north-west Europe) always looms large in British accounts because of the 'Pragmatic Army', a mixed force sent to protect Hannover and the Austrian Netherlands, which sparred with the French and, at the Battle of Dettingen, saw the last time a British monarch led his own army – although George II was there at least as much as Elector of Hannover. This was the theatre in which Maurice de Saxe shone, but the fighting had in the end little impact, beyond making it clear that the United Provinces (the Netherlands) was spent as the great and dynamic military and cultural force that it had been in the previous century. It also began in earnest the humiliating process by which the inhabitants of the Austrian Netherlands came to realize they were so little valued by Maria Theresa (and then by her son Joseph II) that they were open to pretty much *any* bid for a swap of some kind. To go about one's business in Brussels or Ghent dimly aware that your ruler would gladly be shot of you cannot be particularly enjoyable and it would end with the Belgian Revolution, but only after generations of shame. Austrian rule there was erratic and mean-minded, just using up the province's inherent wealth. But it did make Austria into the only truly pan-European power and therefore Britain's natural associate, however bumpy.

The War of the Austrian Succession was stuffed with strange forks in the road. In the end it is extraordinary that from such weak beginnings, Maria Theresa, despite huge threats, did hold on to most of her territories and became a highly successful and impressive ruler, keeping the Habsburg lands intact in the face of their most overwhelming threat before 1914–18. But there is one more what-if: what if in 1744 Maria Theresa had made a treaty with Saxony's Augustus III (a marzipan-like figure) in which the Saxons guaranteed her ownership of the Austrian lands, and in return Maria Theresa agreed that if her heirs were to die her titles would pass to Maria Josepha, Augustus III's long-suffering wife, and another of Joseph I's children? As Augustus was also King of Poland it is possible to see a new state coming into being which might have perhaps permanently tied together the existing Habsburg monarchy with the whole of Poland (at that point, of course, an enormous state) and Saxony – at which point Europe's future would, yet again, have been entirely different. But as it was, Maria Theresa ruled for forty highly successful years and had sixteen children.

Austria wears trousers

Some years ago, wandering around the annual wine festival in the Hungarian town of Szekszárd, with its tiny, pony-fuelled carousel and heart-valve-furring snacks, it was impossible not to notice how many of the folk-craft stalls featured a strange silhouette, in the shape perhaps of an ink-blot or an elaborate cut of meat. On bags, bumper-stickers, jeans patches, drinks coasters – indeed on anything even vaguely plausible (I once saw it incorporated into a rasta woolly hat) – there was the same perturbing shape. I soon started to see it everywhere and it has now (2013) become omnipresent. The silhouette is a map of the 'Crown Lands of St Stephen' and its use is an impotent nationalist cry of rage against the hacking about of Hungarian territory after the First World War, when the enormous territory ruled from Budapest – a sprawling entity on a grander scale than Arizona – was reduced to a traumatized rump no bigger than South Carolina. This sense of fury has waxed and waned and was, for obvious reasons, stamped on hard by the Communists – but it never went away. The many

Hungarians trapped on the wrong side of the borders have lived
with discrimination, violence and contempt from their new rulers
and you do not need to be all that crazily right-wing to feel that
some small territorial adjustments would be wise. In the northern
suburbs of Debrecen there is a classic expression of this sense of
betrayal: a truly obnoxious statue put up in the 1930s showing a beautiful nude woman (Hungary) with an arm and a leg as
bleeding stumps.

It is perhaps only possible to learn so much from a jeans patch,
but the symbolic weight of that shape, wherever it is displayed,
pins the wish for Hungarians to have a clearly defined, ethnically
complete state. But the 'Crown Lands of St Stephen' are a fantasy,
giving a sense of ancient destiny to an arena of political power for
Budapest that in practice only existed from 1867 to 1918 and
which therefore has no more God-given legitimacy than any other
random date bracket. It would be an eccentric history lesson, but
with scissors one could come up with jeans patches of pretty much
every imaginable shape to express the borders of the true Hungarian state, and it is this tragic uncertainty that has been the true
motor for the region's fate.

Maria Theresa's coming to the throne in 1740 gave the Hungarians a startling opportunity to improve their lot, but this was in
the wake of a horrendous century or more. The Habsburg narrative
for the Hungarians has always been about their treachery, men-
dacity, religious splitism and lack of gratitude. As the armies of the
Holy League ended the long Turkish occupation of much of Hungary, its inhabitants were returned to the Christian (and Catholic)
fold and the rule of their king, Leopold I (or I. Lipót). Very few
Hungarians saw this as good. The Principality of Transylvania
had maintained, albeit in flickering form, the flame of a separate
Hungarian political identity. This was an identity closely linked
to Protestantism, and as Habsburg forces marched into Sibiu and
immediately began setting about building the – rather beautiful, if
identikit – Catholic church on the Great Square, that identity was
under acute threat. A frightening precedent had been set in Royal
Hungary, the western areas (principally what are now Slovakia and

Transdanubia) that had always stayed under Habsburg control. These had been subjected from the 1670s to the same iron-fist-in-an-iron-glove re-Catholicizing that Bohemia had experienced in the 1620s. In what amounted sometimes to an ethnic war, generations of soldiers and Jesuits hammered Royal Hungary. This ended up creating loyal, Catholic, pro-Habsburg Hungarians, but it also threatened, as it had for Czech-speakers, what seemed a permanent crushing of ethnic identity. It was hard to be loyal if the price of that loyalty was effectively to become German.

By the 1690s, as the Habsburgs enforced their rule on Transylvania, the once impressive principality of Bethlen Gábor was a distant memory: catastrophic decisions by its rulers had left it devastated by the Ottomans (who lost patience with the pretensions of their vassals) before a counter-devastation by the Holy League. The presence of Transylvanian troops with the Ottoman armies besieging Vienna meant that there was no chance of Leopold's having the faintest interest in leniency. The new rulers set up their headquarters in Sibiu and the once glamorous old capital of Alba Iulia became a mere minor town.

The third and final part of the Hungarian lands – most of the modern state, in fact – as it came under Habsburg control following Turkish retreat was viewed as mere colonial territory rather than a proud Hungarian inheritance. The devastation of this area during the fighting was almost total, with places like Esztergom and Buda effectively re-founded. Swarms of irregular troops from both sides had filled their spare moments by destroying all human existence in their path, with many ancient villages simply ceasing to exist. Indeed, after a while, it becomes baffling as to where fresh Hungarian settlers could come from, so many areas were so utterly burned over.

The seventeenth century saw a number of uprisings and plots by the Hungarians to contest Habsburg presumption and in many ways the issues they raised remained the same until the end of the First World War. Even for Catholic Hungarians the problem was a terrible one. Vienna sat at the heart of a predominantly German-speaking, Imperial hub of power. Once the siege of 1683 had been lifted, Leopold's reign saw the rebuilding of Vienna, including many of the boggling aristocratic palaces still there today – it started to become a great capital for the first time. It swarmed with Germans,* whether from the Habsburg hereditary lands or from the Empire, together with Italian craftsmen, military advisers and mercenaries. There was a near perfect match between the needs of the Habsburg dynasty and the German aristocracy, who filled almost all military and official jobs and who issued a great flow of orders, proclamations and instructions, and who dominated scientific and religious ideas. Some of these were translated into Hungarian, but most were not. To even understand what was going on in the Habsburg lands, Hungarians had little choice but to learn German and, with this, ponder whether they would be better off totally Germanized.

Ever since the original disaster at the Battle of Mohács the Hungarian lands had been used as a buffer and their inhabitants seen as expendable. Now, with the string of great victories, all Hungarians fell into Habsburg hands for the first time. Leopold saw these as his natural spoils, but there were many other views. The truly horrible revolt of Ferenc II Rákóczi, which lasted from 1703 to 1711, caused staggering levels of further devastation, some eighty-five thousand of his Kurucs dying in battle and perhaps four hundred thousand civilians dying from plague and famine. It is hard to imagine that in an era which in western Europe preferred quite formalized combat there could in parallel (often with the same Habsburg troops) be such a bloodbath. Rákóczi's attempt to create an independent state foundered on what would prove the usual basis. The other great powers were willing to use Hungarian discontent to cause trouble for Vienna (variously Russia, France, Poland and Sweden) but lost interest in

---

*   Just to be quite clear, I say 'German' and 'Hungarian' assuming a silent '-speakers' or '-speaking' as this addition would be so cumbersome. I am of course not suggesting the existence of Germany or Hungary in a modern sense. This needs constant self-discipline. Carinthians or Transylvanians had all kinds of loyalties, but none of these were directed at later generations of nationalist historians.

that discontent once they had achieved their own goals. Hungarians suffered the painful fate of being too few in number and too distant to generate much sympathy. This was coupled with a refusal by those other linguistic groups in the 'Crown Lands of St Stephen' necessarily to fancy Hungarian rule. Having seen the departure of the Turks, it did not seem axiomatic that Hungarian masters were necessarily an upgrade. Rákóczi found himself dealing with widespread Transylvanian Saxon indifference, Serbian and Croatian hostility and a lack of unanimity even among Hungarians. Once the Habsburgs under Joseph I could spare the forces to concentrate on him they defeated him. But what choice did Rákóczi have? If the Hungarian nobility were not simply to submit to being a group of politically neutered fancy-dress-shop yokels, then a serious gesture had to be made against German Habsburg hegemony. The Hungarians were clinging to the very edge of political power and – excluded by prejudice, religious bars and language – threatened to become non-people, not unlike the Romanians whom they in turn kept down. The hysterical flavour of much of Hungarian political life, the costumes and obscurantism, stemmed from this sense of danger. As it was, every Hungarian 'rebel' leader until the later nineteenth century wound up exiled, dead in battle or executed. Rákóczi spent the latter part of his life in a town on the Sea of Marmara. It is an incredible sequence of failure, but it did mean that the Hungarians were never eviscerated like the Czechs. And, as with other risings, Rákóczi's created a mythology which made him a near religious figure for later nationalist Hungarians.

The end of the rebellion saw a further overwhelming surge of thousands of colonists into what were now empty lands. This was a substantially hidden epic, as waves of Germans, Hungarians, Slovaks, Serbs, Bulgarians and even Cossacks filled the new territories, taking generations to clear, dyke and build town after town, often from scratch. Large groups of Serbs left Ottoman territory and settled in Szentendre, north of Buda, where they were given special privileges and left behind them, after their twentieth-century return south, a particularly beautiful and iconostasis-packed town.

Many merchants were Jews, Greeks and Armenians and the strange
process by which Hungarians tended to ignore economic activity
of a non-agrarian kind began.

The great Hungarian opportunity for redemption came with the
disasters that nearly overwhelmed Maria Theresa on her father's
death. Betrayed on every side, she had the brilliant idea of theat-
rically throwing herself, a notionally poor, weak woman, on the
mercy of the Hungarian Diet. In two great visits to Bratislava in
1741 she wiped away many decades of loathing between Germans
and Hungarians. Dressed in mourning for her father, holding the
crucifix that had so comforted Ferdinand II at the beginning of the
Thirty Years War (a poor precedent on the face of it), and bargain-
ing ruthlessly, Maria Theresa ensured money, men and supplies and
at least one loyal corner of the Habsburg lands. She camped it up
magnificently, travelling down the Danube for her coronation in
a barge festooned in Hungarian colours, galloping on a horse (a
requirement of being crowned Monarch of Hungary!) and breath-
takingly playing to the gallery. In a perhaps even more hysterical
trip later in the year she held up her super-weapon before the Diet:
a son, the tiny Joseph, whose existence ensured the continuity of
the Habsburg line (albeit via the mother, which remained contentious for some). As the loyal phrase ran: 'The enemy has lost his
chance, for Austria now wears trousers', or at least a nappy. Naturally these occasions in practice must have oozed the most terrible
bad faith, but much to everyone's surprise it turned out that Maria
Theresa was a genius who had, despite her crapulous father, somehow acquired a moral compass and an ability to inspire trust and
respect. The Hungarians reneged on much of the deal and provided a fraction of what they promised, but a new model of
pro-Habsburg loyalism suddenly became available and for the first
time Hungarian troops were sent into western Europe, with sometimes devastating effect.

Any attempt to discuss history purely in terms of jeans patches
must come to grief, but it is not a wholly useless idea. The patch
for eighteenth-century Hungarians would have been drastically different – with Transylvania under Vienna's rule and a large block of

the south forming a new and extended Military Frontier against further Turkish threats, again a vast zone outside Hungarian control. The oddities of the Polish-controlled Zips towns peppered northern Hungary and only a small part of what is now Croatia had some form of Hungarian jurisdiction. In a friendly gesture Maria Theresa handed over the port of Rijeka (Fiume) to Hungarian control, giving access to the sea for the first time since the Middle Ages, and making sense of at least the little hook-shape on the jeans patch.

These manoeuvres between Germans and Hungarians (with other minorities effectively invisible through overwhelming legal disabilities, religious isolation and illiteracy – a situation that would soon change) gave a recognizably more modern form to the Habsburg lands. In many ways it was not until the nineteenth century that the Hungarian regions became fully settled again and this enormous, cellular, diurnal process has to be imagined ticking away in the background. Gradually, a zone that had been perhaps the worst place to live in Europe for at least two centuries took on the appearance that makes it so attractive now. The Hungarians had survived, but whether this was thanks to the Habsburgs or despite them, and within what boundaries, has been the basis of violent argument ever since.

The Gloriette

A visit to the Schönbrunn Palace in Vienna is in many ways a disappointing and confusing experience. Here is the heart of the Habsburg world – a sumptuous summer residence expressing both grandeur and leisure. And yet even a completist such as me cannot get very excited by the building itself. Franz Joseph spent far too long there and much of it is tainted with his own dreary, railway-waiting-room aesthetic. Even the more showy bits decorated by Maria Theresa have a cold dullness to them. The highlight is probably the up-to-the-minute bathroom features put in for the Empress Zita during the closing stages of the First World War, which fully embrace the trivial nature of her and her husband's brief regime. Those running the palace seem aware that it puts on a poor show, so they have tried to improve it with displays of things like old carriages. Most strange of all is a special exhibition of the Empress Elisabeth's hand-made saddles which set up such a sexual-fetishistic and oddly direct relationship between the late Empress and the person staring into them that it is hard to know what to say.

Wandering around Maria Theresa's rooms one has a niggling feeling that the Habsburgs are getting a bit tone deaf when commissioning artists and decorators – with a bit more cash and a lot more taste everything could have been so much better. This frustration evaporates once outside, where it becomes possible to appreciate the beauty of the palace building itself, but even more to enjoy the amazing grounds. I have gone on at too much length in my last book about the miracle zoo with its breakfast house and radiating pavilions filled with rococo exotica. But most wonderful of all in the palace grounds is the Gloriette, a pleasure house and viewing platform on the steep hill above the palace. The Gloriette has many functions, but it is principally a colossal sigh of relief expressed in tons of stonework for the rescue of the Habsburg monarchy from destruction at the hands of the Prussians. It celebrates the Battle of Kolín, where in 1757 Frederick the Great, during the Third Silesian War, at last met his comeuppance and was forced to abort his invasion of Bohemia. This was, of course, a very rare Austrian victory and Frederick himself could have, if he had wished, built an entire shopping centre out of Gloriettes back in Berlin. But, aside from a brief incursion to besiege Olomouc (whose craggy cliff-wall defences can still be seen today and where he took some shots at the Plague Column), the threat to Habsburg territory was now over. There were many Austrian humiliations at the hands of the Prussians still to come but these were generally in Silesia or Saxony.

The Gloriette is in many ways a perfect example of mix-and-match Habsburg cheese-paring, with many of its architectural details, including its charismatic carved bull skulls, hacked out of Maximilian II's old Neugebäude Palace in the suburb of Simmering. But its extravagant and charming pointlessness makes it nearly as fine a monument to Maria Theresa's reign as her breakfast house in the zoo and a happy contrast to her fusty and banal interior decorations. An Allied bombing raid on Vienna wrecked the Gloriette, as well as killing the rhinoceros in the next-door zoo. There is a pathetic photo of the rhino's keeper posing with its armoured corpse, together with a more enjoyable one of Red Army troops with the giraffes inside their enclosure – presumably nobody was in a position to tell them they were not allowed within the fencing. The Gloriette was rebuilt after the War, and with its great swags of carved Roman weapons and massive eagle, it is now a rather odd sort of cafe. It stands there as an absolute and permanent statement of belief in Austrian victory and confidence, in the face of any number of actual catastrophes and defeats. Once they had finished mucking about with the giraffes, presumably the Soviet troops must have enjoyed wandering over to see the ravaged heap of the Gloriette. Silesia was never retrieved but the rest of the Maria Theresa's inheritance had survived an overwhelming assault by a great coalition of its enemies.

The war on Christmas cribs

Tucked away in the midst of the magniloquent, trippy interior of Melk Abbey are two visitors from an earlier time: Clement and Frederick, the catacomb saints. In a bonanza for the Catholic fightback a great series of subterranean tunnels was found in Rome in 1578, filled with the bodies of early Christians. It was assumed that they had been buried there because they had been persecuted and these 'catacomb saints' were exported by the Jesuits all over the Catholic world as superb instances of the primitive sufferings of the True Church. In fact they were the skeletons of pious but ordinary Romans who, having blamelessly lain in the dark for a millennium, now found themselves landed with a random Christian name, canonized and put on a mule cart. Clement arrived in Melk during the great refurbishment, and Frederick was a later arrival, donated by Maria Theresa in 1762. Given the huge number of bodies in the catacombs these saints could be handed out like cookies, and even today a quiet word in the right ear could probably secure one. The Jesuits got a bit out of control as they were also dealing in bits of the martyred St Ursula and her eleven thousand virgins (a spectacular skeleton-pit fraud dug up in Cologne, the equivalent for the Catholic Church of Spindletop for the Texas oil industry). In any event, the two skeletons at Melk lounge in their glass caskets, covered in peculiar body-stockings and jewels, their skulls resting on lurid pillows, and looking oddly like Marlene Dietrich in *Rancho Notorious*.

Maria Theresa's donation of St Frederick was already a pretty retro gesture by the 1760s as Catholic intellectual and emotional culture had moved on. The Jesuits were suppressed across Europe by the Pope in the following decade, except (in a perverse result) in Prussia and in Russia, where Catherine the Great once may have been anti-Catholic but was damned if she was going to be told what to do by some man living in Italy. A new austerity and prayerful privacy reigned. Oddly, this shift moved almost in lock-step with the growth of public musical theatre, as though the now idle impresarios of the Catholic Church found fresh work in opera and oratorio. It is strange that the hysterical emotionalism of, say, Mozart's *Don Giovanni* or Haydn's *The Creation* should channel much the same extreme atmosphere that places such as Melk had done in earlier decades but in a new form. I do not know if it would be possible to make a real link, but it does look as though out-of-control fervency had simply moved house.

Joseph II himself exemplified this move towards a more intellectual Church. Often wrongly thought of as anti-Catholic, he simply wished to sweep away the dirty clutter of superstition and peeling gilt that made places like Melk seem deeply old-fashioned by the time of Maria Theresa's death in 1780. She herself had been sceptical of many of these traditional accretions, but Joseph took the reaction to bizarre lengths. By some definitions one of the most talented of Habsburg rulers, Joseph in everything he did seemed to lurch and overreach. The shape of his reign was a very odd one. After Franz I's death in 1765 he became Holy Roman Emperor, seemingly re-establishing the Habsburg grip on a stable basis. But he then spent some fifteen years under his mother's tutelage, a ruler who by this point knew how to make things work merely by lifting a finger. To make things even worse he had to deal with his mother's contemporary, Frederick the Great, who hung like some appalling spectre over his life, the man who had humiliated his family, but who was also a figure to be admired and whose rationalism and austerity formed a rather sadly obvious model for the strange young man. How different the future if Joseph had modelled himself on his own father and just lolled about eating sweets and looking through a magnifying-glass at bouquets of flowers made out of jewels. Instead, Joseph was racked by an action-this-day fever to modernize and overhaul the lands which, in his view, had failed his dynasty.

The Catholic Church – an institution in every way the ideological partner of the monarchy – was thrown into chaos by a great heap of edicts from Joseph. He had views on everything from banning the making of cribs in the Tyrol to forcing priests to switch to practical and hard-wearing leather vestments (there is a hilariously sad example in Melk). Monasteries viewed as not directly serving the community were shut and the whole tradition of purely private contemplation reaching back to the origins of Christianity was nearly stamped out. As the Jesuits had also been suppressed an enormous number of buildings became available for use as schools, barracks and offices, ushering in the paper- and personnel-driven modern state. The effects can still be seen scattered all over Central Europe, with religious-looking buildings turning out to have oddly secular functions. In Olomouc there is still a carved stone on the side of what is now the Regional Museum declaring how Joseph II had shut down this Convent of the Poor Clares to make it into a school for the town. Jesuit churches were reassigned – so the church which had for many years had its hands full looking after Frederick III's entrails in Linz now became the city's cathedral. The Catholic Church was a land-owner on a vast scale, owning half of Carniola and at least a third of Moravia: Joseph was driven mad with rage by what he viewed as idle ecclesiastical land and grabbed whatever he could. It was a truly revolutionary act, and it was one which would prove to have an unexpected and devastating effect on the rest of the Holy Roman Empire.

Just as bad for Joseph were all those days spent in pointless processions and pilgrimages, days when the population could be building the economy. Most of the Habsburgs' own intricate religious calendar was dumped and processions and pilgrimages were banned or heavily regulated. Many Catholics agreed with much of what he was doing. Atheists remained an almost invisibly small group, and the form of renewal Joseph was carrying out had an entirely respectable Catholic pedigree. This was a process that had begun under Maria Theresa. As an odd side-effect of her ownership of the Austrian Netherlands, the Catholic renewal movement of Jansenism which originated there had made rapid inroads in Vienna. Jansenism, with its cold austerity and cult of the parish priest, was baffling to fans of gold vestments and flying babies, and attracted much suspicion. The old joke was that Jansenism was like the route of the Danube – it starts Catholic, it then becomes Protestant, and it ends up infidel. But Maria Theresa was herself convinced: a fair test of its legitimacy. The rise of Freemasonry has conventionally been seen as a secular challenge even to an over-hauled Catholic Church, but given how much great Catholic music Mozart wrote or that two abbots of Melk Abbey itself were buried with their Masonic aprons tucked into their coffins, this is doubtful. What shook off most of his supporters was, as usual, simply Joseph's relentless, impatient and humourless failure to prioritize. Dismantling greedy Church land-holdings should have been his great achievement, but this got tangled up with stupid rages about Christmas cribs and badgering priests to dress in leather. The end result was not enlightened reform but a chaos of miserable and upset subjects to no great purpose.

Beyond the Church, Joseph slashed at all privileges and ossified habits as though through sheer willpower he could change his domains from a congeries of particularist, multilingual estates into the coherent single entity that he wanted, a proper state, like Britain or France. This was a ridiculous aim: the only coherence enjoyed by the Habsburg lands was that they had fallen into his family's lap. It was typical of Joseph that this never occurred to him – he never seems to have wondered whether in practice rationality was the Habsburgs' worst nightmare. A well-educated, aspirational, unsuperstitious people might well develop other interests than simply offering support for Joseph's latest whim. The sheer stubborn mess of the territories defeated him, but it is interesting that he tried, and he was the last Habsburg except the abortive Franz Ferdinand to throw himself at his inheritance to try to give it proper shape. Symbolically he did this by refusing to be crowned King of Hungary, moving the various state crowns to Vienna and insisting that the Monarchy now was a single and unitary state. German would now be the Monarchy's official language and Hungarians would be forced to use German in all official dealings. Serfdom was to be abolished, the clergy were to be taxed, the nobility were to lose their legal privileges, corsets were to be banned as a threat to childbirth, churches could be built by non-Catholics, the crusty 'Spanish customs' of bowing and scraping at court were to go.

These changes have been overshadowed by the French Revolution and by Joseph's premature death and the subsequent overturning of many of his edicts, but their impact at the time was astounding. If you were a nobleman and a Hungarian, had a lot of serfs and liked corsets and Tyrolean cribs you must have been permanently speechless with horror. It was as though through sheer will-power Joseph was going to take on every sectional group in the country. When he died of overwork, personal misery and tuberculosis in 1790 there must have been many mourning subjects who allowed themselves a small glass of something to mark the occasion.

Joseph's removal of a great range of legal disabilities from the Jews is one of the changes for which he was most revered, with Galician Jews for generations seeing Joseph as one of the great figures in their history. In the mid-nineteenth century the Jewish section of Prague was renamed Josefov in his memory. Some of

these disabilities were so grotesque that it is hard to engage with
the idea that they ever existed. Jews could now remove the yellow
star from their clothing, move freely around the Monarchy, open
their own factories, employ Christian servants, and attend university and visit theatres. They were also permitted to leave their
homes on Sundays and on Christian festivals, bans previously in
place on the grounds that as Christ's murderers it was offensive for
them to be seen in public. These changes inaugurated a new and
powerful relationship between the Habsburgs and the Jews which
ultimately resulted in the greatness of Central Europe's late-
nineteenth-century culture. Joseph's motives, however, were as usual
to do with efficiency – he wished to make Jews into fully productive citizens and he wanted them for his army. There was also the
usual sickness that accompanied all Habsburg thinking about Jews.
As a Catholic, Joseph believed that the Jews' adherence to their
faith was a result of their legal disabilities. Once they were in the
mainstream, took German names and were taught German at school
they would cease to be Jews. The Hungarians came to the same
conclusion with 'their' Jews – full citizenship would lead ultimately to conversion. To a limited extent this did happen over the
following century, just as many ethnically Czechs, Croats, Slovenes
and so on Germanized or Magyarized themselves. This bad faith at
the heart of the reforms – that Jews were to be welcomed into
some imagined mainstream only in the hope that they could eventually disappear – was to have a long and ultimately terrible
history. Jews themselves, of course, knew what was going on and a
great era of debate opened as to the right response to these reforms
and how much compromise might undermine the nature of
Judaism. Germanization too was a philosophy with a catastrophic
future, with its inbuilt assumption that it was the task of other
languages to lie down and become extinct. In the 1780s however these were just a couple of strands in the mayhem of
Josephine reform, with decrees streaming out of the Hofburg – the
Schönbrunn Palace having been mothballed as inefficient and
old-fashioned – at an astounding rate.

Joseph was probably lucky to have died when he did, as even

without the French Revolution, his actions had clearly run completely out of control by then. As the streets filled with homeless nuns, crib-smugglers and angry noblemen, it was unclear if Joseph might in fact have provoked his own revolution. Attempts to abolish serfdom for example flushed out another massive area of disability based on language. The Hungarians of Transylvania dealt with Romanians every day, with most of their serfs being Romanian (or Wallachian as they were then called). Indeed, Romanians were the largest group in Transylvania's tumultuous ethnic mix. The Hungarians themselves hardly formed a coherent group, split like any complex society into competing elements, with noble landowners, an often poor gentry and many small farmers. There was also the very large, separate group known as Székelys, who had traditionally defended the eastern frontiers and, while speaking Hungarian, had little in common with the aristos in Cluj. At some basic mental level, however, the Hungarians pretended the Romanians did not exist and that Transylvania was a thoroughly Magyar land. This tension (or fantasy) was to continue until the cataclysm of 1918, having some of the same flavour as twentieth-century South Africa. In 1784 the hideous Revolt of Horea, Cloşca and Crişan erupted. These men led some thirty-six thousand Wallachian followers across western Transylvania in a fury of anti-Hungarian violence, animated by the excitement around Joseph's reforms. Thousands of Hungarians were murdered and troops sent in with the usual massacres. Horea and Cloşca were ultimately broken with a hammer on the wheel, quartered and then displayed in smaller chunks on poles along the roadside. Crişan managed to kill himself in gaol to avoid this fate. These events suggested that Joseph might be leading the Monarchy into total chaos. Certainly this was the conclusion drawn by his successors, who clamped down and deradicalized, with the French Revolution providing excuse enough to drop further reform. The Revolt of Horea, Cloşca and Crişan, though, would have a long future.

Illustrious corpses

Joseph's reforms were always a strange mixture of the well-meaning
and the merely peculiar. A fine (if terrible) example has been preserved in the Piranesi-like gloom of the Špilberk fortress in Brno.
The fortress has a long history of infamy, and while it is promoted
locally as a family day out, it cannot shake off its miserable role as
both Habsburg and Nazi barracks and prison. One of its worst
rooms demonstrates the strange results of what should have been
Joseph's finest hour – the abolition of the death penalty.

The death penalty had always stemmed in part from the unwill-
ingness of the authorities to fund long prison sentences. Most
criminals' sentences were fines, confiscation of property or expulsion from their city or even country. They could also be mutilated
in some disgusting way, or publicly humiliated, either in the stocks
or through being forced to wear freakish and peculiar metal masks.
Some chilling examples of these survive in Salzburg castle, and to
be forced to walk the streets for a week, humiliated and half
stifled, looking like some shunned relative of the Tin Man must
have been a horrible ordeal. Some religious criminals could be
burned alive, and for crimes against the state they were sent off to
be galley-slaves or executed in the sort of dreadful and exemplary
ways used for the Romanian rebels. So the state had many forms
of punishment, but long terms in gaol were not among them.
Except in the case of debtors, potentially useful political prisoners
or errant noble family members, the idea of long-term incarceration, feeding and looking after criminals for decades at public
expense was not part of the repertoire.

There was, however, a quite widespread feeling that executions
were degrading and unenlightened. Their point was to be great
public spectacles, a stage-managed, living-flesh version of the
moral stories in cheap prints, books and sermons about duty, obedience and the need to curb pride, but they would often get out of
control. We do not know the feelings of the crowd watching
Cloşca's and Horea's prolonged agony, but it is fair to assume that

their status as Romanian folk-heroes was established as much by the execution as by the rebellion. But if there were not to be these horrible fiestas what would replace them? Joseph's abolition of the death penalty was therefore a problem as it meant an alternative had to be found, presumably long-term incarceration.

Parts of the Špilberk fortress were taken out of use in 1858 and its military governor opened it up as a tourist attraction, having blacksmiths make fake torture instruments, fabricating a barely interesting legend about unfaithful wives being walled up in one of the rooms and putting in such fitted-as-standard features as a strappado'd shop dummy. A more serious reconstruction was of Joseph II's 'dark cells' for those murderers who were now spared execution. The new enlightened regime meant that the prisoner spent the rest of his life chained inside a wooden box in total darkness and silence (beyond the distant sound of church bells), with bread and water shoved through a slot by a soundless gaoler. After only weeks of this, prisoners would go completely mad or else simply will their own deaths.

An alternative Joseph found was to put a thousand or more prisoners to useful work pulling barges up the Danube. This was little better than the dark cells, with two-thirds dying of malaria, malnutrition and exhaustion from hauling barges in ropes and chains sometimes through chest-deep water. All one can say about these initiatives was that they represented a very peculiar sort of reformism. But they also offered a preliminary rough sketch for all the forms of chilling, pseudo-rational zeal which convulsed Europe at irregular intervals from now on.

A more attractive example of the pace of intellectual change in the eighteenth century can perhaps best be shown by coming back to Clement and Frederick, the catacomb saints, still shivering in the Danube valley, many miles north of their warm Roman home. It was only sixteen years after his mother donated St Frederick to Melk that Joseph was staying in Florence with his younger brother Leopold, the Grand Duke of Tuscany. He saw there some extraordinary wax anatomical models and commissioned their creators, Paolo Mascagni and Felice Fontana, to fabricate a far

larger, more complex and more detailed group of wax corpses for
his new military medical college in Vienna. It was probably only
very recent descendants of the mules that had hauled St Frederick
over the Brenner Pass who spent the 1780s carrying more than a
thousand wax models over the same route. Now displayed in the
great medical museum at the Josephinum, these astounding objects
have a fair claim to be some of the greatest artworks of the later
eighteenth century, both as reimagined Italian religious sculpture
and in their revolutionary new attitude to the human body.

Certainly, too, as pieces of theatre they are brilliantly presented.
I had no way of telling if this was a legitimate odour in a medical
faculty or a stroke of camp genius by the curator, but the slight
smell of ether in the rooms adds immeasurably to the sense of
Frankensteiny art-yoked-to-science. Far simpler and cruder prepa-
rations of the nervous system or arteries in, say, the Ingolstadt
medical museum or the Hunterian in London are alarming enough,
but the Josephinum presents an endlessly varied set of memento
mori. Lying on their sides, even sharing the same pose as the catacomb saints, these pulled-open and cut-apart people, the wax as
vividly coloured as when they were first made, come startlingly
close to being real. A room of standing male figures, even with
much of their skin removed and internal organs on display, stare
right back at the viewer, their eyes enormous in their flayed faces,
in a challenging and oddly noble way. They make the most accomplished normal sculptural statues of the same period seem merely
inert and formulaic. There is even a sequence of random, dreadful
wax chunks of human torso to help military surgeons identify the
appearance of entry points for different wounds. The models make
humans into functioning (or malfunctioning) machines instead of
divinely ordered receptacles. It is impossible to keep your compo-
sure when admiring how the sculptor has made the muscles stretch
correctly when the skin is pulled away from the upper leg, or when
coming face to face with a big wax prostate. The effect for the
spectator is both religious and scientific: quite soon these ruined
yet grand and moving people create their own complete world and
you walk back out onto the cold streets of Vienna, with cheerful,

duffel-coated students and normal busyness, feeling expelled from something almost too powerful.

Carving up the world

Being a monarch was by any conventional measure not all fun. But if one had to pinpoint the absolute summit of the fun monarchical experience, then it would undoubtedly be found on a bend of the River Dniepr in 1787. It was here that Catherine the Great embarked on her magnificent voyage to the south, eager to inspect her newly acquired territory of Crimea.

Catherine is one of that elite handful of rulers who really loved her role. A German from the micro-state of Anhalt-Zerbst, she came to Russia to marry the heir to the throne, Peter, also a German, from no less micro Holstein-Gottorp, but more importantly a grandson of Peter the Great. It was perhaps as an outsider that she came to so relish becoming a Russian, revelling in the strangeness and grandeur, joining the Orthodox Church, changing her name from Sophie to Catherine and having her husband murdered. Catherine always seems to be on some huge golden juggernaut, hauled along by representatives of the different subject nationalities, while girls throw petals over the entire ensemble and specially trained doves fly in formation overhead, holding in their beaks silk banners embroidered with positive statements in Latin. In 1787 she was living her allegorical fantasy to the full. Heaped in furs and jewels, she watched cheering crowds line the banks of the river, enormous firework displays go off and thousands of Cossacks carry out mock battles, all under the direction of her former lover Prince Potemkin. The River Dniepr, now associated more with rusting hydroelectric plants, can never have looked more glamorous. As Catherine and her guests enjoyed themselves designing triumphal arches, admiring Potemkin's chirpy, all-girl 'Amazon' light cavalry troupe and chatting about which neighbouring state should be attacked next, the only fly in the ointment was a dour Habsburg visitor.

Joseph II, simply attired and travelling incognito, was just the sort of Mr Boring whom the tittering gang on the barge could not stand. Grumbling snobbishly about 'this Catherinized Princess of Zerbst' he did everything he could to lower the temperature. But even with Joseph on board, measuring everything, asking statistical questions and trying to find fault, it must still have been perhaps the world's best outing. The idea of the fake 'Potemkin villages' put up to trick the Tsaritsa, which have been part of everyone's consciousness ever since, was itself in fact a spiteful fabrication. Potemkin had built real palaces, real farms and real cities, albeit sometimes still in rather embryo form. What astounded Joseph as they reached the Crimea was that here was a huge new territory only just snatched from the Ottomans and already teeming with energy and glamour in a way quite beyond Habsburg power. Sevastopol had only been founded four years before and yet already had fortifications and a battle fleet. When they weren't trying out tasty new drinks or clowning around in the former Khan of Crimea's palace – where Joseph seems to have bought himself a Circassian slave girl, a rare but almost welcome lapse into mere hypocrisy – there was serious business to be discussed.

Since Joseph had become Holy Roman Emperor in 1765 there had been an astounding and unnerving transformation in the world to the east of Vienna: two entities fundamental to European history for centuries, Poland and the Ottoman Empire, suddenly looked vulnerable. The first to crack was Poland. The eighteenth century had been full of schemes for partition of various European states. Catherine's predecessor, the Tsaritsa Elizabeth, had intended to end the existence of Prussia, splitting it up between its neighbours: a fate Frederick the Great only avoided through her death and one which the kingdom would only miss by inches once Napoleon invaded it. Bits of Italy were always being hacked about or swapped, and Sweden's empire had been liquidated earlier in the century. Poland was different: a big, ancient state whose rulers had held the eastern marches against Tatar raids and who had rescued the Habsburg monarchy in lifting the Siege of Vienna in 1683. The country had been weakened since that high point, not least through its catastrophic seventy-year period of rule by the vainglorious and inept Electors of Saxony.

The Russians simply used the Saxon kings of Poland as puppets. The Poles tried everything to get out of their terrible position, but neither the Prussians to the north-west nor the Russians to the east had an interest in helping them. When the Poles tried to set up a customs service, Frederick the Great built a fort on the Vistula to fire on the customs vessels. Frederick also entertained himself by flooding Poland with debased fake coinage as a technocratic way of destroying its economy. By the mid-eighteenth-century wars Russian and Prussian troops simply ignored Poland's sovereignty, marching across its lands, requisitioning and plundering without reference to the authorities.

The chaos, bitterness and bad faith came to a head in 1773. Surrounded by stronger states, its economy in ruins and its towns actually shrinking at a time when much of the rest of Europe was booming, Poland was carved up between Prussia, Russia and Austria. The term 'the First Partition' sounds rational and almost surgical, but it was achieved with enormous violence against heavy Polish resistance. Engineered principally by Frederick the Great, the partition took the form of Prussia cutting out a block of land in the north-west and the Russians a far larger, but more thinly settled piece in the east. Maria Theresa was unhappy about the idea (justifiably, given that it was a moral outrage) but in the end she, Joseph and particularly her key adviser Kaunitz could not resist such enrichment and took a broad chunk of territory in the south-east, running along the far side of the Carpathians. This removed about a third of Poland's territory and rendered the remains, which were now to all practical purposes a Russian protectorate, unviable.

We do not know the details of the discussions that Joseph had with Catherine as they meandered down through the Crimea, but once the first partition had gone by without incident (and no European power had objected) there was little reason not to grab the rest. Both Catherine and Joseph could see the possibility of further happy pickings. The interesting question lay in whether or not they could successfully cooperate, or whether they might wind up as enemies. In the short to medium term both sides concluded that there was more than enough cake for everyone. Indeed as the French Revolution and its aftershocks came to dominate all other events, the rest of Poland disappeared almost unnoticed by the wider world, with two further partitions disposing of it – the second not involving the Habsburgs, but the third giving them a huge new area stretching almost to Warsaw.

The issue of the Ottoman Empire was what really enthralled Catherine and which now tempted her to dream of enormous projects. The highly satisfactory Treaty of Küçük Kaynarca in 1774 had opened the way to her snatching the Crimea. She now explained to Joseph her new plans: to create a Kingdom of Dacia out of the eastern Balkans and a Byzantine kingdom at Constantinople, ruled by her grandson, helpfully called Constantine in anticipation. She and Potemkin had already celebrated the Greek heritage which Russia laid claim to by renaming the Crimean Khanate the Taurida Governate and founding or renaming towns with Greek names: Sebastopol (venerable city), Simferopol (useful city), Yevpatoria (a title of Mithradates VI) and so on. It was a mad project, but there seemed little to stop it and each new, enormous accretion of Russian territory made the next jump logical. Joseph returned to Vienna shaken and impressed, confronted by the issue which would dominate the Habsburgs' nightmares until their own lands were in turn partitioned in 1918. He was of course well aware that Prussia had been out of control for decades, so this was a given and Frederick the Great's further aggrandizement in Poland just depressing. But his truly horrible realization was that an independent Poland, however compromised, had been a valuable barrier of sorts and that inviting Russia so far west was a serious mistake. The Kingdom of Dacia did not sound appealing either as it would control the mouth of the Danube which, once cleared of its current unhelpful Ottoman owners, had the potential to become the Habsburgs' key trade route. Were the Habsburgs in danger of being permanently boxed in by a monster?

Bound by alliance with Russia, immediately Joseph reached

home he was faced by a renewed Ottoman war. Constantinople had sensibly decided it should attack first rather than just wait for the Russians to chew it up again. Joseph marched into the Balkans at the head of an enormous army of some two hundred and fifty thousand men, full of chiliastic dreams about trumping Catherine's vision. Unfortunately the army rapidly began to get ill and to starve – at least thirty thousand men died in the first year just of disease – and seemed set to achieve nothing. Joseph himself became very ill and returned to Vienna, where he died in 1790. He lived long enough to hear of a sensational series of Russian victories and then a Habsburg one, the successful storming of Belgrade. These events were marked by no fewer than five celebratory pieces by Mozart and then a *Te Deum* in St Stephen's Cathedral, attended by a very unwell and chagrined Joseph, who had prepared all his life to lead his great, dynastic army to glory and found himself instead coughing in Vienna.

The Ottoman Empire was now finished as a serious menace to Austria and the principal shield-of-Europe purpose of the monarchy for some three hundred years came to an end. But, as usual, you have to be careful what you wish for and the Habsburgs now owned simply a new, impoverished, hard-to-defend block of Balkan land. This bound them, just as carved-up Poland did, to Russian goodwill at the same time as they were desperate to keep Russia away from the Danube. The collapse of the Ottomans also had curious implications for the Holy Roman Empire. The Habsburgs' call on the resources of Germany had been as Christendom's front line and countless Germans had fought on the eastern frontier. There were many reasons for the Holy Roman Empire to collapse in the decade after the old frontier shut down, but it is nonetheless curious that it should have been so soon. A similar dynamic can be seen in 1914, with the last Ottoman troops leaving most of the southern Balkans only a year before the beginning of the First World War. It is as though Constantinople provided a sort of discipline to Central Europe which, once removed, resulted not in the fruits of peace but in imbecilic mayhem.

Joseph, as he lay dying, was horrified to hear that his younger sister Maria Antonia (Marie Antoinette) was now under house arrest in Paris – but the responsibility for dealing with this would lie with his descendants.

CHAPTER NINE

'Sunrise'

Joseph II spent his reign at the heart of a gimcrack, exhausting machine of his own invention, which required him to pull all the levers and crank all the handles. It was as though he was personally atoning for all his predecessors' blank-faced lack of interest in administrative reform. The effort killed him and there is something a bit mad and depressing about the whole performance. His view of himself as 'first commoner', albeit a first commoner who had to be unquestioningly obeyed in all things, led to any number of humiliations. Most enjoyable perhaps was his insistence on dressing in simple military uniform, which once resulted when he was walking outside St Stephen's Cathedral in a priest sidling up to sell him pornographic pictures – which put the priest pretty much at the eye of the storm of all Joseph's hang-ups.

But setting aside all the hectoring and oddness these inconsistencies had some happy results. Joseph's enthusiasm for promoting new German opera resulted in Mozart's *The Escape from the Seraglio*, the opera's jokey Turkism itself an indicator of the Ottomans' declining threat status. Then a further change of mind resulted in a more traditional switch back to Italian and Joseph's personal authorization for *The Marriage of Figaro*, a story whose subversiveness is now almost invisible but at the time seemed a swingeing attack on the aristocracy, and therefore in line with Joseph's own loopy antagonisms. The opera's commission could not have been more traditionally Habsburg – a couple of bright outsiders of a kind who would have been familiar to Rudolph II, the Venetian Lorenzo da Ponte and the Salzburger Mozart. This wonderful magic box remains Joseph's great gift to the world – a softened adaptation of a scathing French play that had notionally been set in Spain (i.e. 'not France'), and turned into an Italian opera still set in Spain (i.e. 'not the Habsburg monarchy'), but which in performance is almost always relocated to a patently Viennese milieu. Joseph's world of short wigs and buckled shoes, all that quite dashing pre-Revolution flummery, is permanently preserved through the accident of its being hitched to a stream of the most beautiful, various and heartbreaking music and singing ever conjured up.

Vienna's ability to attract a disproportionately large percentage of great composers, meaning perhaps ten people in a couple of centuries, is striking. Certain cultures at particular times provide the right facilities – the connoisseurship, the range of players, singers, copyists, venues, instrument-makers and, of course, audiences. Much of this is very alien to us. Our far, far broader access to such music makes us oblivious to how different the circumstances were under which it first appeared. In many cases it was exclusively for aristocratic audiences, or often for almost no audience at all, with a string quartet perhaps produced simply for one patron's personal needs, or a piece designed for a specific player to unfurl in front of some tiny group.

This can be seen most clearly in the career of Joseph Haydn, much of which was spent tucked away in the private employment of the mighty Esterházy family on their estates south-east of Vienna. Here Haydn churned out a simply baffling, almost frightening, amount of music to order. A friend once gave me a boxed set of every one of Haydn's symphonies and even these are unmanageable – like a nightmare where you are trying to cram into your mouth a sandwich the size of a dinner table. I have now spent years trying to take these pieces in, some four hundred movements of music, and it cannot be done. People have done their best to help – they have numbered and ordered them and some have jaunty nicknames ('the Clock', 'the Hen', 'Hornsignal', 'la Chasse'), but the sheer scale defeats even these well-meaning efforts. Some of the symphonies are in practice quite boring and reek of loveless background music for the aristocratic soirées of yesteryear, with brocaded people who have not washed for quite a while kissing hands, fluttering fans and peering through quizzing-glasses. You can hit a really rough patch where you suddenly feel you have overdosed on lavender-flavoured comfits. But it is always worth persevering as something will turn up – a trio that sounds like an overheard, melancholy field-song (67th), a grand blaze of sound which is just right (75th), a strange droning that sounds like Sibelius (88th). It just goes on and on – there's a bit that sounds like the opening of *The Valkyries*, another like nineteenth-century French salon music – but a lot of it, fair enough, sounds like Haydn.

This sheer productivity swamps everything – spectacular piano trios, a great sequence of string quartets, a hundred and seventy-five works for baryton (a defunct kind of bass viol favoured in Esterházy circles), operas, masses, a whole pile of concertos, piano sonatas, scores to accompany a marionette theatre – it is the high road to madness to try to encompass all this stuff. I love his music, but it is a bit disconcerting to realize that you could *die in extreme old age* and still only be familiar with a mere handful of the baryton trios. In that sense his own oeuvre becomes a deeply considered meditation on human frailty, even beyond his own Catholic devotion.

He lived so long that he tipped over into a Napoleonic world very remote from his roots in traditional Austria, one in which he became extremely famous and rich. But this came from the mere chance of living so long. One oddity is his extraordinary work *The Seven Last Words of Christ on the Cross*, written for orchestra but with versions for string quartet, oratorio and a stark piano transcription. In a sort of welter of traditional devotional feeling of a kind Joseph II would have bristled at, Haydn tried to dramatize in music each of Jesus's final exclamations ('Father, forgive them, for they know not what they do' and so on), a commission for the highly severe Good Friday ceremonies in Cadíz cathedral. It is austere to the point of comedy, and is perhaps the last link in those near private sacred works like Biber's *Rosary Sonatas* which had been used to channel the meditations of the Bishop of Salzburg over a century before. One of Beethoven's teachers summed up a

new scepticism by daring to suggest that Haydn's setting of
the words 'I thirst' in practice did very little to convey Jesus's
need for a drink. But then, there always seems to be a comment
one can point to which appears to mark the end of traditional
Habsburg Catholic devotion – and along comes Bruckner, or
Webern.

Without doubt something is waved goodbye to in Haydn's
time, with his comparative isolation preserving forms of baroque
piety hammered elsewhere by Joseph II. A perfect place to observe
this is in Eisenstadt, where Haydn spent so many years of his life.
This is a very sleepy town, part of an old, now drained swampland
focused on the sprawling, surreally unpleasant Neusiedler Lake at
the linguistic frontier where Germans and Hungarians bump into
each other (as perfectly expressed by Franz Liszt/Liszt Ferenc
being born down the road). A highly contested part of the world,
as can be imagined, everything just peters out – into the forests,
into the scuzzy lake, into bleak and tiny villages, an effect much
exacerbated by the old line of the Cold War Anti-Fascist Protection Barrier. It will take many more years before the normal
circulation of people can be re-established, or perhaps the enforced
doziness will become permanent.

Eisenstadt is the home of the 'Mountain Church' where Haydn
was finally buried. The church is a classic of severe Jesuit teaching,
featuring a 'holy staircase' whereby the devotee clambers ever
upward through heaps of tufa, past statue groups dramatizing the
principal acts of the Passion. First put together in 1701, these have
been much patched and repainted and gone through periods of
being so unfashionable that they then required serious repairs. The
tableaux seem as distant from any realistic form of worship as can
be imagined, and yet they clearly fill the same religious world as
The Seven Last Words of Christ on the Cross. For me the highlight
was the scene of Jesus's clothes being split up among the soldiers,
a scene much enlivened by the spiders' webs which filled the
soldiers' fingers.

As a church owned by the Esterházy family, it seemed a good
place to bury Haydn, but he suffered many indignities to get

there. After his death a couple of crackpots stole his head to prove various phrenological theories,* and he was buried with a substitute skull to make it all more dignified. Eventually the real one re-emerged and was donated to the Musikverein in Vienna in 1895. Prince Paul Esterházy in the 1930s managed to find a sculptor so sensationally retro and backward in his enthusiasms (Oskar Thiede) that he could put together a plausibly early nineteenth-century-style tomb for Haydn and he was reburied there in 1932 but still without his real head. Esterházy was subject to a nightmarish show-trial in Budapest after the War and imprisoned until the Hungarian Revolution when he was able to escape abroad. In the meantime, in 1954, the head was at last secured, the tomb re-opened and Haydn was complete for the first time since shortly after his death. In a final, very peculiar twist it was decided to keep the 'original' head there too as it had, after all, been caught up in the first obsequies and retained a sacred enough tinge that it could not really be chucked away. So Haydn now rests easy in Eisenstadt, surrounded by a political framework at an almost mad distance from his own, but with the familiar holy staircase still circling above his heads. Tittle-tattle about a composer's corpse is a shameful diversion, when all that really matters is to put on the opening of the 'Sunrise' Quartet, or the second movement of the catchily named String Quartet in G Major, Op. 64, No. 4, Hob. III: 66 – and be completely happy.

An interlude of rational thoughtfulness

Joseph's death was followed by the short, strange interlude of his brother's reign as Leopold II – a two-year patch of capable, flexible and thoughtful rule almost without precedent within the family. In fact it might not be too exaggerated to say that he was the first

---

* And indeed his skull *did* show a pronounced bump of excellence in the area devoted to music – the sheer stupidity of phrenology must make us freeze with anxiety about the dim things we unthinkingly buy into today.

genuinely shrewd and resourceful (but not disturbing) Habsburg
ruler since Ferdinand I a quarter of a millennium earlier. His completely pointless death (ushered in by doctors messing around with
him in an unknowingly dirty and infecting way) marked him out
too as the last ever genuinely shrewd and resourceful (but not disturbing) Habsburg ruler. His successors were a narrow dullard, a
simpleton, a narrow dullard and a non-entity, and those four get us
to 1918. It is lucky that the interest of the story does not rely on
these figures as otherwise the remainder of this book would be a
trackless waste.

The mayhem of the 1790s tends naturally to focus on France
and its Revolution, but there is an equally strong argument for
seeing a Europe-wide failure in this period which more broadly
promoted irresponsibility and chaotic aggression. In the short time
since the glory days of helping the United States gain independence, France had collapsed as a great power – demoralized,
humiliated and financially broken down – and this had provided a
peculiar and unaccustomed space for Austria and Prussia to muck
about in without fear of French vengeance. Indeed one of the
motors of the French Revolution was a new sense of national
rather than merely dynastic humiliation: that the Grande Nation's
borders were being mocked by countries who would have previously shown much greater respect – most egregiously the Prussian
invasion of the Dutch Republic in 1787 and the Habsburg crushing of revolution in the Austrian Netherlands in 1790.

Joseph II's endless schemes to swap around bits of territory and
generally use the Holy Roman Empire as a sort of goody-bag had
ravaged the political systems along the Rhine and to the east in
ways which also affronted and confused France. He was also well
on the way to wrecking the 'magic circle' which had until then
generally protected the painfully vulnerable religious states and
their tiny confederates. If in the east the Holy Roman Emperor
wanted to sweep away feudal privileges and stamp out old-style
clerical parasitism, then in the west the French Revolution favoured
a far more extreme version of the same thing. The now friendless
little states in between Paris and Vienna could perhaps be fed to

any predator who made the right deal. The protections formerly available because a micro-ruler owned the nicely displayed bone of a saint, or traditionally held up a proud old banner during coronation ceremonies, suddenly seemed a bit threadbare.

Prussian and Habsburg involvement in the First Partition of Poland was also an assault on an existing sovereign state of a kind which would have made the ghost of Louis XIV turn green with envy. He had waded through an ocean of blood just to snatch some grim bits of the Pas-de-Calais, while Vienna had with almost no effort at all tacked on a new territory almost the size of Portugal. All these changes (so many originating in Vienna) meant that any taboo on the wholesale shunting about of territory was long gone well before Revolutionary France began to work its spell. From a British perspective it is very hard not to feel that in the ensuing melee the states that wound up as allies of Revolutionary and Napoleonic France were merely greedy and corrupt traitors. But the land-grab mayhem that dissolved the Holy Roman Empire had a back-dated logic.

Joseph's death left this mess to Leopold. The latter's rule really could not have been more heavily compromised by his brother's actions. Threatened and disliked, its moral authority shot and facing highly destabilizing threats from every side, both as ruler of the Habsburg lands (from February 1790) and as Holy Roman Emperor (from September), Leopold had to remake his office. The French Revolution itself was initially greeted by many European monarchs not as a shocking assault on the nature of kingship, but as a hilarious further implosion of a once-hegemonic rival. As it became clear that this was a most unfortunate misperception Leopold became concerned about the fate of his sister Marie Antoinette, but not concerned to overturn the Revolution. Indeed, a basic problem with each of the Coalitions that faced France was, right until the end, a vagueness as to what the desired outcome really might be. Nobody was interested in marching in to fix up a fresh, powerful, French super-state of a kind that had existed within living memory. And it was by definition impossible to fine-tune something which would be coherent and yet somehow oddly

unthreatening without direct control over Paris, which the final
Coalition would not achieve until 1814. As it was, the shambolic
French state which emerged from the Revolution would be
knocked into shape by Napoleon, thus ending the uncertainty and
anarchism, but not quite in the way the Habsburgs had in mind.

Before his premature death Leopold reorganized Vienna's
position, bought off his many enemies and prepared for war, but
missed out on subsequent and embarrassing developments. Perhaps
his key role was in ending the war with Turkey at the Treaty of
Sistovo in August 1791. Unknown to him, this treaty marked the
last of the wars which had shaped almost the entire course of his
dynasty, from Ferdinand I's first frantic improvisation of the Military Frontier. It is odd really that only a few months later the last
talented Habsburg was dead. A critical element at Sistovo, now the
Danubian Bulgarian town of Svishtov, was the decision to hand
back Belgrade to the Turks. This gesture was designed to be
generous enough to ensure that fighting could come to an end
and troops move to France, but it had head-spinning and quite
unintended consequences. If Belgrade had been part of the new
Habsburg Empire as it emerged during the following decade, then
not only would Vienna have controlled the only major hub in the
northern Balkans, but the Serbs would have become an important
group in the Empire much like the Czechs, rather than just a small
element in parts of Hungary. The history of the nineteenth century
then takes a dazingly different turn. As it was, the Serbs soon
revolted and pushed the Turks out of Belgrade on their own. This
formed the kernel of an independent state that would never have
been allowed to exist if it had still been under Habsburg rule. But
this shows the limits of counterfactual history – a contentious, but
seemingly not earth-shaking decision back in 1791 to hand back
a shattered fortress to the Turks put Serbia on a course which
ended in the killing of Franz Ferdinand in 1914 and the destruction of four empires. But what direction a Habsburg-ruled Serbia
– bitterly and ferociously achieved only in 1915–18 – would have
taken is too vague, unknowable and complex to be interesting.

Leopold's death resulted in his negligible and depressing son becoming Franz II. While it is unfair and unsophisticated to lumber him with the entire blame for the avalanche of setbacks which followed, he certainly did not help. The clever, flexible gestures which had allowed Leopold to fix what had been almost messianic Prussian hostility were quite beyond him. In a system where the Emperor had such a crucial role, Franz's inability to visualize it convincingly had without doubt some impact on the sequence of fruitless one-sided defeats which decorate so many French battle-paintings and the lovely, full-colour *The West Point Atlas of the Wars of Napoleon* which I have on my desk as I type.

Defeat by Napoleon, part one

It would burst the bounds of this book to try to track the course of the coalition wars that followed. Indeed, I was just flicking through the queen of travel guides, the *Baedeker's Austria-Hungary* of 1911 (a possible strap-line: 'the last edition – ever!'), shaking my head in disbelief at the futility of trying to encapsulate so much in just one book when I suddenly felt the icy Fingers of Hubris touch me in a premonitory sort of way. But, smiling bravely and paying no attention to the fingers, I need to keep moving ahead.

The Allied effort remained for many years doomed, not just by French brilliance but, as mentioned, by Allied failure to come up with a new political idea which they could impose *if they were to be so lucky* as to defeat France. There was a good reason why in 1805 Napoleon could entertain himself by riding his horse up the Imperial staircase in the Habsburg abbey of Göttweig en route to occupy Vienna, rather than Franz doing something similar – and yet lugubrious and sprezzatura-free – at the Louvre. The British avoided this political problem by focusing on naval and colonial derring-do and feeding off their own generalized, deep-seated antagonism to France. The Habsburgs, and whichever luckless allies were also going down in flames that time round, did not have this luxury. France had not been successfully invaded for many centuries and on 20 September 1792 this formidable record was added

to by the repulse of Prussian and Imperial forces at the Battle of
Valmy. The battle itself was a Pythonesque shambles, but however
woeful to students of strategy, Valmy and its resulting retreat were
decisive. It was the only shot the anti-French coalition would get
at stamping out the Revolution and their timidity then raised the
curtain on twenty-two years of fighting. It would take the deaths
of many hundreds of thousands of men and the reshaping of most
of Europe before Coalition forces would at last grind their way
through the hundred miles that separated Valmy from Paris.

Post-Valmy, French forces more or less wandered at will into
the Holy Roman Empire and set about a series of political changes
that must have made more thoughtful Habsburg historians and
military leaders sob with rage. The giant wars that had shaped
western Europe since the time of the War of the League of Augsburg all seemed mocked by a sequence of events that had French
armies, despite isolated setbacks, racing through the Low Countries
and to the Rhine. Where were Eugene and Marlborough now?
The British had a shot at taking Dunkirk and, in a rare instance of
direct Austro-British cooperation in the field, were in the autumn
of 1793 both defeated by the French. But British motives in
wanting to pick up Dunkirk were almost comically political and
contributed nothing to any imagined defeat of the French. The
encircling of France by enemies, however ineffective, aided further
radicalization in Paris and the issue of Marie Antoinette's safety
was at last resolved with her guillotining shortly after the Dunkirk
disaster. In the following summer the Allies were cleaned out of
what could now only very inaccurately be described as the Austrian Netherlands at the Battle of Fleurus, where an Imperial,
Dutch and British force of seventy thousand men was devastated
by the French, with the Coalition retreating through Waterloo,
curiously. The Dutch Republic was now invaded and at the Peace
of Basel in April 1795 France got the western bank of the Rhine
too, again once a quite unrealizable dream of the Bourbon monarchy. Surely some of the surviving members of the dynasty must
have relished this at least a *bit*.

Now the dithering, faithlessness and incapacity of the Allies really came into play – at least as important as French success. Franz looked on in horror as the Prussians were bought off, with the French allowing them to create a sort of neutral protectorate over northern Germany, Prussia having already taken another piece of Poland. Prussian importance had now vastly increased thanks to the Revolution. Only months after the Peace of Basel, Prussia, Austria and Russia cooperated to dispose of the final pieces of Poland. Even if moral issues can be set aside – and it could be argued that Poland was so riddled with Russian influence that the options were only partition between the three powers, or a total Russian grab – the action meant that any French move, however outrageous, was happening in a world of comparable outrageous moves. The Battle of Fleurus was to be the last, lamentable outing for the Imperial forces and, even if it survived formally a little longer, the Holy Roman Empire was now up for grabs, with the role of its Emperor teetering close to the edge of redundancy.

Franz continued to fight and in May 1795 a new treaty with Britain flooded the Austrians with money, but now the enterprising young Napoleon made waking up each morning in Vienna and reaching for a newspaper something to be dreaded. The Austrians had a consistent problem with the Alps – armies had to be sent both north of them, through southern Germany, and south of them, through Italy to attack the French without the risk of the unguarded route being wide open to Vienna. But this meant splitting forces with no chance of mutual reinforcement. Sadly, the problem did not seem so vexing for the French as they sent armies by both routes themselves too and defeated the Austrians. 1797–8 saw total mayhem, with such enormities as new republics being carved out of Italy, the Pope in a French gaol and the destruction of Venice.

The Treaty of Campo Formio saw Austria expelled from western Europe, but also tempted into partnership with France. Napoleon's sweeping away of the Venetian Republic removed another historic constant in Habsburg life – the large bloc that both kept Vienna from the Adriatic but also, and very usefully, provided a neutral, rotting wedge between the Alps and the sea.

As the southern Netherlands and the bits and pieces of Habsburg patrimony in the Black Forest disappeared for ever, these might be replaced by fresh territories with a new focus remote from French interests: in Istria, Dalmatia and Venice itself. Culturally this was sensible enough: Venice had always been a key source of ideas, artists, money and trade for the Habsburgs and the coastal territories made sense of the previously somewhat joke port of Trieste, as well as having ethnic links with Slavonia and the rest of the Military Frontier. The Habsburgs were now at peace with France and still ruled a geographically massive European state, but their rule had been warped and remade in a humiliating, shameful way.

Defeat by Napoleon, part two

The inexhaustible pleasures available in Vienna's Military History Museum* include some absolutely prime Napoleonic Wars material. Enormous plaster statues, flags and battle paintings loom through the murk and the walls are hung with implausibly chirpy engravings of crowds cheering the Emperor Franz who, even in the most oleaginous propaganda pieces, looks coldly unpleasant. One striking little survival is a French poster from the aftermath of the abortive Congress of Rastatt at the end of 1799. This classic of Revolutionary language announces the assassination of the French delegates Bonnier, Roberjot and Debry by the Austrian government: 'THEIR BLOOD REEKS . . . IT DEMANDS . . . AND IT WILL *OBTAIN* . . . VENGEANCE!' It all seems a long way from the tinkly pleasantries of the good old days. The delegates' deaths were never properly explained as those concerns were swept away as the War of the Second Coalition broke out, a serious Austro-Russian attempt to crush the French. The discussions at Rastatt began a process over several years which made it ever clearer that

---

*   An amazing institution which will pop up at irregular intervals from now on, more usually called by its bristlingly off-putting German name of the Heeresgeschichtliches Museum.

the Holy Roman Empire was at an end and the Habsburg role was en route to dissolution. Instead of creating a united front against France, German rulers (including the Habsburgs) began chucking about ancient territories like confetti, with the rulers of Bavaria and Württemberg particularly behaving like children at a sugar-heavy picnic. No political boundary offered surety of any kind and duplicitous aggression was the only possible alternative to absolute extinction. All over Europe rulers were either hiding jewels in strange places and disguising their families as implausibly soft-palmed servants, or they were coming up with new designs for palaces and coronation robes, depending on the latest news.

The French themselves had innumerable territorial options and over the coming years Napoleon would inherit the Revolutionary pleasure in fiddling with maps and constitutions, conjuring up such entities as the Parthenopean Republic and then – just as casually – dropping them. Like the Fat Boy in *Pickwick Papers*, the French were always careful to keep some food in their mouths, so that whenever they woke up they could immediately start chewing. One bitter horror for Franz II was the effortless French invasion of Switzerland in 1798. The country that had so humiliated Maximilian I was brought into the orbit of Paris with just a few menacing troop movements and some clever bribes. Even worse was the tightening French grip on the 'Batavian Republic', as the Netherlands had become – the country which had been the nemesis of the Spanish Habsburgs, the focus of a multi-generational conflict that had frittered all the wealth of the Americas, now fell to France with barely a squeak.

The summer of 1799 was momentarily all excitement for the Habsburgs and Russians, who devastated northern Italy and southern Germany, and seemed to offer a serious threat to France. This was the beginning of the cult of Archduke Karl, Franz's younger brother, the commander whose enormous statue stands with Prince Eugene's as one of only two in the symbolically threadbare and incomplete Heroes Square in Vienna. Archduke Karl features in a thousand engravings and was the toast of the Empire, but it was in the context of everyone else being *even worse* rather than for any notable acumen. Compared to some of his rivals (such as the despairingly witless General Mack, humiliated by Napoleon at Ulm) he was a sort of Alexander the Great, but when lined up with figures such as Barclay de Tolly, Masséna, Wellington or – above all by a mile – Napoleon, he is barely a footnote. His achievement was very occasionally to win a battle but his victories only ever proved to be preludes to another fiasco. It could be that his enormous, hyper-charged statue in Heroes Square is there as a subtle, thoughtful meditation on human limits and as a bitter warning to his successors about the frailty of Habsburg power, but this seems unlikely.

Despite its very temporary successes in the summer of 1799, a looming, headachy problem for Vienna also lay in the nature of her allies. It would be possible to write a whole book about the peculiar nature of Europe's geography and its role in ruining every attempt by a single state to turn the continent into a China or an Ottoman Empire. But, keeping the issue under some kind of control, it is without doubt the case that the mixture of barriers scattered across Europe, whether mountains or seas, has had far more impact on the continent's history than religion, ideology, specific national virtues and so on. In 1800 France presented, as usual, staggering problems for any invader. Most of its frontiers were sealed off by seas or mountains and it had the luxury of active fronts which faced onto a rubble of ineffective small states as well as being protected by Alpine passes and Rhine forts. Any Austrian or Russian invaders would somehow have to get past them even before they got to tangle with that year's *levée en masse* of a further four hundred thousand highly motivated and well-led French soldiers.

Two of France's principal enemies, Britain and Russia, appeared in turn effectively impossible to invade, with Britain's geography and money allowing it to pour resources into an infinitely expandable navy, while Russia enjoyed a colossal scale in which invaders simply disappeared. France would test both these defensive systems to their limits, but in both cases they held good. The Habsburg lands by contrast – like the occasional ally Prussia – were vulnerable from pretty much any angle. For years, part of the business of being French was to march across Austrian territory and ravage it as you went. Each of the coalition wars therefore tended to follow a pattern of Britain and/or Russia urging the Austrians on to aggressive military action at no fundamental risk to themselves. The sheer length of the wars and the increasingly Manichean atmosphere in which they were fought makes the reality of the coalitions from Austria's point of view incredibly annoying. The British and the Russians always seemed to be enjoying themselves with issues irrelevant to Austria, while Austria got squashed. Britain kept refusing to commit its own troops to attacking Napoleon and yet always seemed to be able to scrape together the resources to do things like invade Buenos Aires, take over the Cape of Good Hope, or fight the United States, while the Russians would be merrily expanding into the Caucasus or Persia.

The Austrians also had to deal with the profound implications of working out what to do with a Russian ally who, when engaged in western Europe, threatened to swamp Habsburg concerns. Was it a good thing, for example, that Russian soldiers were now marching into such un-Russian parts of Europe as Switzerland? From the British point of view the critical concern was the traditional one of globally crippling France, and these wars effectively ended a century-long global contest in Britain's favour. If the price for Russian support was Russian domination of Central Europe this was (in an eerie preview of 1944–45) fine with Britain. But Vienna had to put up with the practical implications for itself, which were not good. So everybody involved in each new brothers-till-death coalition had reasons to hang back or do a deal.

The very odd (and shortly strangled) Tsar Paul I focused much of his energy on the French treatment of the small island of Malta. Outraged by Napoleon's expulsion of the Knights of St John, Paul himself became Grand Master, and once Britain in turn expelled the French and refused to hand the island to the Knights, Paul withdrew from his already strained alliance with the British. This loopy childishness drove Vienna mad. But it was also chilling to see Russia, under the guise of the Alliance, creeping up ever closer to Austria's own basic interests. Any pleasure felt by the Austrians in despoiling and taking over Venice and its territories was balanced by the Russians taking over (in a leapfrog that would have even given Catherine the Great a happy surprise) the Ionian Islands and Kotor (Cattaro), threatening a future in which Russia had absolute control of the Adriatic. The issue of how on earth to deal with Russia now became an acute one, and indeed the motor for the final century of the Empire's existence, long after Vienna had lost any interest in the future of France.

In a bit over a year absolutely everything went wrong. The Second Battle of Zurich disposed of the Russians in Switzerland; a joint Anglo-Russian attack on Holland went completely wrong; the Brumaire coup brought Napoleon and the Consulate to power in France; the Battle of Marengo ruined the Habsburgs in Italy and the Battle of Hohenlinden did the same for them in southern Germany. The Second Coalition caved in with beautifully uniformed French cavalry only forty miles from Vienna. The resulting Treaty of Lunéville at least gave Vienna full control over the southern Tyrolean territories of Brixen and Trento, a further geopolitical will-o'-the-wisp in the Habsburgs' disastrous nineteenth-century non-destiny in Italy. But these small bits of Alpine picturesque could not hide the principal disaster: that all lands west of the Rhine were now fully incorporated into France, and that the treaty was a general admission of French primacy. From now on it would be Napoleon's decision as to how Europe should be run, without even a residual sense that Franz II was the 'senior ruler'.

Franz II was undoubtedly a feeble figure, but it is unclear if even the toughest of his predecessors could have dealt intelligently with this maelstrom. A striking humiliation of the 'senior ruler' was Napoleon's decision to make himself Emperor in May 1804. This fed into all kinds of Habsburg neuroses. Franz's exact thinking is unrecoverable, but it is fair to say that Napoleon's self-elevation threatened to make Franz the last of his line. The chaos in the Holy Roman Empire had wrecked the traditional structure and made it into *a sauve-qui-peut* mishmash, with Electors vanishing (farewell to Cologne and Trier) and re-emerging elsewhere (Mainz

— but no longer actually *in* Mainz — Salzburg, Württemberg, Hesse-Kassel and Baden). The traditional Catholic Church structure lay in ruins and, of course, the Habsburgs themselves had fatally benefited. Not least they had got their hands on Salzburg, a piece of territory which now seems such a central part of the modern Austria state, but which was then a grab as illegitimate as, say, Poland had been. Salzburg also brought with it the burden that, as an ancient, major ecclesiastical state now gobbled up, it completely sullied and mocked (just as the French intended) any later bid by Vienna to protect the haggard remaining fragments of the Holy Roman Empire. Franz was so aware of this problem that he tried to make the absorption of Salzburg a 'secret clause' in the Treaty — but this just provoked booming laughter — how could the rest of Franz's Catholic friends, or rather *former* friends, *not* know?

The Salzburg issue — along with dozens of others — made clear that a frightening gap had now opened up between family interests and Imperial interests. If the Emperor was meant to protect his hundreds of dependent cities and knights then he was doing a terrible job, as these were incontinently gobbled up in a few weeks of delirium by Napoleon's new German friends. The terrible question now arose as to what the next Imperial election might look like on Franz's death. With a minority now of the Electors being Catholic and Napoleon himself creating a personal gravitational pull without precedent, there was no reason at all to imagine that a Habsburg would even be a serious candidate. Franz now had his one excellent idea: completely illegally and with no precedent he simply announced himself, later in the summer that Napoleon had made himself Emperor of the French, to be the Emperor of Austria. For two further, uneasy years he continued in parallel to be Holy Roman Emperor, but this latter title rapidly became merely the dead outer shell to be shed. After gasps and awkward silences, one by one the other rulers of Europe recognized the new title. As across Germany hundreds of old Habsburg clients had their lands sold and despoiled, as old Imperial symbols were knocked off town halls and city walls, Franz now became thanks to his new title Franz I as well as Franz II — confusingly and uniquely

expressed as Franz I(II). All pretence of looking after the old
Empire was cashed in and a great Habsburg retreat eastwards was
now formalized. Franz was no mere vulnerable archduke in his
personally held lands, but Emperor in his own right, and on a
hereditary basis with no further nonsense about Electors. This
political assertion gave the family another hundred and fourteen
years of power.

Things somehow get even worse

When our children were old enough to take an interest, but still
relatively biddable and portable, we went on several trips to Paris
in the hope that this would inoculate them in favour of France and
give them a graceful ease with both the city and the language in
later life. This worked in only a limited way. Our second son bristled
at the way Parisians could not speak English and were 'sulky' –
both fair points – and I tended to fritter goodwill by coming up
with spontaneous, delusive short cuts for our walks. These generally
turned into route-marches down dusty, evil-smelling and featureless
side streets, enlivened only by occasional umber-faced jack-in-a-
box-like drunkards lurching out at us from doorways. A high point
was reached when the children at last spotted a pizza restaurant
from a British chain, which caused such delight that we spent the
evening eating there rather than tucking into cassoulets. The children
acted as a permanent absurdist pint-size John Bull chorus, applying
our island common sense to everything from the Sainte-Chapelle
to Picasso, with one of the latter's works actually provoking a low
whistle of respect at what he had 'got away with'. All this thoroughly
destroyed the – in any event frail – pretence my wife and I shared
that we were somehow a sort of Belmondo–Seberg team crazily
adrift in the city of alcohol and danger.

We would light-heartedly bring up over breakfast some sort
of cultural destination (the Louvre, the Musée Carnavalet) and
the children's ears would go flat to the sides of their heads, like
threatened cats, clinging to their croissants but alert to danger.

Various compromises would be made about types of food for the day, souvenirs which could be bought and promises not to leave the hotel until late morning: these kept some essentials of the original plan in place, but we shared the common parental problem of wanting some appeal to a higher authority – like the UN – which could find more fully in our favour.

One of our trips was to Les Invalides, where both sons' quiescence was bought by the idea of a museum full of guns, and the daughter's by abusing the fact she was too young to know anything much. The relevance to the Habsburgs of all this is that Les Invalides is the home of their nemesis Napoleon. In a bold gesture designed to shore up his ebbing regime, King Louis-Philippe arranged in 1840 for «*le retour des cendres*» from Napoleon's original burial place on the island of St Helena. In scenes of surely unparalleled nationalist hysteria most of Paris turned out to cheer on the dead man's elaborate cortège. I have never myself been quite clear what I think about Napoleon, but as I ushered my sons into the presence of his quartzite whopper of a tomb, I felt I had underplayed the moment and should have at the very least designed special little cloaks and boots for them and possibly got them to spreadeagle themselves on the marble while I intoned something like, 'I bring you a whole new generation, O Master,' in a sort of Commendatore *basso*. As it happened, we on that occasion had to flee prematurely, as my daughter wandered up to a huge gold vase presented by Tsar Alexander I to his fellow Allies and set off its alarm. The tears of the daughter and exhortations of the guards – it is probably true that she was about to push it over, in an accidental death-to-all-autocrats gesture which would have shaped the rest of her life – made it sensible to leave. But this also meant abandoning any notions I might have had involving lighted torches, a muffled drumbeat and so on. The afternoon ended in an unhappy wrangle in the gift shop over whether a paper-knife in the shape of an antique dagger was a legitimate souvenir, or whether – it could be argued – this made it in all practical senses simply a dagger.

Louis-Philippe's gesture in bringing back Napoleon was an epic blunder as it simply served to heighten the gap between those heroic days and his own low-wattage regime – indeed paving the way for

Napoleon's nephew taking power later in the decade, a figure who
did almost as much damage to the Habsburgs as his uncle.

Napoleon's career will always be in some sense a quite boring
enigma. What was most obvious to contemporaries was his
extraordinary improvisatory energy. But, as we know the outcome,
it unavoidably becomes a story of over-reaching, hubris, futility,
burned-out meteors and so on. It also becomes victors' history –
the almost implacable opposition to Napoleon by the Habsburgs
and the British becomes dogged and heroic rather than merely a
brake on progress and a willingness to see hundreds of thousands
of troops die in futile bids to hold off the forces of the future.

Britain's role is particularly problematic as, by various definitions, it was true that the 'balance of power' pursued by British
leaders meant the 'balance of power in Britain's favour', just as 'free
trade' had a tendency to mean 'free trade in British ships'. In the
end the Anglo-Austrian alliance held, but with Napoleon's destruction it became clear that – in a deeply significant geopolitical shift
– the two countries' concerns were now simply too remote from
one another. The key European motor of the London–Vienna axis,
which had endured spottily ever since the days of William III and
Leopold I, now came to an end. The two countries' interests
simply no longer overlapped except, often bitterly, in relation to
Russia, and they remained substantially at odds until the final and
total estrangement of the First World War.

One summer I quite accidentally found myself repeatedly at the
site of Napoleon's greatest triumph. I had based myself for several
days in Olomouc, only to find that my heart really belonged to
Brno. This resulted in a lot of time spent on buses which, through
sheer good luck, took me along the road down which the Austro-
Russian army marched in December 1805 before being annihilated
by Napoleon at the Battle of Austerlitz. Like all battlefields it,
of course, tells you nothing. Indeed the fields give no more clues
as to what happened than would the sea at Trafalgar, where a
similarly decisive battle had happened a few weeks before. So
shockingly inscrutable was Austerlitz that I abandoned plans to
drive to places like Breitenfeld, Blenheim and Königgrätz, as it

suddenly struck me as absurd to pace up and down various hills trying to establish which group of luckless recruits had stood where. Luckily the casually free-market nature of the modern Czech Republic meant that advertisers at least had taken advantage of the battlefield, and the relatively small monuments were completely dwarfed by a hording for some brand of mineral water that happened to use a Napoleon-style eagle as its symbol and – even better – an advertisement for batteries consisting of a huge artillery piece made out of giant model batteries. These did a lot to perk up the field of destiny, but it seemed a poor strategy to visit further battlefields in the sole hope that I could rely on prankster advertising agencies to do the heavy imaginative lifting.

Austerlitz was a shameful disaster and ended the Third Coalition as well as prostrating the Habsburgs. Franz lost both a block of ancient western Austrian territory to the hated Bavarians and his lightly gained north-east Italian and coastal Adriatic lands to France. Most critically though, the resulting treaty – the Treaty of Pressburg – marked the final gasp of the Holy Roman Empire. Franz agreed that his role in the rest of Germany was now at an end. In practical terms this was merely a final admission, as 1803 had already seen a disgraceful bun-fight called the 'Imperial Recess' at which some hundred and twelve independent ministates, sixty-six ecclesiastical territories and forty-one free cities had been wiped out, absorbed into whichever larger state was both nearby and most pro-Napoleon. On 6 August 1806, Franz II abdicated as Emperor of the Holy Roman Empire, shoving German-speakers into a new world.

The Habsburgs had in many ways been abusive and incompetent in their role, and certainly since Joseph II the Empire had been so messed about as to have become incoherent, but switching from a protector in Vienna to a protector in Paris did little to change the basic problem of German weakness. The Habsburgs had for many generations protected the Germans from the French in the west and the Turks in the east, but this had been a confused blessing as it meant that so many of Europe's battles were fought in German towns of a kind hard to find on a map. The sheer helplessness of people living in places like Essen or Bamberg continued under this fresh dispensation, with the twist that many of their young men would now die invading Russia on behalf of the French rather than being defeated by the French. It was the differing perceptions of what should happen to these people that would be a major theme of Europe's history through to 1870 — and indeed through to 1945, but Austria's role was now to remain limited and provisional.

In the homicidal variant on musical chairs that now followed, hundreds of ancient states vanished almost overnight. Many bishops, knights, dukes, abbesses and petty oligarchs lost out, but others cleverly adapted. There is a funny painting of the young Elector of Bavaria, Maximilian IV Joseph, all dolled up in his wig and jewels, the acme of rococo flummery, which can be contrasted with the surprisingly different painting of him as the brand new (from 1806) *King* of Bavaria, Maximilian I, thanks to Napoleon, sporting his own hair, cut short and severe, and dressed in a dark blue, almost undecorated uniform, faking the stern mien of the simple soldier. This sort of graceless rebranding was going on everywhere.

Franz sat in stunned dullness in Vienna. The Habsburg lands, which can now be called the Habsburg Empire (or, as an acceptable shorthand, 'Austria'), remained an enormous state, but existed only at Napoleon's pleasure. The ghastly fate of Prussia, a ragged, minor French colony since its destruction at the Battle of Jena–Auerstädt in October 1806, was a horrible lesson in just how far Napoleon could go — the equivalent of a gamekeeper nailing the corpse of a crow to a fence to warn other crows off. It was, of course, also extremely annoying in historical terms, as France had managed to wipe out Prussia in a few weeks, something which had eluded Austria since 1740. But Franz's craven sense of caution kept bumping into the problem of hegemony: all attempts by Vienna to treat with Paris as an equal were rebuffed or ignored, for the simple reason that Napoleon did not think for a second that they *were* equals. The new Empire's tattered dignity threatened with each year to slump into mere deliquescence. A final, huge effort was therefore needed and the catastrophic War of the Fifth

Coalition for a few months in 1809 allied Austria and Britain against the whole of Napoleonic Europe. Against a background of almost paralytic gloom and declinist talk, Vienna tried to take on Napoleon, briefly checked him at Aspern-Essling and then went down to absolute defeat at Wagram – beaten not just by the French but by a great array of France's new best friends, such as Bavaria, Saxony and the Confederation of the Rhine. These battles were the largest yet fought and a worrying indicator of future developments. Instead of the often elegant victories of Napoleon's earlier years, Wagram and its successors were afflicted by a crippling gigantism, with almost uncontrollable hordes of under-trained men inflicting horrible, rather random casualties on one another. Wagram ushered in the era of woefully managed slaughterhouses which make nineteenth-century wars (until the Prussians created a new aesthetic in the 1860s) so depressing and unmemorable.

Aspern-Essling was a great personal triumph for the Archduke Karl, and in retrospect it validated everything he had hoped for from the Austrian army and provided the Empire with something to cling to in the bleak times ahead. Just in brackets: one must envy those who had to carry out what must have been one of the handful of truly wonderful jobs in the Austrian army – the successful attempt to prevent part of Napoleon's army crossing the Danube. This was done through the richly enjoyable process of throwing heaps of huge objects into the river upstream so that the flow would hurl them against the French pontoons. There would have been a lot less to relish for Napoleon's engineers, but for the Austrians there must have been scenes of joyous near hysteria as flaming barges, barrels of explosives, gnarled and sharp lumps of handmade flotsam and so on were launched into the current. The *pièce de résistance* must have been when an entire, vast *wooden Danubian floating mill* was set alight and cut loose from its moorings. There are a couple of these magical objects preserved in the great ASTRA Museum of Traditional Folk Civilization in the Dumbrava Forest in southern Transylvania. Incredibly weird and unwieldy, they would ply for trade in the countless, isolated riverside communities, gradually heading east as there was no means

by which they could head back upstream. Anyway, one of these
whoppers came to a glorious end on the morning of 22 May 1809
as, a roaring mass of flame, it hurtled crazily and unstoppably into
the latest French attempt at a pontoon bridge, tearing out a huge
chunk and carrying with it a French general and a number of
pontonniers several miles downstream.

An intimate family wedding

Setting aside floating-mill-based initiatives, the end result of the
campaign was a traditional disaster and the punitive Treaty of
Schönbrunn, the palace chosen as a particularly crushing location
for the heirs of Maria Theresa to sit in. About a fifth of the
Empire's population was handed out, with the loss of Galicia to a
new Polish satellite state, of Salzburg to an ever-cockier Bavaria
and of ancient southern Austrian, Italian and Slovenian lands to
Napoleon's new Illyrian Provinces. With the Empire prostrate,
Franz's advisers felt that there was little choice but to agree to anything Napoleon might ask and hope that they would not suffer the
fate of Prussia. As so often in the past, the core competence turned
out to be dynastic survival at all costs and it was now – in perhaps
the most humiliating moment in an era crowded with humiliating
moments – that the eyes of the court turned on Franz's attractive
teenage daughter Maria Ludovica.

The Augustinian church in Vienna is a classic example of the
strain within the Catholic hierarchy which is highly suspicious of
aesthetic value for its own sake. It is a very ancient, extremely
battered and rather smelly *working* church. A handful of remarkable
monuments are treated as incidental to the overall austerity: it is a
place where monks and congregations go to liaise with their
Maker. The church has an almost Methodist atmosphere in its
refusal to get in the way of direct prayer and serious issues. It is
one of the central Habsburg cultic churches as the Emperors' hearts
are buried there (which, on reflection, doesn't sound overwhelmingly Methodist in its flavour) and it has, since his beatification by

John Paul II in 2004, become the principal site of worship of the Emperor Karl I. But on 11 March 1810 it was the site of the wedding of the Emperor Franz I's favourite daughter, Maria Ludovica, to the Emperor Napoleon I. In an amazing twist Franz's brother, the Archduke Karl, fairly recent victor of Aspern-Essling, stood proxy for Napoleon himself in the ceremony. The ramifications of such an exquisite piece of nastiness almost burst the bounds of this book. Napoleon was, of course, the heir to the French Revolution, an event which had resulted in Karl's aunt Marie Antoinette having her severed head put on a stick in front of a cheering crowd. Marie Antoinette's being packed off to Paris in the first place had been viewed as a disgraceful mistake and came from a long-forgotten earlier pro-French twist in eighteenth-century Habsburg diplomatic history. Maria Ludovica was now being pushed down the same path. Almost as bad, the Augustinian church was already famous for its recently completed monument by Canova to another of Maria Ludovica's aunts, Maria Christina. Maria Christina's cenotaph is perhaps the greatest piece of neo-classicism in Vienna, a wonderful pyramid with stricken mourners and a melancholy lion. Archduke Karl was raised by Maria Christina (who had no children of her own) and her husband, Albert of Saxony, who founded the Albertina art museum.

So Archduke Karl had to solemnly stand at the altar with his niece, in the same spot where so many Habsburgs had been married, and act as proxy for the man who had sprung from events that had murdered his aunt, who had deposed various Habsburgs in Italy, who had spent ten years killing many thousands of Austrian soldiers and humiliating the entire Empire, and had recently taken for himself blocks of territory which Karl's family had owned for over four centuries, the ceremony taking place in the presence of his adoptive mother's memorial. However blackened and desiccated they may have been, the hearts of the former Emperors must surely have convulsed a little in their caskets.

As it happened Maria Ludovica did not have to share the head-on-a-stick setbacks of her great-aunt, instead getting to look sensational in a series of French Imperial gowns, cloaks and tiaras.

Napoleon had married her (having divorced Josephine) because she was posh and because he was anxious to have an heir. The Empress Marie Louise, as she now became, had a son with Napoleon who was proclaimed, in a mockery (by Habsburg criteria) of ancient procedure, as the King of Rome. In a sense it was helpful that Franz I was such a bore as anyone more imaginative would have been driven mad by the idea that a peculiar Corsican who nobody had even heard of until recently could make himself Emperor and threaten to reroute the entire system of succession away from the Habsburg family. Marie Louise had a strange life, partly very enjoyable and partly a pawn of wider forces, with two further husbands after Napoleon (including a fun-sounding equerry) and ruling the Duchy of Parma. It cannot have been easy to be pulled between two families, with every move betraying one or the other. Her much-loved son (very briefly known as Napoleon II) became a sad footnote in royal history – a source of embarrassment but also potential danger to the Habsburgs until his death aged twenty-one from tuberculosis. His extraordinary gold crib in the Habsburg Treasury is a strange reminder of a future that never happened: Napoleon as the founder of a dynasty that ruled a united European super-state. In a peculiar piece of tidying up after the defeat of France, Hitler had Napoleon II's body transferred from Vienna to Les Invalides to be buried near his father. No attempt was made to get hold of his heart, which still sits – in a permanent affront to all the other hearts – in the Augustinian church.

Maria Ludovica's sacrifice on the altar of political expediency came from Franz and his advisers' pathological anxiety, in the wake of the Treaty of Schönbrunn, to save what remained of the Empire from total dismemberment. No humiliation was too great and all flashes of hatred for Napoleon were banned. This worked very well. Nothing the British could do seemed to threaten an end to Napoleon's rule, and so an indefinite future of circumscribed Habsburg watchfulness seemed the only course. It is a fascinating and in some ways plausible counterfactual to think of a permanent Napoleonic Europe, but however many genuine allies the French might have had across the continent, there was something about

Napoleon's default fighting mode which made the whole structure deeply unstable. His ruinous decision in 1812 to invade Russia was entirely logical, as was his inability to come to terms with Britain. Paris, London and St Petersburg all shared nigh-on Mongol superiority complexes, each of which was incompatible with the others and much of world history was to stem from this (with Berlin added in later) until the 1940s. It is very hard for the panoply of ideas associated with being head of an Empire to coexist with others who, by their very existence, mock and undermine your own absolute claims.

The invasion of Russia had all the signs of being the triumph that would seal Napoleon's greatness and potentially bring the entire generation-long war to an end, with a defeated Russia giving France the ability to destroy British India at leisure and thereby force Britain to sue for peace. The Habsburgs managed to limit their engagement with the Grande Armée to providing thirty thousand men to threaten Russia in the south. Once it was clear the invasion had gone absolutely and catastrophically wrong a new coalition became possible and the Austrians cautiously linked up with the Prussians and Russians. This extraordinary change in fortunes resulted in Austria dominating the Sixth Coalition. With Prussia important but relatively small and Russia operating a huge distance from its home base – and with the British as usual following a different agenda – Franz and his chief minister Metternich found themselves much to their surprise, and not entirely through their own efforts, in a position to dictate the future of Europe. The years of peace had been spent by Austria steadily building up an enormous if not very good army of well over half a million men and it had easily the largest contingent in the Coalition. All these soldiers now simply swamped the French – however brilliantly Napoleon manoeuvred he could not deal with this fundamental reversal in the maths. The Battle of Leipzig in October 1813 saw some six hundred thousand troops crashing into each other, the largest encounter in European history before 1914. In a series of truly horrible battles over the following months both sides suffered grotesque losses, but the French could no longer afford these. The strange interlude of Napoleon's banishment to Elba (a tiny island, once part of the Tuscan Habsburgs' patrimony) and his frantic 'Hundred Days' attempt to re-establish himself in France may have ended with the Battle of Waterloo, but even if Napoleon had won that battle he was faced with an infinity of Austrian, Prussian and Russian troops all marching west and making this final bid for power utterly futile.

I apologize for having written so much about warfare and diplomacy and I will try to offer a break from this for a while. The Habsburg Empire that came out of this process was very different from its predecessor, larger but more compact, with a formidable group of allies with a shared conservative agenda, and also a shared wish to forget all the terrible things that had recently gone wrong. As so much of the fighting was so humiliating, the Napoleonic Wars had an uncertain place in the regime's sense of itself. There are a scattering of big monuments to the major figures, but the main business of Franz I seems to have been to proceed with the remainder of his reign pretending none of this stuff had happened. A permanent monument was Haydn's 'Emperor's Hymn', written in 1797 and adopted during what turned out to be only one of many crises, as a peculiarly beautiful and uplifting song of hope:

> God save Franz the Emperor, our good Emperor Franz!
> Long live Franz the Emperor in the brightest splendour of bliss!
> May laurel branches bloom for him, wherever he goes, as a
>   wreath of honour.
> God save Franz the Emperor, our good Emperor Franz!

If ever someone deserved this less it was the gloomy policeman Franz, but the tune (reused magically by Haydn in his 'Emperor' Quartet) took on a life of its own. It became the great English hymn 'Glorious things of thee are spoken', and following what one can only imagine were a number of nervous breakdowns, it was successfully and scanningly translated it into every language of the Habsburg Empire. And finally, as the German national anthem, it was rewritten first to start with what would come to be seen as the chilling assertion:

> Germany, Germany above everything,
> Above everything in the world

and then reconditioned after the world wars so it starts with the much nicer:

> Unity and justice and freedom
> For the German fatherland!

Back to nature

On 24 May 1801, during a welcome break from being beaten up by Napoleon, the Habsburgs enjoyed one of the great cultural events of the new century, the first full performance of Haydn's oratorio *The Seasons* at the Schwarzenberg Palace in Vienna. The soprano role was taken by the Empress herself, not terribly well, but nobody was in a position to suggest she should be replaced by someone else. *The Seasons* became a pan-European sensation with countless performances in every conceivable type of venue, sometimes with that early nineteenth-century equivalent of wide-screen or 3D for movies: the pointless doubling up or tripling up of vocal or musical parts, making the closing ecstatic hymn to God's grace perhaps the loudest human sound yet invented outside the battle-field.

The hysteria around this event was stoked by its being, in the dumbest way, a sequel. Haydn's *Creation* had been a vast success, pushed for by a group of visionaries in Vienna who wished to revive the public religious works of 'old music', meaning Bach but above all Händel. Together with his late symphonies these pieces made Haydn a universal celebrity of a new kind, anticipating Beethoven and deliriously crowning a career which had so largely been spent in the restricted and private world of the Esterházy family. The chief genius behind *The Creation* was Gottfried van Swieten, a multi-talented sometime civil servant, composer and librarian and one of those facilitative figures who make all cultural life possible and yet who tend to fall away from any lasting public recognition.

Van Swieten and his wealthy associates had racked their brains as to how Haydn could cap *The Creation*, a difficult act to follow by all sorts of criteria. They eventually settled on James Thomson's pantheistic long poem *The Seasons*, which van Swieten hacked to bits to provide a suitable array of incidents for Haydn to set. The two hours of elaborate and varied music of *The Seasons* turned out to be Haydn's last major effort and he finished it in a blur of fatigue and mental decay. After an enormously long, varied and marvellous career, the man who would have a fair claim to win any Best Habsburg Subject contest was at last collapsing.

The Creation and *The Seasons* became for the Empire a sort of extension of the normal religious experience (just as Händel's oratorios did in Britain), ritualistic elements in the calendar comparable to major feast days. *The Seasons* is, like all sequels, less good than the original. Haydn himself complained that some of it was just 'Frenchified rubbish', particularly hating the music he was obliged to write imitating frogs on a pond (which is, of course, charming). The score has many wonders – a thunderstorm, a riotous hunting party – but it is perhaps too schematic to have any real forward movement (is it autumn yet?), although it could be said that *The Creation* has the most schematic subject of all and nobody complains.

There may well be later examples, but *The Seasons* is a sort of nostalgic summary of centuries of Habsburg nature-worship. Its concerns are relentlessly old-fashioned and conservative, as carefully vetted representatives of the rural community sing about their place and function – sowing and reaping, picking fruit, spinning flax. Like scenes in medieval miniatures, the people of the countryside are caught beneath a monstrous zodiacal wheel, with the eternal shift from season to season germinating yet further tasks. Indeed one of the threats of *The Seasons* is that once performance has begun it may go on indefinitely, with spring swinging back into view ('Behold, harsh Winter flees') at two-hour intervals with no escape. The tone is almost unchanged from Pieter Brueghel the

Elder's great paintings of the seasons (most famously *Hunters in the Snow*), which came into the collection of Rudolf II's younger brother Ernst when he was ruler of the Spanish Netherlands in the 1590s and which now make visiting Vienna worthwhile just in themselves. Rudolf himself, as one would expect, festooned himself in related seasons-based drawings, paintings and engravings by figures such as Savery, Sadeler, Bril and the wonderful Pieter Stevens. If Scorpio is in the sky and the pigs are rooting in the woods, then you know it is October. As one of the earliest forms of non-religious and non-court art, these images have a peculiar quality of asking their viewer almost to step into them – with even the simplest elements of a few trees and a stream taking on an air of wizardry.

To see portrayal of the seasons as an instrument of social control would be a bit reductive – as with the ancient gods, there is a strong element of relief that they simply provide amusing decorative challenges for artists – and the seasons decorate everything from dinner services to summer-houses in a dopily apolitical way all over the Habsburg lands, as elsewhere. One way of looking at them is as representing a world in which people are relentlessly *at work* and the interlocking demands of each season are all necessary to basic survival, with neglect or failure leading almost at once to disaster. The appearance of a band of soldiers, plague, or flood, or of March's weather in June would sweep the entire sequence away, with selections from *The Seasons* being sung with some sarcasm by any haggard survivors. So even in the decorative context of an oratorio for an urban audience there is an implacable message about life in the country, particularly with so many of the Habsburg lands under a constant and dramatic threat of disaster. Much of the Viennese audience, of course, lived a large part of the year on their country estates and indeed received a large part of their income from them, so *The Seasons* would have spoken very directly to their neuroses.

The oratorio wobbles around a bit in *Winter* as there is not much to do except spin or fend off the advances of a nobleman (in a notably limp sequence) or complain about the cold, but this clears space for the final, immense hymn of praise ('May Thy hand, O Lord, give guidance! Give us strength and courage; then we shall sing, then we shall enter in the glory of Thy realm'), which keeps everyone warm. Although there are pantheistic elements to *The Seasons* which make its sensibilities late eighteenth century, it is also an enormous, specifically Catholic experience – a countryside peopled by hard-working, rooted, God-fearing men and women united in their loyalty to the One Church. It is not surprising that a member of the Imperial family sang in the premiere and everything in the music conforms to Franz I's icy enthusiasm for everyone just doing as they are told.

A principal enjoyment of researching this book has been to engage in a cock-eyed interpretation of *The Seasons* by wandering around the countryside at different times of year, and revelling in more extreme weather patterns than those generally felt in southeast England. All countries furnish their own musical, literary and painterly hymns to their countryside, but it is done very well in Central Europe. I have often found myself humming extracts from Schubert's *The Beautiful Mill-Girl* as I wander along by some blameless stream and it only needs to get a little bit Alpine and heroic before incoherent chunks of Mahler's Third pop up. An otherwise perhaps almost featureless Bohemian valley is ennobled by Dvořák and bleak bits of Transylvania turn spectral and highly flavoured thanks to Ligeti.

The greatest master of this Habsburg *Seasons* pantheism is the Austrian writer Adalbert Stifter, at his peak in the 1840s, whose series of stories and novels is of an almost eye-watering brightness and beauty, with his characters both exalting in and hemmed in by the rural worlds (mountains, meadows, forests) they traverse. You have to pick and choose a bit with Stifter's work – his late novel *Indian Summer* is a book of unyielding tedium, with a featureless narrator paying repeated visits to a house which is in a perfect relation to God and nature, with everyone tending trellises and drying fruit so that you want to scream. I was encouraged that one contemporary German critic said that he would offer the crown of Poland to anyone who could get to the end. So little happens that it could be that the whole novel is (like Perec's *Life: A User's Manual*) a staggering exercise in authorial self-control, with the entire structure devoted to the final page, on which there will be a grotesque, head-busting revelation which depraves and poisons all the previous five hundred pages of boredom, now suddenly rotting and bubbling in all their undraped luridity. But, alas, despite two efforts my high-water mark is shown by page 300 being turned down and I will never pursue this remote chance of a good result.

But setting aside *Indian Summer,* Stifter is a writer who can be read over and over, not for the stories themselves (although these are absorbing) but because he sees everything through such strange eyes: 'Rock Crystal', 'Limestone', 'Brigitta' (a sensational wolf attack!), 'Abdias', 'The Forest Path'. Stifter was a remarkable landscape painter as well as writer, whose almost crazy level of precision in trying to show how, say, a slope of rock is reflected in a mountain lake is equalled in his fiction, where (oddly) he manages in a few words to be *more* vivid than in his paintings. His wonder-work is probably the short novel *The Bachelors*, where a young man, full of vigour and with his whole life ahead of him, walks ecstatically through a series of mountain valleys to visit a mysterious uncle who, crushed with misanthropic bitterness, lives in an abandoned monastery on a lake. If you have managed to persevere, *Indian Summer*-like, with reading my book to this point, then I can only plead with you to drop it and switch to *The Bachelors.*

There is a moment in the novel when as the young man, Victor, is being rowed across the lake (over which towers a mountain, in a scene of photorealist hallucination) to the monastery island a church bell rings out, and the rower stops his work and says the prayer of that hour. Perhaps what is most thrilling about Stifter is that he clearly has some emotional and mental ideal in which God, Man and Nature are perfectly aligned, but this vision is so extreme and hard to achieve (we are too lazy, too venal, too distracted) that it is always threatening to spring into pieces. I went, in a semi-pilgrim frame of mind, down to the far south of Bohemia where Stifter grew up, the remote small town of Horní Planá, looking out over the almost empty hills and mountains separating the area from Austria. There is a little Stifter museum and a genuine feeling of being in the back of beyond, and yet even here the twentieth century has really reached in its claws, with the vandalized stump of a First World War monument and an almost entirely new Czech-speaking population after the Germans were all expelled. Stifter's original visionary community has therefore entirely vanished, but this God–Man–Nature idea was always, outside the frame of its own artistic brilliance, a disturbing and intolerant one. It left out many Central Europeans and it made rural life a moral force in its own right (a message that even I was able to glean from *Indian Summer* despite an increasing preoccupation with my own mental health as I dragged through each page). Like *The Seasons* but more hectically, this vision was very German, very Catholic and with a sense of order and hierarchy which even as Stifter was writing was already under acute threat. For all his worship of nature Stifter spent much of his life in cities, not least Linz, which has a terrific statue to him. *The Bachelors* ends in a sort of frenzy of God-super-vised multi-generational ruralism, but in practice the cheerful Victor would probably himself, by the time his author died in the 1860s, have been wondering about slinking off to some obviously more desirable and sinful city. And virtually all the actors in the *The Seasons* itself would have been on the first train to Vienna, sing-ing about the joys of factories, giant beer-cellars, consumer goods and not having to give a stuff about the seasons any more.

The Habsburg monarchy had always been a sort of patchwork of nearly empty lands (mountains, swamps) and verdant countryside dotted with *Seasons*-style individuals working for their noble mas-ters and (by western European standards) small, generally German-speaking towns acting as goods exchanges and fortifications. The great story of the nineteenth century was the transformation of these towns, as hundreds of thousands of people headed into them, running as fast as they could from the remorseless rural cycle.

CHAPTER TEN

A warning to legitimists » Problems with loyal subjects »

Un vero quarantotto » Mountain people

A warning to legitimists

Growing up, we had a set of French 'Happy Families' playing cards featuring Heroes of France, picked up on holiday one year. While other children were playing the same game sensibly featuring those old favourites Mrs Bones the Butcher's Wife and Mr Soot the Sweep, we were engrossed in swapping cards featuring little paintings of historical personages. So we would swap Marie de Médicis for Bertrand Duguesclin – 'pig-faced soldier of destiny' – or a nicely dressed Henri III for Clemenceau. We must have spent a huge amount of time over the years on this game. What in retrospect seems rather attractive is the way that we never had any idea who any of these people were (except for an unrealistically gamine and available-looking Joanne of Arc) and stubbornly refused to engage in any way with their identities. We never learned anything historical from handling King Clovis or the funny-looking Marshal Ney, and the Duc de Richelieu may as well have been Master Bun the Baker's Son.

I mention this because it was thanks to the game that as an adult reading about post-Napoleonic France, I found myself taking an odd interest in Charles X. He was perhaps the most inflexibly idiotic of all French rulers but his card in 'Happy Families' – an ironic context, given that his family was really not that happy, what with all the executions – made him look dashing and smart in a lovely blue cavalry uniform. I was therefore somewhat smitten with him and have always found his era much more interesting than I should.

The ghost of Charles X stalked his contemporaries like a nightmare. After the turmoil of the Revolutionary and Napoleonic Wars the new world order after 1815 was based around the return to legitimism, the God-backed right to rule based on dynastic succession. Charles X was the true King of France – brother of Louis XVI, uncle of the dead child Louis XVII, brother of Louis XVIII and without a doubt next in the queue. And yet in only six years of rule he managed to alienate almost everybody, behaving as though the Revolution had never happened, insisting on an incense-laden, knee-breeches coronation in Rheims Cathedral and passing a demented, non-market-tested law to make stealing a chalice and host from a church a capital crime (with the felon's offending right hand cut off as a preliminary to his execution). This was not really the tone for the Paris of Delacroix and Balzac and, in a harmless and rather stage-managed version of 1789, Charles was forced into exile.

That a man who had so much going for him – ruling against a backdrop of war-exhaustion and genuine pan-European conservatism – should mess up so badly had a chilling effect on other dynasties. Charles was offered asylum by Franz I, settling ultimately in Görz, a somnolent but lovely Habsburg town north-east of Venice, where he died of cholera. His family continued to be based in Görz, an angry and rather mad group waiting for the call to return, thronged by needy toadies and decayed snobs while real life in France continued without them.

Spending a few days in Gorizia (now split, with the old town of Gorizia in Italy and Nova Gorica in Slovenia), I was overjoyed to discover that my old 'Happy Families' friend was buried in the nearby Franciscan monastery of Kostanjeviča, on the Slovenian side of the border. First puffing up an alarmingly penitential hill to the monastery with rain pounding down so hard it threatened to knock me to the ground, and then stepping gingerly down some chilly steps to the crypt, there, suddenly, in all their desperate flummery were the tombs of dynastic failure: Charles X and the mad parallel universe of his son 'Louis XIX' and grandson 'Henri V'. Henri V made his grandfather look relatively free-and-easy when through the unexpected implosion of Napoleon III's state following the Franco-Prussian War there was a genuine move to re-establish the monarchy. These negotiations foundered on Henri's surreal refusal to rule over a country which used the blood-soaked tricolour flag and his insistence it revert to Charles X's pure white flag. This sort of nonsense meant the moment that had been awaited in Gorizia for some forty years passed over in silence and Henri in due course joined the part of his family residing in the cold vaults of Kostanjeviča rather than that buried in the ancient royal abbey of St Denis.

There is an acute sense of sadness about these helpless tombs, with their dogmatic claims (*Roi de France et Navarre, par la grâce de Dieu*) and long-life legitimist wreaths. Where was the man in the light blue cavalry coat, saluting on his horse, who I had admired as a youth? The family's subsequent fate was chaotic. The monastery was destroyed in fighting during the First World War and the fading Habsburg regime of Karl I had the coffins and their haughty contents hauled off to Vienna. Once the monastery was rebuilt they were taken back in 1932 to Kostanjeviča (then under a brief period of Italian rule) and buried again, with a rather impressive turnout judging from the photos. After the Second World War they found themselves as refugees in the unsympathetic Socialist Federal Republic of Yugoslavia (by about five hundred metres), but survived this interlude to be under the care of the genial Republic of Slovenia. Representatives of the Bourbon family have been trying to persuade the Slovenian government and the Franciscans to let them move the unfortunates yet again, this time to Paris, but their nutty request has been sensibly refused.

I have to admit that I have a weakness for legitimist tombs and once spent an ecstatic afternoon at the luxurious Orléans family burial chambers at Dreux, a playground of white marble, religious peculiarity and thwarted pride without equal. But I cannot pretend, alas, that it has even the faintest relevance to this book. Charles X has, however. His fate ravaged other legitimist rulers. It made Franz I and Metternich ill with worry. Decades of fighting had *not* crushed revolutionary populism back into its box. The only justification for legitimism turned out to be its effectiveness – a contradiction in terms. The gloomy conclusion was that the monarch could only receive the instinctive obeisance of his grateful subjects if they were infiltrated by secret police and watched with unsleeping vigilance. It was in this period that Austria's notorious censorship system blossomed, which managed to be both stifling and inept in a unique mixture. Charles X flouncing around with his Ultra friends, pretending Robespierre and Napoleon had never happened, was not going to be enough. Gorizia beckoned for those who failed.

With the other like-minded monarchs, Franz and Metternich searched the horizon for fresh signs of revolution, hosting congresses around Central Europe to ensure that a united front would prevent the emergence anywhere of pro-Revolution revanche. The great square where they met in 1820 can still be seen – much altered – in the centre of Ljubljana (then Laibach). When these characters met up it must have been hilarious, with row upon row of gorgeously tricked out cavalrymen and the elaborately uniformed rulers giving each other stiff embraces, medals and spurs clinking and everything awash in expensive gentleman's fragrances. Franz may have been cold and unintelligent, but he was an effective Emperor, full to his fingertips with belief in his God-given right to rule. If conservative vigilance could only be maintained – if Austria, Prussia and Russia could stick together – then God would allow him to strike down any threat to his rule. Alas, disaster for Franz came from his own, incredibly legitimate DNA. In a final flourish of Habsburg genetic stupidity he had married his double first cousin Maria Theresa (who sang in *The Seasons*), daughter of King Ferdinand I of the Two Sicilies, himself another legitimist horror. The entirely predictable result was that their eldest son Ferdinand suffered from innumerable physical handicaps and terrible fits, and could not father children himself. But legitimism could not make exceptions. Charles X may have been stupid, vengeful and incompetent, but he was the rightful King of France. For Franz I to pass over his son Ferdinand for a more suitable heir would be dangerous as well as virtually republican. So the inflexible and God-fearing Franz insisted on being succeeded by someone effectively incapable of ruling.

Historical hindsight weighs particularly heavily on the period between 1815 and 1848 because there is such an air of restraint and calm. It was sneered at by later nationalists as an era of people taking piano lessons and adding to their teacup collections, but by almost any measure it was a marvellous time, with the pianist now being able to play Schubert and Schumann and the teacups the shock-troops of a new bourgeois culture. The long period of warfare and revolution had been so complex that we will never be able with confidence to pin any specific behavioural changes to it. Was the new pan-European bourgeois culture something which would have happened anyway with the increasing cheap mass-production of objects and the growth of the non-noble professions? It is certainly striking that although anti-Napoleon forces won the wars, across Europe men still now found themselves wigless and wearing simple deep-coloured materials and women found themselves in post-Empire-type dresses. This is perhaps the period when Vienna most set the pace for other cities (with Paris temporarily being sent to stand in the corner), with its public culture of consumption, cake, civility, public concerts, and with the Prater (a gift from Joseph II to his people) coming into its own.

This 'Biedermeier' period leaves all sorts of subtle traces across the Empire, but it was its private impact which was so appealing. It hardly threatened the nobility in any sense, but even the nobility, whatever their immense privileges, found themselves at least *painted* more informally, even if their actual lifestyle tended still to revolve around several family homes and hundreds of staff. The spread of a sort of cult of children and children's toys and general domesticity is apparent – it is hard not to have Schumann's 'Dreaming', 'Knight of the Hobby-Horse' and 'Blind Man's Bluff' from *Scenes of Childhood* as the theme-tunes for the period or Schubert's genial *Marches militaires*, which could not be less *militaire*. One piece I never tire of listening to is Schubert's tiny *Hungarian Melody* for piano, composed in 1824 and part of the cheerful, tentative engagement in 'play-clothes' nationalism. Schubert, who was born in Vienna and whose father was Moravian and mother Silesian, was much influenced in this sort of music by the Bohemian composer

Václav Tomášek, and here he is conjuring up four minutes of the most lovely, vaguely Hungarian music – thereby swinging in his own person all the way across the Empire.

The introversion and lack of ambition was exactly what Franz I and Metternich were looking for – an acquiescent, devout, quietly consumerist middle class flanked by a nobility providing intelligent leadership and a mass of peasants doing as they were told. It is striking both how successful they were in achieving this – helped enormously by having a shocked and exhausted post-war generation on their hands – and how brief the achievement was. Unprecedented, dizzying social change was unstoppably en route, with the landscape being steadily dotted with factories and pinned together with new rail-lines, the effects of which would make the Biedermeier Habsburg era rapidly look antique.

Problems with loyal subjects

Being the father of his people was always a key skill of the Habsburg Emperor. A wish to be accessible to ordinary subjects, to be concerned equally with issues great and small, was as much part of the state ideology as gaudy crown-and-ermine max-outs surrounded by huzzahing aristos. After all, the logic of absolutism infantilized subjects, but also made them the Emperor's special care. Joseph II had recognized this in his lurching sequence of wild improvisations. It was his perception that it was the great magnates who gummed up state efficiency and that the energies of those beneath them could be released through abolishing guilds, serfdom and other local obstacles. Franz I perfected at a popular level the idea of the family man, never happier than at home either with his actual wife and children or with the wider family of even his meanest subjects. His successor, Ferdinand I, as much as he was able, certainly provoked affection and the cult of Franz Joseph eventually became a fervent one – the simple huntsman for whom no subject's travails were too slight for his concern. Millions of homes were decorated as much with cheap prints of 'the good Emperor' as with Jesus and Mary.

This was a very powerful weapon in the control of the Empire and expressed itself through processions, statues, oaths of loyalty, prayers in every religion, military service and so on. Most strikingly it pinned down an aristocracy that might otherwise have been much more restive and difficult – the Emperor may have been reliant in every part of the Empire on local aristocratic proxies to run things, but he also had a direct line to ordinary people, who could be unleashed with the most extreme ferocity. The Emperor may have posed as the good father, blessing good behaviour and gently chiding unruliness, but in practice unruliness tended to result in somewhat bad-father bouts of near-psychopathic breakdown.

A striking example of this had been the Horea, Cloşca and Crişan Revolt of 1784, mentioned in chapter 8. On the face of it this sounded like a classic incoherent shambles of burning manor-houses and people doing terrible things with scythes in an orgy of primitivism. But Horea had himself met Joseph II in Vienna and throughout the revolt the Romanian peasants who were butchering their Hungarian overlords in the Apuseni Mountains were under the impression they were helping Joseph out. In an earlier tour through Transylvania Joseph had made it clear that the backward-ness and inefficiency of serfdom had to end and he was besieged by Romanians ('Wallachians') handing him memorials about the cruelty of their fate (extraordinarily, accumulating some fourteen thousand of these). In retrospect one can see that this was the point (if not earlier) when Hungarian rule over its eastern regions was in serious trouble. Each of the key pieces of social control – around churches, obedience, education and labour service – began to crumble, with Joseph abolishing such symbolic issues as the peas-ant being obliged to kiss his lord's hand. The great revolt ended in disaster, with the peasants massacred by Imperial troops – whole areas were depopulated, with almost the entire social structure from top to bottom dug out and destroyed. Joseph's paternal con-cern for his subjects proved to be trumped by loathing for disobedience.

The old Hungarian town of Nagyvárad (now Romanian Oradea) has a striking little memorial to this period. Following the suppression of the Revolt, Joseph moved quickly to liberalize the area (much to the rage of the surviving Hungarians). One aspect of this was to allow the Romanian Orthodox to build a church in the town. This wonderful building is known as the Church of the Moon as it has fixed into its front an ingenious gadget: a large sphere painted half black and half yellow which turns a little each day to show the correct phase of the moon, from new to full. This feature is apparently unique in Europe – and you can see why, as a comparable (and more realistic) effect can be gained simply by looking up at the moon itself. But the gadget's idiocy is more than balanced by its charm – and by the beauty of the building itself – a perfect example of a late-eighteenth-century Orthodox church, obliged by the Habsburg authorities to look exactly like a Catholic one from outside and with even its iconostasis looking like a feature of a Catholic church gone oddly wrong, with the same sorts of attractive little religious scenes unaccountably stacked up to form a wall. Right above the iconostasis, tucked into a gold medallion in the roof, is a little painting of a bearded face, which the authorities must have wearily assumed was yet another tiresome prophet. In fact it is Horea himself, painted shortly after he had been cut into pieces, with chunks of him stuck on poles and displayed in Oradea and elsewhere.

There is a great temptation to see everything that unfolded in Transylvania as a reflection of mounting Hungarian–Romanian hatred, with the former only maintaining control of the latter through violence and intimidation. A problem with thinking about historical events is that they by definition deal with breakdowns – but even in the run-up to the First World War there were still many instances of loyalty, friendship and justice between the two groups. Many Hungarians were very poor, not just the Széklers in eastern Transylvania, but also many minor nobles who lived in conditions not unlike those of the Romanians. These Hungarians are the forebears of the nutty provincial figures so beloved of later Hungarian literature, who want only to be left alone with their gypsy mistresses, and refuse ever to open letters let alone telegrams as a matter of principle. This extreme localism meant that, as usual with a colonial class, there was a fatal lack of solidarity – with Hungarians split at the very least between pro-Habsburgs, anti-Habsburgs and quietists but also within each of those groups liberals, reactionaries and even revolutionaries.

This sense of the Hungarians as a colonial class, defined by language and religion, as against Romanians, Slovaks, Serbs and Croats, is new in this period. As various forms of military, pater-nalist feudalism dissolved under both Joseph's reforms and the values of Napoleon it became clear that Horea, Cloşca and Crişan might indeed be the future. With each passing decade dramas around rights, language and religious worship were played out. The twists and turns of Hungarian liberals who wished to democratize Hun-gary sufficiently to share power with the aristocrats but not sufficiently to allow in the Romanian and Slavic majority would be one of the great, tragic subjects of the nineteenth century.

This happened across the Empire in different forms, with German nobles lording it over Czech peasants in Bohemia and Poles over Ruthenians in eastern Galicia. Most emphatically and consistently it was played out in schools. Attempts to prevent the 'underclasses' from having access to education were pursued in a sneak preview of Nazi policy in the 1940s, but gradually broke down, both through the protests of those involved and in the con-tinuing Josephine streak in the Empire which saw the obvious inefficiency of having millions of clueless, semi-literate subjects in a Europe in which even ordinary soldiers needed to be better than this. Conceding schools then resulted in battles over the language of instruction, with the poet Mihai Eminescu's great comment in 1870: 'We are more afraid of Hungarian schools than we are of their Diet, their ministers and their soldiers.' If hordes of Roma-nian tots from illiterate families could be taught in Hungarian then they would effectively *become* Hungarian. But as more Serbs, Czechs, Slovaks, Croats, Ruthenians and Romanians managed to become literate in their own languages (often through Church-sponsored schooling), as movement control based on serfdom

collapsed and as trains offered an amazing new mobility and newspapers allowed those with the right languages to compare notes,
the 'colonial' powers in the Empire became ever more defensive.

Perhaps the most self-consciously paternal of all the Habsburg
provinces was the Kingdom of Galicia and Lodomeria (a Latinized
version of the regions of Halych and Volhynia). We look back on
the kingdom now as a piece of outrageous cynicism, the Habsburg
share of the evisceration of a great European state, given an elaborate new name to avoid any mention of the word 'Poland'. But from
the point of view of Joseph II and his successors it was a purely
Enlightenment project – the rescue of a benighted land from the
feudal bumpkinism of Polish aristocrats. Its capital at Lemberg (now
the Ukrainian city of Lviv) was consciously set up as a beacon of
order and decency and with a quite different aesthetic to the faux
medievalism which was the root justification for Habsburg rule over
much of the rest of the Empire. But the same problem began to
emerge. Hardly anyone was even aware of the Ruthenians at the
time of the Partition – and as in Transylvania the make-up of the
countryside's population was confusing, dotted with settlements of
Poles quite as poor as the Ruthenians and the Jews and all ruled
over by other Poles of immense wealth and power. As the Enlightened state got into action, fuelled above all by the need for army
recruits, it became ever more obsessed with sifting its subjects into
categories, whether religious, racial, linguistic or class-based.

In the longer term the rise of the Ruthenians and their creation
of a 'Ukrainian' ideology that linked them to their fellows to the
north-east, inside the Russian Empire, was to be as fatal to the
Habsburgs (and to the Poles) as Transylvanian Romanians identify-
ing with the increasingly independent Wallachia and Moldavia.
But in the shorter term the most chilling issues lay around the
obedience and indeed the very existence of the Polish ruling class.

If there was a core subject on which the reactionary regimes of
Central Europe all agreed it was the need to keep down the Poles.
The Habsburgs elaborated an ever more complex Galician ideology
which was meant to trump any remaining Polish sentiment and
which ended up actively goading the Ruthenians into political life

to keep the Poles loyal and frightened. In the first half of the nineteenth century the most obvious chink in the anti-Polish army
was the appealingly named Free, Independent and Strictly Neutral
City of Kraków, a five-hundred-square-mile city state squidged
between the three occupying powers as an anomaly created by the
Congress of Vienna. In the 1830s it was decided secretly that if it
were to rebel the Austrians would have the right to annex it. The
Poles, including many exiles in France, hoped to use Kraków as
a catalyst for a general, massive effort to shake off the surrounding
powers – an effort which in retrospect looks desperately unlikely
to succeed. At the beginning of 1846 Kraków and western Galicia
rose in revolt, and this was easily and ferociously crushed by the
Habsburg armies.

There was one terrible variant in Galicia. As insurrectionaries
raised the Polish flag in Kraków and urged Poles across Galicia to
rebel, some Habsburg officials played a new card. In the Enlightenment spirit with which the region had been acquired, they accused
the aristocrats of disloyalty and of representing an old, discredited
past. They urged the region's peasants to stay loyal and to turn on
their masters. The result was a grotesque one. The region's principal town, Tarnów, had its attractive main square transformed by
the arrival of innumerable peasant carts heaped with murdered
Polish aristocrats – at least a thousand were killed and their manor
houses burned down. Somehow, it had become rumoured that the
best way for the peasants to show their loyalty was by bringing the
corpses into the town. The Galician authorities were horrified but
also pleased. The peasants' leader, Jakub Szela, was thanked, given
a medal and set up with a farm in Bukovina, even as the peasant
revolt was itself crushed. Kraków became a miserable Habsburg
barracks town until its recovery in the late nineteenth century.

The events of 1846 had a powerful effect on the Polish nobility, who now had to contend not only with Ruthenian hostility in
the east but, far worse, with the realization that their 'own' Polish
peasants would kill them if they had the chance rather than offer
anything that might be thought of as national Polish solidarity. For
the rest of the Empire's existence the Polish landowners tended to

be an aggressively loyal group, with Tarnów casting a long shadow.
For the Habsburgs any excitement over this Galician loyalty was
probably overwhelmed by the failure of their Enlightenment project as the province remained an impoverished backwater much of
whose population, whether Polish, Jewish or Ruthenian, spent its
leisure hours working out how to leave for America.

That this book is not filled up purely with interesting instances
of racial or linguistic tension across the nineteenth-century Empire
is because of their ultimately rather numbing effect. But this prospect of extreme violence has just to be kept in mind, lurking in the
background, even if some lucky generations escaped it. It is striking, for example, how many characters in the nostalgic post-1918
novels of life in Habsburg Hungary are armed with a revolver or
automatic – not with relevance to the plot, but just as a casual
aspect of their day-to-day lives. For all the positive, normal relations between groups, and the ever-more overblown presentation
of the immemorial Hungarian nobility's hold on Transylvania,
there seems to have been a skittering, frightened undertow to the
banquets, hare-hunts and balls. In Transylvania it was memories of
Horea, Cloşca and Crişan that stalked the aristocratic imagination
– but this would also be added to by the mass Romanian defection
to the Habsburgs in the 1848–49 War of Independence, which
enclosed within it a barely reported murderous race war.

In Galicia it was memories of Tarnów that performed a similar
service for the surviving Polish noble families. Both societies
shared something of the brittle, sports-obsessed cheerfulness of
the British in India – or indeed of Southerners in the pre-1861
United States. These were societies which could resort to any level
of violence in support of racial supremacy. Indeed, an interesting
global history could be written about the ferocity of a period
which seems, very superficially, to be so 'civilized'. Southern white
responses to Nat Turner's Slave Rebellion in 1831, with Turner
himself flayed, beheaded and quartered, can be linked to the
British blowing rebel Indians to pieces from the mouths of can-
nons in 1857. The intermittent ferocity of relations between some
groups in the Habsburg Empire tends to be seen in isolation and

contrasted with the relative docility of life in the countryside of Britain, say, or France – but it is perhaps just a handful of European societies which had a homogeneity sufficient to make them non-violent (and Ireland could also be swapping notes with Transylvania). This hatred, inequality, irredentism and mutual contempt would be played out with ever more terrible results and, in more muted ways, still persist today in the very few areas where the issue has not completely burned itself out.

Un vero quarantotto

Debrecen is now one of the most easterly Hungarian cities. It is a measure of the catastrophe that has engulfed Hungary in the twentieth century that it was once in the middle of the country. The lurch could have been even worse as, with much of the country filled with marauding Romanian troops in 1919, there was a moment when it looked as though the whole of Bethlen Gábor's old Partium region was going to be gulped down by Bucharest, leaving the traumatized Hungarian republic as a tiny reservation not much bigger than Slovakia. As it was, many predominantly Hungarian towns were taken, but Debrecen survived.

The Great Church in Debrecen therefore now has an even more defiant cultic role in Hungarian life than before, if that is possible. The city from which Calvinist (and often nationalist and anti-Habsburg) ideas radiated to all points of the compass has now become the last outpost – it is as though Kansas City suddenly found itself on the border with Mexico. The Great Church is in itself something of a disappointment. The battered, glowering building it replaced, the 'Andrew Church', must have had much of the charisma of the Black Church of Braşov, and had a detached bell-tower and very tall military watchtower from which to scour the surrounding plains for the dust-cloud that would indicate an Ottoman army. Sadly the Andrew Church burned down at the beginning of the nineteenth century, poor timing given the dreary rule-book classicism which plagued the architecture of the period.

Calvinists are, of course, well known for their aversion to figurative religious imagery, and a huge, white-washed, almost featureless classical interior is not much fun. I felt my latent Catholic genes stirring – surely just *one* small picture of Jesus having a hard time wouldn't hurt? The relentless austerity of the main church was disappointing, but at this point in my travels around the Empire I had an almost sixth sense about these things. I remember one occasion in the Upper Austrian town of Steyr when I saw signs pointing to the castle park and I immediately thought, 'I bet there is an orangery there which has been converted into a restaurant where I can have lunch': and there was. Similarly – as soon as I saw a sign saying *Temporary exhibition in the tower* I immediately thought 'I bet this is going to be something a bit mad': and it was.

As though to atone for the monotony of the main church, the tower was filled with an exhibition of extraordinarily manic, precise models of entirely conjectural buildings. Created in the first half of the twentieth century by the Calvinist preacher and writer Lajos Csia, it was a happy example of how the most austere of faiths will suddenly sprout the strangest flowers. The rooms were filled with marvels: visions of the Temple of Solomon, the best ever Tower of Babel, the Temple Mount, all produced in a seemingly clinical, unromantic manner and yet – in their very conception – dementedly romantic. Greatest of all were two attempts to recreate Ezekiel's vision of the renewed Temple in Jerusalem, as revealed to him by the 'man whose appearance was like the appearance of brass' – a riot of strange turrets and battlements, following the man of brass's cubit-by-cubit instructions. There is a long and honourable tradition of antiquarian conjectural fantasy (not least in the work of Athanasius Kircher, discussed earlier), but this is without doubt one of its most convincing and enjoyable expressions, with fascinating hints lurking too of the deep, ancient roots of science fiction.

But in the history of the Empire, Debrecen is not simply 'the vegetable garden of Hungarian Calvinism', or indeed the home of conjectural models of Ezekiel's vision. It is also the home of the tragically abortive Hungarian state of 1849, with Lajos Kossuth's declaration of independence in the Great Church and the anxious, short-lived parliament meeting in the oratory of the next-door Calvinist college.

The events of 1848–49 have an uneasy place in European history. All those involved – on both sides – seem to have been painfully self-conscious about what they were setting out to achieve or to prevent. Without being too reductive, the forces of 'liberalism' and the forces of 'reaction' (both concepts that need to be put in inverted commas as they can in practice both be pretty much ummmed and aaahed to death) had an air of working from a script. This script, of course, had been laid out by the French Revolution. A combination of poor harvests and technological change formed part of the backdrop to 1848, but perhaps more important was the sense of legitimism in decay. Franz I had been so confident of the security of the Habsburg throne that in his old age he saw no problem with his incapable son succeeding as Ferdinand I (as with his father, the numbering starting again to show the fresh minting of the 'Austrian Empire' following the demise of the Holy Roman Empire, otherwise he should have been Ferdinand IV – in Hungary he was King Ferdinand V). Under Metternich's tutelage the government of the Empire in many ways simply ignored Ferdinand, but this meant that too much was required of a handful of officials with no legitimacy of any kind, not the least of them being the increasingly elderly and depressive Metternich himself.

The revolutions across Europe began in Paris where the elderly Louis Philippe, himself brought to power eighteen years before in a coup, wobbled around helplessly. As soon as the barricades went up, panic flooded across Europe. Characters such as Metternich and Louis Philippe, who had experienced the French Revolution in their late teens, knew the drill and fled in an intelligent attempt to avoid having their heads put on sticks. Across the Habsburg Empire major cities fell, from Milan to Venice, from Prague to Vienna. It briefly seemed as though anything might be possible.

A striking and clear strand in the revolutions was that the removal of dynastic rule over pieces of land naturally led to its substitute: national ownership based on language. If people no longer believed that Ferdinand I ruled Milan then something else was needed. Particularly vulnerable were the bits and pieces in Italy like the duchies of Modena and Parma, which had no rationale beyond a specific individual dynast's inheriting them. This issue of ownership crowded into every aspect of life. If an individual wearing odd and expensive clothing no longer owned a territory, then the system by which the people lived on that land also caved in – with serfdom immediately seen as unacceptable and illogical.

1848 was a year of miraculous liberation and excitement, but once its opening phase was over it became clear that it had unintentionally opened a particularly unpleasant Pandora's box. National structures were relatively unproblematic in France, which while far from monoglot, at least had a single dominant language, and at least plausible in Italy, but for German-speaking countries and for the rest of the Habsburg Empire the very idea of 'nation' was an unresolvable nightmare. The new German parliament at Frankfurt almost immediately made this clear – just taking the territory of Bohemia, what would it mean for Czech-speakers to attend an otherwise German-speaking event? Some Germans were encouraging but there was a great temptation to see the Czechs as mere picturesque peasants like the Bretons in France, incapable of political action. The threat of a future devoted to a Czech equivalent of tossing chocolate *crêpes* and knitting striped sweaters was enough to galvanize a Czech nationalism which would drive everything before it – ultimately indeed, only a century later, sweeping away or killing all the Bohemian Germans. At the further end of the Empire, Poles, thrilled by the collapse of central authority, began to gather. But they, in turn, saw no reason to include Ruthenians, who, now no longer serfs, had as much right as anyone to a view on how they should be ruled. But, as with the German–Czech relationship, the Poles could see the Ruthenians at best only in a *folklorique* light, as colourful man-beasts without culture. Less than a century later this tension would be resolved through the deaths of millions of people.

The importance of the change was enormous. If people are

viewed as subjects then in many contexts their language, cultural practices or religion are irrelevant. The Habsburg Empire had long specialized in attractive engravings of the 'Peoples of the Empire' in their different smocks, hats, boots and kerchiefs. A small area of Transylvania might have had a Hungarian aristocratic family in a substantial small palace, employing many of the Hungarian, Romanian, Jewish, German and sometimes Armenian locals. Particular experts might be brought in – German teachers or English horse-breeders or French governesses. The local aristocrat would in this case be responsible to the Austrian rulers of Transylvania, whose authority came from Ferdinand. The different groups in this area might cordially dislike each other – they would rarely intermarry, they went to different churches (although Hungarians and Germans could overlap), celebrated different feasts, ate different foods and navigated each day through a welter of different prohibitions, prejudices and acceptable/unacceptable behaviours. But substantially until 1848 all these groups were neutered. After 1848, however much the new regimes tried to pretend otherwise, everything became about national identity and the way that all these groups in, say, that one small area of Transylvania had competing claims for authority, autonomy and economic control. The consequences were catastrophic. There is no doubt that by many measures 1848 was a great watershed in European history – I am not sure anyone today would particularly fancy going back to a world where most of us would be tied labourers. But it is impossible not to feel a sense of dread about the gap between the excitement of 1848 and the degree to which we now know it was firing a starting gun that would initiate many of Europe's most terrible events.

Once the euphoria of 1848 had subsided, the revolutionaries' lack of a wider, unified purpose became painfully clear and everywhere the revolutions were co-opted or destroyed. There is a wonderful Italian phrase: *un vero quarantotto*, meaning a total cock-up: 'a right '48' – and *un vero quarantotto* about sums it up. Just as doddering or shifty rulers everywhere had known how to play their parts, and had fled by hiding in laundry-baskets or dressing up as common soldiers, so the military leaders knew their parts. The amazingly old General Radetzky had fought throughout the Napoleonic Wars, was absolutely loyal to the Habsburgs, and saw the Italian revolutionaries as merely an uppity rabble. The Prince of Windisch-Graetz further north was similarly incredulous about shop-keepers and other trash in Prague and Vienna having a view about anything at all. Once the initial shock of the revolutions was over these men organized their regular troops and systematically destroyed both the insurrectionaries and anybody else they disliked or who was unluckily in the way. There is something jaunty and almost unserious about the image of 1848 – lots of people in top hats and extravagant neck-ties, smoking cheroots while lounging on a barricade with a rifle, listening to someone playing Chopin in a nearby pub. It also seems relatively frivolous in the light, most obviously, of the French or Russian revolutions. But it is not clear how its actual suppression could have been any worse. The revolutionaries were hopelessly at odds with one another, both amazed by their initial success and then by the sheer complexity of what should happen next – indeed, some of the revolutionaries may have been socialists or Communists (*The Communist Manifesto* was published in February, though it had little impact until later), but many others could in practical terms hardly be called revolutionaries at all. A very broad spectrum of people could agree with the statement 'It's disgusting and embarrassing to be ruled by King Ferdinand II of the Two Sicilies', but a decision on what to do next was much harder.

It was the failure to agree on the next step that allowed the military their chance, and the results were ferocious. The two attempts by the King of Piedmont to invade northern Italy and liberate Habsburg territory were ruthlessly crushed. The heartbreaking attempts by Austrian-ruled Venetia to re-establish its ancient independence, snuffed out by Napoleon only fifty years before, ended in the city's being besieged and shelled into submission. Venice's revolution has never been part of the heroic history of Italian liberation because its leaders had no interest –

except in extremis – in the rest of the Italians, with whom Venice had never shared a political history. It remained a north-eastern, Adriatic, Croatian-tinged sort of place a million miles from Milan. The Venetian uprising gave rise to some great statements, such as Antonio Morandi's:

> Venice arose from the waves purged of Austrian putrefaction, haughty enough never to tolerate a fresh servitude, and beautiful with that beauty the progress of civilization brings with it.

This sort of infectious, wonderful rhetoric could not hide deep problems within the city – with the new, generally bourgeois leadership as frightened of arming and training the workers as they were of the approaching Austrian army.

It was in the Moravian town of Olomouc that the future really took shape. Here a group of loyalist conspirators mounted a coup. The government of Ferdinand I had in the Emperor's name agreed in a general panic to all kinds of concessions to the rebels. If Ferdinand were to be deposed (or rather 'resign') then his successor would not be bound to honour these concessions. The next in line to the throne was the childless Ferdinand's younger brother, Franz Karl, but he and his wife wanted nothing to do with running an empire, so he in turn renounced his rights in favour of his own eldest son, the teenager Franz Joseph. The revolutions were already in deep trouble almost everywhere, but the decisive steps were taken in the pretty ecclesiastical quarter of Olomouc where Franz Joseph was proclaimed the new Emperor, and Ferdinand shuffled off to a long and pleasant retirement in the Bohemian countryside. One of the great oddities of Franz Joseph's reign is its relentless obsession with the dignity of the House of Habsburg, with crushingly stuffy protocols, military uniform collar tabs, hierarchy and choreography – but the reign's entire foundation was an illegitimate fraud. By most definitions Franz Joseph was no more 'real' than Louis-Napoleon Bonaparte, who turned himself into Napoleon III in 1852 – and yet one managed through sheer longevity and dullness to make himself appear the *fons* of legitimacy and the other was always a sly, creepy adventurer.*

This brings the story back to the Great Church in Debrecen. The general crisis of 1848 had seemed to some Hungarians to be the great opportunity to break free at last of Habsburg rule, but as for so many others who misread the year's events and ended up either dead, in prison or spending many years in exile in London, New York or Constantinople, this turned out to be untrue. Inspired leadership and patriotic fervour allowed the Hungarians to carve out an empire of their own, but this only existed through their having a ready-made army in the Magyar-speaking units of the Imperial forces and through the grace of total if temporary Habsburg failure. The curse that emerged elsewhere applied in the Hungarian lands just as brutally. If Habsburg authority was declared void and a group of agreeable Hungarian-speaking polit-icians announced themselves as the true successors, then this tore open ethnic problems of a kind that would in due course destroy the Hungary they were trying to build. Breaking clear of Vienna simply authorized the massive groups within Hungary who had no wish to be dominated by Hungarian-speakers to in turn break clear of Buda. This resulted in a racial war as Serbs, Croats and Roma-nians massacred the Hungarians in their midst. The Habsburgs gleefully egged on the counter-rebels, but Slavs and Romanians would have done this anyway – it was built into the events that were unfolding. The disaster was compounded by the arrival in Transylvania of an enormous Russian army in support of the Habsburgs and which dramatized the degree to which legitimism had really given way simply to reaction – the willingness to kill or manacle anyone who refuses to do as they are told. The Russians were driven to intervene by disgust at insurrection, but also because they could not help noticing how many Poles were joining the Hungarian army: a liberal, republican, independent Hungary pro-viding a shelter for Poles would have featured very high in the

---

* Ferdinand I was quite capable of occasional lucidity. As Franz Joseph lurched through the fiascos of 1866, Ferdinand said: 'This new man, he's losing battles, losing provinces. I could have done that just as well.'

long list of the Tsar's nightmares that focused on the threat posed by personal freedoms. The degree to which Franz Joseph owed his position simply to reaction was played out in incredibly complex patterns throughout the rest of his long reign.

Lajos Kossuth's formal, public declaration of independence in the Great Church at Debrecen on 14 April 1849 was one of the great moments in Hungarian history, and a tragic disaster. It is a marvellous document, but filled with the contradictions and evasions that would doom the Hungarians in 1918. Many Hungarians saw Kossuth's announcement as dangerous and futile, but once it happened there was a clear patriotic duty to support it until General Görgey's surrender to the Russian army four months later. Kossuth began by saying how the Habsburgs were 'perjured in the sight of God and man', which was about right, and therefore no longer kings of Hungary. Hungary was a nation of a hundred and ten thousand square miles and fifteen million people -- a population which 'feels the glow of youthful strength within its veins'. The declaration after a good start then lost all its dignity as it was obliged to discuss the large percentage of the fifteen million people whose youthful strength was in fact directed against Kossuth and his associates.

The Mexican–American War earlier in the decade is a tragic comparison to the situation of the Hungarians in 1849. The Americans had to face a weak enemy whose hold on California and the south-west was slight, with very few settlers and only history and legality on its side. The Hungarians wanted to follow in their footsteps, declaring their own republic and taking back under direct rule all the Croatian and Transylvanian lands that had been alienated from them. But they really could not have had more enemies and Kossuth, instead of just rolling out ringing phrases, had to turn bitterly in the Declaration on the 'partisan chieftains' of Croatia, the Serbians 'whose hands yet reeked from the massacres they perpetrated' and the misled Romanians who had been 'stirred up'. But this was hopelessly inadequate and wishful as a diagnosis – the 'partisan chieftains' under Jelačić were simply loyal to the Habsburgs, with Jelačić the legitimate Ban of Croatia. The region crawled with anti-Hungarian forces. The previous month Franz Joseph had effectively snapped Hungary in pieces, declaring Croatia, Slavonia, Fiume, the Voivodina and Transylvania as separate new provinces and therefore cleverly rewarding all the non-Hungarian nationalities for their loyalty, and previewing the ruin of the Hungarian aristocracy.

So much of the fighting in 1849 remains almost hidden from the records – countless massacres, atrocities, summary shootings, as the surviving Hungarian forces were herded into an ever smaller space. Many leaders fled into the neighbouring Ottoman Empire where, in a perverse inversion of earlier Hungarian history, they had to adopt Turkish names and notionally embrace Islam to avoid extradition. Many others were executed. The most famous of these symbolic acts of revenge was outside the massive fortress of Arad, nowadays in the hands of the Romanian army but with its walls and approaches buried in a mass of luxuriant vegetation of a kind that suggests *Sleeping Beauty*, and with much of its surrounding land now dedicated to the Neptune Water-Park. It was here that thirteen Hungarian generals were hanged as rebels instead of shot as soldiers – a decision by Franz Joseph to humiliate them and, through them, humiliate all Hungarians. Kossuth went on to become a celebrated exile and global voice of liberalism, even though his decisions had provoked disaster at every turn. Franz Joseph, still only nineteen years old, had shown a ruthlessness which is hard to reconcile with his later image as father of his nation – an image almost entirely the result of his appealing white side-whiskers rather than any actual actions or thoughts he might have had.

The other tower of the Great Church, the one without Ezekiel's Vision in it, is famous for its enormous bell. It was originally built in 1636 for the Prince of Transylvania, György I Rákóczi – an earlier Hungarian rebel and inspiration for Hungarian nationalists who had fought both Ferdinand II and Ferdinand III and had the bell wittily made out of melted Imperial artillery he had captured. The bell shared the fate of the rest of the Great Church in the fire of 1802, crashing to the ground and cracking. In 1873 the authorities decided that it should be completely recast and hung up again. It is quite hard to believe this is true, but as a preliminary the magnificent Rákóczi shield, which was part of the moulding, was hammered off and melted into a separate small bell, so that the metal of the new Great Church bell would not have its virtue tainted by rebellion. Sometimes it is hard to be sympathetic to the Hungarians' chauvinism, but the treatment of the Rákóczi bell and the mystical Habsburg dynastic loopiness it betrays shows the mindset that they were up against.

Mountain people

Sitting happily in the Seven Piglets in Lviv, slurping a bowl of Hutsul-style mushroom soup, I felt I had landed in the acme of folkloric happiness. There were benches of rough-hewn wood scattered with sheepskins, low, deeply carved wooden rafters, every surface painted in Ukrainian decorative patterns and a live violin-and-squeezebox band playing, albeit *Bésame Mucho* but that's fine. Waiters in baggy embroidered white shirts rushed around, helpfully bringing me things like piglet with walnuts and sauerkraut of a kind that will sooner or later but not yet give me a gastric ulcer. The whole place is so extreme that it has an almost aversion-therapy feel – patients are brought here who spend too much time listening to folksong arrangements or have devoted entire rooms of their house to hand-painted Easter eggs. Anyway, the aversion therapy didn't work for me, as the pancakes laden with forest fruits arrived with a flourish.

An obsession with folklore can take many forms, running the gamut from a timid interest in fabrics to the barrel-chested roaring and good fellowship that characterizes the once notorious Girl Fair at Muntele Găina. Folklore tourism has been important ever since the railways were invented, and the tension between 'remoteness' and easy access, between celebrating a unique way of life and polluting it can never be resolved. The remarkable Hutsul village of Yaremche in western Ukraine is a prime example. It is genuinely marvellous. The River Prut, the colour of serpentinite, thunders under a bridge and the Carpathians (no doubt bear-filled) glower around the little town. There are horses with embroidered saddles and two teenage boys with golden eagles of alarming power, size and shagginess on their shoulders. There is even that Ukrainian favourite, a stall where you can dress up in a Red Army uniform and pose for photos with a variety of startlingly heavy automatic weapons.

Of course, the whole thing is an elaborate tourist construct and has been so for many years, otherwise I would not be there. Stall after stall sells industrial quantities of sheepskin coats, traditional samplers and carved wooden coasters, and coach after coach arrives filled with people to buy them during the short summer season. People have been coming to Yaremche as a daytrip from Ivano-Frankivsk or even Lviv – in the intervals between political and military upheavals – ever since it was an option.

Folklore has an oddly intimate role in the Habsburg Empire. Partly this came from the obvious fact that so much of the Empire was made up of unproductive and annoying mountains (albeit mountains sometimes filled with valuable minerals). Life in these areas, across the Alps, their Balkan spurs and over to the Carpathians, was probably more characteristic of the Empire than any other environment. Their inhabitants were fiendishly difficult to control – the gap between straggles of snowbound houses along high valleys and the beautifully regulated order of a walled town must have driven administrators mad. With thousands of thinly populated valleys, it was also unclear that there was much need to control them. Just taking a train up through the passes of the Tyrol it is obvious that until recently this cannot have been much of a tax base. Entire regions were cut off for a large part of the year (the key to Adalbert Stifter's great short story 'Rock Crystal') and rarely produced much economic excess. The little they did (hams, embroidery, fleeces) were sold at summer fairs so they could buy the things they could not make or repair themselves, a context in which gypsies have always been a crucial element – in a symbiosis of the most sedentary and least sedentary.

Life in these valleys was extremely harsh. No tourists in their right mind would visit Yaremche in winter. In a sense their inhabitants were lucky because there were many times when their remoteness and poverty protected them from the historical events in the plains – but an exceptionally bad winter or terrible flooding or a fire might do as much damage as a Turkish army and plague in a valley could kill all its inhabitants. So much of this is barely recorded, but these communities must have been re-founded frequently, presumably from neighbouring valleys. In any event the attraction of the high meadows for grazing was invisible to most humans, who considered the whole way of life dreadful. When the Italians took over the South Tyrol in 1918 they imagined they could restock the region with Italian-speaking hill farmers and remove all the Germans, but even the most hard-scrabble, hollow-eyed *contadino* considered it insane to spend his brief existence wrestling with moufflon in ten-foot snowdrifts and the project foundered. This was a life that could only be endured if you were born to it.

The most famous example of mountain people banding together is the Swiss Confederation. The often formidable difficulties in communicating between the different elements of the alliance in fact helped to keep the genuinely federal nature of their arrangements. The maze of passes within the Swiss Alps could either be a green light for banditry and short-term business thinking, or it could allow for peaceful trade and prosperity and the Confederation regulated this to everyone's gain, as well as offering protection against outsiders. The Confederation's resolute hatred of the Habsburgs (themselves originally in part Swiss) climaxed in the Swabian War of 1499 when after a series of disasters Maximilian I was obliged to leave them alone. The mayhem caused by such a small country in the late fifteenth and early sixteenth centuries is breathtaking – and, indeed, although the Swiss founding principle might have been an anti-Habsburg one, their role in killing off Charles the Bold and thereby ensuring Habsburg supremacy must have earned them at least a Christmas card from the Emperor.

Switzerland came and went in its impact on Europe, with its

mercenaries severely mauled in the Italian Wars, but the associated Three Leagues (the League of the Ten Jurisdictions, the Grey
League and the splendidly named League of God's House) to the
east of the Confederation caused intermittent violent chaos into
the seventeenth century, driving various military commanders
into total mental breakdowns by their sheer obduracy and localism.
It was only the arrival of Napoleon that ended their independence
and folded them into Switzerland.

The Habsburgs were always confounded by the way that while
mountains are excellent defences they are also extremely difficult
to defend. The Carpathians, as became clear in war after war well
into the twentieth century, look like a terrific natural bastion on a
map but each pass is sufficiently far from the next that they were
hard to reinforce and could therefore turn into the worse kind of
static fortress, soaking up troops and supplies while the enemy
simply goes round the corner and does something else. In the First
World War one of the most depressing experiences (in a crowded
category) of the Austro-Hungarian army was the 1915–16 defence
of the Carpathians, which had seemed smart on paper, but proved
impossible for the usual reason – that so few people live in the
mountains because there are so few supplies and they get covered
in snow for half the year. The result was thousands of deaths from
the cold and a total collapse in the survivors' morale.

The Habsburg cult of the mountains and of mountain folklore in
fact had military origins. As so few people could live in the mountains there was (if they were not wiped out by fire, flood or slave-
raiding) an excess population each year – classically split between
women who would work as servants and men who would join the
army. Stefan Zweig's story 'Leporella' is the perfect exposition of the
fate of women – the Tyrolean girl who ends up in Vienna working
for a worthless and libertine nobleman with catastrophic results.
Virtually the entire course of Habsburg military literature is filled
with tough Slovak, Ruthene or Serb squaddies, assigned by their
German or Magyar officers the same sort of 'martial virtues' the British projected onto the Highland Scots, Sikhs or Jats. The Habsburgs
had also always used large formations of irregular troops, drawn in

many cases from the Dinaric Alps and festooned in outlandish hats, boots and jackets. This gave the Habsburg military an entirely different profile to western European formations. The Military Frontier districts guarding the Empire against the Ottomans also had many regular troops, but it was groups such as the mainly Croat Pandurs who became famous, with a romantic cult quite at odds with the realities of border atrocity warfare. Many of these highly decorative irregulars were at such key events as the relief of Vienna in 1683. Given that a vital element in the Allied force there was a mass of Polish hussars with high, feathered wings on their armour and that they were fighting Ottoman camel troops in coloured turbans, the whole thing must have looked like a fancy-dress party or circus parade gone very badly wrong.

This fascination with exotic folk costume readily shifted, as the army's clothing became more regularized and banal, into a more general curiosity about those parts of the Empire that still maintained forms of folk dress. The same forces that created railways, accurate long-range rifles and mass colour printing in the mid-nineteenth century also created both nationalism and a civilian cult of folk costume: as millions of peasants flooded into the Habsburg cities, as multicoloured, easily spotted uniforms were put away and as mass literacy became available, real folk costume vanished for most people but became enshrined in other ways.

It is impossible to exaggerate the importance of folklore to the emergent nationalisms. In the search for authentic new heroes, there was both a military thread and an outlaw or bandit thread, where a motley selection of figures who had stood up to authority became enshrined in countless rhymes, songs, tales and portraits, with their folk costume (often a blind guess, of course – even the figure himself often had a shaky real historical existence, let alone his clothing) a symbol of integrity in the face of besuited German or Hungarian oppression. Everywhere had a bandit king – Juraj Jánošík, friend to the Slovaks and Gorals, or Oleksa Dovbush, scourge of the Poles and friend of the Ruthenes and Hutzuls, now a major Ukrainian hero whose attractive Carpathian rock hideaway I hiked through recently.

The Hungarians themselves were torn on this issue – they wished to distance themselves from Germanizing greyness, but also wanted to appear progressive and modern. Indeed all nationalist groups became irreparably tangled up on this point and could never decide whether rows of girls waving hoops covered in flowers or rows of men in steel helmets and puttees were the way ahead. In the end they settled for both. There is a particularly shrill cartoon by the Slovenian artist Hinko Smrekar which brings the folk costume question to its acme. Drawn in 1918 it shows Woodrow Wilson standing next to a piece of meat-grinding equipment and shoving into the machine a grotesque crone labelled Old Europe, vampire-toothed, skeletal and in a dirty wig, a crucifix around her neck, holding a gallows and whip. As she disappears into the machinery out of the bottom bursts a group of very fit-looking young women in folk dress, dancing away and helpfully labelled as Yugoslavia, Czechoslovakia and Poland, with an unidentified further figure with ear-rings and dark, curly hair which I would guess might be the spirit of Questionable Additional Lands Grabbed by Romania.

CHAPTER ELEVEN

The Temple to Glorious Disaster » New Habsburg empires »
The stupid giant » Funtime of the nations » The deal »
An expensive sip of water

The Temple to Glorious Disaster

Vienna's Military History Museum was Franz Joseph's pride and joy. In many ways it brackets perfectly the entire Habsburg experience, defined by two huge hunks of metal: a fifteenth-century 'supergun' from Styria of staggering size and impracticality* and an armoured cupola from a Belgian fort devastated in 1914 by a twentieth-century supergun, the Škoda heavy siege mortar. This cupola was somehow hauled to the museum across hundreds of miles as a tribute to Austro-Hungarian engineering and industrial prowess and to show its loyalty to and value to its German ally, shortly before all such concerns became nugatory.

The museum was built as part of the Arsenal complex in southeast Vienna, one of a series of Imperial urban strongpoints packed with weapons that could quell a future 1848 – a role they were never called on to fulfil. Designed quite arbitrarily in a sort of Moorish style more associated with harems than soldiers, it is one of the first examples (and a relatively charming one) of the sort of brain-destroying architectural eclecticism which would wound and goad generations of Habsburg intellectuals and designers into finally giving birth to modernism. Franz Joseph was deeply engaged in every aspect of the building and it was set up as a temple to the greatness of the Habsburg military traditions. The entrance

---

* The craze for such weapons was a brief one, ended by the impossibility of retreating with an object of such monstrous weight and value – one of Maximilian I's sudden and frequent exits from the battlefield was enlivened by disasters involving many of his Swiss mercenaries having to be diverted to hauling along one of these futile behemoths.

way is crowded with life-size white marble statues of generals –
many of them prime figures in the Habsburg cult of victory
followed by defeat, making the entire hall into a sort of Temple to
Glorious Disaster. The beards, ruffs, tricornes and weapons change
but the outcome tended to be the same. At the head of the main
staircase there is a bust of the young Franz Joseph with *Kaisertreu*
written under it – the conventional term describing the unques-
tioning loyalty and adulation felt by the soldiers for their supreme
commander. As all these very boringly conceived statues were
carved and hauled into place through the 1850s and 1860s this
was a sentiment that was to be put under considerable pressure,
and more than a few senior officers must have given a derisive
'Ha!' as they walked past the Kaisertreu bust.

It has always been important to the British to think of the nineteenth century as broadly peaceful once Napoleon had been finally
defeated, with the Crimean War as an exception plus a couple of
'cabinet wars'. An air of slight stuffiness hangs over much of the
century, but in practice Europe was just as turbulent as in the twentieth century, albeit with an incomparably lower death toll. The
British are among the most egregious fantasists, as their Victorian
peacefulness only existed by pretending that the dozens of colonial
wars in which they were engaged were not happening. Indeed, the
near universal habit of seeing European and colonial wars as unrelated is unfortunate, as in practice it was just as dangerous to be a
ruler targeted for destruction in Europe as it was to be one in India
or Africa. If there had been a suitable venue, figures as diverse as the
King of Hannover, the last Mughal Emperor, the Duke of Modena
and the Nawab of Oudh could have had bitter conversations about
the fickle nature of the mid-nineteenth century.

Austrian policy was fiendishly difficult. With the crushing of
the Hungarian rebellion there seemed to be a possibility of great
things, and indeed for short periods the Empire had a quite
extraordinary reach, both in its own right and on behalf of the
German Confederation, the loose association of German states of
which Austria was the most senior member. At one point during
the Schleswig-Holstein crisis in the 1860s the Habsburg navy was

in the North Sea, engaged in the Battle of Heligoland with the Danish navy and, following defeat, taking refuge in the waters of the British naval base on Heligoland. The very idea of a British base just off the German coast (soon to be swapped in fact with Germany for Zanzibar), let alone Habsburg warships being in the North Sea, let alone fighting the Danes, seems scarcely imaginable, but this was part of a crisis that dominated Europe. In a similar moment of glory Habsburg troops occupied the mouths of the Danube at the outbreak of the Crimean War, creating a buffer between the Russians and the Ottomans. For a couple of years it seemed that a Habsburg fantasy going back at least two centuries was about to be realized with the entire river system under Vienna's rule, but none of the other powers thought this a good idea and with the end of the war the soldiers were obliged humiliatingly to back out and make way by the end of the decade for a united Romania, a nightmare far worse for Vienna than somnolent Turkish rule.

In the end none of the opportunities came off and the period from 1849 to final humiliation in 1866 was catastrophic for the Habsburgs – but catastrophic in an annoying way, as so many of the problems stem from a mulish failure by Franz Joseph and his advisers ever to do anything right. It would be far too complicated and tiresome to give all the details of the congresses, treaties, meetings between monarchs and armistices that stud the period. Places which have never before or since been important suddenly took on a world-historical role. I have a friend who used for family reasons to have to go to the western Schleswig coast for Christmas and, not speaking German let alone dialect, he was obliged for a few days, as gales howled over the dunes and the tiles rattled on the roof of the farmhouse kitchen, to listen to his wife's relatives at mealtimes collapse with laughter – while he munched his way through the usual burnt pig selections and potatoes – as they came up with incomprehensible but clearly ever more elaborate insulting terms to describe him. Schleswig has featured in almost no conversation before or since the 1860s, but at this one moment in time, across Europe there was a sudden rush to atlases. Statesmen would narrow their eyes, stare at some imagined horizon, puff out their chests and claim some overwhelming, scarifying national interest in places with barely any population or even any animals.

The extreme instability of the period came from the collapse of the semi-solidarity of Europe's rulers following the 1848 revolutions. Suddenly a policy of mere reaction seemed untenable, not least because of the arrival of the Emperor Napoleon III in France, the great lord of misrule in this period and as creatively damaging in his way as Bismarck was to be. It was the Habsburgs' disaster to suddenly appear, at different times and in different constellations, a backward and unhelpful element in the European system. This was most clearly shown in the Crimean War, where Britain and France uneasily allied themselves against Russia in a bid to protect the Ottoman Empire from further predation. The Austrians owed the Russians everything for their help in defeating the Hungarians, but now, only four years later, they found themselves siding with the Allies out of fear of Russian ambition to take over Moldavia and Wallachia from the Ottomans and thereby block the Danube. Franz Joseph was in an impossible position – he moved his troops into Transylvania in a threatening manner, forcing the Russians to keep an army on the border which would have been useful elsewhere, but then could not make up his mind to attack. The Russians were half mad with rage over this betrayal and their recent and useful alliance with the Austrians was at an end. In happier times, a grateful Franz Joseph had given a statuette of himself to his best friend Tsar Nicolas. Nicolas now took the statuette off his desk and gave it to his valet.

But Franz Joseph knew that for Britain and France it was – at some level – quite a pleasure to attack Russia, as the Russians had no way of getting back at them, their navies making it wholly implausible that Cossacks would ever put, say, Tunbridge Wells to the torch. A declaration of war by Austria would have ensured at once that all the serious fighting would be on Austrian territory, starting with Transylvania, a province whose topography was entirely familiar to the Russian army from its very recent visit. There was a strong chance that the Crimean War (famous, as it turned out, for its grinding and inconclusive character) would have ended with the Russian occupation of Vienna and a situation not unlike 1945. Prussia managed to stay neutral without annoying anyone, Austria managed to alienate absolutely everyone (including Britain and France) and all this in a context where even the weakest knowledge of Habsburg history showed that alliances were essential for survival.

Appearing feckless, dithering, inconstant and backward, Franz Joseph's regime made vague gestures to embrace new allies, but to no avail. One surprising result of the Crimean War was the temporary collapse of Russia as a European power, the new tsar's interests redirected to the Far East and even to a fairly liberal course, the combination of the two removing what had been a reliably swivel-eyed and scarlet-faced Force of Reaction. Even if Austria could have made up with its former protector, Russia was no longer capable of doing any protecting. Prussia should have been a source of comfort as its unbalanced monarch Friedrich Wilhelm IV was obsessed by hierarchy and loved deferring to the Habsburgs as the senior sovereigns. But even he found himself constrained by German nationalism and any hope of a military treaty had to result in Prussian command over the army, which Franz Joseph could not agree to. The French were far away from Austria and in any event ruled by a dangerous revolutionary maniac, the nephew of the Habsburgs' nemesis. The British more or less gave up on the Austrians over their chronic indecision during the Crimean War, and this really marked the last gasp of one of the great constants in Central Europe: the British use of Austrian troops to pin down the French and get killed in huge numbers, while the British helped themselves to colonies in the rest of the world.

This sudden vulnerability was stark – no more Holy Alliance, no more automatically friendly German Confederation. In a visionary moment in 1854 Lord Palmerston mused that a general reorganization of Europe could be made whereby Prussia would be given Schleswig-Holstein and in return give Posen (a chunk of eastern Prussia) to a newly re-founded Kingdom of Poland; and Austria would get the Danubian principalities in exchange for

evacuating its territories in Italy. If only this had happened peace-
fully the entire course of Europe's history would have been
different. But, as usual with such counterfactuals, different does not
mean better. Similarly, as soon as anyone talks about Prussia's step-
by-step takeover of Germany and its fatal consequences, there is
always the assumption that if Austria had defeated Prussia, and
Vienna become the capital of a united and rather different Germany, the outcome would have been in some way nicer: an idea for
which, by definition, there is no evidence at all.

In the case of Italy, the speed with which a series of invasions
and revolutions united it is staggering. In the spring of 1859 the
Habsburgs in most of the north and their clients in the centre
(Modena, Parma and Tuscany) seemed absolutely dominant. Their
large army and control of both Lombardy and Venetia, much reinforced since the revolutions of 1848, made the idea of any form of
Italian independence a joke. But by the spring of 1861 a parliament
was meeting that represented the whole of Italy except Venetia and
Lazio. As in 1914, the Austrians were driven beyond endurance by
the goading of a small irredentist power, in this case the militarily
tough north-western kingdom of Piedmont. Piedmontese provocation in Habsburg Lombardy resulted in the Austrians demanding
that Piedmont disarm. Prussia and Britain had both expressed irritation with Piedmont, and Austria confused this with military support for itself. When Piedmont ignored the ultimatum the Austrians
attacked and, following a secret treaty, Napoleon III gleefully sent
in thousands of French troops to support the Piedmontese. Defeated
first at the Battle of Magenta, the Austrians were defeated again at
the immense Battle of Solferino, in which some three hundred
thousand poorly led and baffled troops killed each other in horrifying numbers before the Austrians withdrew. Napoleon tricked
Franz Joseph into an armistice to allow them to talk man to man.
Here the dull and starchy Franz Joseph was completely outwitted
with vague promises of helping out his relatives, who had by now
been thrown out of Modena, Parma and Tuscany. Napoleon
suggested that it was much better for Austria to withdraw from
Lombardy and keep Venetia than risk dismemberment at some

international congress. Italian unification leapt from Napoleon's control, with much of Europe simply sitting immobilized and aghast as various ancient cities, with courts that had often been the nursery of the greatest artistic and intellectual moments in Europe's history, and over which so many battles had been fought over the centuries, suddenly became engulfed by the new Italian state and reduced to municipal councils.

Franz Joseph's response to the Battle of Solferino (the awfulness of which led to the foundation of the Red Cross) was to end the war. This was an extremely old-fashioned thing to do, and a trick he would repeat in 1866. With our more recent experience, from the Franco-Prussian War onwards, with fighting which mobilizes entire societies and generates total demands, and which only ends by one side collapsing in complete disarray, this attitude seems odd. The Austrians, despite losses of some thirty-five thousand in a couple of weeks, still had many troops, a powerful defensive position and the possibility (as Napoleon uneasily realized) of intervention by Prussia. And yet Franz Joseph preferred just to pack it in. From our perspective it almost makes the losses seem frivolous. The Habsburg army was designed to fight and if the stakes were so high why give Lombardy up so easily? Franz Joseph seems to have developed a fatalistic attitude that it was better to be defeated honourably than simply to hand out family territory on the off-chance that this might appease whichever predator he was dealing with. This resonates with all his ancestors' behaviour too and it is more a comment on the increasingly odd and backward Habsburg presence in Europe than a criticism of Franz Joseph that he recognized this.

Italian unification, however much of a mixed blessing this may have been for many Italians, seems now to be as inevitable as German and Romanian unification and Franz Joseph's dully correct position – while it put a whoopee-cushion under Kaisertreu – kept many more people alive than some more apocalyptic policy. But as the white marble statues filled up more and more of the Military History Museum's foyer, there must have been some very bitter conversations between officers having to deal with the shock of

Habsburg expulsion from Lombardy of all places, with its family
associations lying in a tangled heap from at least the fifteenth century. But the Museum – which still has FJ monograms on the doors
to the toilets – would be putting up special displays featuring quite
a few more humiliations before it could all settle down.

New Habsburg empires

Travelling south from Graz, it is always exciting to be crossing
another linguistic barrier. The west–east wedge of German and
Hungarian settlement across the middle of Europe is suddenly
broken through, and places with names like Kaindorf an der Sulm
give way to places with names like Šentilj. The modern state of
Styria and country of Slovenia compete with one another for
harmless, outdoors daffiness, with local websites a great mass of
mushroom festivals, special stitched costumes and hiking opportunities. But all this admirable neutralism has to twist around a past
of German–Slovene hatred, perhaps most brilliantly expressed in
Peter Handke's great novel *Repetition*, with its picture of bitter discrimination and a shared landscape viewed through two quite
different pairs of eyes.

Modern Slovenia is stuck together from the rubble of the
Empire's end, with its core made up from the Duchy of Carniola
with bits of Styria, Gorizia, Istria and a small piece of the old
Hungarian county of Vas. The northern Slovenian city of Maribor
was the site of violent fighting in 1918 as this German-speaking
city (Marburg an der Drau) in a sea of Slovene-speaking countryside was grabbed by Yugoslavia, but only briefly as Hitler, in
Habsburg mode, carefully reincorporated it into Styria in 1941,
with the town's ancient Jewish population dispossessed and sent to
the camps. There are some grim photos of Hitler, Bormann and
others complacently surveying this citadel of Germandom from the
charismatic Old Bridge across the River Drava. All the Germans
were then expelled in 1945 and Maribor became an authentically

if traumatically Slovenian town. The expulsions are commemorated in a plaque on Graz's Castle Hill.

It is hard to shake off the harshness of Maribor's fate or the lack of continuity with the Habsburg past – the town's gloominess may be my own over-self-conscious projection. Under the late Empire it was a harmless minor way-station en route to the Hungarian-ruled kingdom of Croatia-Slavonia and the medley of the Austrian Littoral – it was a linguistic border town but not a political one. The great theme that beckons with every mile of the railway trundling down towards Ljubljana and Trieste is the one of the Habsburgs' futile southern destiny.

The slightly hysterical air of reaching a different cultural and linguistic world is based not least on the sudden prevalence of heaped piles of seafood. The best restaurant in Maribor is an Adriatic fantasia, a sort of cornucopia of bits of octopus, lemons, small things with fins, all thrown together with heaps of Mediterranean herbs. By the time you get to Ljubljana everyone is pretty much fish-mad, with perhaps the definitive seafood obsessive's restaurant tucked into the arcades under the great Jože Plečnik's magical Triple Bridge. Maribor itself is quite notably far inland and has as much claim to be a seafood Mecca as Birmingham, but it is quickly clear that this all stems from a reasonable Slovene yearning to be as Mediterranean as possible. Here they can play the decisive card that makes them *not German* – it's all calamari, oregano and prettily coloured drinks for them, leaving behind a sad world back in Graz of people having to pretend that river fish don't taste of mud.

For the Habsburgs this temptation to leave the sauerkraut behind and get a bit of sunshine was simply too great. Their ownership of Venetia was something new, a reward from the Napoleonic Wars, but it proved to be a total curse. The Venetians were, like all inhabitants of declining states, personally blamed for their fate – they were too indolent, sensual and corrupted and did not deserve to survive. There was no sense at all that it was not the Venetians but Venice itself that was the problem, that it was the terms of trade stuck at the top of the Adriatic that had gradually made the whole area a backwater. What had been one of the focal points of maritime history had, in an age of trans-global voyages and the resettlement by Europeans of entire continents, become merely an appendix. Whoever inherited Venice would have exactly the same problem. But for planners in Vienna, adding the small Habsburg ports of Trieste and Pola to the Venetian inheritance would make the Empire into a great oceanic and commercial power.

It was unfortunate for the Habsburgs that the Venetians had no interest in any such vision. Venice's quite separate political development from the rest of Italy gave it a certain resistance to Italian nationalism, but this did not for a second imply anything other than loathing for the Austrians. Despite all the indicators (for example, the self-immolatory Venetian Republic of 1849) the plan remained that the old Venetian properties would become an indissoluble part of the Empire, defended by a new navy and by the mighty Quadrilateral – the latter yet another of these notionally 'impenetrable' fortress systems which simply soak up troops who might otherwise be mobile and of some use.

A principal architect of this Habsburg vision was Franz Joseph's younger brother Maximilian, who was put in charge of this southern strategy. At the implausible age of twenty-two he was already head of the Austrian Navy and, almost as a private whim, organized a small but proper battle fleet and sent out a major scientific expedition around the world in the manner of other countries with navies. His monument remains the extraordinarily desolate seaside castle of Miramare, just west of Trieste. Built in the 1850s as a sort of Disneyish dream-home for Maximilian and his wife, it was still incomplete when he took the Habsburg global destiny far too seriously and was persuaded to head to Mexico to become an emperor in his own right, only to be crushed by political forces way outside his control: humiliated, imprisoned, executed and finally immortalized in Manet's paintings. The castle sums up the futility of all political striving, having hosted wave upon wave of short-lived visitors – men who would briefly stand in the hallway, look at its weary post-Scott medievalism plus running hot water, and wonder. Habsburgs, nationalists, Fascists, royalists have all passed through. There is even a terrific suite of *razionalista* cupboards and chairs from a time in the 1930s when the Duke of Aosta, Viceroy of Italian East Africa, lived at Miramare, complete with two sensational Italian Fascist painted maps, one of Libya filled with camel cavalry and a giant SPQR standard, the other of Italian Somaliland, decorated in a spirit of some desperation with a big crocodile and a selection of the corals and anemones, which apparently bejewel its coastal waters. Just as Maximilian died in Mexico City, so the Duke of Aosta died of malaria in a British POW camp in Kenya, meaning two cursed owners in the same castle. You can definitely see why there were no further takers.

The castle is crowded with elaborate objects and paintings which seem only to mock Maximilian's fate – many of them only installed after he left for good. There is a very strange painting of him as a teenager with his younger brother Karl Ludwig (the future father of Franz Ferdinand) inspecting the bottoms and breasts of slave-girls in a Smyrna market. I have never been able to work out how to even start researching who thought that was a good idea as a theme for a painting – perhaps it started off as a private memento. Maximilian's time in the navy is commemorated by his having his private office as an exact copy of his office on board his flagship, with lots of nautical-looking struts – a hearty joke which must have rather paled by the time that work was completed. There is a painting of the seemingly unenthusiastic ceremonies in Venice (a small bonfire and a handful of boats – it's no Canaletto) when he was appointed Viceroy of Lombardy–Venetia. And here too is the actual table at which he signed his assent to become Emperor of Mexico. There is also a spooky range of posh gifts which he never saw, from top well-wishers such as the Pope, plus an unused Japanese-themed smoking-room and a chapel still futilely decorated with a Mexican eagle. Best of all is an oil painting by Cesare dell'Acqua (perhaps the worst painter of the nineteenth century, albeit in a hotly contested field) showing the Argonauts in olden times rowing into the bay of Miramare and being waved at by lots of semi-nude locals.

But most bitter of all is the Imperial Mexican throne room, lined with paintings of Habsburg ancestors and with a huge map of the world colouring in all the places once owned by the family, designed to show Maximilian's inheritance in Mexico as a renewal of that of Charles V, the whole thing decorated with an uneasy mix of conquistadors and grateful First Nations types. It is possible, of course, to become too gleeful or too morose in the face of such beautiful examples of the vanity of human wishes. It would be interesting to know how New Zealand troops billeted at Miramare in 1945 as part of the Trieste protection force, standing in the throne room, felt about it all. The castle just spills over with examples of the decay and delusions of empire.

Maximilian lived long enough to get news (perhaps while wearing the special imperial sombrero preserved in the Military History Museum) of his vindication as a naval visionary: the bizarre Austrian naval victory at Lissa. His new fleet, under its commander Wilhelm von Tegetthoff, despite being outnumbered, managed to prevent an Italian landing on the Dalmatian island of Lissa (Vis), part of the frenzy of events in 1866. Tegetthoff devastated the Italian navy through the implausible method of using a metal ram, in a crazy throwback to the Roman Empire. Tegetthoff became a Habsburg hero. He also confused a generation of European naval engineers, who spent years mucking around fitting rams to everything, objects which never in fact tactically came up again. Unlike the futile mainland heroics, his actions also changed geopolitical history. The Italian expedition to Vis was there to establish Italy as the legatee of the entire Venetian state, including its old Dalmatian territories. Its defeat prevented this and despite short periods of Italian rule in the twentieth century, the eastern coast of the Adriatic solidified (with mass deportations of Italian-speakers) as part of Croatia. Admiral Tegetthoff sported the same bizarre whiskers as Maximilian, as though his cheeks were being attacked by two synchronized voles. As a native of Maribor, his victory was commemorated in the main square by a massive, lugubrious bust, sadly dismantled later in an outburst of anti-Habsburg feeling, despite his accidental contribution to the South Slav cause.

The Habsburg navy never came to anything. The problem always remained that the Empire was a land power and any diversion of resources into the Adriatic simply meant a loss of heaps of steel for the army, but still resulted in too small a navy to make a difference. In the First World War the British and Italian navies easily blocked up the Strait of Otranto with a miscellaneous heap of ships, ropes and nets and made the Adriatic a sort of enormous watery prison for Vienna and Budapest's expensive fleet. This navy's only, very dubious gift to the world was the steely Admiral Horthy, who tried and failed to break the Allied cordon and whose courage brought him to sufficient public notice to kick off his long career as the Habsburg 'Regent' of what would then be a land-locked Hungary. In the aftermath of Tegetthoff's early death, a ship was named after him and, in a final gesture of global ambition, sent up to the Arctic. In an epic of futility and ice its crew discovered a genuinely pointless archipelago now proudly named Franz Joseph Land.

In the century since the Habsburg Empire came to an end, workmen across Central Europe have been busily engaged in taking down any mention of Franz Joseph on countless statues, plaques and street names across the former Empire and it is at the very least odd that the largest-scale use of Franz Joseph's name survives in an area so remote that even its Soviet owners could never be bothered to change it. So the inheritors of the bold, imperialist and naval future for the Habsburgs were not the Venetians, and certainly not the Mexicans, but a few baffled and perhaps quietly loyal seasonal walruses.

The stupid giant

Intermittently, through the series of short but brutal wars of the 1840s to 1870s, Richard Wagner was working on first the libretto and then the music of *Siegfried*, an opera finally premiered in 1876. I am not quite sure why I like this opera so much and have such weak feelings about the rest of Wagner's enormous output. Perhaps it is the way that such excessive resources – length, orchestra, design – frame such simple action: no choruses, hardly anybody on stage at all, and then there is the unprecedented coup of only male voices for hours and hours, so that when the Woodbird arrives it is like a spell being lifted. The third part of *The Ring of the Nibelung*, *Siegfried* at its heart has a scene of the darkest intensity, where the parties interested in the fate of the dragon Fafner are dotted around the forest, awaiting events. The music has an almost extraterrestrial quality and you can see why so many people in the later nineteenth century and onwards were driven mad by Wagner – he makes so much else sound merely salon and ephemeral. Fafner is the last of the giants, who has used a magic shape-shifting helmet, the Tarnhelm, to turn himself into a dragon and has hidden himself in the depth of the forest to protect his treasure, including a magic ring which, in more intelligent hands, would give its owner dominion over the world. For Fafner, ownership is pointless – he lies on an infinite heap of gold which, in such a woodland-walks context, has no value. Fafner lives only to guard something he cannot use.

I fear it is easy to see where this is heading. To me – needing psychiatric assistance by now on Habsburg issues – Fafner is the nationalist critique of Habsburg monarchy. The watchers around his lair are, admittedly, sociologically unconventional, as they consist of a god, two angry dwarves and a blond simpleton – but you could see Wotan as the Aristocrat, Black Alberich as the Demagogue, Mime as the Worker, and Siegfried as the hero of the dawning age who will forge a new reality through his great deeds. Imposing *Siegfried* on the period only works in some respects, but it is quite interesting. The Tarnhelm stands for the shape-shifting political quality of the times: from 1848 to 1871 astonishing experiments are carried out across Europe – abortive republics appear from Rome to Venice to Paris, superstates are created in Germany and Italy of a kind which would have appeared idle fantasies to an earlier generation. Everything seems up for grabs, with figures like Kossuth, Bismarck, Mazzini and Garibaldi ushering in new, conflicting realities.

The Habsburgs are universally viewed as the stupid giant, their rule exposed to unbearable strain by events in Germany and Italy.

To be fair, Franz Joseph *does* try to use the Tarnhelm himself to improve his situation, switching from absolutism to bits of democracy, from activism to inertia, from centralism to federalism, but almost always in ways that appear too late, cynical, and incompetent. He keeps changing shape under his magic helmet, but you can still see the side-whiskers. Oddly, it is not as though the Habsburgs do not have allies, but they turn out when put to the test to be weak and unsure, whereas the allies that really matter are all in some way alienated. Very much like the marvellous scene when Wotan tries and fails to convince Fafner that he is in mortal danger, there were many people (including even Bismarck) available with advice for the Austrians which would save them. But, like Fafner, they just lie there confusedly awaiting their fate. Once the dragon is rather easily killed, the watchers across Europe wait to find out who will end up with the magic hoard (the blond simpleton, unfortunately).

Throughout the pan-European crisis of 1866 the Austrians continued to view themselves as a granitic pillar of moderation and consistency, baffled at the way almost everyone refused to believe them. Venetia had been under the rule of the Habsburg army since 1848 and with only the most footling concessions made to local, burning resentment. Attempts to smother everything in floral garlands, fireworks and a cheerful brass band were absurdly at odds with the reality. It was as though Vienna imagined it could portray its rule as a sort of *tableau vivant* of loyal and laughing peasants looked down on by a portrait of a benevolent Franz Joseph: Emperor, yes, but also father. If one could pan back a little from the *tableau vivant* the rustic group would be seen to be entirely surrounded by armed guards, busy censors and imprisoned bourgeois notables. Vienna (in a bind that would be endlessly repeated) could make no genuine concessions to the Italians without implying they were a special case: in other words, that Italian nationalism was real rather than the mere sick chimera of a few sallow intellectuals. This meant that many Venetian figures who hated the idea of being ruled by the alien Piedmontese felt trapped into thinking that even this would be better than being held in a state of suspended animation by the Austrians.

Triumphant tours around Europe by Garibaldi helped fix in the liberal public mind an image (which in any event needed little fixing) of the Habsburg Empire as a backward prison camp, alienating opinion in Britain most importantly. But even on the notionally reliable reactionary right Franz Joseph was in trouble. The Russians had never forgiven the betrayal of the Crimean War and were no longer available to terrify the Hungarians. Unrest in Romania in early 1866 briefly raised the idea that the Habsburgs simply dump Venetia and compensate themselves by taking over Romania. This provoked the enraged response from the Russian state chancellor Gorchakov, 'If I had the nature of a *sheep*, I should revolt at the very idea.' So that got nowhere. The Italians had even offered the previous year to *buy* Venetia, cash, which the Habsburgs could have used. But Franz Joseph chose to consider this an almost unbelievable piece of coarseness. A further problem lay in Vienna's refusal even to acknowledge the existence of the Kingdom of Italy, making negotiation almost impossible except through dodgy third parties, such as Napoleon III. Napoleon was torn over Venetia. In the end he was committed to nationalism and saw the conjuring up of the Kingdom of Italy as his life's work. But he could not help being somewhat uneasy about the massive growth of Prussia's power and his own lack of friends. Should he perhaps now become friends with Austria?

The final disaster for Franz Joseph lay to the north, where he shared in more fully fledged form Napoleon's worries. It was quite cruel that someone as limited as Franz Joseph should have been up against Bismarck. But again, he made his own problems. Because the rubble of minor German monarchs tended to be pro-Austrian there remained an unrealistic sense of Habsburg power over the region, a sense stoked by the slavish attitude of the Prussian kings, particularly Friedrich Wilhelm IV, who loved the idea of the Emperor as the olden-times-style senior German ruler and was still panicked about Prussia's vulnerability, obsessing about its near extinction in the Napoleonic Wars. Bismarck had no such concerns, and saw the contradiction between Prussia's sky-rocketing economic position and its subservience to Austria within the German Confederation. As an odd sort of conservative, Bismarck did not want to destroy the Habsburg Empire, but he saw that it was (as a multinational mess) incompatible with a German national state. If the Habsburgs disengaged from the Confederation and focused elsewhere – the Balkans looked nice – there was no reason for war, but, as in Italy, Franz Joseph's sense of honour made backing down quite impossible. It was not surprising that Franz Joseph spent so much time obsessed with a picture-book view of older Habsburg history, focusing more on horse-breeds and heraldry than political events. Hunting through the past for a time when things were better seems a fair response when you find yourself waking up each morning still having to deal with two alligators like Napoleon III and Bismarck.

Geographically alert readers will have noticed that the previous paragraphs have roamed around Europe hunting for possible friends for Franz Joseph and come up blank. Essentially the only ones left were a number of exiled rulers, including the ex-Duke of Modena, whose final act was to leave his enormous estate to the young Franz Ferdinand – making him, some years before he found himself Franz Joseph's heir, extraordinarily rich. These people were of very limited real political value, but keen either to go back to their old territories or find new ones. More plausible, seemingly, were the non-Prussian German monarchs, but for years their economies had been drawn ever further into Prussia's orbit and they were themselves in any event a mixed bag. We can be grateful to Ludwig II of Bavaria for paying the money that allowed Wagner to complete *Siegfried* and build his dream theatre in Bayreuth, but he preferred dressing up as ancient Germanic heroes to being a real king. George V of Hannover (who had inherited the territory instead of Queen Victoria as Salic law prevented her from doing so) was a frothing reactionary of a kind even other reactionaries would skirt round at drinks receptions. The Grand Duke of Baden was essentially pro-Prussian. All in all, this was not a very shipshape crew, and their responses to the events of 1866 mocked Vienna's hopes.

1866 saw mayhem break out across Europe. The combination
of allies, neutrals and semi-neutrals meant that actual fighting
lasted only six weeks. It is a curious contrast with 1914: both were
a surprise to almost everyone involved, but 1866 was militarily
resolved with bewildering speed, whereas 1914 turned out to be
sickeningly unresolvable. It shows the contingent and peculiar
nature of major crises. Prussia had little military experience, Austria
had plenty. Nobody knew then that all Austria's allies in Germany
were useless. France's position was very unclear. The Austrians
were goaded into attacking Prussia by disagreements over the Confederation and Schleswig-Holstein. But the Austrians had become
used to throwing their weight around in the Confederation with
the implied quiescence of Prussia and did not know that Bismarck
now had fresh plans for them.

Franz Joseph went to war with elaborate and old-fashioned
intentions: to crush the Italians, humiliate the Prussians, take back
Silesia (in a bonkers nod to Maria Theresa) and give one of his
exiled relatives a new dukedom in the Rhineland. Critical to this
plan was a secret deal with Napoleon whereby France would
remain neutral and be given Venetia for his trouble, which could
then be handed to the Italians. Insanely, this meant that Habsburg
troops were fighting in large numbers to defend Venetia, a region
which under all circumstances was now lost. They had their usual
self-indulgent few weeks defeating the Italian army, but of course
this meant that there were insufficient troops in the north to deal
with the Prussians, a probably crucial margin.

Part of Franz Joseph's plan was to use the German Confederation to outlaw Prussia and so authorize the other German states to
attack Prussia. Bismarck responded by declaring the Confederation
finished. Prussian troops then effortlessly carved through the minor
monarchies, with Saxony, Hannover and Hesse-Kassel in tatters
within about forty-eight hours. After the Hannoverian soldiers
surrendered, the Prussians disarmed them, gave them railway
tickets home and then ended their kingdom, a territory that had
been one of the key factors in European and British politics for a
century and a half.

Highly unfortunately the Austrian war effort in the north was in the hands of Ludwig von Benedek, a fine example of a Habsburg commander who froze up under his sheer incapacity. He seems to have, after the first moments of excitement, become catatonic, simply waiting for enormous Prussian armies winding through various Bohemian passes (which could have individually been knocked off before they came together) to join up and destroy him. Some four hundred and twenty thousand men crashed into each other at Königgrätz, in the largest but also dullest battle in European history. The sheer helplessness of Benedek makes it awful to read about – not from any sympathy for the Habsburgs, but from a sense that so many people died and so much trouble was taken to such pitiful ends. From the Prussians' point of view it was more a question of traffic management than anything else once it was clear that – to their astonishment – the Austrians were just going to stay put until they were outnumbered and pinned down.

It is very odd that an Empire that defined itself in military terms perhaps more than any other except Russia should have been so useless at fighting. All dreams of taking back Silesia or of forging a Grand Duchy of the Rhineland vanished with sensational speed. The old German Confederation was replaced by total Prussian control over most of Germany and the end of Vienna's role in western Europe, with only a handful of southern German monarchs staying independent. Italy, despite defeat, took over Venetia through the humiliating agency of France and came a further large step closer to unification. Napoleon realized far too late that he was now left quite alone with a monstrously enhanced Prussia on his border – a fact which would be resolved with the destruction of his own regime and the abasement of France four years later. This disappearance of Austria from western Europe really is one of the great shifts in the continent's history. It may have long ago been removed from the old Austrian Netherlands (now independent Belgium) but before 1866 there were Austrian troops up in Holstein and in the Confederal fortresses along the Rhine. All this went up in a puff of smoke and the attitude and thinking which had linked Franz Joseph back to Maximilian I and Charles V was at an end. This was hardly to be regretted, but it was startling: the Habsburg Empire was now merely a regional power, and a cowed one.

Meanwhile the Military History Museum was gamely continuing to finish its decoration and put further white marble Habsburg military heroes in its lobby. Ever more lavish display cases were installed, full of the notably gorgeous uniforms of the past – plus medals, sashes, battle paintings, elegant weapons, captured Turkish tents. There must have been *really* awkward conversations around the ticket booth by the late summer of 1866 as almost every aspect of the museum now appeared coarsely sarcastic. Last time I was wandering around the museum there was a temporary exhibition of such oddness I cannot help thinking of it as having been a dream. This featured a video of an Austrian army fashion show held in the grand hall in 2006. There, below frescoes of the frowning generals of the Thirty Years War and heraldic shields of the old Empire's territories, was a stage draped in camouflage. With Euro-style electronic dance music playing, army recruits uneasily strutted back and forth modelling the latest range of Austrian military wear: fatigues, combat gear, skiing clothes, military bras, SAS-type clothing, plus drop-dead formal wear for that special occasion. The effect was stunning – momentarily it all seemed an outrage to end all outrages: the silliest possible spectacle, with girls and boys pouting and waving their bottoms around, making a chimp-house of the entire Military History Museum. Wake not the ghost of Prince Eugene! But by the time they sashayed off, it seemed in fact perfectly judged and in the living spirit of the Battle of Königgrätz. Here was an army whose principal use was as a sequence of bodies on which to project attractive, matching uniforms rather than to fight. This is, of course, admirable – there is nothing at all to be said for being a country good at fighting, and the rapid collapse at Königgrätz with a brisk surrender to follow prevented many more battles and deaths. The fashion show cheerfully embraced both modern Austrian neutralism and a past of upbeat incompetence.

Funtime of the nations

The rise of nationalist music is one of the Habsburg Empire's great gifts to the world. Its rich musical life, its concert halls and its conservatoires meshed together across a vast area to find exceptional players and receptive audiences, all in the cause of music that was setting out to destroy it. The music is more prominent than it would have been at the time because the other avenues of cultural nationalism – newspapers, periodicals, discussion groups, epic poems – are in many ways closed to us. The music, together with paintings, sculptures and folk dress, is what is left. As with so much of the Empire's life, it was provoked by the love–hate relationship with the German language – with German music, like German bureaucracy, the unstoppable flood of the mainstream. What started as a tentative or even merely peevish and backward attempt to hold on to something of their own traditions ended with the non-Germans making something remarkable. It is striking how close German comes to winning in the early nineteenth century. Figures such as Smetana famously had to battle to teach themselves Czech, and there are innumerable cases of nationalists who in private continued to feel more comfortable in other languages. But the challenge of a German hegemony, pouring into the Empire not just from Austria but from the whole vast expanse of northern Europe, made the creation of various national musics a seemingly life-and-death issue.

Shortly after the Cold War ended I went to a chamber concert in Prague Castle. It was extremely cold and sitting still listening to the music was a peculiarly intense experience. The room had a window looking out over the Old Town and, hearing the wonderful, chiming, declamatory sounds of a Dvořák piano quintet, music for a moment really did sound like the secret weapon that destroys all invaders – an illusion, of course, but a potent one.

In a way the nationalist explosion fitted in well with Habsburg priorities. The *folklorique* had always been an aspect of the Emperor's job and Franz Joseph was very adept at switching uniforms, medals, hats and crowns depending on what part of the Empire he was visiting. The Hungarian aristocracy was particularly keen to join in, with its enthusiasm for outrageous costumes involving fur, feathers, gold chains and frogging creating a surreal mishmash almost unrelatable to any real time or place. Nationalism effortlessly left off from the old engravings which assigned each part of the Empire a particular form of dress. Everyone hunted high and low for what they felt would be the most authentic elements in their region, meaning the least tainted by Germanism. This tended to equate genuine with rural or mountainous. Figures like Dvořák spent much of their energy creating sound-pictures of the Bohemian countryside. These are beautiful and great works of art, but as an image of linguistic or cultural purity their implications were chilling. Surely what most exemplified Bohemia was in fact the booming Czech–Jewish–German city of Prague? What really best characterized the entire Empire was its chaos of nationalities, and its best hope lay in an ideology (already supplied by the Habsburgs) of cooperation, or at worst grudging wariness. The disaster of Central Europe lay in the language wars which now engulfed everybody and which made on the face of it harmless issues like what music you listened to or what braiding you had on your shirt into ever more violent badges of exclusion.

Most of the rest of this book is about this subject. We know it ended in catastrophe, but of course at the time it was exciting, new and very creative. It is also possible to say, at some gloomy level, that nineteenth-century liberalism was always doomed to fall into the nationalist trap. Just as Joseph II ended up provoking rebellion and hatred everywhere, so an insistence on uniformity, rationalization and freedom of expression ends up with race-hatred. If it is not acceptable for everyone in the Empire to use German to communicate, then *any* counter-suggestion excludes another range of languages. In Hungary the Croats pleaded for Latin to be kept as the official language because they knew that the alternative was that they would have to learn Hungarian. The strange role of Latin in Hungary had itself originated in the Middle Ages as elsewhere in Europe, but somehow it had maintained itself as a *lingua franca* that stretched across the kingdom, allowing Slovak to speak to Romanian. It may be just loopy obscurantism to suggest that Latin should in fact have been imposed on everybody, but it would have solved this problem, and more plausibly than one of the constructed languages such as Volapük or Esperanto (the latter celebrated in an unbeatable museum in Vienna). But for a linguistically scrambled zone of Europe to have to choose a single specific language of command, school and bureaucracy raised the stakes for those excluded incredibly high, way beyond folk-dances and Hutsul authenticity.

Boycotts, abuse, marches and ever more aggressively chauvinist festivals broke out across the Empire in the latter half of the nineteenth century. These all seem a bit charming compared to the racist torture-chamber that was revealed in the following half-century, but it was this eruption that laid the ground work.

The weakness of Vienna after the disaster of 1866 allowed everyone to pounce, with, for example, the first Slovene Congress being held in Gorizia, or the Italian-speaking South Tyrol sending petitions to be split from the German-speaking north. The Czech example was a particularly grim one. With Bohemia such a tangle of Czechs, Germans and Jews and with German the dominant language of commerce and government, Czechs felt they had little choice but to assert themselves. 1848 had marked the point where Czech and German liberals faced impossible choices. The Germans naturally looked to a future ruled by German-speakers in Vienna or in Frankfurt – but equally naturally Czechs saw neither option as even faintly appealing. As the century progressed the situation became ever more ferociously polarized, with mutual shop boycotts so severe that in the end even Jews were successfully pressured into serving customers of only one language or the other. This wretched, Ulster-like atmosphere was ultimately only resolved, catastrophically, in the 1940s.

Bohumil Hrabal's wonderful 1976 novel *Too Loud a Solitude* sums up where all this would end. The narrator meets and falls in love with the lovely Manča at a dance. She wears folk costume, braids and beautiful long ribbons in her hair. She rushes to the latrine before the dance begins, not realizing that in the process she is dipping her ribbons in the 'pyramid of faeces' under the plank. As she leaps and whirls, her ribbons centrifugally fling a medley of excrement into the faces of the other dancers.

The deal

1866's most important political pouncers were undoubtedly the Hungarians. Here was Franz Joseph's regime in total disarray – his army humiliated, his allies dethroned, his ministers' judgement almost comically adrift. With Vienna kicked out of Germany, perhaps it could also be kicked out of Hungary? The arguments against a total break were considerable. The war of 1848–49 showed that even a severely weakened Austria could turn nasty by summoning the genie of the suppressed nationalities. There was also a chance that outside help could be called in – if not the thoroughly alienated Russians, then perhaps the newly forgive-and-forget Prussians. The misplaced confidence that Kossuth had felt about Hungary's ability to be an independent state fuelled a more general anxiety: could an independent Hungary really hope to exist in such a rough neck of the woods? Austria might be viewed with fear and contempt, but was far better than the only other obvious 'protector', Russia. And with an ever more assertive Romania, what if Hungary was left on its own to fight off some future Russian–Romanian invasion of Transylvania? These were all grounds for clinging to Vienna – and all nightmares which would indeed cause sleepless nights in the following decades.

The genius at the heart of the negotiations was Ferenc Deák, who had opposed Kossuth's extremism and saw the value to Hungary of being linked to the rest of the Empire, both economically and militarily. Negotiations between Vienna and Buda had been going on for some years, but now suddenly snapped into place. Franz Joseph's government was frenziedly preparing a fresh war of revenge on Prussia and could only do this by leaning on Hungarian support, not unlike Maria Theresa back in 1740. A radical overhaul resulted (although in the end the war of revenge got shelved): a new state linked by the person of the Emperor and common defence, foreign affairs and (for shared issues) finance ministries. The negotiation dripped with bad faith on both sides, with a powerful Austrian camarilla always seeing it as a short-term deal with the Hungarians to be followed by retribution in due course. At the end of the century Franz Ferdinand dreamed of opening his reign with a swift military occupation of Budapest and there was always a poisonous undercurrent of mutual hatred threatening to break the surface. But much to everyone's surprise the new state of Austria-Hungary survived. The Hungarians had sufficient independence to mostly do what they liked with their territory, with an attractively substantial pan-European stage on which to act.

Territorially the two halves were now called Cisleithania (west) and Transleithania (east), the River Leitha forming a chunk of the border. Vienna therefore kept everything except what might now be called 'The Crown Lands of St Stephen'. Transylvania was at last ruled from Budapest and over the next few years the old Military Frontier was dismantled, with areas such as Syrmia (which included the great fortress at Petrovaradin and the Serbian cultural hub of Sremski Karlovci) passing to Hungary, together with the Banat (based around Timişoara) and the Slavonian and Croatian Military Frontiers. These zones were enormous, complex and settled with innumerable linguistic groups not necessarily enthusiastic to become part of Hungary. The last two of these (the Slavonian and Croatian Military Frontiers) greatly increased the size of Hungary-ruled Croatia, previously just a small block based around the insignificant Zagreb, a military town which had only received its first mayor in 1850. It was now that Croatia received much of the strange shape it still retains today – a sort of default area of land filling in, like grouting, the gaps between Ottoman Bosnia and other Habsburg holdings. Coastal Dalmatia remained out of its reach though, staying as the surviving piece of the old province of Venetia as an Austrian possession. In 1868 the Croatians negotiated specific sub-rights from Budapest that delineated the Kingdom of Croatia-Slavonia, which distanced it in a not dissimilar manner to Hungary's distancing from Austria. But in practical terms Croatia-Slavonia was hemmed in and with little room for manoeuvre of its own.

The two halves of the Empire carried on in parallel, held together by Franz Joseph's startling longevity. Both halves boomed, being immeasurably richer by the beginning of the twentieth century. Austria had been neutered and infantilized by its defeat by Prussia – when the new united Germany emerged in 1871 it became Franz Joseph's central aim in life *never* to be alienated from Berlin again. It became axiomatic that Imperial security could only be guaranteed by holding Bismarck in a clingy embrace. Hungary was even further neutered and infantilized politically by being in Vienna's shadow and using the security guarantee provided by their association to underfinance its own armed forces. This Berlin–Vienna–Budapest axis now settled in, and of course with no sense at all of what a bitter future generation would owe to it.

An expensive sip of water

It could be argued that Bohemia's two great contributions to Europe have been to do with the manipulation of water – whether in lager or in spas. Certainly while Europe has many spas scattered in the most unlikely places, it was western Bohemia that had the most prestigious and enormous ones: Franzensbad (named after Emperor Franz I), Marienbad (the Virgin Mary) and Karlsbad (Emperor Charles IV). There was also Teplitz, which was as grand as any but suffered a catastrophic late-nineteenth-century disaster when coal miners accidentally dug into its principal underground spring and – in a spectacular subterranean burp – filled it with arsenic, corpses and pit props in a way that overnight obliged seekers of health to make other arrangements.

Marienbad (Mariánské Lázně) fills an entire valley with hotels, shops and sanatoria of the utmost haughty grandeur. A seemingly endless esplanade of white stucco flanks a park filled with splashing fountains, ancient trees and little bridges, all framed by soothing hills smothered in firs. In its pre-1914 heyday famous guests crowded in, everybody from Gogol to Twain, Mahler to Paderewski. In an earlier period Chopin took the waters and Goethe experienced his last, sad romance here. Most famously Edward VII (the last monarch actively to relish ruling Britain) stayed at the Hotel Weimar and chatted with Franz Joseph.

Things have been a bit bumpy since – with a devastating collapse in pan-European aristocratic clients after 1914, a period as a Nazi military hospital during the Second World War (Günter Grass rested up here), the expulsion of almost its entire population (who were German-speaking) after the war's end and its battered resurrection under the Communists as a people's spa. This last has been set aside now in favour of trying to recreate the pre-1914, Europe's playground atmosphere. Once more people parade up and down the old Kaiserstrasse as they admire the hotels, buy jewels and amber and stop for a cake and ice-cream. Once again, genuinely dying people and mere malingerers hiss at each other across dining rooms, fortunes are lost at roulette and nannies and mistresses clutter the parks. There is lots of hilarity around the spa itself with drinkers using special china sipping cups to try the different springs as they gush from individual taps. I grew up in a spa town, so medically touted waters hold no fears, but even I had to blench at the hard-core Cross Spring, an atrocious blend of metals and sulphur, which gives its sippers some insight into the experience of a victim of poisoning.

As in its golden era, Marienbad has an attractively brittle quality based around most of its treatments being a pointless fraud. The hotel facades seem determined to outstare sceptical visitors and get them to reach for their credit cards. Marienbad doctors were famous for their ability to batten like vampires onto rich, pettish hypochondriacs and many careers were made clowning about with mud, hot water and invoice pads. As real twentieth-century medicine built its bypasses around places like this, luckily for Marienbad many people did not notice and Central Europeans still swear by treatments of puzzling lack of efficacy.

The struggle between classiness and charlatanism is as old as

the very idea of the spa and there has always been an entertainingly 'mixed' crowd. I noticed gently walking down through the
park an attractive young Russian family in expensive leisurewear,
somewhat let down by the massive scorpion tattoo on the husband's sandalled ankle. This suggested that perhaps the entire
clientele once stripped off would sport acres of Russian prison
tattooing and almost all be engaged in exciting fringe free-market
activities.

Of course, it is profoundly boring here. You can only sip nasty
water, munch chocolate cake or buy amber bracelets for a certain
percentage of the day. Rubbing out a key underworld rival with a
silenced machine-pistol in a mud bath – with bullets making different sounds as they clack into the tiling or plock into the mud
– does not take much *time*. Even the Russian Orthodox Church,
built for members of the Tsar's family, seemed oddly listless and
unengaged with its environment. I tried to shake off this sense of
futility by walking in the surrounding hills which, while attractive,
were very empty of spa patients, as though nobody could even
bring themselves to wrestle actively with their condition, real or
imagined. As usual, rambling around was rewarded, this time by an
immense cemetery with battered monuments to the old German
community now elbowed aside by hundreds of newer Czech
graves, perfectly showing the process by which ethnic change puts
down serious roots through death.

The only real disappointment was to discover that *Last Year in
Marienbad* was not filmed there. This strange masterpiece has wandered about in my head for so many years that it was perversely
upsetting to find that my enthusiasm for going to see Marienbad
had been misplaced: it turns out it was filmed in palaces around
Munich and *of course* it could not have been filmed in Czechoslovakia at the height of the Cold War – duh!

The film's atmosphere does somehow hang around the real
Marienbad, though, a sense of time suspended, of a peculiar lethargy. If towns and cities are the focuses required for us to live out
our daily lives, then spas are something else: a space in which the
sick are meant to get well but also where, uneasily, the well are

meant to enjoy themselves in a constrained and tasteful way. They are quiet places because it is vulgar to be noisy, but it is also insensitive as people really are ill. This atmosphere hangs over Aharon Appelfeld's short novel *Badenheim 1939*. Appelfeld grew up in the Bukovina, in the Carpathians. The Nazis murdered his mother and he worked in a labour camp before escaping into the forest where he lived for three years, still only in his early teens, surviving until picked up by the Red Army. He reached Palestine in 1946 and became an Israeli citizen. This background is essential to understanding the sheer rage of *Badenheim 1939*. A Marienbad-like spa gradually wakes up for the season, as the orchestra arrives, the cake shop opens, variety acts set up in the hotel and guests flood in. As the day in, day out routine of the spa settles down it becomes clear that the gentility and calm are an illusion and the authorities are keen to discover who among the guests are Jews.

The genius of *Badenheim 1939* is the way that it panders to the idea of the spa as a place which is necessarily harmless and charming, while allowing tiny glances of horror to intervene, which until the end almost everyone refuses to notice. It is a much more subtle book than simply an attack on Jewish passivity – Appelfeld sees the whole idea of the great Central European spa as an evasion and in effect a monstrous trick. This framework for polite, empty circulation, a regulated, closed environment for the right kind of people, now seems to stand for a lost and enviable pre-1914 world, but in practice it has always been toxic and peculiar.

CHAPTER TWELVE

Mapping out the future » The lure of the Orient » Refusals »
Village of the damned » On the move » The Führer

Mapping out the future

The obsessive conservatism of the Empire under Franz Joseph had many sources, but perhaps the key driver was its unhappy involvement with the Balkans. The last great land-grabs under Joseph II had (in collaboration with the Russians) finally wrecked Ottoman fighting power. From Vienna's point of view the future for the Balkans had to lie in a sort of picturesque, unthreatening decay – Turks lolling in caravanserai, sipping coffee and reminiscing about past greatness. Any other outcome was simply a threat. For the Hungarians it became axiomatic that any actual extension of the Empire would be a disaster – to bite off a bigger bit would just result in more Slavs or Romanians, who would further dilute a Hungarian presence already spread thin. Locked into such a view was its opposite: for those still actually under Ottoman rule living south of the Empire's borders there were for many two clear goals – first to remove the Ottomans and then to liberate their fellows trapped inside the Habsburg Empire. The Habsburgs were equally clear that a Russian presence in the region was unacceptable. With the Ottoman Empire's decay looking ever *less* picturesque, the vacuum would logically be filled by a partition between the Habsburgs and the Russians, much as with Poland. But the Habsburgs' distaste both for further territory and for any hint that the Russians might control the mouths of the Danube led to a freakish result. Having spent centuries fighting the Ottomans, the Habsburgs suddenly became solicitous of their health and conspired with the British to prop them up and keep the Russians away. If Vienna had historically often felt humiliated by being London's patsy, then one can only imagine the humiliation in

Constantinople, as the whole place filled up with vulpine false-friends from Europe swearing eternal friendship with the Sublime Porte purely to mess up St Petersburg. It was this stand-off which created a peculiar force-field around the Balkans in which national-isms that might otherwise have been stamped out came to full bloom. It created a slow-motion disaster for the Empire, which during a century or so first threatened (if blooms can threaten) and then destroyed it.

The four hundred years of Ottoman rule in the Balkans had created a very different society. The ruling class was entirely sepa-rate from the bulk of the population, in language, religion and culture. The areas bordering Habsburg territory consisted of Serbs ruled by Muslims, and Romanians ruled until the 1820s by Greeks (the Phanariots) on behalf of Constantinople. In the Slavic areas (Serbia and southwards – the Romanian principalities of Wallachia and Moldavia never had a Muslim presence) Christians operated under all kinds of constraints, with elaborate codes for where they could live, what they could wear and what jobs they could do. A mounted Christian had to get off his horse in the presence of a Muslim, a Christian could not wear the colour green, no new Christian churches could be built (giving an ever-deeper cultic reverence to those kept going since the original invasion). This started to crumble in the eighteenth century as the stuffing fell out of the Ottoman project. Military defeat, disease, economic failure and banditry (both through renegade Turks and restive Serbs) thinned out the population, but gave particularly good reasons for Muslims to pack up and move nearer to the capital, decisions which brought economic life almost to a total halt.

The Serbs started the great home-grown rejection of the Otto-mans, carving out their own autonomous zone in the early nineteenth century and in sudden surges picking up further land and independence. Western Europe always treats the Balkans as alien, and it is true that it had a very different atmosphere. A couple of examples are music and food. The court cultures of west-ern Europe, right up to the south-east fringes of the Empire, were saturated in fine music and fine food. The entire Habsburg landscape was given a deep, even coating of musical interpretation, whether Smetana and Dvořák in Bohemia or Haydn and Schubert in Austria or Bartók and Kodály in Hungary. As soon as you head south from Hungary or the Carpathians this music stops. And with food, the greedy, complex and extravagant Habsburg world of layered cakes, a mad use of chocolate, subtle soups and fine wines goes off a cliff. This is obviously an enormous subject, ludicrously compressed here, but the very idea of such complex foods trickled down in the west from royal courts, famously with the development of the idea of the 'French restaurant' in the aftermath of the Revolution. Indeed, we all eagerly guzzle a range of court foods – with many Indian and Chinese restaurants in the west also serving essentially court Mughal or Qing banquet foods, albeit in mutilated forms. In the Balkans the old Muslim ruling class were so remote from the population they ruled that their expulsion or killing ended any connection with such a world, with all those pilaffs, sherbets and baklavas once enjoyed in Pécs or Belgrade retreating to Constantinople together with the great Ottoman music, clothing and rituals that had accompanied them.

The Ottoman collapse left a peasant society, extremely poor, with very little education, eating basic, local foods washed down with fruit brandies. This was true throughout the entire region, as much in Albania as in Greece, Macedonia or Bulgaria. A very flat social system created an atmosphere very remote from that of Hampshire, say, or Saxony. The two Romanian-speaking principalities of Wallachia (the area south of Transylvania) and Moldavia (to the east) were somewhat different as they had managed to keep enough independence to have elements of a Romanian land-owning class, albeit under Greek-speaking control. But even Romania battled against poor education, an alien court and the far worse problem of being in the way of the invasion route in any fighting between Russians and Ottomans.

The nineteenth century played out a highly complex battle for independence and control, which gave the Habsburgs kittens. In its simplest form the Habsburgs provided tutelage and support for the Serbs, the Russians for the Romanians. As both nationalities became better educated and more economically complex (shifting to cash rather than local barter) so relations became strained. The Habsburg south of Hungary, around what is now called Novi Sad, had many Serbs living there, mainly the result of previous mass movements to escape Ottoman control in the seventeenth and eighteenth centuries. These Serbs provided bureaucrats, thinkers and soldiers for the new autonomous Serbian state to the south, but they also lived in what would logically be a potential area of Serbian expansion. By 1867 the last Ottoman troops had left Serbia and Serbia was truly independent. The Habsburgs used their control over the country (buying all its pigs and plums) to keep a friendly regime there, but the resentments were overwhelming and the still explicitly Catholic ideology of the Empire in any event repulsed the Serbians. Serbian attempts to expand into Ottoman Bosnia and to gain access to the sea were blocked in 1878 by a 'temporary' Habsburg occupation of the territory and in 1913 by the Habsburg creation of Albania – perhaps the only state to be invented simply as an act of spite.

The Romanian story had a related trajectory. There, Romanians in the Habsburg Empire (in Transylvania, the Banat and Partium) provided intellectual fuel for Romanian nationalism and, despite the Carpathians splitting them from other Romanians, gradually began to make sense of a single language-based entity. The two Romanian principalities of Moldavia and Wallachia, under Russian influence, worked towards some form of union from the 1840s and as remaining Ottoman privileges crumbled, a single state seemed likely. Russia, as a protector, did not have the exquisite scruples of the Habsburgs about chewing through fresh territory. During the Napoleonic Wars Russia had accidentally on purpose absorbed eastern Moldavia, calling it Bessarabia – the core of what is now the grim country of Moldova. On the face of it there was little to stop Russia absorbing the rest of Moldavia and moving on. The Russians also had plans to turn Bulgaria into a further, massive satellite, to be followed by Constantinople. This never happened, but the boundaries in the area remained very fluid. The rival intentions and fears of the three empires circling the region created an elaborate magnetic field of sufficient, if erratic, repelling power to allow the relatively small nationalities to keep some hold over their own destinies. Britain and Russia's mutual dislike and suspicion, everywhere from the Mediterranean to the Himalayas, made Britain a natural ally for the Habsburgs, but there was no avoiding the problem that Britain's navy could not have much impact on Russia, whereas any land war would involve the Habsburgs doing the heavy lifting. The Crimean War saw a high tide of cooperation, but the British only seriously damaged a small area along the Black Sea with their fleet, and the Habsburgs realized they were simply not strong enough to fight the Russians alone on land with any chance of success. So although they reached the Black Sea, they maintained neutrality against Russia. The notional monarchical solidarity between Moscow and Vienna now came to an end, but the latter's timidity meant that they at least did not fight each other until 1914.

In the later nineteenth century as Belgrade and Bucharest were transformed into ever more plausible and sophisticated capitals it became clear to some key elements in their elites that their national revolutions were incomplete and that their brothers trapped within the Habsburg Empire cried out for redemption. The disparity in military force between these small countries and the Empire made this seem a somewhat comic aspiration, but so much of the national legend of both territories came from Sremski Karlovci, the principal Serbian town in southern Hungary, and Sibiu, which had a similar role for Romanians in Transylvania, that this was a powerful rather than frivolous or marginal aspiration. The Serbian revolution of 1903 ended any cooperation with the Habsburgs and eventually led to the wars which partitioned the remaining Ottoman territories in Europe. As the Habsburgs used every diplomatic trick to box in the Serbs and kick them away from Albania, the Serbs found themselves permanently trapped inland. Straightforward Serbian nationalism, in this pressure-cooker, mutated into Yugoslavism. If the Serbs were not strong enough to take on the Empire, perhaps they should ally with other Slav peoples? This would make it legitimate to absorb Habsburg-ruled and substantially still

Muslim Bosnia (the temporary occupation had become permanent in 1908), and Croatia and Slovenia, even though none of them had any real historical links with Belgrade, aside from the usual medieval nonsense. As with almost all Balkan issues this would need a fatal weakening of the Imperial power. This seemed unlikely until the Serbian-sponsored killing of Franz Ferdinand in Bosnia in 1914, perhaps the most amazingly successful terrorist act in modern history, one which – after terrible suffering – fulfilled all the most far-fetched Serbian fantasies, and those of Romania too.

This is a very brief summary – the whole subject is so fascinating that it deserves much more space – but it is curious that whereas the Habsburgs could lose out in Italy in the 1850s and in Germany in 1866 without any serious questions about their future, it was in their traditional backyard, impoverished and with a small population, that their nemesis lurked.

The lure of the Orient

I may have just been in an unusually good mood because the Gregor Mendel (father of genetics) Museum was unexpectedly closed, but with a spare afternoon in Brno I found myself radiating benignity as I went into a courtyard and up some stairs and through the door of what may be one of the nicest places in the world: the Good Teahouse (Dobrá čajovna). Brno is a civilized and beautiful city and the Good Teahouse clinches its case. A series of rooms filled with wall-hangings and Persian carpets, heaped cushions and little tables, the teahouse may teeter on the verge of parody, but it is nonetheless a remarkably complete Orientalist fantasy. Moravian students smoke hookahs and sip tea, the latter ordered by tinkling a small bell on each table. There are few enough opportunities in Central Europe to loll, and here at last is a place which is a sort of essence of lolling.

Orientalism, with its uneasy mixture of languor, sex and cruelty, is one of the great organizing principles in Western life. It is, of

course, unrelated to any actual, real part of the world but is instead
constructed from vague ideas about Ottoman or Arab or Persian or
Moghul or Chinese life (most of the world, in fact) as filtered
through various texts, objects and paintings. Its beauty lies in its
immense range – within each country, indeed within each individual, there is a private Orientalism, (with a bit of a male bias)
from munching pistachios while lying in a pile of girls to the conquest of whole races in an epic of cruelty – and all achieved just
by letting the imagination roam a bit while sitting on the bus.
Much of my own Orientalism came from the comparatively real
experience of having spent some months selling books in the
actual Middle East. I have the happi-est memories of sitting around
(lolling even) with booksellers in Jeddah or Riyadh, sipping the
most perfect mint tea and swapping courteous and engaging stories
with my elegant host (Sudanese servants and Indian accountants
lurking in the background) before eventually getting down to business. To be honest I am unsure that I contributed much myself
in the way of courteous and engaging stories, but the experience
had a profound impact on me – couple this with an enthusiasm
for Mary Wortley Montagu's *Turkish Letters*, the paintings of John
Frederick Lewis and Eugène Delacroix and an infinite tolerance for
The Arabian Nights and I had my complete kit.

Central Europe's fascination with the Orient has its own
specific flavour – although again it has to be emphasized that
Orientalism is so various that it would be horrible and depressing
to claim a simply Austro-Hungarian form of it. Most obviously it
was based on a specific and direct fear of the Ottomans. There
is a lovely seventeenth-century engraving of Pécs in southern
Hungary, showing it as a completely Turkish place – a quite small,
walled town filled with domes and minarets, the picture decorated
with camels (then common as beasts of burden right across the
Balkans) and slippered Turks preparing coffee. The 'cultural
exchange' between Christians and Ottomans in Central Europe
(principally desperate, fanatical fighting plus large-scale slave-
raiding) was a vigorous one. One very odd aspect of this can
still be seen in churches on the old border, in the crook of the

Carpathians in south-east Transylvania. Here the entire human landscape is designed around defence against Turkish raids. But because of the severe Protestantism embraced by many Transylvanians and the accompanying hostility to all images (a hostility, of course, shared by much of Islam) many churches in the region have very surprising decorations. This is most famously the case with the great Black Church of Braşov, the final, craggy, massive western Christian church before the mountain passes marking the crucial frontier with the eastern world of Orthodoxy and Islam. Despite the Black Church's almost oppressive symbolic importance, the interior is decorated with Turkish carpets, nailed to or hanging from the walls – their beauty but also their abstract design making them permissible embellishments, despite their obvious Islamic symbolism.

Central Europe's relations with the East were based on fighting and on trade, forming one of the key conduits (along with Venice) for the transfer of beautiful fabrics, coffee, Turkish tobacco, jewels and all the other rather worrying indications that the Ottoman Empire was a great (and for very many years unbeatable) civilization. I have already written about the actively military aspect of this relationship, but fighting had fallen into almost total abeyance by the nineteenth century. The concern with the Ottoman Empire now became for Vienna an awkward mixture of wanting to prop it up as a threat to Russia and wanting to carve it up to gain territory (a plan always vetoed by the Hungarians): a dilemma never resolved until the collapse of the Habsburg, Russian *and* Ottoman Empires within a few months of each other.

The Hungarians had a particularly odd relationship with the East because by the 1840s they felt under so much pressure on so many fronts. The highly influential ideas of German intellectuals, from a number of perspectives, stated that the Hungarians would shortly die out, doomed as a linguistic oddity to be swamped in a sea of Germans and Slavs. This suggestion understandably added a nerve-racked edge to Hungarian nationalism. The Ottomans shared some of this view of Hungarian terminality and after the Russian invasion of 1849 stamped out the last embers of Hungary's bid for independence there were high hopes in Constantinople and among the large Muslim communities along the eastern reaches of the Danube that the logical thing for the Hungarians to do was to convert en masse to Islam.

At a time when all the peoples of Central Europe were scouting around for bogus stories of national origin, one clear embarrassment was the thinness of everyone's roots when compared to the deeply ancient and complex worlds of the eastern empires. The Hungarians had a particular interest in this as they felt they could trump the Slavs by making a virtue of their own presumed origins in Central Asia. This had many fascinating spin-offs – and indeed could make in its own right a long book – and is a topic not helped by my own susceptibility to the gravitational pull of all things eastern.

Sándor Csoma de Kőrös was a polylingual Transylvanian, born in 1784, who became obsessed with the long-standing idea that the Magyars were descended from the Huns and decided to travel to Central Asia looking for clues. He ended up trapped in a grim, completely unmanageable piece of intellectual machinery of his own devising, battling with Tibetan texts in remote monasteries, subsisting on handfuls of rice, swathed in woollens, unfolding the mysteries of Vajrayana Buddhism and doing very little, as it turned out, to prove Magyar origins in the high Pamirs. Intermittently supported by the Asiatic Society in Calcutta, Csoma de Kőrös revolutionized understanding of Tibet, creating a grammar and Tibetan–English dictionary as well as engaging in the rather thankless task of translating infinite amounts of stuff about Vajrayana Buddhist ritual, his work being described by the French traveller Victor Jacquemont as 'unspeakably boring . . . there are some twenty chapters on what sort of shoes it is fitting for lamas to wear'. This engaging, modest man, almost incredibly far from home and without another Magyar for thousands of miles, is one of the great heroes of Oriental studies and should have a little shrine to him in the Good Teahouse as a key initiator of the hippie obsession with Kathmandu. He eventually died of fever in the Terai jungles on a final, fraught expedition.

Arminius Vámbéry was a similarly modest figure, brought up in extreme poverty and hardship in northern Hungary but blessed with an uncanny facility for languages. Inspired by the *Arabian Nights* and also by the same Hungarian fascination with their ever more nebulous homeland, he took the startling decision while working as a tutor in Istanbul to disguise himself as a mendicant Sunni dervish and, using his ability to soak up foreign tongues, to visit the almost unknown emirates and khanates of Central Asia. So in 1861 he set out on his extraordinary journey, recounted later in one of the greatest of all nineteenth-century travel books, *The Life and Adventures*. This inexhaustibly marvellous, brilliantly lit and funny book is a sort of *hyperpuissance* of Orientalism – earthquakes, scorpions, fatal salt bogs, cruel khans and turquoise-mines. By the time he encounters a group of Turkmen raiders in Khiva emptying out bags of human heads and carefully collecting their dockets from the khan's clerk so they could cash them in for particularly gorgeous silk robes ('the suit of eight heads', 'the suit of twelve heads', etc.), it is all getting almost too much. As he travels by camel over the Tigerland Plateau, herds of thousands of wild asses raise great clouds of dust, while in the immense central deserts travel is only made possible by the Pole Star, known in the region as the 'Iron Peg'.

Vámbéry never went back to Central Asia and spent the rest of his long life in Budapest promoting the idea that Hungarian and the Turkic languages share a common origin – an idea not generally viewed with favour by most philologists. It was however attractive in bolstering Magyar self-identification with Central Asia and providing fresh grounds for the burgeoning relationship between Budapest and first Ottoman and then Kemalist Turkey, a relationship which set aside centuries of mutual hatred in favour of a more nurturing, shared hatred for the Russians. This cult of Central Asia ('Turanism') was to rebound somewhat by refining a magnificent weapon for the Romanians, who went on entertainingly about the Magyars being merely 'Asia's discharged magnates', whereas they were themselves the pure outpourings of Trajan's centurions' loins and the true gatekeepers of European civilization.

This unhelpful debate has never been resolved.

The world of the khanates described by Vámbéry has a very specifically Magyar flavour – he compares the Oxus to the Danube, he compares the flat, mirage-bewitched landscape near Isfahan to the Hungarian Great Plain, he seems much more excited about the novelty of the sea than a British writer would. Above all, in a highly self-conscious way, his book can now be read to describe a world rapidly vanishing in both Central Europe and Central Asia in which human communities were constrained by the capabilities of animals – the distance an animal can be ridden without food or water – a world of remote inns, bandits, chronic shortages and purely local knowledge. As telegraphs, rails, guidebooks and maps spread over the Earth, these constrained and semi-distinct environments disappeared, whether in the Kingdom of Galicia and Lodomeria or the Emirate of Bokhara. Vámbéry got to Central Asia just in time. Only ten years after he left, Khiva fell to a Russian army, beginning a long and miserable association with Tsarist and Communist forces which has left the region a degraded ecological catastrophe.

There is a great moment in the book where in a northern Persian village, Vámbéry, clothed in rags and muttering extracts from the Koran in his habitual dervish disguise, realizes that two locals are chatting about how he is obviously just a foreigner dressed up. Later on, in Herat, he is face to face with the sixteen-year-old Afghan ruler of the city, who prowls around him, swearing that he is an Englishman. Vámbéry is lucky to be there so early in the proceedings and to have such bizarre powers of dissimulation that he could stare down the prince, bamboozling him with Islamic proverbs. A generation later the whole place was so crawling with British spies that, in a sandy version of *The Man Who Was Thursday*, entire caravanserai would have been filled with walnut-juiced fake mendicant dervishes from different parts of the army or secret service, all offering each other pious blessings and engaged in a continual round of ritual ablutions, when in reality the whole lot were near neighbours back in Surrey.

Places like Herat became the front line in a cold war between

Russia and Britain, not one that featured Hungary notably. This gives a relatively unpolitical, cultural purity to Vámbéry's Orientalism (although he was paid by the British to support their position, a fact that only came to light in 2005) and confuses the argument that Orientalism was simply a means of imperialistic manipulation and control over the East. For Austria-Hungary the stakes on the Oxus could not have been lower, but the importance of this purely cultural Orient to Central Europe was considerable. Of course it could always be just a minor grace note, such as Franz Ferdinand's Turkishly decorated 'harem room' at Konopiště Castle, where he used to hang around smoking with nice friends such as Admiral von Tirpitz and Kaiser Wilhelm, rather than using it for the purposes that the room's name suggests (unlikely, given his churchy uxoriousness). But it becomes a sort of core blizzard of sensuality and fatalism for late-Habsburg composers, most importantly through the renderings of Persian and Chinese verse by the German poet Hans Bethge, who provided the texts for Mahler's *Song of the Earth*, Szymanowski's *Symphony No. 3* and *Love Songs of Hafiz*,* Schoenberg's *Four Pieces for Mixed Chorus*, Webern's 'In der Fremde' – the list goes on and on. There is also Béla Balázs's adorable collection of fabricated Chinese fairy tales, *The Cloak of Dreams*, packed with magic parasols, screaming skulls and fish made from silver which make a sound like tiny silver bells as they brush against each other in their pond. But that's quite enough.

I should not leave this topic though without mentioning Aurel Stein. Although he worked for the British Empire he was the acme of Central European engagement in Central Asia. A tiny bachelor Hungarian Jewish convert from Budapest, he was inspired by tales of Csoma de Kőrös and Vámbéry to march into the heart of what he winningly called Desert Cathay. There is a marvellous photo in the British Museum of his party heading off across the murderous Taklamakan Desert, all sand dunes, eerie shadows, muted heroism

---

* Szymanowski is strictly speaking a Russian Pole, but his manner and values are so Habsburg-friendly as to make him an honorary subject. And I like him too much to miss him out.

and camels laden with dubious old loot. He tracked back and forth over some twenty-five thousand miles during his long and restless life, battling with opium-addled diggers and the horrible spiders of the Turfan Depression, losing toes to frostbite in the Kun Lun Mountains (and only saved from losing a leg by the adventitious appearance of a Moravian missionary doctor in Leh) while discovering all manner of ancient Chinese wonders, abandoned many centuries earlier after battles with nomad raiders. Stein died in Kabul aged eighty-two while planning yet another Silk Road expedition. He was perhaps the greatest of all the Hungarians who failed to come up with any evidence for their national origins, but nonetheless did amazing things for us all.

Refusals

The Habsburgs always had to deal with a powerful strand within their Empire not so much of dislike of their rule but resolute indifference. There was the day-to-day refusal of many peasants to see any Imperial official as anything other than a boring menace, the sense that any outsider was bad news. This remains true today. I once chatted to a Transylvanian Székely who said how in their entirely Hungarian-speaking town anybody heard talking in Romanian was assumed to be visiting purely to defraud them or make life worse in some way. This must always have been true all over the Empire as German- or Hungarian-speaking officials fanned out, investigating recruitment or taxation or farming methods and leaving a trail of misery behind them.

An extreme variant on the wish to be left alone came from the more severe monastic contemplative orders such as the Trappists and Camaldolese. I have had a soft spot for the former since I found myself for several years in a row selling books at a medieval studies conference in Michigan with the booth next to mine occupied by a couple of cheerful figures from the Abbey of Gethsemani in Kentucky who sold the bourbon fudge which the Trappists specialized in – a beautifully localized adaptation both to the state they were based in (the bourbon) and to the vow of virtual silence (the fudge). This idea of a great and unbroken sequence of prayer, stretching out over centuries and quite independent of secular vanities, was a profound challenge to any ruler and one of the reasons Joseph II stamped out such groups as 'unproductive': if the purpose of living within a specific geographical space was to channel resources to the centre for the greater glory and security of the state then there could be no room for Trappism. The magnificent Camaldolese abbey outside Kraków only survives today because the Habsburgs absorbed the region in 1846 and by then no longer shared Joseph II's harsh vision.

A larger group was the Hutterites, who originated in the Tyrol during the Reformation and whose leader, Jakob Hutter, was burned at the stake in Innsbruck in 1536. They managed both to be heretical in their beliefs and utterly enraging to any form of authority – refusing to accept orders, wear uniforms or even hold a weapon. Their communal existence, impervious to Habsburg authority, drove them first to Moravia, then to Transylvania, occasionally protected but mostly hounded. They found themselves by the mid-nineteenth century on the Nogai Steppe before sensibly having a rethink and heading to the American and Canadian prairies, where they have thrived ever since, still speaking their antique Tyrolean German.

A more powerful affront to the Habsburgs lay in the Hungarian minor nobility, who obsessively pursued their right to hunt, drink and reproduce free of wider obligation across enormous areas of land. These local landowners had a coherent and appealing ideology, based around resistance to Habsburg rule. They gloried in great earlier revolts, viewing Franz Joseph as illegitimate ('the Hangman' as he was often referred to for his method of killing the Hungarian generals at Arad in 1849) and prepared to be ornery, tiresome and lazy in a way which can only be admired. There are so many great examples. György Faludy has a fine one in his memoir *My Happy Days in Hell* of the pre-War Hungarian petty seigneur who when the first snow fell would send his coach down into the village to collect his three favourite card-players and then not let them go until the spring thaw arrived. It is easy to see why the central administration was driven mad by these people's refusal to give a fig about the wider world, but there is no particular reason why we should either share that annoyance or be personally upset about the tatty nature of the Habsburg tax base.

By a long way the most powerful critique of the Habsburgs lay with the Jews. For much of the course of the Empire, Habsburg attitudes towards the Jews and Jewish attitudes to their home form a sort of Möbius strip with both sides ascribing to the other views and ideas which enforced their own world ideology. The Hatam Sofer of Bratislava in the early nineteenth century laid out with crushing clarity the Jews' position: that they were ruled over by 'the abomination of the land', that they were the 'captives of the war of destruction' and that any form of innovation in behaviour was forbidden, to the point that any Jew who strayed was simply no longer a Jew but an atheist. Much of this position is still maintained by the Hasidim – that suffering purges sin and that something even as simple as a change of dress style can unravel everything.

All Habsburg legislation in relation to the Jews was carried out effectively without reference to their needs or any real knowledge of their ideas. Maria Theresa could be anti-Semitic and obsessed, even as she removed some legal disabilities, with such issues as what action a Jew must take if he finds himself in the street as a procession of the Host goes by. Joseph II was impatient with this stuff but, as with his anti-contemplative legislation, his own improvement of the Jews' lot was unconcerned with their welfare but obsessed with their becoming 'good citizens'. Each stage in Jewish emancipation was pushed by bureaucratic efficiency and not by liberalism.

The traditional Jewish view was that they were marooned in the barbaric, vainglorious and hypocritical shambles of Central Europe by God as atonement for past sins. It was correct to acknowledge the rulers who protected them, but this implied not a peep of endorsement for their laughable values. Some of Joseph II's plans were therefore deeply threatening. If the root of Jewish survival was the maintenance of strict behaviour patterns over many generations then his 'rationalist' insistence that book-keeping and invoicing had to be in German rather than Yiddish or Hebrew raised terrible questions. Each removal of blocks on Jewish activity was therefore a snare – Jewish children being allowed to go to school was on the face of it an improvement, but as those schools were ostentatiously Christian in their ideology they were simply a means of destroying Jewish solidarity.

The Partitions of Poland meant the transfer of most of Europe's Jewish population from Poland to the Prussian, Habsburg and Russian states. The great majority fell to Russia, which had no tradition of dealing with Jews and proceeded to make a disgusting nightmare of 'the Pale'. Berlin and Vienna had long experience with Jewish populations and simply extended their own more or less disreputable ways of dealing with them. Prussian Jews were unlucky enough to have the ridiculously low-grade Friedrich Wilhelm III, a mystical and babyish Christian who once shut down an experimental new synagogue in Berlin (which allowed men and women to sit in the same space) on the grounds that if Judaism lost its aura of irrational obscurantism it might become attractive as a faith. This binary atmosphere – either pressure on Prussian Jews to become German-speaking Prussians or the Russian view that Jews were irretrievably alien – made the Habsburg experience relatively sane.

As the nineteenth century proceeded the old views of the Ḥatam Sofer seemed ever less plausible to many Jews in much of the Empire. The sheer poverty and remoteness of the Jewish towns on the eastern side of the Carpathians kept them relatively traditional, but as the last serious disabilities were knocked away, the world of the mainstream became irresistible. By the 1880s a quarter of Vienna-ruled Jews could speak German and over half of Budapest-ruled Jews could speak Hungarian. They became part of the great population boom and resultant rush to the cities over the century's last decades. The scramble that so inflated the populations of Vienna and Budapest was of course mainly made up of non-Jews, but the novelty of Jews being released from the sidelines and benefiting particularly from the great boom of the period in professions previously those of a tiny group (medicine, journalism, banking) made them conspicuous. The Hatam Sofer's descendants viewed these men and women as no longer Jews: some happily agreed with this view, particularly those who drifted towards socialism, but the majority saw themselves as no less Jewish than those still trapped in the yeshiva.

Habsburg Jews as part of a multinational state were by definition better protected than those in Germany and Russia as there could be no state ideology that could plausibly discriminate *more* against them than many other groups. It was unthinkable in the other empires for Jews to become army officers, but there were thousands of Jewish army officers in the Habsburg forces. The final period of the Habsburg Empire was famously dominated by the achievement of its Jewish subjects − it seems boring to come up with the usual list, but a meaningful or cherishable European civilization cannot be imagined without them. Sigmund Freud's parents moving from Galicia to Moravia then to Leipzig then to Vienna stands in for countless others. In the history of modernism, I particularly like the idea that James Joyce made Leopold Bloom's father a 'perpetrator of frauds' from Szombathely.

Even in the *relatively* benign Empire however there is no point at which there was anything like stability, and the ghost of Maria Theresa insisting that Jews stay indoors on Sunday out of shame at being Christ's murderers was never dispelled. The massive surviving late-nineteenth-century synagogues in the Empire, most famously the Great Synagogue in Plzeň and the Dohány Street Synagogue in Budapest, have so many powerful and disturbing associations that visiting them is not really an aesthetic experience. But in as much as it can be, they are clearly victims of the same woeful gigantic industrial eclecticism as the museums and opera houses scattered across the Empire in the same decades. The two thousand Jews of Plzeň had the indignity of constant interference in the design of their synagogue to ensure it was as 'Oriental' as possible, to make it quite clear it could in no sense be confused with a Christian place of worship, with an early design turned down for having insufficiently exotic towers.

This insistence on difference kept bubbling up in frightening ways. A notorious case was the revival of the blood libel in 1882 in the Hungarian village of Tiszaeszlár, where local Jews were accused of abducting a Christian peasant girl called Eszter Solymosi and getting a kosher butcher to kill her, draining her blood into a bowl for use in Sabbath matzos. The defendants were eventually let go on the straightforward grounds that there was no evidence (the girl was eventually found drowned in the river), but the media, including disturbing numbers of Catholic priests, had whipped up an anti-Semitic frenzy and there were attacks on Jews across Hungary. Scarcely credibly, at the time of my writing the far-Right Jobbik party have been promoting a cult of Eszter Solymosi's grave and raising questions about what really happened to her in the Hungarian Parliament. The more we pride ourselves on being intelligent and thoughtful the more we turn out to be Morlocks.

Jewish unease within the Empire was stoked by the Tiszaeszlár scandal, but at least there was a widespread official recoil from its repulsive imbecility. This did not mean Jews could feel that they stood on stable ground. The move to assimilate meant assimilation through speaking German or Hungarian, the 'master languages', and this meant that in a world of ever more unhinged nationalism Jews became a particular focus of hatred for politicians and demagogues pushing a Slovak, Romanian, etc. agenda, while at the same time not appeasing German or Hungarian Christian anti-Semitism. Outside the Empire horrible events filled the newspapers. Most immediately frightening were stories from Romania, where the government decided that Jews, like Gypsies, were by definition not Romanian. With the end of international supervision after 1878 the Romanians proceeded with violence, fraud and intimidation on a scale that provoked a mass exodus, with some sixty-seven thousand Jews (a quarter of the entire population) leaving for the USA. The vastly larger Jewish population in Russia was subject to repeated and ferocious violence, with thousands dead. The Empire became an island of relative decency, but with poverty as much as anti-Semitism driving huge numbers of Jews out of Galicia to the

USA and elsewhere. Assimilation proved enormously successful for many, but every decade provided its own frights and challenges for Jews throughout the Empire, and nobody could assume any genuine, lasting normality.

Village of the damned

I have often turned over in my mind the idea of writing a book about zoo architecture. This neglected form of building is so rich and so peculiar and it has never really had its due. It is an amalgam of shop-window display, storage facility and prison and its most direct clients (the animals) are unable to notice it, whereas its more casual clients (the visitors) treat it as an almost invisible frame. The buildings tend to be very solid so that their inhabitants do not get out and kill everyone. Their robustness therefore accidentally preserves them, unlike the trappings of many other areas of entertainment, circuses, say, or fairgrounds. This longevity gives a visitor today a surprising link to the popular atmosphere of the past – the period from the late nineteenth century to the 1920s when zoos stood at the apex of 'a day out', the populist direct descendants of the cabinet of curiosities.

One of the oldest and most marvellous is the Budapest Zoo. So often when meant to be en route to some more up-scale cultural highlight I have found myself instead wandering off to admire its demented entrance gate, decorated with *art nouveau* mandrills, bears and elephants in perhaps the single most fun sculptural commission ever tendered for. Much of the zoo found its current form in the years of urban joy before 1914, with several of the same Hungarian eclecticists who did so much to heroically decorate buildings across the capital let loose to do pretty much what they liked. Chief hero is probably Kornél Neuschloss-Knüsli, who conjured up not only the great entrance gate, but also the scarcely credible Elephant House – a fantasy on Central Asian mosque architecture with blue-tiled roofs, a minaret and somewhat un-Koranic decorative hippo-rhino-hippo-rhino head decorations around the guttering.

The elephants themselves merely chomp away, oblivious to their odd double-relocation – first to Hungary itself, and then to a faux-Tamerlane backdrop also very remote from their true home. Indeed, the Elephant House is possibly the maddest of all Hungarian 'Turanian' fantasies about national origins in some vague but grand part of Central Asia, with the unique displacement activity of also granting the nation's elephants a shared Hungarian ancestry. During the period of the First World War, when the Hungarians found themselves, untypically, in alliance with the Ottomans, the smart new Elephant House caused great offence as it was effectively a mosque being used to harbour beasts, so the minaret had to be taken down for a while.

The wonders of Budapest Zoo are almost infinite. Not least there is the Aquarium underneath the Palm House. Here the fish seem to have been chosen – parrot- and lion-fish, clouds of tangs – so that they match the beautiful mosaics and even a creature as sinister as a moray eel becomes ennobled, the shimmering gold of its flanks making it seem like a Klimt escapee. Indeed of all such places in the world (and I have been to *a lot*) this is the one where your head is most clearly plunged into the glass-harmonica planet of Saint-Saëns' *Aquarium*. Drenched in drifting colours, floating in the spirit of the fin de siècle, it is shocking to come out into mere standard-issue daylight and distant car and playground noises.

All zoos are palimpsests created by bouts of director activism, changing styles, a sudden influx of funds. The Budapest Zoo had a grim interlude in its existence as collateral damage during the 1944–45 city siege. Most of the animals were killed and the buildings devastated – so what we see now, as in so much of Budapest, is the result of many years of dedicated reconstruction work. In the general nightmare of those months people had other things to think about than the zoo. At one point a lion escaped into the Underground and came up to scavenge dead horses for a while before a squad of Soviet troops was sent, in one of the war's more unusual missions, to finish him off. Almost the only survivors were some hippos who, when electrical power was lost and most other animals froze, wallowed happily in a pool of the warm artesian water which wells up all over Budapest. There were two hippos trapped in Trieste harbour during the 1866 War – the delicate process of unloading them from their ship's special tanks trumped by tiresome military priorities – but to my frustration I have been unable to find out if these are linked in some way to the 1945 Budapest hippos, with the possibility this would create of a parallel history of Central Europe seen through the endurance of one brave African artiodactyl family.

The whole place is in a sense a tease for its central work of genius. The one area of zoos I typically tend to avoid is the children's petting zone, where a handful of demonic white goats blankly chew, and an abject sheep, patted until its wool only exists in patches, shivers in a corner. But the Budapest Zoo is quite different. At its heart lies a work of extreme satirical savagery: the Guinea-Pig Village. This genuinely frightening, brilliant piece of work consists of an enclosure filled with small, simplified wooden models of a typical Central European provincial town, with its town hall, school, pompous bourgeois homes (for the doctor, the lawyer), a church and rows of cheaper houses. But, of course, it is filled not with people but with guinea-pigs. I have had a short clip of the village in action loaded onto my phone now for four years and the main reason I refuse to upgrade that phone is fear of losing it. To add to the febrile atmosphere, the clip has the happy accident of a police siren going on in the background, and the lucky viewer can see dozens of guinea-pigs racing through the main square to gorge on a bucket of carrots that has just been thrown into their community. As a piece of conceptual art the Guinea-Pig Village has a genuine sneering ferocity that can never lose its power to shock. As the animals rush from their respective parts of the enclosure they really *do* appear to be small, box-shaped, wiry-haired versions of town councillors, shopkeepers and local professionals, all in meaningless pursuit of carrots. It would not work with any other small creature, but there is a stuffy self-sufficiency about guinea-pigs that anyway makes them look as though they are off to some grim, patriotic gala dinner, even without the wooden town hall to help the effect. There are even little wooden cars, in one of which a guinea-pig had stayed sitting, immune to the appeal of the carrots because he was clearly dying – but with none of his friends noticing or caring. Fortunately we do not need to choose, but weighed in the artistic scales: how many stories by Kafka or essays by Kraus would be needed to balance the power of the Guinea-Pig Village?

On the move

The urban contempt for small-town life encapsulated in Budapest's petting zoo is an only slightly wonky segue into discussion of the huge changes that racked the Empire in its final decades. Everywhere, people were flooding out of their guinea-pig villages and filling up the big cities. There was a push and a pull about what happened. In the early nineteenth century in many areas of the Empire money was only used intermittently. Communities remained self-sufficient and based around barter, with regular visits from itinerants, particularly Gypsies, who could supply missing items from the outside world, but wherever a railway protruded there would be a fresh and irresistible bridgehead for the cash economy. One Ruhr factory could turn out in a day all the little metal objects, better made and cheaper, needed for entire regions. New necessities such as sugar, tobacco and more interesting alcohol poured in a chaotic flood across the continent. Nowhere was ever completely cut off except seasonally, but the sheer effort of horse transport had made objects from the outside world relatively rare and expensive. Now people were showered in marvellous things, often quite modest but with profound impacts: hairclips, mirrors, screws, needles, make-up, cooking oil – objects partly transformed by cheapness and partly by their disposability. The flood of machine-made clothing had as deep an effect on Central Europe as it did on India.

Just as railways injected extraordinary things into places previously hidden by distance, climate or mountains, so they also allowed for far larger populations to be reliably fed and housed in cities of unparalleled size. Between around 1870 and 1910 places such as Lviv, Graz, Brno and Trieste doubled in size, Prague grew by four hundred thousand inhabitants, Budapest by five hundred thousand, Vienna by twelve hundred thousand. There was no precedent for this astounding flood of people. They swamped all existing social structures, reshaped landscapes and created a new sense of excitement or of dread, according to taste.

Incidentally, it is generally around here that anybody writing about the Habsburg Empire is obliged to have a section on people like the Empress Elisabeth and her son Crown Prince Rudolf, but really if these people are of interest you should probably just look them up on Wikipedia, which has excellent entries. In Britain there is a cruel and entertaining system of classification for films, where each movie is given an age approval rating with a little sentence to follow up, most helpfully something like: *Contains strong sex and language*. I once saw a poster for a French film with a man and a woman in hats smiling at each across a table in the countryside and the clearly bored film censor had given it a rating followed by: *Contains scenes of mild emotional involvement*. I find it really hard to think about Elisabeth and Rudolf for even a moment without this phrase coming to mind. There she is drifting around Europe, glumly riding her horse, being a wistful soul-sister to the hopeless Ludwig II; there he is being vaguely liberal, binge-drinking, miserable and unable to cope. She has the ignominy of finally being stabbed to death by an anarchist who had hoped to kill somebody else, but on being disappointed by his victim's no-show fell back on her. Rudolf ends up with an odd-looking teenage girl in a double-suicide – but perhaps they were murdered? Or not. These scandals of yesteryear definitely contain scenes of mild emotional involvement. It is perfect that Elisabeth and Rudolf have ended up as the stars of the Imperial Furnishings Warehouse Museum in Vienna, which contains Rudolf's desk and a hilarious exhibition showing all the old palace bits and pieces used as props in the trilogy of films about Elisabeth from the 1950s starring Romy Schneider (Part 3: *Sissi: Fateful Years of an Empress – Contains scenes of crushing lack of interest*). Their lives seem to map perfectly onto the rooms of the museum, filled with old hat stands, flimsy posh chairs, fire-screens and so on. Franz Joseph himself often has an air of being actually constructed out of these objects, as he trundles back and forth for decades, almost immune to why his Empire was interesting, diligently signing things, hunting, shuttling to the Imperial Villa in Bad Ischl with its special pathway to his mistress's house. I don't think anyone needs even to be particularly on the political left to feel that in this period interesting life is elsewhere.

The one great value that Franz Joseph does bring to the extraordinarily churning landscape of his Empire is something approaching blindness to nationalisms. If the Empire was to have any point then it had to struggle against overt racism. A political entity which had been a plurality of family lands brought together by accident, which had gone on to become a military machine and a Catholic bastion, became in its final decades somewhat by default an island of, if not tolerance, then certainly of relative restraint – much to the growing anger of many of its inhabitants.

The village identity of the hundreds of thousands of new migrants to the city had been shaped by tradition and by religious practice. The villagers of Galicia, for example, identified themselves simply as Jewish or Catholic or Uniate or Orthodox. Many had no idea what language they spoke – it was just the dialect of the village. The spread of trains, of education and of books and newspapers changed this, redefining how people felt about themselves even before they moved to the cities and had to 'choose'. This choice (just as in the United States) could within two generations represent a total jump, whereby in the Empire's case a Slovak, Romanian or Jew, say, could become Hungarian, changing language, dress, diet, profession. So the village couple from the Banat arriving in Budapest in the 1870s could have Magyarized adult children by the 1890s and have themselves long changed their own tastes and behaviours almost beyond recognition. Mass rallies, religious affiliation, occupation would shape a nationalism for people who had proved to be formidably flexible before donning a specific and final costume.

There are famous Jewish examples: Mahler's father was an inn-keeper from central Bohemia, his grandmother a pedlar; Kafka's grandfather was a ritual slaughterer from southern Bohemia. Not all this great movement resulted in a Habsburg destination. I am so in the midst here of my personal heroes that it is impossible even to type this without feeling deeply moved, as though the opening of Mahler's *Second Symphony* were playing in the background (which it is, in fact) – but here are two further: Billy Wilder's epic (although also quite common) journey from Galicia to Germany and then to America to fulfil his destiny and make some of the greatest Hollywood movies; the grandparents of Philip Roth leaving Galicia and therefore making possible my favourite writer – who in turn has done so much to bring Central European writing to an English-speaking readership.

The Jewish example is particularly clear as the process of travel by earlier traditionalist Jewish standards was unacceptable – leaving behind communities could only result in behavioural disasters and engagement with 'the abomination of the land'. But by all kinds of measures this was true for countless non-Jews too, who had to discard a welter of ancestral shibboleths and learn entirely new ways of behaving in the huge new cities. From the top of the Petřín Hill in Prague you can see the rough outline of the much older built-up areas, all gnarled and tangled up around the river, but then there is a totally rebuilt late-nineteenth-century Josefov with its extravagant, indeed peculiar, apartment blocks, the great monuments in the New Town to Czech nationalism from the same period – and then beyond that a sea of housing in every direction for the countless new workers from the countryside.

As the villagers arrived in the cities it was very unclear to them exactly who their new masters were. The aristocracy may have made money from land deals for the new housing, but were irrelevant to most of these new inhabitants. Any surviving sense of deference had been shaken off with the move. Confronted with a tangle of trams, newspapers, sermons, political parties, schools, there were crucial decisions that needed to be made about assimilation, diet, acceptable habits. As good an example as any is the

Bohemian town of Plzeň. Until the later nineteenth century this was very clearly a German place called Pilsen, part of a broad framework of German-speaking places whose inhabitants viewed Czech as the rural language or as that of their servants. Its famous beer was created by a Bavarian, Joseph Groll, and lager was viewed as an entirely German drink (as was the case too in the predominantly German town of Budweis, now České Budějovice). The Plzeň beer works is still here, but is now simply an enormous computer-controlled hangar, in which green bottles whip by, supervised by the handful of surviving workers whose main job is to clean up occasional smashed glass. The whole place smells eerily soapy and is a long way from the world of twinkle-eyed old men in leather aprons and funny moustaches it was clear that everyone on the tour had been looking forward to. As merely one of many holdings in the depressing SABMiller multinational's portfolio, Pilsner Urquell is at this point just a brand meant to convey a vague sense of Central European pub chumminess – a good fellowship cruelly mocked both by the factory and its ownership and grimly remote from the old ideals of the Velvet Revolution.

The German oligarchs who had always run Pilsen found themselves completely adrift within a few years of the railway coming through. Pilsen was a major hub and an enormous repair shop sprang up, employing thousands of (mainly) Czechs. Even worse, in 1866 Emil Škoda was made chief engineer of Count Waldstein's weapons factory in the town. Within three years Škoda bought out Waldstein, and then become one of that extraordinary group of capitalist inventors who presided over the vast explosion in *things* involving metal and electricity. It is good that this is a mere passive book I am writing, or I would now be excitedly getting out and bringing over to you one of my favourite possessions, *150 Years of Škoda in Photographs and Documents*. The photos form a uniquely eloquent and hair-raising meditation on late-Habsburg life, with dwarfed men next to ship's turbines, naval guns and a giant steel-geared wheel with *30,000 kg* helpfully written on it. Here was a temple to the precision manipulation of metals on a monstrous scale, with sprawling floors crammed with semi-assembled weapons, cases of rivets, pails of grease and chains swinging from gantries. What *is* the right political dispensation for such a transformative Pandaemonium: for its owners, for its Czech ex-peasant workers, for its products? Austria-Hungary was never remotely an industrial power on the scale of Germany or Britain but it still made astounding things of a kind that would have been viewed as forms of black magic by an earlier generation. It is in the spirit of the age that figures such as Bruckner and Mahler should start producing music that matches the endeavours of the Škoda Works. Haydn's 'Sunrise' Quartet seems a very long way away.

Pilsen in the space of a few years therefore became Plzeň. Czechs poured in from the countryside and the issue of who had allegiance to whom and why became critical. The spread of mass political parties, literacy and money created a new public space which quite rapidly ran out of control. Forms of nationalism are very easy for an outsider to deride. They are obviously poisonous, depressing and end in catastrophe for everybody. There was always a Habsburg argument that nationalism could be restricted to forms of the picturesque (costumes, foods, parades – not unlike in the United States). There was a socialist argument that nationalism was a demagogic sham and a trap for the workers. There was also a liberal argument for the dangers of hating someone simply because they spoke a different language or attended a different church.

But these different arguments against nationalism could, for obvious reasons, find no common ground with one another. In addition, it was very hard indeed not to become infected. What did it take in practice for a Hungarian liberal to agree that the majority Romanian areas of Transylvania should be handed over to Romania, or that the Serbs could help themselves to southern Hungary? Such views were mere eccentricity. The longer I have spent thinking about this book the more horror and disgust I feel for nationalism, which seems something akin to bubonic plague, but clearly such a perception only gets anyone so far. Even the most intelligent and articulate figures in Europe embraced it in some form and could no more shed it than they could shed their own skins. Once the language you used (and the newspapers and books you read) and the religion you grew up with became part of a public sphere, rather than an entirely local issue, there was no going back. Plzeň was a perfect example. After years of escalating Czech language demands, the Badeni Decrees of 1897 announced that in Bohemia all government business had to be conducted by men who could speak both Czech and German. This was an intelligent retreat from the previous all-German position, but overnight turned Germans (who generally had not learned Czech at school) into second-class citizens and Czechs (who *had* been obliged to learn German) into the new masters. Bohemia was torn apart by riots and boycotts and the Decrees were withdrawn. But what *was* the solution, if Plzeň's richest and biggest employer and his employees were Czech? And what did this mean for Bohemian Germans, who now felt baffled and abused, and could contrast their fate with that of other German-speakers just a few miles down the road, in the Second Reich?

It was only a keen sense that without the Habsburg umbrella fratricidal hatreds could run riot that kept discipline across the Empire. Many dreamed of a nationally pure independent homeland, but many too stayed aware that the region's tangle of ethnicities made that idea very dangerous. Even as central a figure as Tomáš Masaryk, who served in the Parliament in Vienna from the 1890s, recognized that Czech independence was unrealistic: Prague may have been overwhelmingly a Czech city, but the islands of German-speakers in places such as České Budějovice, Brno and Český Krumlov meant that even if Bohemia could somehow cut away the German-speakers along the western and northern borders (the Sudetenland) some form of compromise with the remaining Germans was necessary. It was only the cataclysm of the Great War that changed Masaryk's thinking.

Much of the nationalist running within the Empire was made by the groups who were causing 'trouble' for the dominant German and Hungarian nationalities and had external sponsors. Serbia and Romania had many co-nationals within the Empire who might have had until now almost unrelated histories but who, it was suggested, should now unite with others who happened to speak the same language. Ultimately many Habsburg Serbs and Romanians would come to agree with this assessment – but until the disasters of 1917–18 most did not. There was little in the brutal way that Belgrade or Bucharest ran their affairs that made them look preferable as rulers. For example, the 1907 peasant rebellion in Romania, which ended in a bloodbath that killed some ten thousand people, gave a serious pause for thought and added to the sense (which was also felt by many Habsburg Serbs) that the national flame was perhaps in rather more competent hands inside the Empire, even with all its humiliations, than in the uncouth nation states.

It is often said that Vienna was brilliant at playing the different nationalities off against each other, manipulating them like circus animals with a mix of treats and threats. In practice, for much of the time Vienna was merely incompetent, battling to deal with a cauldron of socio-economic change and sometimes taking blind stabs at a solution (such as the Badeni Decrees), which merely caused further chaos. The situation in Bohemia, though, was characteristically difficult in a way that helped Vienna. Short of a language-based civil war to clear the province (which happened in 1938–45) there was genuinely no answer to the conundrum. In Galicia it was fun to support Ruthenian cultural expression to keep the Poles worried, but the only 'solution' to the region's problems was the declaration of a total ethnic and class war – and, again, this did in due course happen. Whether these were permanently preventable is too frightening and tangled a counter-factual to have any meaning. Both the Austrian and Hungarian sides of the Empire spent inordinate amounts of time scribbling calculations of relative ethnic strengths on the backs of envelopes. The first German ethnic political parties in Vienna's half made the ingenious suggestion that Dalmatia should be handed to the Hungarians and that Galicia should be made a separate administrative kingdom: with all those Slavs gone a German majority could then turn on and overwhelm the Czechs and Slovenes. The Hungarians, doing their own maths, were understandably just as keen *not* to be handed Dalmatia. It was very useful to Franz Joseph to see how many of the Slav groups owed a natural allegiance to him because of fear of what their

German and Hungarian masters would do if unchecked by the
genuinely supranational element in the Hofburg. But even this
allegiance was a wobbly one. The Poles may have been trapped by
circumstances, but what if the millions of other Slavs – Czechs,
Slovaks, Ruthenes, Slovenes, Croatians, Serbs – were to feel that
their oppression by the 'master nationalities' could be ended by
another external sponsor, perhaps by Russia?

The Führer

Germans too were of course moving into ever bigger towns, with
places such as Linz, Graz, Wiener Neustadt and Steyr growing as
well as Vienna. Steyr is in fact an excellent parallel to Czech Plzeň:
a matching but ethnically German military-industrial complex. In
Steyr's case this was based around the sprawling gun works. Local
supplies of iron had meant that Steyr had produced weapons since
the Middle Ages, but in the usual nineteenth-century way growth
now became frenzied, with many thousands of workers turning
out rifles and automatics designed by Ferdinand Ritter von Mannlicher. In the local museum there is – aside from innumerable
examples of Mannlicher and his successors' gun designs – one very
remarkable object. This is a photo showing a delegation of Abyssinians visiting the Steyr Mannlicher works in around 1910. They
are photographed during a machine-gun demonstration. The gun
is just about to be fired and most of the photo consists of men in
top hats, tailcoats, pince-nez and elaborate facial hair putting their
fingers in their ears. The members of the delegation are picturesque
and remote in a different way, but one Abyssinian, a young man
with a cartridge belt and strikingly short hair, just happens to be
staring at the camera. He is someone *quite* different: his level, cold
glare makes him look like a visitor from the future, a 1960s African Marxist in a crowd of decayed stuffy nincompoops. This is a
photo that should be on the wall of all schoolrooms where history
is taught. I do not mean for anti-colonial reasons, but because of
the cross-currents that swirl around the image: the terrible weapon

on display being treated as a trade item; the way that the Austrian industrialists look more 'exotic' now than the Abyssinians; the assumption that the Abyssinians must have been patronized and even derided by their hosts, but it was the hosts who within a decade would be destroyed, with Steyr Mannlicher shut down by the Treaty of Versailles. It is interesting, too, simply to think about why the picture was taken in the first place.

German-speaking political alienation from the Habsburgs stemmed both from a general lashing out at other minority groups, as in Bohemia, and from a new working-class self-assertion in the Austrian industrial centres. A powerful narrative of German grievance began to be articulated from the 1870s onwards. When German-speakers had been splintered between numerous different European small states, being a German in the Habsburg Empire had been a badge of pride. The rise of Prussia had challenged that pride, but now the creation of the German Reich actively ridiculed it. Were Austrian Germans to become mere marginal Alpine pictur- esques like the Swiss?* In Bohemia, an ancient part of the old Holy Roman Empire, German towns were becoming overrun with Czechs demanding their rights; in Carinthia it was the same with Slovenes. The Germans glared at the Hungarians' half of the Empire, which they saw as a parasitic burden on German-speaking tax-payers; and at the Jews, who seemed to be newly confident in ways that Germans increasingly were not. As Franz Joseph's gov- ernment made ever more frantic attempts to balance nationality against nationality, it found to its dismay that it was in the process shaking loose its German core.

One chilling sample of this new streak of German paranoia was Georg Ritter von Schönerer, an Austrian landowner who, like many, was traumatized by the Battle of Königgrätz and came to worship Bismarck, feeling that Germans trapped within the Habsburg Empire should break free of Franz Joseph's dead hand and unite with their fellows. Schönerer was a terrifying figure: racked with hatred for the Habsburgs, for the Catholic Church that

---

* After much horror and bloodshed the answer would be: yes.

backed them up, for Czechs who should know their place, for liberals, for socialists – and above all for Jews. As head of the Pan-German Party and an MP he was a key figure in fuelling the violent loathings that made the Parliament in Vienna into a dysfunctional shambles, destroying any sense of rational debate or give-and-take. He invented the 'Heil' greeting and had the title of 'Führer' bestowed on him by his followers. He saw himself as the protector of all Germans, succeeded in getting a prime minister dismissed and created for German-speakers their own fangs and paranoia quite as bad as anything offered by other linguistic groups.

Schönerer was too haughtily aristocratic to be a mass figure, but he did not need to be as he was trumped by 'Handsome Karl', Karl Lueger, the Mayor of Vienna. He lacked Schönerer's eccentricity, and was ostentatiously pro-Habsburg and a populist of genius. More than anyone in the pre-War world he seized the opportunities provided by the new mega-cities, working to make Vienna a bearable place for its hundreds of thousands of new inhabitants through vast waterworks and tram systems. Much of what still makes Vienna work is thanks to Lueger. From 1897 to his death in 1910 he dominated the city. He was devout, a great organizer, adored by the Germans and nearly as anti-Semitic as Schönerer – whose campaign to ban the arrival of more Jews in Vienna he had supported in the 1880s.

While I am writing this there is a campaign to rename the road now called the Doktor-Karl-Lueger-Ring. Lueger once referred to the Jews as 'beasts of prey in human form', said that wolves, leopards and tigers were closer to humans than Jews, and agreed that a good solution to the 'Jewish problem' would be to put them all on a big ship and sink them at sea. It does not seem too uncontroversial to say that the nature of these comments probably trumps his role in improving Vienna's sanitation systems. It is impossible not to feel that by walking on 'his' section of the Ring, or by looking up at his grand statue facing the Stadtpark you are effectively being forced to endorse him.

Schönerer and Lueger disagreed on many issues but between

them developed a particular model for Austrian German politics and a separate ethnic awareness that hardly existed before. Until then, to be a German inhabitant of the Empire was an undefined and effortless tag, as it had always been. To be a German anywhere in the Empire had given certain, seemingly natural privileges and implied particular forms of organization. Other 'races' suffered from religious disabilities, illiteracy or poverty in ways that kept them below and separate. As the nineteenth century progressed this ceased to be true, with groups who had been mere labourers or serfs or shut out from most professions suddenly feeling just as entitled and articulate, just as well-dressed and culturally astute as their former masters. In 1908 the teenaged Adolf Hitler arrived in Vienna, one of many thousands of badly off German-speakers from Upper Austria looking to the big city to find their fortunes.

CHAPTER THIRTEEN

The sheep and the melons »

Elves, caryatids, lots of allegorical girls »

Monuments to a vanished past » Young Poland

The sheep and the melons

At numerous points while writing this book I have had real difficulty believing my luck. Despite ludicrous setbacks, humiliations and the curse of my language incompetence, I had a motive and excuse to visit many miraculous spots. I never felt this more strongly than in the central Romanian city of Sibiu.

Sibiu is a classic 'Saxon' foundation under the protection of the Hungarian kings, ruled under a German legal code ('Iglau law') which defined the settlers' obligations and privileges. As Hermannstadt it became a major German settlement, and only Braşov was further east. In few places is there still such a strong sense of this past, with its colossal, glowering Saxon church, its Upper Town on a great block of rock and its Lower Town with its crooked and sunless streets (where I stayed in a small guest-house and each morning seemed a new gift as I would step out into what appeared to be one of the Expressionist sets from Paul Wegener's movie *The Golem*). Battered watchtowers, like brick and wood prototypes of the Martian Tripods in *The War of the Worlds*, still stand sentinel, looking out towards the mountains for long-vanished Wallachian and Turkish enemies, and street after street is crowded with architecturally chaotic but somehow inspired buildings.

That Sibiu changed in the first half of the twentieth century from a south-eastern Hungarian border town to a central Romanian one is just one small example of the horrible wrenches experienced by the inhabitants of the Empire. The dominant group in Sibiu, the Saxons, like all dominant groups, claimed some immemorial stability and social order, using history to shore up their unique ownership of the town since the fifteenth century or earlier. This was untrue, as Sibiu's past was, as one would imagine from its location, an absolutely chaotic skein of revolts, battles, convulsions, plagues and religious tension. But perhaps until the mid-nineteenth century it could still broadly be said that Sibiu was a German-speaking town roughly fulfilling its old function as a guild-based entrepôt, making and circulating things and services, still guarding against Wallachia, then under an uneasy mix of Ottoman and Russian rule and potentially in the military front line again after the Crimean War broke out in 1853.

What began to happen in the later nineteenth century in Sibiu, as in hundreds of other places across the Empire, was a demographic revolution. It seems so important somehow for Europeans to imagine themselves as stolid, immobile and timeless – and yet almost everywhere people were on the move. A special case has always been made for sheepishly acknowledging that millions of European fellow countrymen were hot-footing to port cities to head off to settlement colonies, but there is a blankness about the same process when it happened within the continent. A marvellous (and ginormous) history of Europe from 1850 to 1950 or so might just completely ignore kings and queens and be filled with Irish building London, Neapolitans heading to Lombard factories and Slavic and Romanian peasants heading for Habsburg towns. The same push-and-pull that made uprooting to the Americas or the Pacific plausible for millions also drove an *internal* mass movement. Sibiu was always small but its size nonetheless ballooned, from some thirteen thousand people in 1850 to nearly thirty thousand by 1900. The ethnic composition changed, with the Saxon population nearly doubling, but the Romanian more than tripling. In the same period a small Hungarian population of fewer than one thousand grew to nearly six thousand. In miniature therefore Sibiu laid out the almost impossible problems facing forms of governance in the Empire. By luck Sibiu, as part of Transylvania, was ruled directly by Vienna into the 1860s when democratic (or at least mildly democratic) elections were proclaimed in 1861 to be held in 1863.

1861 turned out to be the crucial year for Romanians. In the deal that would be done in 1867 to create Austria-Hungary, Transylvania was assigned to the Hungarians. But by 1867 this scheme was too late – the Romanians had found a political voice and objected violently to being handed over to their new Hungarian overlords. In 1861 the remarkable Transylvanian Association for Romanian Literature and the Culture of the Romanian People (ASTRA) was founded in Sibiu. It started from an extremely low base in Transylvania, but with the most simple (and therefore exciting) tasks to be done – schooling in Romanian, the establishment of a basic Romanian literature and the creation of a separate Romanian economic sphere away from German or Hungarian concerns. The amazing polymath George Bariţ was a perfect example of this generation of Romanians, working on the first Romanian encyclopaedia, teaching, writing, energizing, going to Vienna to represent his constituency before 1867 blocked that off – and working first as secretary and then as president of ASTRA.

Bariţ was much hated by Budapest as a key figure in pleas to Vienna not to put Transylvania under Hungarian rule, but figures like him multiplied uncontrollably and in 1892 the great Transylvanian Memorandum was sent to Franz Joseph asking for equal Romanian rights. The absolute failure of this appeal (which Franz Joseph refused to even read) and the imprisonment by the enraged Hungarians of most of those who signed it showed the unresolvable nightmare of ethnic entanglement now unfolding. With the wretched ease of hindsight it is obvious the land-grab of 1867 was a terrible mistake for Hungary. Hypnotized by visions of some ancient medieval state and by apocalyptic fears of their own national extinction the Hungarians tried to create a state which was even bigger than Italy and failed. The many Hungarians who lived in Transylvania were in incoherent blocks that could not be put together into anything defensible. Even worse, they were in any event used to living under diverse regimes and with strange neighbours, so even fellow Hungarians could not be relied on in practice to view Budapest's rule as a plus.

This hindsight is useless and even by 1867 it cannot have been

clear how the pace of change would crush everyone. We can now
see that ASTRA and its associates were going to be important, but
it would have required a strange sort of genius to have understood
this at the time – some schools and a little Romanian-owned paper-
mill were not something to warn the Chancelleries of Europe
about. But events moved on. By 1900 the neighbouring Kingdom
of Romania was a substantial, fully independent state and providing
a welcoming home for any Transylvanian Romanians fleeing their
Hungarian overlords. And within Sibiu alone Romanians had come
a long way from being a semi-literate and impoverished group
spurned or used casually by Saxons and Hungarians alike. Indeed
ASTRA had inspired millions of Romanians both inside and outside the Empire. This was the result of Bariț's activism but also of
the actions of his great ASTRA contemporary Andrei Şaguna. A
monk and bishop, he had through relentless petitioning and planning (and motivated in part by a total hatred of Hungarians, a
hatred which was warmly reciprocated) gained official recognition
in 1864, with only three years to go before the shift to Budapest
rule, of the independent Romanian Orthodox Church. By 1900 the
results were clear in Sibiu, with building proceeding on an ASTRA
museum and on a spectacularly beautiful Romanian Orthodox
Cathedral, which now forms part of a sort of religious Restaurant
Row, with almost all conceivable denominations having a major
church within about five minutes' walk of one another.

   This triumph of 'Romanianism' was a critically significant event
in the Empire – it meant that if Hungary stumbled politically or
militarily, its entire eastern area would be painfully vulnerable to
subversion from Bucharest. Despite the breathtaking incompetence
and bad timing of the Romanian government throughout both
world wars, Romania grabbed Transylvania and held on to it (aside
from a brief interlude in the Second World War when it was partitioned). And since then mass emigration by both Saxons and
Hungarians made renewed rule from Budapest impossible, although
an idea still harboured by particularly reckless politicians.

   For the Hungarians, 1867 was a moment of immense excitement, with the dazzling prospect of a serious kingdom of their

own. This excitement was raised to frenzy in the new, unified city of Budapest in 1873 (sticking together Buda, Pest and Óbuda). But it was impossible not to recognize that they faced a formidable range of new 'subjects'. Within five years protests had come not just from the ASTRA Romanians, but from Serbs in Nagybecskerek, Slovaks in Turócszentmárton and Croats in Zágráb (now, tellingly, the towns of Zrenjanin in Serbia, Martin in Slovakia and Zagreb in Croatia). A further edge was given to these political and linguistic movements (the two cannot be split) by the way that so many of these groups lived in mountainous or otherwise poor land. Often, particularly in Slovak northern Hungary or in Transylvania, they were under the supervision of a Hungarian landlord class of an increasingly bizarre level of old-fashionedness, making the ethnic issue also one of access to resources. The huge estates no longer provided an adequate economic motor, preserving one lifestyle and shutting out others.

In the face of such resentment, the process of 'Magyarization' really was relentless – a Slovak could sit in his mountain fastness in a folk costume or he could move to Budapest or Transdanubia, learn Hungarian and get a factory job. Then, as now, the crushing dullness of the countryside, the low life-expectancy, the vagaries of dearth and disease, made even the worst-paid city jobs glamorous. For a much later generation this was still the case – Herta Müller, a Nobel prize-winning Romanian German, vividly describes in her novel *The Land of Green Plums* how the only options in the Banat countryside were to grow melons or to tend sheep, and how the only excitement came from when the sheep got loose in the melons and smashed them up with their hooves. This was no different in nineteenth-century Banat and somewhere like Budapest offered staggering temptations. The entrance price was to become literate and learn a new language and this process generated a further 2,000,000 or so 'fresh' Hungarians between 1850 and 1910. The largest group in this converted total were Jews, about 700,000, followed by Germans (500,000), Slovaks, Romanians and South Slavs. The effect was startling. One oddity of the Hungarians' own focus on land-ownership and estates and of so many historical reversals was a consistent lack of an urban culture, with Germans, Jews, Serbs and Armenians at different times and places doing most of the civic work. This changed finally by 1900. Even in 1848 Budapest was still a German-speaking town, but by 1900 a vastly larger city was 80 per cent Hungarian. Across much of central Hungary the Hungarians had become urban, with the traditional landed interest ever less representative. In the same period the Hungarians were also helped out by enormous numbers of the 'nationalities' simply leaving – almost a million Slovaks, for example, heading very sensibly for the United States, where some would have a key role in creating the ideology and negotiations that in the depths of the Great War led to the –slovakia bit of Czechoslovakia.

As the First World War approached it became ever more complicated to be a Hungarian politician – not only did many suffer from a pathological aversion to the Austrians and their relentless attempts to undermine the Compromise or at least revise its terms, but there was upheaval across much of the kingdom. However many Magyarized, it was never enough. There had been a hope that the Slovaks might simply disappear altogether, but this did not happen and the process, as with Germanization in Austria, seized up, as literacy spread and local politicians and priests protected local language schools. The Slovaks only proved a serious threat once the Empire had collapsed in 1918, but the Romanians became ever more grimly opposed to Hungarian rule and had a clear plan – unification with Romania. The Serbs were split, but for many there was an obvious foreign sponsor just over the border in Belgrade. The Croats by definition also loathed Magyarization but were held back by anxiety over being themselves absorbed by the Serbs, or indeed the Italians. They were also distracted by a wish to be united with Dalmatia, which stayed under separate Austrian rule. Everyone became obsessed with percentages, with minute census examinations of each county to spot hopeful pro-Hungarian trends. This became a form of panicked timidity, with the Hungarians ever more neurotic about any further move by Austria-Hungary into the Balkans, simply because more Slavs would change the ratios further against them. Budapest went numb with anxiety both over Bosnia-Hercegovina's annexation in 1908 (more Slavs!) and Franz Ferdinand's plans for a new Compromise which would have put South Slavs on the same footing as Germans and Hungarians. Admittedly, a key motivation for Franz Ferdinand's vision was his borderline-pathological hatred of the Hungarians, but the replacement of 'Dualism' by 'Trialism' was a logical next step, even if furiously resisted by elements in the Empire.

There is probably no limit to how interesting (to me anyway) these population issues are but I need to stop. The nationalism which had in many ways proved abortive in 1848 had become compelling for ever more people as the century proceeded. None of these needed to matter in a life-or-death way as long as the Empire held the ring, which it still did effectively in 1914 and indeed perhaps into 1918. But events increasingly seemed to play to national more than Imperial audiences. Janáček's piano sonata *1.X.1905* has its unusual title because it was written to commemorate the killing on that date by Imperial police of a man in Brno who was simply demonstrating in favour of a Czech university. This incomparable piece of music has an awful prescience – conveying a sense of running men on suddenly hostile boulevards, the panic of the crowds later anatomized by Elias Canetti and which would become one of the most disturbing features of Europe from 1914 onwards. Janáček's outrage over this single death was completely swamped by later events which make the Habsburg Empire now seem very mild – but it did not seem mild at the time.

As nationalisms locked more and more solidly there was one commentator who seemed to many at the time simply eccentric but whose short 1896 tract *The State of the Jews* was perhaps the single most extraordinarily effective of all nationalist documents. Just as Czechs or Croats pointed in a mystical, philological fashion to medieval kingdoms or Romanians made crazy appeals to Roman Dacia, so Theodor Herzl looked back to the Jewish state before the destruction of the Temple and the dispersal of the Jews across Europe and the Middle East. Herzl's family were from the far south of the Military Frontier, from the small river town of Zemun (now

a suburb of Belgrade), but had moved to Pest, where Herzl
was born in 1860. His parents were entirely Germanized Jews
who, provoked perhaps by the increasingly fevered anti-German
atmosphere in Budapest, moved to Vienna in 1878. Herzl was
characteristic of a torrent of individuals who had shape-shifted
across the Empire. The conclusion he reached when he wrote *The
State of the Jews* was that the Empire was coalescing in a way which
would exclude Jews and then kill them. It was as if everybody was
playing a form of nationalist musical chairs that would end with
places for everyone but the Jews, who would be left standing.
Anti-Semitism was unappeasable – no attempt to integrate and no
betrayal of Jewishness could ever persuade the new Central European nationalists that Jews 'belonged' even if Jews had been there
since the Roman Empire. The only solution was to create a Jewish
homeland in Palestine, and for Jews to leave Europe before it was
too late.

Herzl's revolutionary ideas met with derision, but also with
curiosity. Palestine had received a handful of Jewish visitors, was
remote, expensive to reach, but also, and most importantly, did not
feature for most Jews as a very worthwhile location. As an idea and
as a focus for religious identity it was compelling, but the modern
reality of the dusty Ottoman eyalet made Herzl's suggestion merely
ludicrous to many – it had the air of a hotter and even worse
version of Galicia. From an uncertain beginning, however, the
Zionist movement grew, and it was impossible not to see this –
Herzl did – as a logical side-effect of the increasing exclusionary
nationalist hysteria gripping the Empire. Herzl was an extraordinarily compelling figure and he criss-crossed Europe looking for
and finding support. The motives of those he talked to varied in
sickening ways. Russian ministers particularly were thrilled by a
solution which would allow them to expel 'their' Jews. Wilhelm II
came closest to seriously pursuing the idea of a Jewish homeland
on a visit to the Ottoman Empire, but for the traditional motive
('The tribe of Shem', he declared, would be 'directed to worthier
goals than the exploitation of Christians'), and in the face of Ottoman resistance he backed down. Herzl and his supporters became

ever more desperate for a result, driven on by news of terrible pogroms in Russia. This led to the strange, ultimately abortive discussions with Britain. The British had any amount of colonial land at their disposal and serious thought was given to building the homeland in Cyprus, then on the Mediterranean coast of Sinai, west of Gaza (a scheme which the young Lloyd George was involved in) and then in British East Africa. This last became a formal offer: a Jewish block of land in the Kenyan Highlands. Looking back it does seem astonishing that Herzl, a not particularly well-known Viennese journalist, could conjure up his ideas almost from thin air, win thousands of supporters, create a powerful Zionist movement and then persuade the British to come up with a homeland, all in not even eight years. The problems with Kenya (or 'the Uganda scheme' as it was inaccurately known) was the obvious one: that it was just a new place of exile plus monkeys and elephants and entirely adrift from anything approaching the Land of Israel. With Herzl's early death in 1904 Zionism lost its hero and the Kenyan option dissolved.

Herzl's book is filled with the most extraordinary statements: 'Am I stating what is not yet the case? Am I before my time? Are the sufferings of the Jews not yet grave enough? We shall see.' But he was wrong. Zionism was a quintessential Habsburg movement and Israel in many ways the perfect expression of the mutual exclusionism that was wracking the Empire,* but the context in which Israel was in fact founded was inconceivable at the time of Herzl's death. The incredulity with which *The State of Israel* was greeted by many Jews was entirely honourable and intelligent, marking, among many other things, their commitment to a long-standing Empire which successfully protected them. Jews would be both the Empire's greatest cultural element and then its greatest memorialists. A great chasm existed between even Lueger and Hitler. Herzl was right to see a deeply sinister strain in turn-of-the-century European life, but it took a series of catastrophes without

---

* Israel is now of course one of the very few countries left in the world still having to struggle with severe majority–minority issues of a once very familiar Habsburg kind.

a precedent since the first Ottoman invasions to give them an
atmosphere in which they could breed.

Elves, caryatids, lots of allegorical girls

When writing about any particular time or place there is always a
severe worry that the chunks and scraps left behind are so de-
natured, chaotic and historically loaded as to be unusable. Historical
and technological change mutate and ironize cultural remains so
thoroughly that the listener or viewer or reader can be cornered
into just choosing either a purely aesthetic response (transported on
wings of song) or a detective response (Berg's music as evidence the
First World War was about to break out), both of which manage to
be boring and reductive in their own ways.

Hugo Wolf's work is among the most extraordinary Habsburg
products of the 1880s and '90s, with songs such as 'To an Aeolian
harp' ('An eine Äolsharfe') and 'The Converted' ('Die Bekehrte')
beautiful in an almost alarming, too-bright way. But the way that
we experience them today is crazily at odds with their original
context. For example, I enjoy listening to them in our kitchen,
with a bowl of nuts and some beer, generally with the background
sound of large passenger planes roaring overhead every few minutes and our second son in the sitting room playing a computer
game like *Afghan Rough-House* or *KriminalKrew*. This is hard to
relate to the salon of a Vienna society hostess, all ruche, inlay work
and satins (and that's just the hostess), with the recital being listened to by a handful of posh whey-faced neurasthenics. More
uncanny than the need to filter out the sound of a Glock pistol
dispatching Taliban in the sitting room is the simple act of repetition. Even the most poisonously demanding patron could not get
the singer and accompanist to sing 'To an Aeolian harp' dozens
and dozens of times in one evening just because they liked it so
much. Our sheer familiarity with specific pieces of music in a specific performance is completely at odds with the spirit in which
they were both composed and appreciated.

Going to an actual Wolf recital, I felt driven to the edge of terror by the idea that in front of me were a soprano and pianist of real flesh and blood, who would have to manage from scratch the high-wire act of getting through even one of these songs without any of the lurking mistakes, splutters and mental blanks that could take them by the throat at any second. In this sense a recording is effectively unrelated to Wolf's aims. And, of course, it is not as though Wolf is all fun – it is hard to imagine some of his cuter material, such as 'Elf Song' ('Elfenlied' – tippety tap!), can ever have had many takers, or the dirgy ones which just seem to go up and down for five minutes like voice and piano exercises. But, again, this is a huge difference – not only do we listen to pieces of music exponentially more often than in their original contexts, but we are also terrible completists. Just sticking with Wolf: I am sure fans, singers, patrons, even the composer himself, must have thought 'Elf Song' pretty much a disgrace and only raised the idea of playing it in a spirit of comic threat. But now we must listen to the whole gamut of songs, good and bad, meticulously edited, complete and nailed down to a definitive listing. Even that unvarying sequence is a total affront to the *Lieder* spirit – thank goodness for digital randomizers, which could be further improved if they could also run ahead, intelligently assessing and wiping songs before they are even played.

The gulf between our experience of these songs and the composer's intentions is nothing compared to other problems pressed on us by history. We know that Wolf died young of syphilis and haggard with self-loathing, feeling in the end that his songs were mere minor work. We also know that his death in 1903 marked in some ways the end of the *Lieder* tradition, with the great composers who followed him never establishing a similar level of public enthusiasm for their attempts at the genre. Even Wolf's background as a German Slovenian is problematic, as the disappearance of German Slovenians is a minor tragedy of the twentieth century. And of course – the big one – our awareness that all this confident-seeming late-nineteenth-century culture, with its gloom and grandeur, is all about to come to an end in cataclysm. This last is without doubt the most infuriating and boring struggle of them all. I hate the way that it gives everything a layer of sad varnish completely at odds with its lived experience, but what can be done? The entire structure of this book, even the page number reached, is doomed to press on towards an over-the-cliff denouement invisible to the protagonists, but also in no way inevitable.

Wolf introduces a form of super-aestheticism which was in many ways to be a key strand in the sensibility of the 'Late Empire', a sensibility somehow confected from a strange tangling up of *l'art pour l'art* and parade-ground philistinism. The famous cultural clashes of the pre-1914 Empire – the banning of Strauss's *Salome*, the outcry over Klimt's paintings for the Great Hall of the University of Vienna, the shock at Loos's Goldman und Salatsch building (the 'Looshaus') or Freud's *Three Essays on Sexuality* – all seem to us a battle between idiocy and modernity. But this narrative of a battle between the future and reaction, between prescience and timidity (which we all so enjoy and is *so* self-selecting and self-flattering) is not true, with the reality much less clear. Like everyone, I cannot think of anything more fun than imagining some spindle-shanked courtier in knee-britches, frock coat and a quizzing glass, surrounded by images of the Virgin Mary and St Leopold, denouncing some piece of modernism as a bestial and lubricious mockery of all that is decent. There were indeed court factions of this kind, but they were never very significant. More characteristic was the straightforward dullness of Franz Joseph himself, whose sheer lack of curiosity (except about things like hunting rifles or uniform tabs) made him so lulling an influence on all things cultural. After he opened each of the major cultural forums around the Ring, a depressing official painting would be produced of him standing with various figures in uniform or court dress, surrounded by another pharaonic pile of red marble and gilding which could now be filled with music or stuffed animals or paintings. He would make some much quoted comment (the Kunsthistorisches Museum: 'This turned out rather well') which was meant to make him sound simple and direct, but which more accurately reflect his chilling imperviousness.

These amazing museums are the winding-up of the great collections – a final public presentation of his ancestors' manias, from Ferdinand of Tirol's heroic armours to Franz I's rocks and ammonites. This relentless cataloguing and displaying, this fixing onto walls of specific sequences of pictures by Rubens or of death's head hawkmoths, was a pan-European obsession in the nineteenth century. The sheer, wearying vastness of corridor after corridor and the bombastic marbled framework adds to a sense of stuffy backwardness, but the display process was actually revolutionary. Everything that had once been private or restricted was now on public display. Rudolf II's mania for Spranger's porny Roman goddesses, Ferdinand II's devotion to big altarpieces, sudden gusts of oology, a bouquet of flowers made from precious stones given to Franz I by Maria Theresa – these all now became part of public sensibility. This was a dizzying sea-change matching and entangled with other later-nineteenth-century issues such as loss of faith, or the spread of literacy and electricity which, when taken as a complete package, make the changes we are undergoing in the early twenty-first century seem comically trivial.

The floridity of these buildings has always been used as exhibit A in suggesting a bogus and cloying past from which the great experimenters of the fin de siècle were trying to tear themselves. Perhaps the acme of this is the Musikverein in Vienna, which may have miraculous acoustics but is also a temple to the bad taste of the 1860s. While half enjoying a Schubert concert there recently, I was frequently distracted trying to imagine the origins of the nude female caryatids that line the walls. These gold oddities are not exactly erotic, as from the waist down they are mere tapered plinths. Their identical faces are unnerving too. But they are chiefly striking for their breasts, and I would love to have access to the minutes of the working committee for the Musikverein at which these breasts must have been discussed. Presumably, once the reckless and by no means in-the-bag decision to have nude female caryatids lining a public building had been taken, there must have been a number of awkward debates about the breasts, with different factions arguing for different levels of realism, heft and

enjoyableness, and concerns raised as to how much they might be
a distraction at Brahms's next recital. The end result was a fatal
compromise whereby the breasts stayed, but only as rather odd
cone shapes. Still, the agreeably starchy atmosphere of Vienna's
temple to music is undoubtedly enhanced by rows of gold breasts
dominating the interior. If a concert there was filmed in the spirit
of a 1920s surrealist experiment, with a bearded man in white tie
crazily pounding away at a piano while row upon row of immobile
haute bourgeois gawp and yawn and sex-doll-like caryatids loom
above them, it would have seemed authentically avant-garde – and
yet the whole place could not be more High Victorian.

The confusion of motive and motif in the Musikverein repre-
sents a sort of dam-burst for Imperial taste throughout its delirious
final half-century. The Empire almost disappeared under naked
female allegorical statues representing Plenty, Harvest, Drama, Justice and a variety of river systems. Wandering the streets of Lviv
today perhaps the chief hazard is being hit by a falling piece of
allegorical woman. Almost every pediment or turret has a tribute to
the limber models and girlfriends of late-nineteenth-century sculptors, who must have been working on an industrial scale. City
budgets today which should go on hospitals or roads must presumably be redirected to the near-hopeless task of keeping under safe
repair the complex stone coiffeurs and sternly pointing fingers of
the Spirit of Galicia or Industry Allied to Art. It is odd that a century associated with repression, hypocrisy and buttoned-down
reserve should have left behind it such a nubile trail. This atmosphere of thinly veiled sex-put-to-allegorical-use trailed its way into
everything, always with the same weakly insistent Classical gloss.
Painters like Hans Makart created an endless sequence of nauseating, lurid canvases of a kind which seem to mock all the art
traditions of the past, and can hardly be looked at now, the pig-
ment equivalent of the massive Ring buildings. He can easily be
seen as a beaux-arts dinosaur, but he was hugely popular and the
break between Makart and later modernist heroes is much less
clean than one would hope.

There is a fun argument – which seems plausible to me – that there must have been a highly secret group who agreed that, from 1860 or so, all public commissions in the Empire would be for incredibly lavish, hot-house and over-ornate buildings, statues and frescoes. These would end up putting such overwhelming intellectual and aesthetic pressure on the Empire's genuinely creative artists that modernism would be forced into existence, the result of a near-cosmic aesthetic struggle-session whereby if you heaped up so many tons of malachite and/or allegorical girls representing the Vistula River, Art would suddenly break through to the other side. This secret group has never admitted its existence, but if the Empire ends up as the truest home of the clean modernist line, the flat roof and the plain chair then, wandering around its cities today, it seems easy to see why. Branches of the group provided valuable help in places like Berlin and Brussels, where there is a similar sense of huge, heaped-up, flaccid, wretched buildings (Berlin Cathedral!), but the Habsburg Empire is without doubt its headquarters.

This is where we are beset by the demons of what-we-now-know. It is possible to see a heavy and discredited official Imperial culture undermined by end-of-century mischief-makers, a clean demarcation between 'Victorian' and 'modern', but if we do so we have merely inherited the self-flattering rhetoric of the period. We see these objects because they are all that remains of a culture made up as much of conversation, reading the newspaper, family visits, public processions, preparing food, attending church or temple. We have almost no access to the sensibilities that might have been moved to helplessness by a Wolf song or Rilke poem, but which may have been equally or more engaged by the performance of a specific actor, or by Easter mass or by news of the Austro-Hungarian annexation of Bosnia. It was these unknowable sensibilities that cross-hatched over this whole era, providing all kinds of continuities, both among patrons and among artists. In a way, many of the great works of the Empire's final period are directly and straightforwardly the descendants of Makart's bacchanaliae and the decorations of the Musikverein. Klimt was taught by Makart and while his manner is his own, much of his subject matter and approach could not be more old-fashioned. Mahler's symphonies are a musical equivalent of the Ring buildings, with their demand for Imperial levels of resource (and Mahler himself of course spent most of his life in the employ of the court). And if Makart had lived long enough he would have been entirely in favour of removing the ban from Mahler's conducting *Salome* at the Hofoper, as it provided just the kind of sex-death spectacle long familiar to its fans in other forms. Even Freud's revolutionary work in that sense has its roots deep in Habsburg culture, with the human mind revealed as a previously unguessed-at mass of richly decorated surfaces, hidden props and repaintings.

I do not mean to suggest here a sort of hyper-conservatism where all change is merely minor adaptation – but even figures such as Webern or Schoenberg who live and die by being *new* can be seen, in their different religious interests, their demands on their musicians and on their audiences, as enshrining a sort of elaborate refinement that is almost camply backward. So much of the great artistic life of Vienna, Budapest and Prague consisted of 'luxury modernism' reliant on small groups of patrons quite as pettish and weird as any of their predecessors. We are today looking at scraps which survive because of the material they are made from: the infinitely reproducible book or music score, the ability to turn Klimt's pictures into posters, drinks mats, key-fobs, paper napkins. These are allied to the survival of specific spaces and skills: museums, publishers, printers, musicians who have at different points in the twentieth century been acutely constrained, twisted and censored across much of the former Empire. The world of this culture's original audience – complex, multilingual, religiously diverse, experimental and self-confident – has vanished under annihilating hammer-blows. It was more silly, self-contradictory, occasionally mediocre and in many ways provincial (for every eye across Europe focused on Vienna, a thousand must have been focused on Paris), with the clear artistic shape we can see now very unclear then. Klimt's and Schiele's real fame was posthumous, indeed even post-1945. During Mahler's lifetime many Viennese lovers of music admired him far more as a conductor and impresario than as a composer, but he was also hated by many, for his arrogance and bombast, and as a Jew, a Jew destroying German music. Mahler and Wolf between them are two of the last and greatest enactors of the love affair between the outer rim of German-speakers and the German heartland – as magician-setters of poems by the Franconian Rückert, the Frankfurter Goethe, the Silesian Eichendorff and the Swabian Mörike. Their settings of these poets alone make Mahler and Wolf figures who in my own, somewhat skew-whiff pantheon, have special places right at the top. But the meaning of being a German and a Slovenian for Wolf and a German and a Moravian and a Jew for Mahler was becoming ever more problematic, and had implications from which both men were sheltered only by their premature deaths.

Monuments to a vanished past

The Habsburgs used a very successful series of strategies to keep everything together. They engulfed nationalism in what could be thought of as 'threatening niceness' – concessions, co-option, investment, occasional arrests and lots and lots of barracks. The traditional bulging-eyed, heavily uniformed philistinism of much of the court and government became ever more accentuated. This created an odd sort of protective cover for all sorts of remarkable artistic and intellectual experiment, with the clashing, overlapping national groups all scoring off each other, but in a mutually defeating way. The authorities were rather like those Australian scientists who kept on importing new creatures to eat pests, which in turn became new pests – each clever manipulation and promotion of an ethnic or religious group scuppered the most immediate threat, and then created a fresh problem. By 1914 it is fair to say that the air was heavy with irrationality, but there was little to suggest that the Habsburgs were played out. Mischievous or aggressive public symbolism could be threatening, but it was all a long way from a genuine crisis like that of 1848, and without the War it could have gone on for many years. At no point were Habsburg security forces stretched and, given the monsters that were about to emerge from their caves, it is unsurprising that these decades appear now as a sort of Arcadia.

Within their short period of triumph, from 1867 to 1914, the Hungarians ran amok. This atmosphere is still preserved in the wonderful group of buildings in Budapest from the 1890s, built for the delirious celebration of one thousand years of the Hungarians in Europe. The enormous Millennium Monument features a group of charismatic statues of shaggy chieftains on their horses, a riot of barbaric yet noble splendour. The arrival of the Magyars is shown as providential, as Central Asian fighting men, who are also intensely European, yet also moustachioed sort of Red Indians, reaching the Promised Land. This is quite as chiliastic and extreme a vision as Herzl's, and definitely has little to do with Habsburg ideas about sharing nicely. In a classic example of how Franz Joseph milked this sort of nuttiness, he placed himself at the heart of celebrations that by definition had a heavy undertow of anti-Habsburg sentiment; if only because these established a prior claim and a separate Magyar trajectory. It was partly Franz Joseph's sheer lack of imagination, but also cunning policy, that he ignored potential insults and took all the fur-and-antler flummery of the Hungarian aristocrats as toothless pageant rather than fiery nationalistic reproach. The Millennium Monument has been much hacked about, as would be expected of such a politically freighted site. It used to have some Habsburg statues but these were taken down and replaced with a sequence of great Hungarian leaders culminating with Kossuth – all figures who would not have allowed a Habsburg even to feed their dog. The Vajdahunyad Castle next to the Monument carries on the same theme: a group of replicas of famous Hungarian buildings from around their territory brought together and rebuilt. This was a temporary, wooden exhibition, but its popularity was so huge that it was rebuilt in stone with some of the flavour of a proto-Disneyland. The centrepiece is a copy of the Romanesque church at Ják – much more convenient and snug than the original and with the clear message of Hungary as a beacon for Christianity, just as the repro bits of Transylvanian castle show it as the shield of Christianity. These monuments are now in many ways painful to look at as Hungarians have had such a grim time since this period of exuberance. But at least we can now enjoy them just as witty and bonkers works of art rather than as pieces of heavy chauvinism.

For the Austrian 'half' there is similarly no sense at all of restraint or retreat in the Empire's last decades. The small, remote province of Bukovina had been picked up as a negotiating thank-you present from the Ottomans in 1775 and was a shambles of mutually antagonist minority groups held together by a Vienna-backed hierarchy. Intelligent concessions and divide-and-rule kept Bukovina going and created pro-Austrian groups who clung together out of fear of the obvious alternative rulers on the province's borders: Russia and Romania. The capital, Czernowitz, received the standard full kit: electric tramways, an opera house, a whole lot of art nouveau, a bust of Schiller and a comically dreary Austria Monument, put up in 1875 to mark a century since the Turks ceded the territory, and featuring a statue of a lumpy woman with an ivy-entwined sword and a palm-leaf. When the Romanians invaded in 1918 the Austria Monument bit the dust – but its torso was rediscovered in 2003, with copies being sent across Europe as a symbol of Bukovina's links (by now somewhat thin) with the West. Inevitably an artist took one of these torso copies and put a head in a burka on it, perhaps the most leaden and pathetic piece of conceptual art yet attempted, but equally perhaps a witty genu-flection to the nullity of the original monument itself.

It is hard to completely enjoy Czernowitz (now the Ukrainian city of Chernivtsi) as its fate in the twentieth century has been so awful. The survival of so many attractive buildings and spaces is obviously trumped by the non-survival of most of the population for whom these were built. Gregor von Rezzori (his very name a perfect Habsburg amalgam) in his great, astonishingly vivid memoir of growing up there, *The Snows of Yesteryear*, described the complex world which still existed in Czernowitz even in the 1920s, in the person of his childhood nurse:

I was nourished by her speech. The main component was a German, never learned correctly or completely, the gaps in which were filled with words and phrases from all the other tongues spoken in the Bukovina – so that each second or third word was either Ruthenian, Romanian, Polish, Russian, Armenian or Yiddish, not to forget Hungarian and Turkish.

Almost all these languages have now disappeared from Bukovina and the very existence of von Rezzori's family appears strange. Following the Russian invasion of 1914, the von Rezzoris were able to call on the huge geographical reach of the Empire, fleeing through a Carpathian pass and settling in houses first in Trieste and then Lower Austria, before returning to now Romanian-ruled Bukovina, with the author ending up at school in Transylvania. This incredibly broad fluid Habsburg frame of reference would be barred by innumerable hostile borders until 1989.

The traumas of much of the western parts of the Empire are better concealed by more recent prosperity and rebuilding, but the haggard nature of so many Galician and Bukovinan towns makes it much more raw and obvious that these are places where everything has gone just completely wrong. Contemporary Chernivtsi makes its money as an enormous market on the edge of the European Union, with products trucked in from as away far as south-east Asia to leak across the chaotic borders into Romania. This at least makes it a busy, bustling place with a real, albeit semi-criminal, purpose. Much of Chernivtsi, with its battered pavements, snarled-up traffic, broken-down lorries, heaped boxes and enormous roadside advertisements, has a very Indian feel and it is curious to come face to face with such clear evidence that townscapes are a side-effect not of culture ('Indian chaos') but of specific formulae involving local GDP, tax revenue and government reach.

Chernivtsi is home to one completely astonishing building which has somehow survived all the numerous regimes* that have

---

* At least ten in the twentieth century, each acutely threatening to one or more of the city's communities, whether by class, religion or language, and not counting the huge political shift of 1991.

swept the city: the Metropolitan's Palace. This surreal marvel is a summa of Vienna's attitude towards its role and its commitment to pharaonic architectural overreach, not unlike the British building New Delhi just as their own rule over India was about to stop. By some measures the Metropolitan's Palace was the most expensive construction project in the entire Empire and yet it was built for what was never more than a charismatic backwater. Its origins lay in the aftermath of the 1867 Compromise. Habsburg Orthodox populations had previously been subordinated to the authorities in the now Budapest-ruled Serbian town of Sremski Karlovci. For the Austrian half the solution lay in upgrading Czernowitz (already a significant religious focus) as the Vienna-ruled equivalent. The strange geography of the new state here achieved its strangest form. Vienna's continuing direct rule over Galicia and Bukovina brought into existence a four-hundred-mile scythe of territory between Russia and Hungary, at the far tip of which was Czernowitz. In a tidy piece of madness the new Metropolitan See was responsible for the Orthodox populations of both Bukovina and Galicia, and Dalmatia – with all the many thousands of square miles of territory between the territories under Hungarian rule. Baffled Adriatic Serbs now suddenly found themselves owing allegiance to a man living in the Ukrainian borderlands.

The Metropolitan Palace, as it gradually took shape in the 1870s, seems to have got completely out of control, the building equivalent of the sorcerer's apprentice unable to stop the spell he has unleashed. The result is a Burgundo-Hanseatic-Grenadan-Hutsul-Byzantine mishmash of a heroic kind, and a classic piece of Habsburg collaboration: with a patently insane Czech architect, Josef Hlávka, armies of medievally inspired German and local decorators and specialists and seemingly no one doing the budgeting. Gregor von Rezzori's father had an office there for some years and it must have fitted perfectly with his historicist-reactionary enthusiasms. The complex has come through some terrible times, but is now one of the world's most attractive university buildings. With its little courtyards, magic garden and loopy eclecticism, the whole place made me wish to be reincarnated as a Ukrainian undergraduate. Indeed, so charismatic and enjoyable is Hlávka's vision that it seems a bit pointless for architects to come up with new, less good solutions for institutional needs – instead of just being hidden away in Bukovina, exact copies should be made for any city that wants one.

The existence of this building shows the strange balancing act that Vienna had to keep up every day, always with different interest groups, aggrieved parties, collaborators and enemies needing to be nudged, bought off, incarcerated, ignored. It also raises very difficult issues of distance, both physical and temporal. To wander along, as at some elaborate buffet, looking at different options and behaviours is effectively an activity unrelated to living one's life within one of them. To stand outside these issues is to be invisible and irrelevant. The last generation of Habsburg officials, such as von Rezzori senior, prided themselves on this being their stance, and yet we can now see the innumerable ways in which they fooled themselves, their scientific rationalism a delusion. But there really was a form of Imperial colour-blindness, the kind celebrated later by writers such as Stefan Zweig and Joseph Roth (not coincidentally Jews), and which did have a real, transparent value. This was at its most extreme in Bukovina, perhaps Europe's greatest *macedonia di frutta*, and a culture (which also produced Paul Celan and Aharon Appelfeld) unique but now long dispersed.

Young Poland

Even when baring their teeth at one another, Russia, Germany and Austria-Hungary generally cooperated to ensure that 'their' Poles were reconciled to their fates as inhabitants of a non-country. Austrian-ruled Galicia was in Imperial terms a great success although only by default: the Poles who lived there were deeply aware of how much worse their lives would be in the German province of Posen or in Warsaw, the third largest city in Russia. The presence of an ever more educated, vocal and insistent Ruthenian element in Galicia, an absolute majority in some regions, gave the Poles further reason for loyalty to the Habsburgs. But within that Polish loyalty attitudes ranged from genuine belief to contemptuous cynicism. The relative loyalism of Galicia meant that it tended to be held up as an example to other provinces, but this loyalism came at a very high price. For much of the rest of Europe, Galicia was synonymous with impoverished misery, with at least a million Galicians (many Jewish) emigrating and squalor and gloom prevailing outside a handful of spruced-up town centres. Economically the stakes were perhaps too low for the Poles for it to be worth being too fractious. Despite great bureaucratic ingenuity it seemed that nothing could be done with the region. The one peculiar exception were the oil deposits around Drohobych, which created the strange little semi-Americanized enclave of prosperity which Bruno Schulz later turned into a sort of wonderland in *The Street of Crocodiles*.

Kraków, a much smashed-up backwater, had been tacked onto Galicia in 1846 when it fell to Austrian rule after a failed rebellion. The capital of Galicia remained Lwów, far to the east, and Kraków at first seemed merely haunted and debilitated by its earlier greatness, with the Wawel Castle reduced to a dreary Habsburg barracks, its lovely Renaissance pillars covered up. But almost by default Kraków, as a provincial town rather than a major governmental centre, and as the biggest of these not in the brutal hands of the Germans or Russians, became an open space for rebuilding Polish culture. One curious moment came in 1873 when the Germans celebrated the four-hundredth anniversary of the birth of Nikolaus Kopernikus, a figure who Poles were under the impression was Mikołaj Kopernik, Kraków student, hero and Pole. Copernicus was clearly a linguistically and ethnically complex figure of a kind quite common in the era in which he lived. But the blustering German argument threw up the chilling possibility of Polish culture as well as land being dismantled before the eyes of the surviving Polish intelligentsia. It was in Kraków that there was a context in which such a future might be averted.

Kraków benefited from the same speedy industrialization and growth as elsewhere in Europe, becoming a substantially new

Polish Christian and Polish Jewish city and at last shaking off its era of stagnation. It was the home of Jan Matejko, who single-handedly painted virtually every major event in Poland's history in a lurid, feverish, Verdi-esque and incredibly enjoyable style which makes me wish that British history had had such luck. This frenetic act of recovery meant that by his death in 1893, Matejko had ensured that every Polish schoolchild would grow up with the most vivid sense of his buried nation's past, laughing at the discomforted Turk, sneering at the proud Prussians' grovelling submission to the Polish king, warm and alive to the thrill of the Union of Lublin. Perhaps more than anybody Matejko's histrionics hauled Polish identity out of the danger zone, with the paintings' public display spreading a renewed pride far more effectively than any history books.

'Young Poland', which grew up from the 1890s, is one of those artistic movements frustratingly little known to the rest of the world. This is in part because so much of it was entangled in formats which are rarely translated (plays, poems) or are site-specific (buildings, stained-glass windows). My own ignorance was total, but it is hard not to stand in awe of such figures (once you have encountered them) as Stanisław Wyspiański, who seems to have been wonderful at everything he turned his hands to (interior design, plays, poetry, furniture), or Feliks 'Manga' Jasieński, a charismatic Orientalist who brought Japanese culture to Kraków and who rightly has a sort of shrine to his sensibility in the Wyspiański Museum. Much of 'Young Poland' was politically harmless, except in the sense that the very idea of a vigorous Polish culture could not avoid having implications. Much of Wyspiański's most beautiful work consists of paintings of children and domestic life and it seems utterly without menace, but he could not escape a more vigorous nationalism that surged everywhere in turn-of-the-century Europe. One compelling oddity, and a fine example of Wyspiański's ability to turn his hand to pretty much anything, is the fantasy he created with Władysław Ekielski of a total architectural renewal of the Wawel hill. This shabby Habsburg military complex and parade-ground was at last evacuated by Austrian troops in 1905,

opening up amazing possibilities for rebuilding and effectively
reconsecrating the greatest of Polish national sites. Wyspiański and
Ekielski reimagined it as the Acropolis of the Polish Nation, a sort
of fairy castle of turrets and domes, museums and new government
buildings flanked by an enormous hippodrome. It is a charming
vision, preserved in an incredibly charismatic model, but all over
Europe people were sketching similar ideas of unlimited grandios-
ity, some of which actually got built (such as the gross, mournful
Neue Burg in Vienna). As a model, however, Wyspiański and Ekielski's vision cannot be bettered. When they were creating it genuine
national independence, rather than mere dangled forms of autonomy, was surreally unlikely, but all the cultural groundwork had
been done by 'Young Poland' and the Poles, as it turned out, only
had a short while to wait.

I realize that things are getting a bit pell-mell around here, but
we cannot move on without a quick mention of the multi-talented
Stanisław Witkiewicz. He is owed the world's gratitude for inventing the Zakopane-style of architecture, a modern and substantial
version of the wooden buildings and carvings of the Goråle
mountain people of Poland's far south. I am rarely happier than
wandering around Zakopane, which, even with its almost uncontrollable crowds of visitors from Kraków, is still a thrillingly
enjoyable town. It is here that one of my favourite composers, the
intermittently great Karol Szymanowski, lived, creator of among
many other things the wonderful Goråle pantomime-ballet
Harnasie. It was here too that Joseph Conrad – who had grown up
in Kraków and Lwów but had left Poland forty years before –
found himself on a nostalgic visit stuck by the outbreak of the First
World War. Eventually a sympathetic American consul arranged for
him to be extracted from Austria-Hungary. As Szymanowski and
Conrad are two of my spiritual godparents (not a role they would
have volunteered for), to be in *their* mountain town made everything seem more beautiful and significant than it perhaps really is.
Witkiewicz's vision of a town of authentic, severe yet extravagant,
wooden houses continues to prevail in some parts of Zakopane.
I would love to live there, surrounded by Zakopane-style butter-
moulds and milking-stools, wearing a folkloric blouse and walking

in the Tatra Mountains. It has been a tourist trap for at least a century, but sitting at a table munching a vast plate of mountain-style meat listening to Goróle musicians, you feel that it is absolutely fine to be trapped.

CHAPTER FOURTEEN

'The fat churchy one' » Night music » Transylvanian rocketry »
Psychopathologies of everyday life » The end begins

'The fat churchy one'

The Archduke Franz Ferdinand is one of the modern era's terrible ghosts, doomed to re-enact year after year his floundering final hours, ostrich feathers everywhere, his body bulging in an absurd uniform. He is always en route to that wrong turn which will bring him face to face with the depressed young man, sitting in a Sarajevo cafe mulling over the pathetic failure of his assassination plot, who is suddenly presented with this incredible reprieve. Betrayed by his useless security arrangements and daft, pop-eyed, moustachioed appearance, Franz Ferdinand seems to cry out to be killed and usher in a new and awful world.

Franz Ferdinand spent almost his entire adult life rehearsing and war-gaming his upcoming role as Habsburg Emperor. From the age of twenty-six to his murder a quarter of a century later, he impatiently awaited his despised uncle Franz Joseph's death. Of course we will never know if he would have been a 'good' Emperor. It may well be that he had just waited too long and that whatever qualities he might have possessed had long curdled, lost in a maze of ritual, uniforms, masses and – above all – hunting. His shooting skills made him legendary, belonging to that disgusting and depressing era when the aristocratic hunting expedition became married to modern military technology, unbalancing the entire relationship of hunter and hunted, so that shooting partridges became like a proto-version of playing *Space Invaders*. Franz Ferdinand totted up the dazing total of some three hundred thousand animals killed. The little woodland critters on his Bohemian estates must have indulged in a certain amount of high-fiving on receipt of the news from Sarajevo.

Franz Ferdinand's reputation is doubly ruined – not just by the dumb, chaotic, portentous nature of his death, but by his comic role at the opening of Jaroslav Hašek's *The Good Soldier Švejk*. The devastating opening chat between Švejk and his landlady – where Švejk assumes that the Ferdinand whose murder has been announced must either be a Ferdinand who works as a chemist's messenger or a Ferdinand who is a local dog-shit collector ('Neither of them is any loss') – has for many thousands of readers buried the Archduke for ever. The last straw is the landlady's crushing correction: 'Oh no, sir, it's His Imperial Highness . . . the fat churchy one.'

In the modern Czech Republic, Franz Ferdinand's home at Konopiště is a hugely popular tourist site and is at the heart of the renewed cult of the Habsburgs as happy rulers of a better time. Having frittered much of my life wandering around Central European castles, I think I can say with some authority that this is the most interesting of them all. Despite damage and theft by the Nazis, the interior of Konopiště accurately reflects its appearance when Franz Ferdinand and his family left it for the last time, en route to Bosnia. It is comparable perhaps only to Freud's house in London as a picture of the inside of a particular mind. It also brings to mind Bartók's *Duke Bluebeard's Castle*, with each door opening to reveal a fresh aspect of the heir's psyche. Franz Ferdinand was a great mental and physical cataloguer – a man who felt that he could know everything by systematizing everything – and he used Konopiště as an extension of his own memory.

As he shot animals around the world (everything from rhinos to gemsbok to emus) Franz Ferdinand carefully wrote down each kill, leaving a complete and dismaying record. Hundreds of these animals were stuffed and mounted, leaving whole corridors of the castle bursting with antlers, tusks, beaks, snouts, glass eyes, feathers and bristles. Just a moment of inattention while wandering past these heads could result in being gouged by something or releasing a nauseating shower of sawdust and skin. Wherever Franz Ferdinand travelled he had photos taken, and corridors are filled with his global wanderings, across Egypt and Australia, Canada and the United States (where he had, to his bafflement, actually to hand in his gun before visiting Yellowstone National Park). He collected weapons, many superb pieces being from his cousin the Duke of Modena, who bequeathed him not only heaps of wheel-locks, silver-chased partisans and jousting armour, but also so much money that he became one of the richest men in Europe – independently of any Imperial money, much to Franz Joseph's impotent fury. Entire rooms are stuffed with ingenious metal objects for killing people, in glass cases, in decorative patterns, hanging from the ceiling. Franz Ferdinand also collected statues of St George (although his favourite saint was St Hubert – patron saint of hunters) and every nook and niche is filled with beautiful, strange or indifferent sculptures of George, with or without dragon. In all this monstrous accumulation of *stuff* there is something eerie and excessive. There is even a wing of the castle built specially for his cousin and friend Crown Prince Rudolf's use, filled with objects of a kind which the young Franz Ferdinand thought would please him. Rudolf killed himself without ever visiting the castle, but the wing, with its wood panelling and air of masculine, tweedy, outdoorsy common sense plus a slight whiff of eau de Cologne, was kept as a perverse shrine.

By the time that you have taken all this in – plus Franz Ferdinand's obsessive diary of his geographical location for every day in his life (the page open on a shooting trip to Welbeck Abbey, where a loader flirted with changing all human history by accidentally nearly killing him) plus his multi-compartmented leather travelling cases – it is clear that there was something very peculiar about the castle's owner. Undoubtedly very clever, conscientious, focused, hungry for information, he was also humourless, narrow, grasping and an insatiable, unappeasable cataloguer of a chilling kind. Whether at Konopiště or at the Upper Belvedere Palace, his Vienna base, Franz Ferdinand spent year after year wondering how to reform the Empire and which Hungarians he would gaol first, poring over maps and books, cross-examining whole crowds of experts, all in preparation for when he would *at last* take over. He imagined for the Empire a definitive reorganization which would

THE UNITED STATES OF AUSTRIA

tidy it up, rationalize it and essentially bring it into line with his game diary, St George statues and serried flintlocks. We will never know if the plan for a United States of Greater Austria would have worked (there were many variants and it is unclear how seriously he took them) but on paper it seems tantalizing: fifteen ethnically coherent states with Vienna as the (very powerful) federal capital. To look at the map (designed by the Romanian Transylvanian Aurel Popovici) is to see a future which never happened – or only happened in part under the obscene, transient tutelage of the Nazis. The existence of such states as Szekler Land, Trentino and German Bohemia would have saved a lot of agony and the map has become an anguished commentary on what has happened in the century since it was proposed.

Franz Ferdinand was an unusual Habsburg in that he was poor at learning languages, and his complete failure to master Magyar may have been one of the reasons he hated Hungary so much. For his map to have worked the first obstacle had to be the destruction of the Hungarian state. The years of obfuscation, special pleading and hypocrisy by the Hungarian aristocracy so enraged Franz Ferdinand that he – a lifelong hater of democracy – became a warm supporter of a broad franchise just in Hungary (not in Austria) purely to enrage and then ruin the Hungarian aristocracy. He wanted to recreate the atmosphere of prostration that had prevailed back in 1849 so as to reshape the current botch and make a Habsburg super-state. These fascinating possibilities of course fall foul of the acute problems in achieving them. However friendless the Hungarians may have been, such a drastic reordering could have attracted malevolent Russian interest as well as Italian, Serbian and Romanian outrage of a kind that might well have led to some similar conflagration to that provoked by Franz Ferdinand's murder. It also assumed that each nationality would have remained, once the Hungarians had somehow been disarmed, happy and merely *folklorique* within the bounds of Habsburg federalism. Why would the Bohemian Germans be willing to keep living in their little woodsy province rather than unite with the Second Reich? The plan (and Franz Ferdinand had many – so he may have spotted this flaw himself at some point) also failed to notice that it was the Hungarians who were the gendarmes, the most zealously brutal and anti-nationalist enforcers. Their neutralization would knock from the Habsburgs' hands their most powerful weapon. In any event, some of the variants enshrined in Popovici's map would ultimately be tried, with truly horrible results – but both the ruthless re-cutting of boundaries and the implicit violence had important origins in Franz Ferdinand's mind.

In many of Franz Ferdinand's political dealings there is the air of someone dreaming about how one day he will thrash all his servants in the hope that this will enforce obedience. But this was in many ways just his unpleasant personal manner and he was certainly no warmonger. One of the worst counterfactuals around his death is his role in the July Crisis, had he not caused it by being dead. He was no titan, but could he have shaped a more intelligent Austro-Hungarian strategy than the gang of fatalists and jittery oddballs who gathered around the ancient Franz Joseph? If much of the July Crisis was caused by the utter moral failure of Europe's civilian leadership, then it is plausible to think that Franz Ferdinand's enormous authority may have imposed a different pattern of thinking. He was always convinced that the motor for a stable and successful Europe was a German–Habsburg–Russian alliance, an alliance which had been, after all, highly successful for much of the nineteenth century. This perception that the three empires should support each other for dynastic, anti-democratic and anti-Polish reasons was very plausible – and indeed the perhaps needless alienation of Russia proved as great a disaster for Europe as the split between Britain and Germany.

These various combinations and options and possibilities ran back and forth in his mind as the years went by at Konopiště. But it was all against one very appealing piece of background. He may have been rude, narrow, sneering and an enemy to furry friends the world over, but he was a very good husband and father. With the usual historian's despair at the wayward, unguessable nature of private life, it has to be said that Franz Ferdinand was unimpeachable here. Despite freezing disapproval from Franz

Joseph, he insisted on marrying Sophie Chotek, a Bohemian aristocrat who was by Habsburg standards too common to be a
suitable partner. They seem to have been devoted to each other and
Sophie spent the rest of her life being snubbed and humiliated by
the creepy court in Vienna, way down the list of precedence, sitting at some poky side table at banquets while her husband was up
on the Emperor's table. All this reinforced their decision to spend
as much time as possible at Konopiště with their three children,
Sophie, Maximilian and Ernst. A condition of the marriage happening at all was that any children could never succeed to the
throne – a piece of vindictive madness but one that, as it turned
out, at least saved the Empire from being ruled in the middle of the
First World War by a fourteen-year-old Maximilian III.

The family provides the other really surprising and moving
aspect of the castle. The nursery and the family rooms preserve a
very privileged but nonetheless charming, modest and thoughtful
existence, far removed from all the stuffiness and parade-ground
shouting which made Franz Ferdinand so unloved in other contexts. The paintings and photos of the family, the toys, the
drawings by the children take on a value which, while obviously
sentimental, is nonetheless inescapable and upsetting – capped
by a final photo of the entire family looking cheerful on holiday
in Croatia just before Franz Ferdinand and Sophie headed off
to Sarajevo, and then a final, final photo of the children posed in
black and looking mournful in a staged and dated way after the
news of their parents' murder. The children were too obviously
threats to the Anschluss and were lucky to survive. The sons were
imprisoned by Hitler as soon as Austria was absorbed and two of
the daughter's children were killed fighting for the Third Reich.

As if this dense, almost suffocating array of associations, shocks
and cross-fertilizations filling Konopiště were not enough, there
is a final treasure: the gloomy little station of the local town of
Benešov has somehow still kept the decorative door-frame that
once led to the special waiting room reserved for guests en route
to or from the heir's home. This door-frame may not be much but
it has survived an incredible number of tribulations, and what curi-

ous, ornate figures once walked through it! In the summer of 1914 Kaiser Wilhelm II and Grand Admiral Alfred von Tirpitz arrived for a visit. This was one of the key meetings prior to the First World War and infuriatingly there is no clue at all as to what was discussed. Franz Ferdinand was against preventive war of any kind – well aware of Habsburg weakness, and impatient (by this time *more* than impatient) to carry out his internal reforms and regenerate the Empire as a great power on the modern German or American model. The three men, probably sitting in Franz Ferdinand's 'harem room' with their cigars, would have had the most frank and interesting conversation imaginable, filled with random gusts of anti-British, anti-Russian and anti-French ranting with occasional polite pauses to allow Franz Ferdinand to be anti-Hungarian and anti-Serb. We would know so much more about the true parameters of the German–Habsburg relationship, which was to create the summer's fatal dynamic, if there was only some kind of record. Both the Grand Admiral's and the Kaiser's bedrooms have been preserved. Tirpitz's is decorated with a straight-talking albeit freakishly bearded militarist in mind – it is the room of a man's man, no nonsense and with a portrait of Wallenstein. In a weird contrast, the Kaiser's room is decorated with a rose-themed pink wallpaper and lots of fussy Bohemian glass and spindly furniture. It is hard to imagine that Franz Ferdinand gave orders for such an insulting chamber for the Nibelung Supreme Warlord, but someone lurking in the castle must have thought it funny.

Night music

This is probably as good a place as any to come clean about Béla Bartók. Through all the travels and all the reading behind this book a number of composers have provided the soundtrack, but none more important than Bartók. Shortly after beginning my first proper job I met up with a friend who had just discovered him and insisted I sit and listen to the opening bars of *Duke Bluebeard's Castle*. At last my life had the shadowed, mystical, darkling and morbid accompaniment that made sense. I may have been sleeping on a fold-away bed in the storeroom of a crowded rental semi on the edge of a Basingstoke industrial estate, microwaving chicken pie and sweetcorn, but in my mind colossal dramas were being played out.

As so often these completely accidental encounters at the right age can have a total impact. I can no more imagine my adult life without Bartók than I can imagine it without my family – and without Bartók I cannot see how I would have written this book. Several writers and artists spun me round to put me face to face with Central Europe, but it was Bartók who over some twenty-five years turned it into an enduring conundrum, his face in countless photos a sort of enigmatic father figure to me. However much I love to listen to Szymanowski, Janáček, Ligeti, Dvořák, Zemlinsky, Berg, Mahler, Wolf and Schoenberg, these are all composers who for me follow behind the trail he blazed through my head.

In a book not unfree of self-indulgence there is a huge temptation here to go on indefinitely about Bartók, but I will try to rein myself in. I was very lucky not to have seen *Duke Bluebeard's Castle* on stage until the entire opera was safely lodged in my imagination as it is, in the cold light of the opera house, a rather embarrassing oddity. The drama is set around the duke bringing his bride, Judith, back to his dark and gloomy castle. The couple love each other but Judith insists (reasonably enough) that the seven enormous doors of the castle's interior be opened, both to brighten the place up a bit and because there can be no secrets between them. The duke grudgingly complies and the doors are unlocked one by one, to reveal a torture chamber, an armoury, a treasure house, a magic garden, a great vista of forests and meadows, a lake of tears and, finally, Judith's own awful fate.

Even writing this stuff out it is impossible not to feel a bit uneasy about the leaden nature of its grinding symbolism, cod psychiatry and so on. The blame for this lies with Béla Balázs, who wrote the libretto and also did a similarly awful job for the scenario of Bartók's ballet *The Wooden Prince*, although he was himself a fascinating figure – a classic example of Magyarization, having been born to German-Jewish parents as Herbert Bauer. Whatever his failings on the stage his fake Chinese stories *The Cloak of Dreams* could not be more perfectly enjoyable. But clearly Bartók found it sympathetic and the Budapest of the time was a mass of such stuff: *Bluebeard* should probably be seen as cut from the same wonderful material as the Zoo or Ignác Alpár's Vajdahunyad Castle or sculptures of the *Turul.* * Unfortunately for Bartók these objects do not depend for their success on being displayed on a proscenium stage to well-heeled people sitting in rows. Balázs and Bartók created something which looks ridiculous on stage (two people warbling away surrounded by doors), but which quite inadvertently turned out to work brilliantly on headphones or through massive speakers. No set-designer can hope to get near the music itself, which conjures up visions of disembodied horror and ecstasy in a mentally infinite regression of Piranesi's *Imaginary Prisons*. As with so much of Bartók's music it makes me wistful that I have never had much to do with mind-altering drugs.

Duke Bluebeard's Castle was my introduction to the baffling joys of Magyar. When Bluebeard becomes Kékszakállú (much better!) and things are said like

> Aranypénz és drága gyémánt,
> Bélagyöngyel fényes ékszer,
> Koronák és dús palástok!

then you know you are lost. I have spent so much time trying to pronounce Magyar properly and it is the language that now sits at the heart of my personal rage and sadness about my language impotence – the certainty of dying with still no access to such strange, mellifluous sounds.

Bluebeard (or, ahem, *A Kékszakállú Herceg Vára*) was the beginning of a long journey I should not threaten you with. But for me

---

* An eagle-like creature with a central place in Magyar mythology. There is a huge statue of one on Budapest's Castle Hill, but the biggest (with the somewhat narrow boast that it is Central Europe's biggest freestanding bird sculpture) is on a hill outside the town of Tatabánya.

Bartók has offered the permanent promise of an aural book of endless interest and with an infinite number of pages to turn. Most of
Bartók's orchestral showpieces, apart from *Bluebeard*, the piano
concertos and the *Music for Strings, Percussion and Celeste*, have never
struck me as having much value. It is in the works where he is
most completely unfolding his innermost strangeness – the chamber music, the pieces for piano – that he becomes so hypnotic.
With aching self-consciousness I once read Musil's *The Man Without Qualities* while listening over and over to *Mikrokosmos* and these
two gripping and heroically ambitious works are welded together
for me even if to a colder eye or ear they would have nothing in
common. *Mikrokosmos* is a vast set of over a hundred and fifty
piano pieces initially setting out as simple little teaching pieces for
Bartók's son ('Dotted Notes', 'Syncopation') but by the final 'Six
Dances in Bulgarian Rhythm' capering off to the Lunatic Asylum
of Virtuosity. I have never dared find out after how many pieces
into the sequence poor little Péter Bartók blubbed and ran off. The
first of the exercises, which even I could play, already sound absolutely Bartókian and have made it possible to speculate that his
music is so odd because he just heard or imagined things differently (or 'wrongly') – but this is, of course, unverifiable. Patches of
Mikrokosmos are merely proficient and colourless, but extraordinary
things like 'Subject and Reflection' and 'From the Diary of a Fly'
are, for me, the articulation for thinking about Hungary and race
back and forth in my head, enlivening even sitting on a bus in
Transdanubia.

Bartók's existence (as with so many Austro-Hungarian artists)
is terrifyingly at odds with later political and racial convulsions.
Almost nowhere associated with either his upbringing or interests
now lies inside the Hungarian state. He was born in Nagyszent-
miklós, now the Romanian town of Sânnicolau Mare, then moved
to Nagyszőllős (where he tinkled away as a child prodigy), now
the Ukrainian town of Vynohradiv, then Nagyvárad, now the
Romanian city of Oradea, and then Pozsony, the Slovakian capital
of Bratislava. Only in his late teens did he get to Budapest. The
peasant-song research which was so critical to Bartók's music was

carried out mainly in what is now Slovakia and Romania, with the composer dressed up in a painfully earnest walking costume. It is almost as though he was born just in time to exist as a composer, fed from sources which would soon be stopped up.

He lived the entire historical sequence, beginning with the anti-Habsburg contempt of his early tone-poem *Kossuth*, which has a derisive snatch from 'The Emperor's Hymn' that caused anxiety to the authorities – a needless anxiety given the work's dreary stiffness. He then lived through the nightmares of the Great War, was associated with the post-War Communist republic, but eventually rebuilt some bridges with the traumatized, grey Horthy regency while never dropping his own commitment to what he happily called 'the brotherhood of man'. The mutual hatreds that drove Central Europe to destruction could not be split apart from music, however private much of Bartók's music became. An initiative as simple as a plaque on his birthplace in Romania collapsed into recriminations over what languages it should use. Equally gloomily one of his greatest works, *Cantana Profana: The Nine Splendid Stags*, was based on a Romanian *colindă* (a form of Christmas carol) but had to be translated into Magyar to make it acceptable for performance in Hungary. His bristling hatred of Fascism eventually drove him to emigrate to New York, where he was ill, miserable and lived just long enough to see his country destroyed. Ten people attended his funeral.

Normally I am resistant to visiting the museum homes of famous writers or composers as there seems such a limited link between what they contain and what we value – desks or pianos or knick-knacks seem very low on the list of reasons for being interested in someone, particularly once a cafe, shop and ticket desk have been hacked into place. But I felt I had to make an exception for Bartók's house in the Buda Hills, where he lived for much of the 1930s. I also made an exception for Szymanowski's house in Zakopane, which was fascinating – and which showed that in fact I had been entirely *wrong* for years about writers' and composers' houses and had left a now irreparable and silly hole in much of my writing.

Bartók's house could not be more remodelled, but this is still the street he walked up, the garden he looked at, the spaces he moved through. It was a suitably dark, bare-treed and wintry day and everything seemed to call for *Bluebeard*'s 'Lake of Tears' music. The house holds a miscellany of Bartók things which almost accidentally emphasize his proto-hippyness. In most photos he dresses like a gloomy bank clerk, but here is a photo of him in a colourful chemise and sandals sitting devoutly in front of a *folklorique* painted wardrobe, and the wardrobe itself now stands next to the photo. Most wonderful are the little objects he liked to collect – trays of beetles, flowers, coins, minerals, sea-shells, cigar boxes filled with odds and ends, a chess set, a pocket maze, an edelweiss. The museum's major treasures were what you would expect (diplomas, scores, paintings), but these tiny objects were nearly unbearable – here was the man who had written *Mikrokosmos,* inventor of the churring 'night music' that is scattered throughout his work, whose sensibility seemed as perfectly expressed by a folding chess set or a pressed flower as by his actual music.

Transylvanian rocketry

For some years I have had an underdeveloped fantasy about the museum directors of western Romania and how at their annual Christmas lunch the impatiently awaited highlight – between gulps of gum-burning brandy – is always the announcement of the winner of the dullest exhibition-case award. As one of the handful of individuals who has ambled around pretty much all the museums in Transylvania, Partium and the north-eastern Banat, I could certainly be a plausible guest and make helpful suggestions. In a crowded field the winner most years must be the incomparable display case at the Sighişoara Museum that simply features two late-nineteenth-century books open to show illustrations of a man demonstrating a back-strengthening device. Others might have their displays of callipers, decorated bellows or drinking vessels – but there is no escaping the low whistle of admiration provoked by this doozy. And so yet again the director of the Sighişoara Museum – polishing his glasses with his napkin in quiet pride – almost disappears under the hearty back-pats of his colleagues.

Even typing this I feel a total heel. How can museums which have been hit by every imaginable ideological wave be anything other than timorous? How could a world where several generations of looting soldiers, corrupt mayors and acquisitive politicians from the capital cities hold sway *not* have exhausted, drained-out museums? Post-1989 – with the rejection of the last twinges of the nationalist–Communist narrative – what *is* the story that a museum is meant to tell? Lack of funding, but perhaps more importantly lack of interest, has meant that many museums are shut completely or have huge areas closed off (including, sadly, the reputedly fascinating sections on the grim end of the Hungarian War of 1848–49 in the Arad Museum).

Control of museums, like control of teaching, was always a key nationalist aim throughout the Empire, with the exhibits bent to demonstrate specific ancient claims to the land, to enshrine terrible deeds of the past and to celebrate current achievements. This is still the case in places such as the National Museums of Prague and Budapest, with the former currently showing two exhibitions, one of proud Hussite remnants and the other simply called Great Czechs. In the parts of the Empire now ruled by Romania there is a sense of ideological exhaustion which generally makes this unacceptable. Everyone who has survived has been through the mill in a way that makes the past simply too awful to be worth enshrining. So in that sense old pictures of patented back-straightening devices celebrate the exorcising of that past. Perhaps this too is why some of the truly exceptional Transylvanian museums, such as the Ethnographic Museum in Cluj or the ASTRA park outside Sibiu, work so well. By restricting themselves to the nineteenth-century obsession with folk costume or architecture they skirt more difficult questions and, with all passion spent, allow an entirely aesthetic rather than political response.

Across Transylvania, wandering through the endless display cases of river-fish tridents, enema pumps and horse-brasses it has to be said that there is always going to be something interesting. Even the jaw-slackening Sighişoara Museum has its moment of greatness. Up inside the battered and superb great watchtower, there is a display of cuttings about the Transylvanian visionary Hermann Oberth. As a teenager before the Great War, Oberth became obsessed with the idea of space travel and doodled on bits of paper, inventing the multi-stage rocket. By the age of fifteen he had created a rocket powered by guncotton. During the war he experimented with ideas about weightlessness and invented a small liquid-fuel rocket. By the early 1920s he was sketching out space stations, lunar-landers and spacesuits and the physics behind a giant space mirror that would control the temperature of the Earth. Oberth was a terrible figure in many ways but from his mind stepped most of the basic principles of the space programme. He was Wernher von Braun's teacher and involved with both Nazi and then American rocket designs. It could be claimed that it is very peculiar that most of the intellectual and practical thinking behind the quintessential two-edged twentieth-century achievement was set out in such a notionally dozy and remote part of the world as Transylvania. But then I hope that by this point in the book I have made some kind of case for even places like Sighişoara being in practice at the very heart of Europe. I have lost count of the number of times I have found myself somewhere satisfyingly 'remote' only to realize, by being there, that it has become nearby. If the key origins of V2s and ICBMs lie in southern Transylvania then we probably need to think about our history books differently.

I realize with a chill that this section could go on almost indefinitely and it would be possible to bludgeon the reader with items from page after page of my notes, which should perhaps just be quietly binned. I see a note here, for example, I made in Sibiu: *Picture of eighteenth century horse-driven mint: four horses needed to work coin-stamping machine! Use to kick off section on coins?* But this all has to stop somewhere.

Just in passing, given the stresses and terrors inflicted on this part of the world, it must be pointed out that what have tended to survive for display in Romanian museums are very heavy or rugged objects. Through the brutal winnowing process of the past century, things too heavy to loot or too inert to burn now have a disproportionate hold on the displays. Not just swords and tankards and metal dishes, but such surprises as a heavy stone that convicted malefactors had to wear round their necks with the notice 'Live a Christian life and beware of evil – then the stone will not hang on *your* neck'. Or perhaps the most enduring of all – the enormous statues created during the Great War to raise money for war bonds. For a certain sum pledged the individual could hammer a nail into the wooden statue, generally of a medieval knight, sometimes with the family name written on the nail's head. As thousands of nails accumulated, the statue became a sort of iron monster. This was an Austro-Hungarian invention copied by the Germans. There is a just spectacular example in the Altemberger House Museum in Sibiu, an implacable sort of crusader-robot about ten feet high with a blankly sinister armoured face. These creatures have a strange claim on our attention – their materials have kept them, bar a little oxidizing, just as they were, as expressions of willing or unwilling local patriotism, to raise money for the Empire to fight the Russians. Their iconography is meant to whip up a sense of the crusader West fighting the barbarian East, of Christian morality against pagan depravity. This is obviously trash history, but also quite interesting as so many of the combatants on both sides did see themselves as medieval knights. There is, for instance, a statue in London's Hyde Park showing the British as St George and the Central Powers as a dead dragon, a mere heap of superbly rendered metal scales. This was a universal cliché. So these money-raising robots are a very clear-cut reminder that the Central Powers saw themselves as on the side of right, fighting for specific and noble values against the barbarians that surrounded them. The nails are a final monument both to an Empire about to cease to exist and a community (in Sibiu's case half German and a quarter each Romanian and Hungarian) which invested (literally) in that Empire and which has also ceased to exist.

Psychopathologies of everyday life

Writing about the last decades of the Empire is a useful way of delaying the point at which it implodes. There is no point in rehearsing yet again the vigours and wonders of that period before 1914, when Freud waved cheerily from a tram at Schiele and the Second Vienna School sang a capella to delighted cafe-goers. Fuelled by waltzes, nicotine and sexual perversion, the Empire hurtles to its doom leaving an astonishing meteor streak across the sky.

It would be absurd to deny that this was a very remarkable culture, and indeed it is the reason (as for everyone) why I first became interested in the Empire. But I have become ever more struck by how much this narrative was almost entirely created *after* the War – and indeed in many cases, particularly in Britain, was still being constructed into the 1990s. For Britain, Austria-Hungary could probably have been summed up as a barracks-ridden, aristocratic and actively philistine place. There was some appreciation of Vienna's music, but this was generally viewed as having a merely museum-like quality – the land of Johann Straus II and Brahms. Budapest and Prague, which we would now think of as crazily wonderful, hardly figured. Even the one great musical sensation from Austria-Hungary, Strauss and von Hofmannsthal's *Der Rosenkavalier*, ecstatically received at both Covent Garden and the Met in 1913, added to the sense of decay by being set in the era of Maria Theresa and, however ironic and beautiful, to the sense of its being an embalmed culture, which even had to bring in a German composer to provide its music.

It is really very alarming to see just how little anybody knew or cared about Austria-Hungary. A giant figure such as Mahler (who died in 1911) was valued as a conductor (the reason he went to New York) and some of his music was known, but most of his symphonies did not receive their British or American premieres until many years later – in the UK the Second Symphony only in 1931 and the Third only in 1961. The *Adagietto* from the Fifth had

been played on its own as a 'lollipop' at the Proms before the war
– which seems about right – but the whole symphony was not
played until 1945. The US was similarly slow to get to grips with
this music. And as for what we would now see as the great tumble
of extraordinary music from Schönberg, Berg, Zemlinsky, Webern
and others, it was almost as though it did not exist. The pieces
which for me at any rate are the terrible soundtrack to the end of
the Empire, Berg's *Three Pieces for Orchestra* or Zemlinsky's startling
Second String Quartet, were unplayed. Bartók's *Duke Bluebeard's
Castle* was written in 1911 but was not premiered until 1918 in
Budapest which, in the context of the time, did not make this a
hot ticket for Allied music-lovers. It was eventually given its stage
premiere in the US and UK in the 1950s.

Writing from the period was also quite disregarded. Kafka had
published a handful of stories (*Description of a Struggle* and *The
Judgement*) but it was many years before these were familiar in the
West. Freud, in his late fifties when the war broke out, was, outside
very narrow circles, more or less unknown – *Interpretation of Dreams*
and *The Psychopathology of Everyday Life* were only just being published in New York. Painting and architecture fared no better.
We may all love Klimt now, but at the time he was completely
swamped by the overwhelming, blazing presence of the Paris art
scene. Adolf Loos had built nothing yet outside the Empire and
perhaps the two most appealing figures of the entire period, Josef
Hoffmann and Koloman Moser, were busy conjuring up wonders at
the Wiener Werkstätte more or less ignored by the wider world.

So the society which now strikes us as headily varied, tolerant
and inventive carried on its work almost unnoticed in London or
New York. This matters only in the very narrow sense that this was
a society only really appreciated in the rear-view mirror. The horrors of the War and the subsequent civil wars, massacres and
invasions sealed into place something which subsequently appeared
lost and precious, a process built on and elaborated by countless
exiles and by the two great post-War authors Stefan Zweig and
Joseph Roth, the latter not really being widely read in the West
until the 1990s. The steady accumulation of interest in the Empire

was, of course, long delayed by distaste for the region, which
bridged much of the gap between 1918 and 1939. During this
time figures like Bartók and Schönberg became admired partly
because of their own loathing of their countries' regimes. This distaste was naturally maintained easily across 1939–45 and then left
the entire region derelict and friendless (again, except through émi-
grés) until the end of the Cold War. So a process began in 1914 of
turning Central Europe into Eastern Europe, where cities such as
Lviv, Debrecen or Cluj, which had been part of a culture rooted in
mainstream European values, and part of a framework that made
towns from northern Italy to Transcarpathia look pretty much the
same, were banished into outer darkness.

But it is perhaps just as striking that the inhabitants of Austria-
Hungary themselves did not seem to know what they would be
missing. Many of the creative figures we now most admire were at
the time part of very small coteries and it was probably true that
the dominant tone of the Empire really *was* much more set by
parade-grounds and barracks, perhaps with a spa attached. But also
it was a place absolutely dominated by nationalist issues to which
everything else seemed subservient. The parliaments in both Budapest and Vienna were reduced to virtual paralysis by waves of fury
about schooling, military languages of command and so on, with
deputies banging their desks, throwing ink-pots, fighting duels,
and having to be periodically shut down by troops. We may value
a handful of remarkable individuals who were made by the Empire,
but their shared strangeness (and frequent Jewishness) shows the
pressures of living in a Europe which was harsh, ignorant, callous
and militarily obsessive. Perhaps the cultural survival and indeed
veneration of figures such as Kraus, Freud, Hašek, Kafka, Schiele
and Webern flatters and distorts how we think of the Empire. It
would be a grotesquely demeaning thing to set up and it would be
visited by nobody, but perhaps a major exhibition should be put
together celebrating all the figures who were often very successful
at the time but who are now forgotten – the heroic realist sculptors, the anti-Semitic cartoonists, the insipid society portraitists, the
writers of slim bestsellers on how German Austrians should join

the Reich or why Jews, Romanians, Ruthenians and so on are bio-
logically made to be untrustworthy.

One interesting example of the era's real concerns is shown in
Janáček's spectral choral piece from 1909 *The Seventy Thousand*.
Janáček is a perfect example of a great composer only fully discovered in the West in the 1980s whose work now so retrospectively
colours the early twentieth century as to provide a sort of soundtrack for it. *The Seventy Thousand* uses a startling blend of male
voices, in whispers and shouts, to create an atmosphere of despairing hysteria. Janáček has a benign air, almost entirely because in
old age he looked like a children's toy, but in practice he was a
thoroughly unpleasant Slav nationalist of a dotty kind.[*] This piece
is very odd, a setting of one of Petr Bezruč's bestselling *Silesian
Songs*, about the fate of Czech-speakers in the Duchy of Teschen/
Těšín/Cieszyn. The song saw the Czechs as crushed between the
two millstones of German and Polish and doomed to disappear:

> One hundred thousand of us have been made German
> One hundred thousand of us have been made Polish
> ...
> A crowd, we look on vacantly
> Just as one calf watches the slaughter of another.

So what *was* the right number of people to speak a particular
language? All over the Empire there were different obsessions –
generally fuelled by isolating a specific area like Teschen and then
having a mental breakdown about some demographic shift.
Nobody made choral settings of poetry pointing out that there
were plenty more Czechs just down the road and that Czech culture was thriving as never before (expressed not least in the works
of Bezruč and Janaček). This crazy ethnicity-meets-mathematics
environment stemmed from the fall-out of intellectuals as diverse as
Friedrich List and Charles Darwin, fuelled and spread (awkwardly)
by literacy and forms of democracy. It was a definite problem that

---

[*] Exhibit A: He must be the only person in history ever to exclaim, as his train
crosses the border into Tsarist Russia, 'Now we enter the land of liberty.'

the Empire's parliaments made language the route to power. This sense of an unending scramble for a place in the sun, a place that could only be reached by stamping down on the heads of others, lay at the heart of the European disaster that now unfolded. Retrospectively the Habsburg version seems a bit childishly harmless, but it was bitter and vicious enough at the time, and the Empire was the laboratory as much for Nazism as for Zionism. Schools, newspapers, elections, cafes, government jobs became battlegrounds for linguistic competition. The governments veered between repression and electoral concession. In February 1914 a classic Habsburg gesture was made in Galicia, when the parliament in Lviv at last allowed in some Ruthenian deputies, albeit not in proportion to their share of the population and with Poles still having the whip-hand. With, as it turned out, only months to go before the Russian invasion destroyed Galicia this last attempt to satisfy minorities pleased nobody: it was seen by Poles as a frightening concession and by Ruthenians as merely an unsuccessful piece of cynicism to try to buy them off. Similar elaborate and angry dances were going on between Germans and Czechs in Vienna and Hungarians and Romanians in Budapest.

The logical conclusion to the situation seemed not so much the break-up of the Empire as some cataclysm in which the survivors of some inter-galactic war would at last impose a world in which everyone would speak Hungarian or everyone would speak German, and in which questions of democracy and representation would be resolved by turning non-Nibelung races back into illiterate slaves. However far each language group might successfully spread, they would by definition always be impinging on another people, who could then be claimed as a threat. Each group ground and splintered against the next, in the manner of *The Seventy Thousand*. The situation was kept under control by the Habsburgs and their loyalists, who were found in irregular but considerable patches across the Empire and who for reasons of their own could see the potential disaster ahead. Many of these individuals had a genuine attachment to the Empire as a whole and to the dynasty, values particularly spread by the army. Others were neutralized by anxieties about the alternatives: Bosnian Muslims fearful of Serbian rule and western Croatians of Italian rule and Galician Poles of German or Russian rule. Others – Italians, Serbs and Romanians – were split between those who yearned for Anschluss with Rome, Belgrade and Bucharest and those who looked down on these corrupt, badly run new nations and feared being chewed up, swallowed and then forgotten by them.*

This need to keep all these groups in play had the unexpected effect of making the Habsburg authorities (dynastic and martial) in modern terms very liberal, while many groups who one would think of as liberal (urban, middle class, civilian) were frothingly nationalist. Czechs sat quietly at home reading about Hussites slaughtering German invaders, Ruthenians reminisced about massacres of Polish landowners and Romanians and Serbs listened to epic poetry about their ancestors' unlimited ferocity-cum-nobility. All these fantasies would be put to the test. But nobody at the time could have imagined that they would end up most potently in the hands of the Germans – in some ways the least thought-about minority in the Habsburg Empire: a Western ruling elite, but equally fulfilling every role from shopkeeper to ordinary soldier to agricultural worker, dotted irregularly everywhere from the Tyrol to the Carpathians.

The largest immune group was the Jews, except those sufficiently assimilated to wholly share German or Hungarian views. There was no nationalist politician, pointing with trembling fingers at a medieval map, wearing his people's flag in his lapel, robustly singing some nineteenth-century anthem, who did not see the Jews as an obstacle. Even the most assimilated Jewish Hungarians would suddenly find themselves excluded by middle-class Protestant Hungarians, who would drift off into pathetic fantasies about pure ancestry from ancient horsemen. Herzl understood what this might

---

* A not inaccurate fear as once the thrilling judder of unification had happened all these places became total backwaters, with once significant cities as various as Trieste, Cluj, Novi Sad and Braşov experiencing a geographical equivalent of the bends so violent that they became consigned to decades of a Shropshire-like level of somnolence.

mean, but in a sense all nationalist politicians understood it – that the logic of their views had to mean the disappearance of all those who did not share their 'race'. This could be achieved by everyone being penned inside separate frontiers (the solution since 1945, with the Soviets and then the EU as neo-Habsburg gendarmes), but there were terrible alternatives to be tried first.

The end begins

Austria-Hungary's monuments to the dead of the First World War tend to be small and private: the work of relatives, or groups of surviving individuals from specific regiments. This is understandable – a war fought for dynastic and Imperial reasons which ended with total defeat and the eradication of both the dynasty and Empire, followed by a maelstrom of social and economic disasters, ticks none of the boxes likely to result in a thoughtful public commemorative programme. None of the successor regimes had any interest in enshrining such a catastrophe, with no form of words really available that could both acknowledge what had happened (some 1,100,000 dead) and come up with any even faintly consolatory rationale. Some small towns (Szekszárd and Rust for example) have simple 'standing soldier' monuments in the same style as those in Britain and France, and major cities have them generally tucked away, in side chapels or school halls, with many destroyed by one regime or another. The only really moving exception I came across was in Most na Soči, a tiny Slovenian village on the railway line between Gorizia and Ljubljana where I had planned to travel on to Kobarid, the site of a major battle in the autumn of 1917. The atmosphere of the station, with battered flatbed railway trucks, silent, dripping mountain trees and the reek of resin and sawdust, was so wonderful that it made me pause fatally, emerging into the courtyard just in time to see the day's only bus to Kobarid trundling off across a bridge over the spectacular cyan-coloured river. Filling in the time until the next train back and trying to retrieve something from the fiasco I wandered around the area until I suddenly found myself facing an immense, flat, vertical rock face into which was carved in colossal lettering:

HIER KÄMPFTE DAS XV. KORPS
MAI 1915 : OKTOBER 1917

Here the XV Corps fought. At the monument's base are steps and a sort of altar and stone torches. These latter used to be lit to create a suitably warrior-pagan atmosphere. Of course everything was soggy moss, mould and rust streaks, but this only enhanced its strange dignity. I have to admit a research defeat, being simply unable to find out how such a monument has survived, with both its post-Habsburg Italian and Yugoslav owners not exactly in favour of the Empire. Perhaps its bald declaration was sufficiently abstract to be respected. It certainly sums up all that can be said about the Habsburg armies – they fought, but in the end they met everywhere with disaster and defeat. How such disaster overtook and eviscerated the Empire, which had lasted so successfully for so many centuries, is a great and complex subject that requires whole books rather than a few glib paragraphs and is, of course, both a Habsburg story and a European one.

Perhaps the single most striking aspect of the last decades of the Empire is the speed with which its concerns became fatally irrelevant to the rest of Europe. After its crushing by the Prussians in 1866 the Empire continued to behave like a major predator, without noticing that it had become a prey animal – a lion that was actually a gnu. In the wake of the defeat Habsburg forces marched out of the federal fortresses on the Rhine and evacuated Holstein and ended their long engagement with western Europe, removing the last traces of a possible shared interest with Britain.

In an era defined by the dramatic expansion of Europe into the rest of the world, the Empire only participated as a provider of impoverished emigrants to North America. Two strange exceptions happened in 1878. One was the peculiar expedition to the Arctic Ocean, crewed by shivering Dalmatians, mentioned in chapter 12. But even this was a private expedition so – mercifully – it did not establish Habsburg sovereignty over Franz Joseph Land, thus saving

the Empire both from foolish investment in the harvesting of
hardy mosses for world markets, and a serio-comic further battle-
front in the First World War.

The other exception stemmed from Bismarck's urging, after
1866, that the Habsburgs follow their destiny in south-east
Europe. This was a region about which the Germans cared little,
but which, it was true, had been at the heart of Habsburg ideology
since the days of Ferdinand I. In 1878 the process of Ottoman
decay resulted in further lumps of Turkish Europe falling off in
the face of Russian aggression. But here the narrow scope of Habsburg concerns shows in a chilling form. Russia's interests were
now transcontinental – scooping up places such as Tashkent and
Samarkand, moving along the Ussuri and Amur rivers into the Far
East and in the same 1878 war snatching further chunks of the
Caucasus. By contrast Austria-Hungary only had eyes on Bosnia-
Herzegovina, which it occupied, along with the wonderfully
named Sanjak of Novi Bazar, notionally to restore order and only
on behalf of the Ottoman Empire, which already had its hands
full.* This feeble pretence was met with ferocious Muslim resistance
and some five thousand Habsburg casualties. Strangely, one of the
most prominent war memorials in Graz – on the road that leads
to the Arnold Schwarzenegger Stadium – marks the invasion of
Bosnia.

The acquisition of this small, bitter and impoverished region
(from which many Muslims now fled) was in itself almost pointless,
a parody of Prince Eugene's sweeping triumphs. It had three purposes: to keep apart the two micro-states of Montenegro and
Serbia; to prevent Serbia's own occupation of the territory; and to
act as a jumping-off point to grab in due course the port of Salonika. The first two were sensible enough and identified an alliance
which would prove extraordinarily dangerous, if embarrassingly
so, given the disparity between the Empire and its teeny Balkan
enemies. The Salonika plan was discreetly shelved, although the

---

* Bosnia-Herzegovina was fully absorbed in 1908 and the Sanjak returned to the
Ottomans.

idea of the Habsburgs as an Aegean power dominating the whole Balkans is fascinating – and it hints at an alternative history where there is nothing at all preordained about Greece's eventual ownership of the city, after many further twists and miserable turns.

Any thoughts of further expansion into the Balkans by the Empire were nixed by the impossible attitude of the Hungarians. As all Hungarians now lived inside the Empire any territorial extension would result in a larger percentage of non-Hungarians – and the addition of yet more Slavs. This pathological, zero-sum, ethnographic obsessiveness drove Vienna mad and resulted in Franz Ferdinand's secret dreams of marking his future coronation by invading Hungary. But, again, the Hungarians had a sort of point – any further extension south which enfolded further Serbs could only be supervising the creation of an internal Yugoslavia. Indeed in 1913 the result of the Second Balkan War was the final expulsion of the Ottomans and much more territory for the Serbs, which made Bosnia-Herzegovina their next piece of unfinished business. The assassination of Franz Ferdinand in Bosnia the following year was therefore both beautifully apt, and part of a far wider pattern which would indeed destroy the Empire.

The disappearance of the Ottomans has a curious trigger quality. There were Turkish troops in the Belgrade fortress as late as 1878 – they marched out on the declaration of full Serbian independence – and on the Adriatic in 1912. Despite disaster after disaster it was only in 1912–14 that they retreated to the small block of land around Edirne still held by the Turkish republic today, the final remnant of Turkey-in-Europe. It is as though their departure removed the discipline which had prevented the region's other major actors from turning on each other.

The Habsburgs watched immobilized as pie-carving Romanian, Bulgarian, Montenegrin, Greek and Serbian armies resolved the region's future in the Balkan Wars almost without reference to them. This was a desperate and humiliating situation. How could these small countries be taking such violent and far-reaching action while completely ignoring their colossal neighbour? The answer was that they were all well aware of structural Habsburg timidity.

For all the war-games, parades and bluster, the Habsburgs had gone from being a pan-European power in the 1850s to a local one, frightened of its neighbours. It is perhaps an implausible image, but Austria-Hungary and Germany in global terms had in a generation become the Babes in the Wood, clinging to each other, surrounded by colossal powers operating in a global, not a European framework. In a world in which America and Russia were both deliriously expanding and where colonies were seen as the currency of economic, masculine assertion, Austria-Hungary and Germany hardly counted, with even Belgium a more convincing Imperial power. Of course, these were Babes backed up by Škoda and Krupp, but in both Vienna and Berlin there were acute anxieties that their styling themselves 'Empires' seemed increasingly sarcastic, given their now relatively small, boxed-in landmasses. It is strange that the term 'World War' in 1914 did not really apply to the Central Powers, who essentially fought a war merely around the rim of their European borders. This sense of encirclement, decline, of an agenda shifting against them had a powerful impact on Vienna, Budapest and Berlin's ever more irrational world view.

Much of the discussion about blame for the disaster comes from arguments about which of these capitals did most to bring it about, but this can never be resolved. And with each passing year it becomes clearer that blame can be more usefully handed out to all the major European countries, which seem racked by a sort of disastrous febrile skittishness. For those clambering out of the catastrophe of 1914–1945 (or indeed 1914–1989) it was crucial to give reasons for what had happened of an appropriately cosmic grandeur – either a monstrous German plot or a systemic failure within capitalism. The idea that the unfolding of the war could have been simply the result of a cock-up, of truly contemptible civilian decision-making allied to a balance of forces which *happened* to make the war unwinnable by either side, seems far more plausible now. These old cosmic explanations allowed political leaders to take no responsibility for what happened – when, of course, every capital city throughout the conflict was filled with

civilian men who allowed themselves to be flattered and hypnotized by what they thought could be achieved by unleashing
military power.

One final act of will by the Habsburgs led to the creation of
Albania. The Albanians were a group who moved from having no
agreed form for their alphabet in 1909 to full independence five
years later. They were an extraordinarily cosmopolitan and widespread people and had had a powerful impact on Mediterranean
history, both fighting for the Ottoman Empire and undermining it
– Albanians had ruled Egypt and fought and administered everywhere from the Red Sea to the Caucasus. A large part of the world
had been open to them and the collapse of the Ottomans was a
disaster. They found themselves shut into a tiny and vulnerable
national area for the first time, grudgingly proclaiming independence only when it was clear that Turkey-in-Europe was at an end.
Serbia saw how it could obtain a sea coast at last and invaded the
region. This was the perfect nightmare for the Habsburgs: a Serbia
with ports, which its Russian ally's navy could use first to box in
the Adriatic and end Habsburg access to world trade, then as a
base for ferrying in an unstoppable expeditionary force. Fortunately other European powers could see that this would not be
brilliant for them either and cooperated to create an Albanian
buffer-state, with Serbia nonetheless keeping the Kosovo vilayet, a
decision which would have profound consequences in the 1990s.
The old Sanjak was split between Serbia and Montenegro.

It is a striking measure of Habsburg weakness that it could only
manage a geographical spoiling action, and only then with the
cooperation of the Italians, who also relished a weak new state in
the Adriatic – but who otherwise could not have been more inimical to the Empire, despite being its notional ally. From the
perspective of the seventeenth or eighteenth century the Balkans
should have been the final horizon of the great Habsburg mission,
their troops effortlessly filling in the peninsula down to the Peloponnese, but it was a horizon which now vanished in a haze of
vacillation and timidity. Romania and Serbia could with growing
confidence look on other Romanians and Serbs still 'trapped'

inside the Empire as hostages who would one day be redeemed. The Serbs felt the same about Bosnia-Herzegovina. Gavrilo Princip, born an Ottoman subject in western Bosnia in 1894, was entirely characteristic of bitter Christian Slavs who – harassed by the Habsburg police – made their way to Belgrade looking for revenge.

CHAPTER FIFTEEN

The curse of military contingency

In common with much of the rest of Europe, Austria-Hungary managed to be imbued with a militarist ethic while not really fighting anyone. After the humiliation of 1866 the army which stood at the heart of the state only saw action occupying Bosnia. The small and futile Habsburg navy had a curious outing as four ships and some three hundred marines became an almost unnoticed element in the international expedition to 'restore order' in China after the Boxer Rebellion. This fact is only of interest because one of the members of the expedition was Baron von Trapp, who was on board the armoured cruiser SMS *Kaiserin und Königin Maria Theresia* on the Yangtze. This was of course very many years before, played by Christopher Plummer, he sang 'Edelweiss' and won my ten-year-old daughter's heart for ever, committing us as a family to playing the *Sound of Music* DVD so many times the digital coding almost wore through.

This pacific stance meant that despite countless manoeuvres, table-top plans, wave upon wave of uniform and weapon reform, nobody had any real experience of war. This was true too for Germany, where the army also became just a pleasant rite of passage – years of hanging around in a terrific uniform and making friends who would form drinking clubs, reunion dinners and mutually back-scratching business arrangements that would define the future shape of their millions of participants' lives, but no fighting. This was, of course, entirely admirable. Franz Joseph loved reviewing troops and artists spent their entire careers doing paintings of him looking at smart cavalry regiments. This harmless activity could have put an entirely rosy glow on his reign if he had died before

1914 (as by almost any reasonable criterion he should have done) but the continuity of his values until 1916 shows how a poisonous sense of violence was a latent constant year after year. The military remained overwhelmingly the state's principal preoccupation and the biggest factor noticeable in the Habsburg landscape. Dominant buildings in the cities, such as the Wawel Castle in Kraków or the Buonconsiglio Castle in Trento, were massive and unlovely barracks (the latter's beautiful frescoes all whitewashed over) and the world wistfully recreated in Joseph Roth's *The Radetzky March* or Stefan Zweig's *Beware of Pity* was – looking between the lines – a narrow, macho, dreary place. Perhaps the clearest sense of the scale of Habsburg society's commitment to the military was that by the end of 1914, 3,500,000 of its trained citizens had been activated for service. All those years of polishing boots, drill, small-town brothels and drinking contests before passing into civilian life meant that, even years after, you would suddenly find yourself reached out for, so that you could die or be wounded in some hideous way.

This was true across the whole of Europe. The lack of an ideological element to this obsession with military contingency makes it hard to understand now. Generals were constantly coming up with fresh plans for dealing with fresh enemies, with the stakes strangely low. Perhaps the only ideologically motivated European country was France – by far the most militarized as a percentage of population – grimly bent on its eventual war of revenge with Germany to regain Alsace-Lorraine. Otherwise everyone seems to take turns in being allies or enemies, to little effect. There was a common obsession with isolation (except, for much of the period, in the case of Britain, which had little stake in the Continent beyond peace in the west) and layer upon layer of public and secret treaties offered various forms of security while at the same time provoking counter-reactions. The actual combination in place in 1914 seems now like a mere accident, with quite different possibilities if war had broken out a couple of years earlier: in which case at the very least Italy would have fought alongside Germany and Austria-Hungary; or a couple of years later: in which case

Russia and Britain would almost certainly have been totally antagonistic again.

As had often been the case in the nineteenth century, Germans,
Austrians and Russians needed to cooperate to keep the Poles
down but also so their rulers could visit each other's houses, swap
uniforms, have banquets and hang around sounding off about
the evil of liberals. This was a great source of stability. The one
constant was a grim determination by Franz Joseph to stick to
Germany under all circumstances. His early reign had been marked
by isolation and military humiliation. Moving in lock-step with
Berlin gave him a magic shield. Russia was a problem, though.
Bismarck had kept Russia quiet through the deeply secret Reinsur-
ance Treaty, which in its most secret inner sanctum agreed even to
allow Russia to attack Constantinople with impunity. Bismarck's
dyspepsia was brought on by knowing that France's delirious fantasies of revenge could be realized through a treaty with Russia
and to avoid this a nod and a wink to Russian expansion anywhere
else was preferable. Bismarck's departure in 1890 put everything
into the hapless hands of Kaiser Wilhelm, who refused to renew
the military treaty as he felt instead that he could rely on his
sparkly personal magnetism to stage-manage the relationship just
by speaking to the Tsar, man to man. This provoked total panic
among the now isolated Russians, who in 1892 duly signed up
with France. That a further twenty-two years went by before war
broke out shows that the set-up was not fatal in itself. But it did
hold the potential for turning a local problem into a pan-European
one.

For the Germans eastern Europe became ever more of a backwater. Their interests – particularly via Hamburg and Bremen
– were in trade, and the bulk of their most dynamic industrial areas
were in the west, as were their best customers. With the exception
of Silesia, the German eastern areas which had so defined the old
state of Prussia no longer counted for much, and yet it was the east
that saw the disasters of the twentieth century. From the early
1890s onwards Vienna and Berlin initiated ever more fevered and
elaborated war-games to work out how to deal with the Russian

menace. Germany was oddly placed as it had no interest in taking any Russian territory and Russia had no interest in taking any German territory. In that sense the countries, allies for much of the nineteenth century, were only antagonistic because of Russia's alliance with France. Germany was also entirely defensive in the west: by 1914 it had given up its absurd plan to take on Britain's navy and it just wanted France to carry on buying things. But, again, it was France and Russia's alliance that turned Germany from a sated power into a paranoid one, its planners obsessed with the need *if there were to be war* to knock out first France and then Russia, in a military operation of more and more unfeasible vastness. But the plan's principal author, Alfred von Schlieffen, had died of old age in 1913 without his ever more elaborately deranged heaps of train times, scribbled arrows and diktats ever coming close to being used.

Austria-Hungary's situation was quite different as it had to deal with *active* interference by Russia. As in Austria-Hungary, Russia (whatever its rulers' dreams) could not simply be run as a giant prison cell, nor were its elite able to function as cold and disengaged technocrats immune to wider trends. For Russia, particularly Russia totally humiliated by the 1905 war with Japan, a tear-stained, proud interest in their Slav 'little brothers' the Serbs and Montenegrins came to take on real importance: both as a genuine piece of mystical craziness and as an ideology based on the surprisingly hard late-nineteenth-century fighting that had taken Russia itself further into the eastern Balkans in its wars with the Ottomans. If the Habsburgs had occasional but rapidly suppressed thoughts about taking over Salonika, the Romanovs had more concrete plans, kept warm since Catherine the Great, to take over Constantinople. If they were to do this then they would need a quiescent or friendly Balkans. Bismarck had thought it worthwhile to buy Russian friendship by letting them into Constantinople, and the British and French had a similar secret clause in their agreement during the Great War, and it is odd in a way that it never actually happened.

This pan-Slavism was a variant on other standard-issue

nationalisms across much of Europe, cutting across more local boundaries in a confusing manner and finding its fullest expression in Yugoslavism. Pan-Slavism was also, of course, highly selective – the Czechs were warmly embraced in St Petersburg when they sent delegations there to annoy their Habsburg masters, whereas, oddly, Russian–Polish toasts of friendship never seemed to happen. One indicative fruit to drop from this peculiar tree was perhaps the most futile of all declarations of war when, during the Russo-Japanese War, Montenegro, in solidarity with its 'big brother', declared war on Japan.

Generations of Habsburg senior officers launched plan after plan for dealing with a response to some unacceptable Russian incursion, either in support of France or in support of Serbia, with staff colleges overrun with rival scenarios, bitter arguments lasting whole lifetimes, and no actual war. The peace was so extended that the evil genius of Habsburg planning, Conrad von Hötzendorf, had, despite being in his sixties, no actual combat experience, nor had Oskar Potiorek, the Governor of Bosnia-Herzegovina, who led the fatuous invasion of Serbia in 1914. Entire careers had gone by with an only theoretical understanding of warfare, at a time when technological change in almost every imaginable field meant that a huge gap could open up between the most modern theory and actual practice in only a few months.

It was understood perhaps instinctively by the Austro-Hungarians that anything other than a very limited war would be a disaster. This was clearly seen by the Hungarians, who had everything they wanted (their own empire, autonomy, a thriving capital city) and who worked to sabotage anything seriously military at every turn. Their reasons may have been self-serving, but as a group they were perhaps the most genuinely uninterested in war in the whole of non-neutral Europe. This meant that the Habsburg army was understrength and underfinanced and it is a routine part of any book on the First World War to blame the Hungarians for this, but given the glamour warfare had for so many in the years leading up to 1914 and the excitement it aroused, it is appealing to see the accidental pacifism of local selfishness in action. Once the war broke out, however, the Hungarians saw that it was their privileges that were at stake, and it was their land that would be invaded if the Central Powers' front line broke. So, having starved the military budget for years, they now fought with great vigour and ferocity, but it was too late.

Conrad – a very odd man – was principally famous for his self-confidence, and for his declaration on numerous occasions that war was the answer to any political question. He was at last believed in the summer of 1914 – and yet it turned out that all his obsessive planning was merely incompetent. Years had been spent working out the balance of forces in the event of war with Serbia and with Russia. Much of this was spent in wishful hoping that Serbia might be successfully isolated because of Russian fear of Germany. This hope had its roots in the shattered and humiliated Russia of 1906 after its war with Japan and abortive revolution, but by 1914 the Russian army was re-equipped, enormous and fully committed to its alliance with France. Conrad endlessly juggled with the quandary of having not enough soldiers and needing to send them to two separate places.

An extreme but interesting argument could be made that both Germany and Austria-Hungary should have just doodled a few sums on the back of an envelope in 1914 and realized that they would lose. Against the solidity of the French–Russian alliance Germany invented a fantasy whereby most of its troops would invade France and defeat it in a few weeks *so that* the troops could then be redeployed east to defeat the Russians. The Austro-Hungarian variant was that Serbia had to be quickly defeated *so that* all those victorious troops in the Balkans could then be redeployed to the other end of the Empire to take on the Russians too. Neither side had any serious plan to deal with the result of even a slight delay in defeating the enemy they chose to tackle first – the logic of this blind-spot was that a delay would make it almost insuperably difficult to win. But it was a measure of the conditions under which these often highly intelligent figures were operating that nobody seems to have drawn the logical conclusion. For Conrad the obvious answer as the July Crisis unfolded was for

Austria-Hungary simply to put a bare minimum of soldiers into defensive positions in the south to hold off the small Serb army. Everyone else could have been thrown at the Russians, who were the threat who could in fact erase the entire Empire, as they could have done quite easily in their 1849 intervention in Hungary if they had not been feeling so benign. Conrad assumed that on the eastern front he would be standing shoulder to shoulder with the Germans, refusing to even admit to himself the reality – that if most German troops were in France then in fact almost the entire weight of the Russian army would fall on his own drastically smaller forces.

I go into this in such detail because much of the war simply played out this situation, its grim logic only fended off by German tactical brilliance. An already questionable war plan was further compounded by Britain becoming a belligerent rather than a neutral, something for which the Germans had simply made no plans and a country which, indeed, the Germans could not defeat (unless they ran down their armies in favour of surreally large numbers of U-boats). The Schlieffen Plan therefore continued to unfold despite the sudden arrival of yet another enemy for Germany with roughly the same GNP. *Even worse*, the notional third pillar of the Central Powers, Italy, decided to be first neutral and then, in May 1915, an enemy. This was fundamentally because of Austria-Hungary. Just as Germany had no stake in the Balkans, it had no interest whatsoever in the frenzied nationalist atmosphere south of the Alps. Berlin was driven purple-faced with rage at the Habsburg failure to negotiate seriously with the Italians who, predictably, wanted Dalmatia, Gorizia and other Italian-speaking bits of the Empire in return for joining in. The Habsburg view was that this would have been a betrayal of everything the Empire stood for, but flicking through picture-books about his ancestors Franz Joseph could have found there plenty of grotesque bits of betrayal in return for a wider strategic good. A more subtle German argument was that the Italians should be given what they wanted and then, once Germany and Austria-Hungary had won the war they could, as Europe-wide hegemons, turn on and destroy the Italians, taking back as many bits of its territory as they liked. But the proud tradition of Habsburg obtuseness prevailed, and a quite futile further military front opened up to add to all the other ones which could also not be adequately manned.

Sarajevo

Franz Ferdinand's arrival in Bosnia-Herzegovina on a visit of inspection in June 1914 therefore put him at the centre of a number of enormous and overlapping ridges of pressure. Some of these were very long term and specific to the strange situation inside the Empire. Not the least of these was Franz Ferdinand's own anger and boredom over his endlessly deferred accession to the thrones, as his hated (by FF) predecessor hung on in an unchanging sequence of dreary routine, just getting older and even older. Not the least of the grounds for this hatred was, as discussed earlier, Franz Joseph's insistence that Franz Ferdinand's wife was too common to have proper status at court. In Sarajevo, however, Franz Ferdinand was visiting in a military capacity rather than as heir to the throne, so the creepy world of the Hofburg went into abeyance and his wife was allowed to walk by his side and sit by him at banquets and in their touring car.

All kinds of irredentist and separatist problems threatened the Empire, but none in itself could have been anywhere near fatal. Many national groups hated being in the Empire, but almost nobody could come up with a scheme that allowed a plausible separation. There was a further safety valve through emigration. If you really loathed the Habsburgs or your Hungarian landlord you could go to the United States. Some went on nationalist grounds, but most simply because of poverty, with Galicia remaining a developmental disaster. During the War a key Habsburg headache was that there were so many languages in the Empire (Conrad von Hötzendorf himself spoke seven) and such huge casualties that officers and men simply could no longer be trained to understand one another. It was almost inevitable that sooner or later a Slovak military unit was formed, with officers who had been taught English at high school commanding men who had learned English so that they could emigrate to the United States. This English-language unit was an ingenious Habsburg solution, but the reasons for its existence did not imply any great faith in the Empire's future.

The Empire therefore had considerable reserves of strength, but they turned out to be reliant on peace, as some of its rulers seem to have sensed. Franz Ferdinand himself, although very close to Conrad, was notably cautious. Franz Ferdinand's enthusiasm for bringing Slavs into the governing structure and engineering a sort of 'approved Yugoslavism' made his visit to the southern Empire particularly resonant. His ideas were well known so when he arrived in Bosnia-Herzegovina he was by a long way the most desirable imaginable candidate for assassination for any Serbian nationalist group. This was not just because any day now he could become a harsh, cold and effective Emperor but because Trialism could create a form of Slav solidarity which explicitly excluded the Kingdom of Serbia itself.

The sheer scale of the plot against him, with Franz Ferdinand and his wife running the gamut of no fewer than six assassins, had no real precedent and was a very pure expression of the forces which had emerged from the massive recent changes that had surged across the Balkans. The Habsburgs had been in danger of simply looking old-fashioned for some decades, but both Vienna and Budapest had been subject to sufficiently radical constitutional twists and turns to make this incorrect. The Empire was nothing if not modern and contemporary, albeit with a funny superstructure of archdukes and so on, but in that sense little different from Germany or Russia or indeed Britain. It was perhaps the assassination itself that tipped the Empire into seeming irredeemably quaint. It was astonishing that the couple stayed alive as long as they did, with would-be assassins losing their nerve or mis-throwing their bombs, pitting fanatical teenagers against someone too fat for his uniform and wearing ostrich feathers.

The sacred relics of the assassination – the car, the bloodstained jacket, Princip's pistol, the chaise-longue on which the archduke died – understandably have pride of place in the Military History Museum in Vienna. The car, a totally spectacular Gräf and Stift Double Phaeton, is clearly the real culprit. Being pulled along by several horses in a coach is both potentially very fast and explicitly very high up, together with ample space on the back for security guards and around the carriage for cavalry. Moustachioed, automatic-wielding insurrectionaries would find such a vehicle a severe problem, whereas the Gräf and Stift, once stopped, left the archduke and archduchess with no protection of any kind. Princip simply had to walk up to them as though they were, rather oddly, sitting in the middle of the street. So the last serious Habsburg was effectively destroyed by new technology.

From the world-view of the teenagers and their political masters in Belgrade – and perhaps by any standards – it was the most successful assassination in modern world history. It killed Serbia's most determined opponent, it destroyed the entire Empire and it created a massively enlarged Serb-ruled state only finally dismantled in the 1990s. What would now be called the 'collateral damage' also puts it on a special level, with nobody across Europe the next morning having for one moment, as they read about the undoubtedly major and shocking story of the killings, any sense of what would happen next.

The Przemyśl catastrophe

The opening phases of the War were filled with grotesque shocks for everybody. All those years of military manoeuvres, secret codes and technological upgrades were held up to mockery. The French invasion of Alsace (the non-confidence-buildingly named 'Plan XVII') failed, the Russian invasion of East Prussia ended in Armageddon, the Germans' Schlieffen Plan became an incoherent disaster within weeks. Austria-Hungary's nightmare was therefore a shared one. Effectively the entire European military caste had been shown to be recklessly incompetent. Their notional political masters proved incapable of acting intelligently to end a conflict which it was rapidly clear threatened to destroy European society. The immediate scale of the horror offered simply no precedents. All generals dreamed of nineteenth-century actions where grit, cunning and boldness could win a decisive result. The Battles of Königgrätz 1866 (twenty-three thousand dead and wounded) and Sedan 1870 (twenty-five thousand dead and wounded) had been complete victories on a scale sufficient to devastate the defeated side's entire political framework. What they got instead was the First Battle of the Marne with some five hundred thousand dead and wounded and no hint as to how the war might end. The very scale of the mutual massacre made it impossible for anyone in a position of power to admit defeat – and yet it was in these weeks that it might have been possible. Indeed it is striking how negligible and weak the principal leaders were and how willing to be swept along by events – not a Bismarck or Salisbury in sight.

At least until the end of 1916 all the major fighting powers remained robust, each with a victory plan and each with sufficient economic strength and manpower to keep going. For the first time in European history humans were viewed in the same light as crops, with hideous calculations about each male 'year group' becoming old enough to be trained and kitted out to replace its ruined predecessor. This was a fundamental change in the way that populations were imagined and had a long and bitter legacy throughout the century: rulers who had before 1914 often barely impinged upon their subjects now carried out dreams of absolute control over life and death. Calculations which started with entire bureaucracies working out how to replace the regular armies erased in 1914 led by a direct line to everything from the Nazi 'hunger plan' to the Great Leap Forward.

The exception to this military robustness was Austria-Hungary. Of all the major powers it was the only one where a dangerous gap quickly opened between its pretensions and its performance. After the initial shock, each of the major combatants, whatever the setbacks, girded itself for the next year's fighting with fresh men, fresh plans and even greater military supplies, but the Austro-Hungarian base proved inadequate.

As a large part of the Habsburg army pointlessly headed south to attack Serbia (because this was the *casus belli*), it became clear that the Russian army in the east was offering an immediate and overwhelming threat to the Empire. This required a humiliating and chaotic rerouting of trains en route to the south back to the east. With typical helplessness it was decided that the easiest way of doing this (to shunt them back to their starting points in the major cities and then head them out again) would be unacceptable for morale. Only days before, huge crowds of weeping family members, brass bands, hoarse cheering and thousands of flowers had seen the soldiers off and there would be consternation in Budapest if the same trains now sheepishly trundled back to the platforms. Of course such consternation would have been reasonable, because the manoeuvre did indeed indicate an overwhelming cock-up – after all that money, planning and prestige, Austria-Hungary's military staff effectively lost their war in a quick handful of decisions, as soldiers dawdled down branch lines, dozed at remote stations and the railway personnel had nervous breakdowns.

As had been the anxiety all along, the result was failure on both fronts: too small an army attacking Serbia and too few to hold off the Russians. In a series of disasters without parallel, hundreds of thousands of Austro-Hungarian casualties were generated on both fronts, with the Serbs having before the end of the year completely defeated an invasion which was notionally the only pseudo-rational element in the fighting (to avenge the death of Franz Ferdinand). In the east the Russians annihilated Habsburg forces, taking over much of Galicia and Bukovina within weeks. Battles were provided with names to give a shape and a geographical focus that they totally lacked, as vast and confused armed groups crashed into each other in a mockery of Napoleonic concision. Accounts at the time describe scenes of total chaos, with much of the population fleeing, whole towns in flames and – as it turned out – no real Habsburg plan for taking the Russians on, with elite cavalry units sent out into the devastated countryside and simply never seen again, swallowed up by the terrain as much as by enemy machine-gun units.

As Cossacks posed for photographs in the ravaged city centre of Lviv, Austria-Hungary's last hope for avoiding total disaster lay in the Galician town of Przemyśl. Some five hours by train east of Kraków, it had long been designated as the military heart of Galicia, the terrain's unhelpful flatness relieved there by a moderate-size river (the San) and some moderate-size hills. Since the 1870s layer upon layer of fortifications had gone up, with the usual bickering and underfunding. The area today remains littered with their fragments, some of a size which makes it seem as though a spaceship (oddly made out of bricks) has blown up above the site. On the road out to the Ukrainian border, next to a giant Tesco, I even managed to stay in a hotel built around one of the hundreds of surviving chunks. The fortification was never completed, or rather it spread out over such a huge area that nobody could ever have declared it complete – even with ten times the number of strong-points and a garrison of millions it would still have had weaknesses. In any event the Russians before the war had secured from their spy in the Habsburg military, Colonel Redl, all the details of the Przemyśl fortifications (and of the Habsburg invasion plans for Serbia – which they thoughtfully passed on to Belgrade).

In the short term, in September 1914, Przemyśl's fortifications were a success as the Russians were obliged to besiege the town. Without Przemyśl there would have been little to prevent the Russians from advancing into southern Poland and north-east Hungary and the war could have taken a quite different turn. An epic now unfolded with both sides committing ever greater resources to enforcing and to breaking the siege. In October a Habsburg army briefly got into the city and the Russians retreated. There is an extraordinary photo of the town centre filled with an infinity of people, every surface crammed with the astonishing diversity of Przemyśl's inhabitants, civilian and military, a diversity best expressed in men's and women's hats and umbrellas (it is raining), as for one last time the subjects of the Empire pose for a cameraman

on a high balcony: Poles, Jews, Hungarians, Austrians, Ruthenians.
This was a brief respite though as only three weeks later disasters
elsewhere along the front once more isolated Przemyśl. Habsburg
relief forces tried to break the Russian front, battling through the
Carpathians in temperatures below -15 degrees Celsius, suffering
scarcely credible casualties, with exhausted troops desperately
trying not to fall asleep, knowing they would then either freeze to
death or be eaten by wolves. By early 1915 Habsburg troops had
suffered a total of some eight hundred thousand casualties on the
Eastern front. One final attempt to relieve Przemyśl generated a
further fifty thousand. Eventually, the half-starved garrison surrendered in March 1915, having killed all its horses, burned all its
supplies and blown up all its heavy artillery and major forts in
what must surely have been the largest use of explosives in human
history to that point. Eight generals, two thousand five hundred
officers and some hundred and seventeen thousand troops surrendered and the Russians marched in. Przemyśl was going to become
just another Russian city, Peremyshl, under military law and with
the usual chilling ban on Polish in schools or offices. En route to
Siberia, Habsburg prisoners-of-war were marched through Moscow
in a great parade which eerily prefigured that of the shattered remnants of Heeresgruppe Mitte less than thirty years later.

These catastrophes ended Habsburg Europe. The final scene
of Miklós Bánffy's brilliant *Transylvanian Trilogy*, written in the
1930s, does not concern itself with the war, but shows all the
young men whose lives the reader has followed over so many pages
excitedly putting on their devastatingly smart cavalry uniforms in
July 1914 and heading off to their units. It was simply understood
by Bánffy's readership that they would all die in Galicia shortly
thereafter. Already in early 1915 there were mass defections of Slav
troops to the Russians. This is the era immortalized in *The Good
Soldier Švejk* when bitter Hungarian troops mockingly put their
hands up in surrender when they saw Czech troops. With the fall of
Przemyśl, the remaining army became 'a militia', ever more unreliable and capable only of defeating the Italians.

In the summer a renewed offensive against the Russians chased them out of the ruins of Przemyśl and there is a strange genre of postcards featuring Habsburg soldiers posing rather sheepishly inside blocks of smashed concrete and weird Brobdingnagian metal hoops and cones from wrecked fortress cannon. An even odder photo shows officers standing to attention outside the town hall as some strikingly burly and ferocious-looking troops march past. But these troops are different: they are carrying an immense Bavarian flag and wear spiked helmets. These are Germans a long way from home. Their presence meant the eclipse of Austria-Hungary: the Habsburgs now became mere adjuncts to their vastly more powerful ally, unable to defeat even Serbia and Romania without the German army. Already some Germans were talking about carving out their own empire from the Imperial corpse. For Przemyśl itself, events since 1914 had converted a multi-ethnic backwater into a principal stage on which the disasters of the new era were played out. The Germans left in 1918, but returned in 1939 as the town and the River San that runs through it became the front line between Nazi-ruled and Soviet-ruled Poland. In the following years most of the population fatally crossed both of their new rulers on racial, linguistic, political or class grounds.

Last train to Wilsonville

For Austria-Hungary the most severe damage was perhaps not even done by the annihilatory battles it found itself fighting, but by the strange gangs of intellectuals and artists who it could not even hope to defeat and for whom the Great War was a sort of dream come true. Europe was really not a normal environment at this time. One small example is the *grotesco* Italian poet, propagandist and fighter pilot Gabriele d'Annunzio, who celebrated the first day of Italy's attack on Austria-Hungary with:

> Our vigil is ended. Our exultation begins . . . the blood is spurting from the veins of Italy! . . . The slaughter begins, the

> destruction begins . . . All these people, who yesterday
> thronged in the streets and squares, loudly demanding war, are
> full of veins, full of blood; and that blood begins to flow . . .

Pronouncements like this drew huge applauding crowds rather
than a frontal lobotomy, and were not uncharacteristic of the sort
of unhinged disgustingness which now engulfed Europe.

Within moments of Franz Ferdinand's death, the area around
the rim of the Empire began to seethe with peculiar figures like
d'Annunzio, concocting entirely mystical reasons for such-and-
such an outcome to the war. The most straightforward of these
were the Romanians. The origins of Romanian nationalism lay in
cities such as Sibiu and their 'redemption' was uncontroversial,
except for the immense numbers of Germans and Hungarians who
would be swept up too in such an annexation. The Poles looked
for some form of disarray in either the Central Powers or the Russian Empire which would give them the space to re-establish their
own state. The total surprise that all sides wound up imploding,
clearing the ground for a genuinely independent new Poland, only
revealed itself in 1918.

More extreme were the Serbs, Italians and Czechs. The Serbian
government found itself in the summer of 1914 threatened with
invasion by Austria-Hungary, but also – to its amazement – as the
ally of Russia, Britain and France and therefore surely on the winning side. Ethnographers, linguists, geographers and historians
swarmed over Belgrade, coming up with almost limitless possibilities for a future Serbian mega-state. Serbia had already been in
discussions before the war with Montenegro about joining forces,
but a near-cosmic 'Yugoslavism' now took over, with everything
to the north including such cities as Klagenfurt, Timişoara and
Szeged seen as ripe for absorption into the kingdom. There were
also serious discussions with Bulgaria about a pan-Balkan federation: a state from the Adriatic to the Black Sea of a similar land
area to Germany. Everywhere earnest and bespectacled figures were
coming up with reasons why Slovenes were (despite an unrelated
political history for many centuries) in fact 'little brothers', or why

Croats (despite being ruled by Hungary since 1102 and being Catholic and using Roman rather than Cyrillic script) had some freshly discovered deep affinity with the Belgrade regime. Nobody ever really worked out how Muslim Bosnians or Albanians would fit in at all, but a new, southern version of the Habsburg Empire minus the Habsburgs now took clear shape. It is striking that among the few surviving would-be assassins in Sarajevo one wound up teaching at the University of Belgrade and another ran the ethnographic department at the Sarajevo Museum. Essentially 'Yugoslavism' was a series of mere academic nutty assertions – but like many nutty assertions it took on an extraordinary solidity.

The Italian state was fuelled up by generations of hatred for Austria-Hungary. Garibaldi had spoken of the 'cesspool of humili-ation' into which Italy had been tipped by the slinking, desperate way it had received Venetia from the hands of other European powers, after having had its own armed forces whipped by the Habsburg army. The decision-making processes within the Italian government were bewilderingly incoherent (although in 1914 no European state exactly shone). Despite being part of the Triple Alliance with Austria-Hungary and Germany since 1882 there had been regular bolts of nationalist dementia about the really quite small and unimportant areas partly filled by Italian-speakers and ruled by Vienna – the valleys of the South Tyrol and the region to the north and north-east of Venice in which the dominant city was Trieste. Italy had plenty of ports (and indeed was quite famous for already having a whole lot of coastline), so adding an extra one should have been of no interest, particularly, as it turned out, when Trieste's significance only stemmed from its supplying the whole of the Empire – once in Italian hands it withered away. Many Italian politicians disdained the rubbish of 'irredentism' – the lib-eration of all Italian-speakers – but it was nonetheless almost a religion for others. Quite rapidly it shaded into a broader land-grab, with the small scatterings of Italians sprinkled down the Dalmatian coast becoming an excuse to take over that area too – plus the Albanian port of Vlorë, which had already been seized in 1914. This held out the prospect of the Adriatic becoming an

'Italian lake', despite much of it being strikingly devoid of Italians. The South Tyrol issue similarly started off as irredentism and ended as a land-grab, with the Italian-speakers around Lake Garda and Trento shading into a large block of Germans well before the Brenner Pass, now proclaimed by Italy as a 'natural border'. So – as with the other countries lurking on the fringe of the Empire – Italy's claims were no less and no more mystical than those of the Habsburgs themselves. In this sense they were falling in the footsteps of a grand old tradition of nonsense, fuelled by academics of a kind who would have been wearily familiar to Maximilian I. But they became serious as the weakness and military incapacity of the Habsburgs in the opening months of the war ushered in a golden age of hostile cartographers and philologists.

Most academic of all were probably the Czechs. As the war turned against the Central Powers it became ever more plausible that the Empire might collapse completely, in which case the Czechs could either be absorbed into some expanded German-speaking state or have a fleeting chance to carve out an empire of their own. All the ingenuity of the usual figures was obliged to whip up a plausible conjunction between Czechs, Slovaks and Ruthenians which would allow a new multi-ethnic state (which also included millions of Germans and a lot of Hungarians) to undulate its way from west to east in the small gap between other German- and Hungarian-speakers and many Poles. This was, again, an act of will. Slovaks and Czechs had much in common, but ultimately the state had no real historical roots beyond some vague appeal to an imagined set of shared Slav values which excluded a large part of the population. This mysticism perhaps met its apogee of absurdity in October 1918 when the Czech ideologue Masaryk and his associates posed in front of the Liberty Bell in Philadelphia as they proclaimed the independent Czechoslovak republic *in Pennsylvania*. This photo crystallizes the really extraordinarily donnish and prissy figures – fuelled by folk costume, epic poetry, grammatical niceties and prettily coloured maps – who now seemed to inherit the Habsburg Earth. Posing with the Liberty Bell was meant to imply a shared democratic inheritance, but the delegation had been in

Pennsylvania in the first place to find some almost comically unrep-resentative American Slovaks with whom to do a deal. Notionally apostles of modernity, they come across as monuments of the purest fust. The new state used a Hussite motto (*Pravda vítězí*: 'Truth shall prevail') and promoted pride in a notionally authentic Bohemian heretical past, despite most Czechs being Catholic. Masaryk then crazily hailed the enormous German population as a 'colonizing avant-garde' in contrast to the 'settled' Czech-speakers, as though the Germans, living throughout Bohemia and Moravia since the Middle Ages, were somehow interloping wetbacks. This shameless photo with the Bell was followed up by another breathtaking piece of sucking up with the suggestion that the new state's second city should be called Wilsonovo ('Wilsonville'). The city in question only had German and Hungarian names – Preßburg and Pozsony, awkwardly reflecting its actual German-Hungarian heritage. Per-haps mercifully Wilsonovo was dropped for the plausible-sounding new name of Bratislava, itself stemming from an old mistranscrip-tion of the name of the medieval Prince Braslav.

What is striking about all these groups is that they all inherit varieties of Habsburg weirdness. None of their statements, visions, assertions, acts of violence are in any sense actually worse, all improvising on variants of old Habsburg wishful thinking. The results only seem more hollow and ridiculous because they are more recent, with Bratislava merely a very recent example of what must presumably have been countless misunderstandings and bits of ineptitude behind many older place-names. The war carved out a fresh batch of multi-ethnic states which proved to be merely smaller versions of what they had replaced, and no more rational than, say, Ferdinand I's magic narwhal tusk. Their visions of great-ness also, of course, fatally overlapped with and contradicted one another. The following decades showed the degree to which the Habsburgs' legitimacy had been based on being able to defend their hotchpotch state – something which their successors all proved tragically unable to do.

A pastry shell

While the first years of the war brought nothing but disaster and humiliation to the Austro-Hungarians, much of the remainder seemed an extraordinary triumph. This proved an illusion, but it was sufficient to give a disastrous semi-confidence to the regime until shortly before the war's end.

The nadir was the summer of 1916 when a colossal Russian attack – the 'Brusilov Offensive' – further devastated Galicia and Bukovina. The incompetence which had dominated Habsburg conduct of the war had been in some measure sheltered by matching fiascos on the Russian side. It is curious that in two such hidebound armies it should just happen to have been the Russians from among whom a single commander, Aleksei Brusilov, emerged brilliant enough to stop the floundering and change the strategic balance. No such lucky chance ever occurred on the Habsburg side – and nor could it have. Conrad and his commanders were living agreeably at the distant headquarters in Teschen (nearly four hundred miles from the front, which makes the chateau generals of the Western Front seem positively hands-on) and refused to interrupt a 'gala dinner' when the news of Brusilov's attack came, with Conrad confident the Russians could not get far. As one account put it, the Habsburg front 'crumbled like a pastry shell' and in only three days the Russians took an extraordinary total of two hundred thousand prisoners (nearly half the Habsburg forces opposing them). By the time the offensive had been stopped through German counterattacks and general exhaustion the Habsburg army had more or less ceased to exist as an independent force, with a total of some seven hundred and fifty thousand casualties, over half of them prisoners.

As was the case with any victory on the Eastern Front, the spoils were simply an accumulation of barren marshes and forests and burning villages, and the Russians gained nothing from their new territory (much of it wrecked anyway by them during their earlier scorched-earth retreat). But whoever owned the remnants of Galicia, it was absolutely clear that the Habsburg Empire's future was now fatally reliant on that of Germany. There had been grand plans for a reordering of the Empire to put a Habsburg on a revived Polish throne with its capital at Lublin (now in the Habsburg zone of occupation), but the Germans began to look much more coldly on their allies, with the first serious discussions about absorbing the German-speaking areas into the Reich of a kind which would be realized in 1938. Future offensives were led by the Germans, generally with Habsburg troops only a minority element.

The chaos of the Brusilov Offensive suggested to the Romanians that the time had come for them to declare war on the Central Powers or risk missing out on what appeared, by the summer of 1916, to be the strategic endgame. Their invasion of Transylvania resulted in the easy capture of Braşov and mass panic as the invaders had little to prevent them reaching Budapest. It turned out that now their test had come, the Carpathians were only really a major obstacle on maps, and generations of planners droning on about eastern ramparts had been wrong. The Romanian timing however was catastrophically wrong. The Russian offensive petered out and joint Habsburg, German, Bulgarian and Turkish forces turned on Romania and destroyed it in a few weeks. In early August the Romanians were marching through south-eastern Transylvania, but by early December Bucharest had been captured in one of a handful of genuine lightning campaigns, of a kind of which generals had dreamed back in the summer of 1914. The Braşov Museum has a rare First World War atrocity photo – of a grinning Hungarian soldier posing next to a ditch filled with the corpses of Romanian soldiers dusted with lime: a photo which must have appealed first to vengeful Hungarians and then to counter-vengeful Romanians when they finally marched in to take over the area in 1918.

Franz Joseph died in November 1916 and on the face of it he left the Empire in a position of triumph that Conrad must have longed for at many points in his career. On every front the strategic

dilemmas which had made the previous decades so unattractive
had ended. Habsburg troops occupied Belgrade and Bucharest,
they had their own occupation zone in what had been Russian
Poland, and at regular intervals their troops in the south-west
humiliated the Italian army. In 1917 scarcely credible prospects
unfolded as the Russian front collapsed. An early Habsburg
embarrassment in the opening days of the war was the release
of a Russian citizen captured near Zakopane, Lenin, who had been
allowed to proceed to his Swiss exile. Now the Germans carefully
arranged for his reintroduction into the prostrate Russian Empire
to foment further chaos. A final pleasure in November 1917 was
the Battle of Caporetto, a joint German–Habsburg campaign
against Italy which tore off a huge hunk of the Italian north-east,
threatened Venice and inflicted some three hundred thousand Italian casualties, mostly prisoners. All that was needed to end the war
was a final German campaign in the West to finish the British,
Americans and French.

Everyone knows now that this was a will-o'-the-wisp, but until
the failure of the final German offensives in the summer of 1918
victory still seemed genuinely plausible. German strength gave
Austria-Hungary the semblance of a great power, but in every
theatre of conflict it was in practice a mere haggard extra and in
the one theatre that mattered – the Western Front – it was hardly
even present. But for surviving elements in the Austro-Hungarian
army the situation appeared fabulous, with Russia in pieces and no
serious enemies on any of its fighting fronts. However, the arguments about how to take advantage of this showed immediate
problems. The new Emperor, Karl I, was effectively an incapable
cipher. In the early twenty-first century churches have shrines to
Karl, who was beatified in 2004 and is therefore en route to sainthood. Being useless seems a funny path to religious greatness and
I stare at my Blessed Charles bookmark and medallion in some
disbelief. Suddenly moved into the starting blocks by Franz
Ferdinand's death and uneasily aware that Franz Joseph could die
at any moment, Karl had spent only two years trying to work

out how to become ruler of a multinational empire. He was crushingly described by one of his generals: 'you hope to meet
a thirty-year old ... but you find a man with the appearance of
a twenty-year old ... who thinks, speaks and acts like a ten-year
old'.

Franz Joseph's death, following the killing of so much of the
army on which his dynastic rule rested, weakened and hollowed
out Imperial loyalty. Karl may have been himself weak and
hollow but he did understand that the triumph of the Habsburg
position was unsustainable – that the army was falling apart and
the entire Empire was starving from the Allied blockade. Each
week that the war continued brought total collapse nearer. In the
spring of 1917 he made a secret bid to get Austria-Hungary out
of the war through negotiations with France. These got nowhere
as the issues which concerned France could only be settled by
Germany. Indeed Karl's 'man of peace' posture was merely
a reflection of terminal Habsburg provincialism – that he had no
stake in the Western Front, where the war would be decided. In
the spring of 1918 the French gleefully revealed the secret corres-
pondence and Karl's already feeble reign became completely
circumscribed by the enraged Germans. It was probably at this
point the Empire had no future – even some increasingly inconceivable victory by Germany would have resulted in drastic
reorganization. Germany had already ballooned out crazily to the
east. This was Hindenburg's Wallenstein-like Ober Ost territory,
forty thousand square miles from the Black Sea to the Gulf of
Finland, carved out since 1915 by the destruction of town after
town using giant searchlights, massed cannon and Zeppelins, in a
now-forgotten sequence of victories hideously similar to those of
1941 in the region. There was a preview too of how high the
stakes were viewed by both sides, with the Russians in Vilnius
destroying everything they could before retreating in an enforced
mass evacuation. The fighting in Galicia is also overlaid in our
minds by what happened later, but in the First World War pogroms,
looting and reprisal shootings by Russian troops accompanied

both their invasions of the territory.* By 1918 the Germans were juggling with client states from the Gulf of Bothnia to the Volga – but this was not the Habsburg experience, which was mere helpless exhaustion, a corpse held upright by its overbearing ally.

Discussions within the Empire about what to do with their new provinces showed that even total victory only created fresh problems. For example, bringing the captured Serbian lands into the Empire simply meant that the Serb lands were now unified. This was not meant to be the point at all. The original 1914 'punishment expedition' was designed to cow, humiliate and disarm Serbia. Instead, after an extraordinary national epic, surviving Serbs had been evacuated by the British and French to Corfu and now had a refitted and aggressive army fighting primarily on the Salonika Front – a zone to the south of Bulgaria from which the Allies intended to march their way directly up into the Empire, but which was held in stalemate until late in 1918. It is hard to be aggressive if the prospect of any new territory fills the notional hegemon with dread. The Germans were dealing with ever larger and more complex client states, but the Habsburgs had little to do with this. Hungarians could feel happy that Belgrade was so devastated and so many of its inhabitants killed or fled that it could now be seen as merely a 'Hungarian provincial town', but there was no medium-term hope for coping with millions of surviving enraged Serbs, any more than there was any way that the starving Empire could feed its hundreds of thousands of Italian prisoners. The ideological basis for grabbing further lands seems to have just packed up, and this intellectual conclusion made it difficult for the surviving elites throughout the Empire to battle the forces that would make it fall apart in the winter of 1918. Perhaps it had been back in 1878, with the half-hearted occupation of Bosnia and the Sanjak, that a sort of colonial weariness had set in – but in any event the temporary triumphs of 1916–18 marked the final reali-

---

* Wholesale massacres by Ukrainians and Poles, both of each other and of Jews in the year after the War officially ended, meant that by 1919 the old Habsburg Galicia had effectively ceased to exist.

zation, far too late, of the sort of fantasies that had once fervently preoccupied Leopold I, Charles VI and other of Karl's ancestors through so many hours of devotional prayer.

The price of defeat

The process by which Habsburg civilization began to collapse began almost as soon as war was declared in 1914 and the first of what would be some eight million uniformed young men began to leave. Of these over a million were killed, almost two million were wounded; over a million and a half were taken prisoner, of whom almost a third died in captivity. Within a year there can have been no street not filled with fearful or distraught families. Beyond this obvious disaster there was an economic catastrophe. Austria-Hungary was painfully easy to blockade. Once Italy entered the war the British were able to close the Adriatic, which completely shut down the Empire's only ports – the great entrepôt of Trieste and the now futile and neutered naval base at Pula. Supplies could only arrive from a handful of neutrals via Germany (and, of course, Germany kept much of these for itself) or, even more tortuously, via the Ottoman Empire once the Balkans had fallen to the Central Powers in late 1915.

Europe had become wealthy on the basis of its international trade and many of its component elements had become ever more specialized about what they needed to create for themselves and what they could import. This trade was paralysed in 1914 and never really recovered until years after 1989. All the inland towns of the Empire essentially existed as places in which goods could be exchanged, with each further circulation of each item allowing a further profit to be clipped, fuelling an entire, unbelievably complex world of merchants, bankers, lawyers and those who worked for them. This system collapsed. The most central, semi-trivial but essential things associated with the Empire disappeared – most obviously the famous cafes no longer had coffee or chocolate. Even if (for some odd reason) you were to set aside the issue of the

immense numbers of families wrecked by combat deaths and mutilation, inflation had on its own destroyed the middle class that had
made the capital cities and provincial centres so prosperous. Perhaps this was an even greater factor than the combat deaths in the
Empire's demise: the millions of pleasantly complacent bourgeois
of the summer of 1914 emerged at the end of 1918 desperate,
impoverished, fearful and angry. Everywhere you can see the high-
water mark – the lovely Partium town of Oradea must have been a
permanent building site from the 1890s to 1914, a playground of
Hungarian eclecticism of the most unrestrained kind (including the
scarcely credible Black Eagle Hotel complex, all multi-coloured
flowers, stained glass and cheerful bobbles). But this all stopped
and never restarted, leaving the town centre architecturally frozen
as it was when news of the assassination arrived. Even before the
war ended Vienna was already shrinking, the result of starvation
and sickness, but also of the general seizing up of its Imperial functions.

The army monopolized supplies of every kind. There was a
fevered search for even the smallest scraps of metal to make weapons – in 1917 alone almost ten thousand tons of church bells were
melted down for their copper, but even items like door-handles
and the casings from shop display windows were seized. The lack
of rubber meant that everything down to the pockets of billiard
tables was grabbed by the army in a feverish and futile attempt to
put tyres on military vehicles. The lack of new cotton (once
blithely imported from the USA or British-controlled Egypt) meant
that clothing began to wear out and had to be replaced with hemp,
which had to be grown on land formerly devoted to food. As a
final flourish, the great Spanish influenza pandemic that killed
perhaps twenty-five million people around the world landed particularly crushingly on the Empire, infiltrating cities that already
hardly functioned and seeming to focus on digging out the final
elements of Habsburg culture, killing Klimt in February 1918 and
Schiele and his pregnant wife in October. There is an understandable lack of commemoration of these terrible events. One that

has always stuck in my mind is Zemlinsky's extraordinary Third String Quartet, with its neurasthenic, grey, pulseless atmosphere, like 'licking a cold, dirty window-pane', as someone once said.

It is hard to see how societies can hold together under such circumstances. At the time it was thought that the Empire broke apart because of military defeat and nationalist agitation. These were undoubtedly important, but since 1915 the Empire had existed only as a sort of husk. Those who had most effectively bought into the idea of the Empire had been its young military elite, the aristocracy who spoke lots of the languages and cared about the structure as a whole and about the framework created by the Emperor, and these were mostly dead within months of the war beginning. The legitimacy of the entire structure was then beaten to pieces by economics – an absolute impoverishment which mixed with wave upon wave of both civilian and military deaths. The Russian revolution of February 1917 served notice on the Emperor Karl only weeks after his coronation: his uselessness in that sense was beside the point. Strikes and mutinies crippled the entire Empire by the end of 1917. On 16 January 1918 some twenty-five thousand women were standing in line at Vienna's main meat market waiting for food.

It was the absolute collapse of legitimacy that (as in Russia) provided the space for new ideas. The whole of Central Europe began an experiment that lasted for much of the century and submitted its populations to previously inconceivable levels of violence. The forces that now rampaged through docile, pompous but civilized backwaters were only there because everything else had failed. Oradea, for example, was invaded by Romanian troops after the Armistice and its Hungarian citizens were subjected to violent discrimination that has carried on intermittently ever since, with Hungarians today making up less than a quarter of the inhabitants. In 1927 a meeting of the Legion of the Archangel Michael in Oradea resulted in half the town's synagogues being burnt to the ground. There was never a point at which normal life could exist in a stable form.

Triumphs of indifference

One oddity of the War was that the British and the Habsburgs only ever fought each other in glancing, minor ways. The British blockade was fundamental to the starvation of much of Central Europe, but this was a remote form of warfare, came from control of the North Sea and Mediterranean and required little active animosity to be hideously effective. Otherwise, some British troops were shifted to the Alps in the aftermath of Caporetto to stiffen the Italian line, and Austrian specialists and observers encountered the British on the Palestinian and Salonika fronts, but the Habsburg forces effectively fought a separate war. This was also true for the Americans, for whom the Austrians were mysterious, but also – through the narratives both of innumerable Galician immigrants as well as visits by Czech intellectuals – a symbol of stifling European backwardness, a crusty prison of the nations. Because there was so little actual fighting this could have been an advantage to Karl as the Allies' passions were barely engaged by the continuing existence of his Empire. But, as it proved, this also meant a fatal lack of information, a willingness to rely on a handful of experts for advice, and a careless indifference to the Empire's collapse which made it an easy sacrifice.

The Emperor Karl seems to have left almost no impression on anyone who met him – a banal, peevish, stroppy figure, his best chance was to decorate his audience chamber with the portraits of any number of comparably unengaging ancestors, and argue that the dynastic principle had at regular intervals thrown up makeweights even more helpless than himself. Sadly, his ineffective predecessors were propped up by a royal framework designed to maintain the dignity of even the least dignified. Wandering around the Schönbrunn Palace, stifled by the retirement-home gentility of Franz Josef's old furnishings, with the glamour of the Russian Revolution unfolding up the road, Karl was a disappointing figure in every respect. It is a shame that the last Emperor did not go out in a reckless blaze of glory, roaring out a medieval battle-cry as he was gunned down, surrounded by beautifully dressed bodyguards, in a final battle with revolutionaries in Heroes' Square. But there had been no precedent for such swagger since Maria Theresa's youth. Karl had few options but he managed to manage all of them poorly. Much of the rage and bitterness Karl had to deal with stemmed from the sense – particularly once peace with Russia had been made in March 1918 – that the Empire was on the verge of validating its terrible casualties. Everything that had ever given a Habsburg citizen an ethnic or strategic headache seemed at an end with the borders not only secure but all the countries beyond them prostrate. No Russian army could ever invade Hungary again, no Serb army Croatia, no Romanian army Transylvania. All that remained was to stand by and wait for the Germans to defeat the British, French and Americans and all would be well. By the spring of 1918 every conceivable Habsburg goal had been met. And even in the unlikely event of defeat there seemed no specific threat, as the Allies had not made any commitment to break up the Empire and an armistice would make no difference to the patent implosion and degradation of their enemies.

Of course, we know that this view was wrong – but the Allies themselves began 1918 exhausted and appalled at how little impact they had made on the Central Powers. With the German army hugely reinforced by the end of the Russian war and division after battle-hardened division moved to the Western Front, the initiative still lay with Germany if not with Austria-Hungary, which became a virtual military observer. But Karl had effectively run out of armies: even with the wholesale evacuation of soldiers from the major fortresses and standing down of the Carpathian defences there were simply very few Habsburg troops left and no supplies. Some final bright ideas resulted in the requisitioning of race horses and instructions that new conscripts should bring their own underwear from home, but these were not going to balance out the depletion of factories, the collapse of transport and chronic anaemia in all aspects of Central European life.

One of the issues that dominated 1918 was the return of Habsburg prisoners of war after Russia's surrender. The extraordinary total of a million and a half men had been captured, of whom perhaps a third had died. Scattered all over the former Russian Empire, they made their way back home as well as they could, one of the first of the horrible mass migrations that were to mark region after region of Europe until the late 1940s. The return of the prisoners, often seriously ill, understandably often imbued with a hatred for an Empire that had humiliated them, and frequently Communist and/or criminal, threatened to outweigh any surviving value in the still existing army. There are no real figures, but it was estimated that perhaps two hundred thousand deserters were roaming around the Empire and punishments were brought back that would have brought a happy smile to the lips of figures like Radetzky and Windisch-Graetz, such as tying them to stakes or locking them in irons. Attempts to process all these haggard survivors and put them back into the army went completely wrong with an overwhelming percentage of the POWs unfit by any physical or political benchmark.

In many ways the Empire's resilience had been remarkable, but by the end it was assailed by such a multiplicity of problems that the major power centres inside and outside the Empire started to make other plans. The symbolic last straws are so numerous you could build a hut with them. The best one was the sinking of the *Saint Stephen*, the only Hungarian battleship ever built, the fruit of a desperate desire for power-projection and the pride of the futile naval base at Pula. It had nothing much to do during the War as it was so painfully vulnerable to the Italian, French and British navies waiting for it as soon as it reached the Mediterranean. Finally leaving harbour in June 1918 as part of a frantic bid to disrupt the blockade, it was intercepted by Italian torpedo boats before it even reached the blockade line and destroyed with the death of most of its crew. Hungarian dreams of naval grandeur came to an end.

For the Central Powers the killing blow came in the surprising shape of the Bulgarian front. For years the Allies had been penned up around Salonika, derided by the Central Powers and a source of embarrassment to the Allies themselves. In September 1918 a joint French and Serbian force at last broke through, threatening the entire Balkans. Neither Germany nor Austria-Hungary had an answer to this and Ludendorff threw in the towel. There were simply no troops left – they were all committed to occupation duties across their vast but economically morbid eastern Empire, or to grimly holding out against overwhelming superiority in the West (with the USA planning an army by 1919 of some four and a half million men).

The months that followed were complex, exhilarating and frightening. Suddenly, in a way with no precedent since the Turkish invasions, it mattered profoundly where you or your ancestors had chosen to live. A decision taken for romantic, economic, arbitrary or despairing reasons perhaps many generations before would now dictate the state in which you would live: and in the cases of millions of people this would in the coming thirty years result in their pauperization, expulsion or murder.

As it became clear that the War was ending the various nationalities began to move against the Habsburgs. Many commentators have seen this as a tragic sequence of events but it is impossible to exaggerate how little credit remained to the Empire – not just contempt for Karl and the Empire's rulers but, worse, indifference and a sense that any future dispensation made them irrelevant. The Empire was a haggard, starving ruin with predators both within it and around it. It was simply not recognizable as anything like the entity that had declared war so confidently in the summer of 1914. Militarily, yet another last straw was the Battle of Vittorio Veneto in late October – an Italian triumph after so many decades of humiliation at Austrian hands. As the last thirty thousand or so Habsburg subjects to die for the Empire duly did, it was clear that everything was lost.

The somewhat chaotic minutes still exist for the final, late October meetings of the Common Ministerial Council in Vienna when for the last time Austrian Germans, Czechs and Hungarians met with Karl in scenes of hopeless indecision and lack of realism. On 18 October Karl had announced a *Manifesto to My Faithful*

Peoples announcing a federation of six new states under his rule: Austrian, Ukrainian, Czech, Polish, Hungarian and Yugoslav. But this was all far too late and proclamations were breaking out all over the place, completely ignoring the wishes of Vienna or Budapest. The Council made ponderous comments about the rights of the Crown of Stephen, shook their heads over 'the sphinx Wilson' and generally gave the sense of confused figures roused up from a retirement home. Outside, the new era, of boulevards filled with running, menacing crowds, panicked police and angry veterans, was beginning. On 11 November, in a final piece of peevish indirection, Karl refused to abdicate but instead 'relinquished participation'.

The Empire ended and its subjects looked out onto a new and − as it would prove − terrible world.

Conclusion

If I think about how I have divided up my time in researching this book, I am struck by the enormous accumulation of hours just spent walking. In city after city a much more characteristic activity than any other was the criss-crossing of residential areas. It became a sort of sickness. I would just take a rough compass direction and make sweep after sweep through areas of private homes – Communist-era tower-block estates, rows of tiny nineteenth-century artisanal housing, streets filled with the decayed great villas of the old haute bourgeoisie. Shortly after the end of the Cold War, I spent some days staying as a guest of an elderly couple in the suburbs of Dresden. Their house was extremely bare. They had no phone and no television, and were kind, gentle and stunned by the utterly unexpected change of regime, a change to which they could hardly react. Their lives orbited around a small allotment in the next block from their home. This allotment had been converted into a demented, Technicolor arbour crowded with trellised flowers so brightly coloured they were hard to look at. In the summer the couple would take out a couple of fold-out chairs from a tiny shed and sit under the flowers.

I mention this because it has stuck in my mind for some thirty years, but also because it seemed such a reasonable response to an impossible situation. All over central Europe there are countless such gardens. On many streets the pavements have been made wide enough to plant flower gardens and everywhere there are tiny plots that receive the most lavish care and thought and contrast drastically with the many, often very haggard public spaces.

Wandering along these streets I found myself endlessly rolling over in my mind the same quite simple questions, goaded by the usual mixture of the clinking and banging of washing-up, barking

dogs, children's voices, music from a radio. Each of these towns is
a place filled with the normal life almost everyone aspires to – a
daily round of family and work, food and sex, conversation and
sleep. But they are also places that have been subjected to waves of
utter catastrophe, of a kind outsiders such as me cannot begin
to understand. The sounds of washing-up, dogs, kids and music
would have been consistent for all of the last century, but the
identity of those making those sounds would have been different.
There can hardly have been a home in the former Empire into
which the most terrible forces – intellectual, political and military
– did not reach a hand. This would have begun in 1914 with the
first of a flood of telegrams announcing the death or mutilation of
family members but the demands made on all these homes now
went on for generations. This is most obviously the case, of course,
in the great former Jewish sections of cities such as Prague, Vienna,
Budapest and Kraków – here a various, thriving, vigorous culture
had been annihilated within twenty-five years of the Empire's end
and millions of people murdered for mystical and intellectual reasons so perverted that they raise effectively unmanageable questions
about the real nature of Europe's civilization. The Kazimierz dis-
trict of Kraków remains intolerable – the sounds of family life are
the same, but they are made by different people. But this is true
across the entire region. In cities like Lviv or Ivano-Frankivsk
almost the entire population was killed or expelled – for being
Jewish, for being Polish, for being German, for being wealthy, for
being pro-Nazi or pro-Communist. The Galician Jewish town of
Kolomyya is now a bustling, messy Ukrainian town, but with no
Jews at all. When the Cold War ended its statue of Lenin was taken
down and the pedestal turned out to be filled with old Jewish
gravestones.

Almost everyone within the old Empire seems to have taken
turns to be destroyed by one aspect of the twentieth century or
another. The Lychakiv Cemetery in Lviv is in this sense one of
the most remarkable, over-charged sites of memory in the world
– an extraordinary domain in which it is possible to confront the
many groups, racial, linguistic, social, which created the uniquely

complex and curious culture of Galicia, but who were almost all destroyed. The battered, moss-caked and pompous family mausoleums of the city's great Polish families rub shoulders with Protestant, Uniate and Orthodox graves. The huge memorial built in the 1920s to mark the successful defence of Lviv (or rather Lwów) by its Polish citizens against invading Ukrainian troops has (amazingly) been recently rebuilt. For decades this was a ground zero of nationalist political terror, smashed to pieces in turn by vengeful Nazis, Soviets and Ukrainians and ultimately turned into a truck depot. It is a measure of the post-ideological exhaustion of the present day that the Ukrainian and Polish governments were able to agree to the grandiose monument's rebuilding (it was reopened in 2005) – but also an indication that the issues around the monument are at an end as, after all, Lviv no longer has any Polish population.

The poet Adam Zagajewski wrote in 1991 an essay called 'Two Cities' about his memories as a very young child of the mass expulsion of surviving Poles from Lviv after the Second World War. In one of the biggest of many acts of overwhelming brutality, Stalin decided to solve the problem of the mixed Polish–Ukrainian areas of old Galicia by moving the entire Polish state west into what had been German territory – much of it the old Habsburg territories of Silesia seized by Frederick the Great. The surviving Germans in these Silesian towns, many of which were little more than rubble, were all kicked out and expelled Galician Poles moved in. Many Poles were relocated to places like Gleiwitz, which now became Polish Gliwice, some three hundred and seventy miles west of Lviv. Zagajewski's essay is about the extremes of the human experience in Europe and is remarkable in all kinds of ways, but the image that sticks in the mind is of those new inhabitants of Gliwice who refused to admit that they had even moved. They talked to their neighbours as though nothing had happened, wore their ancient clothing, referred to each other by now meaningless courtesy titles and tried to imagine that nothing had happened to interfere with the Habsburg idyll in which they had grown up. Effectively they walked around Gliwice imagining that its geography was that of Lwów. And, of course, they all tried as hard as possible not to notice the arrival of the People's Republic, a new system to replace the horrors of Nazism, and itself representing, in Zagajewski's words: 'fear, blood draining out of the face, trembling hands, talking in whispers, silence, apathy, sealing windows shut, suspicion of one's neighbours, signing up for the hated Party membership'.

The speed of this absolute catastrophe, from 1914 to 1950 or so, engulfed virtually everyone within the Habsburg Empire, for different reasons. Hundreds of instances race through my mind all the time and could just turn everything into a jumbled catalogue of horror of a pointless kind: the German towns with no Germans, the Polish towns with no Poles, the Hungarian towns with no Hungarians. But also, of course, the countryside: the countless tiny Jewish villages scattered across Galicia and Bohemia. In London a museum in the Westminster Synagogue preserves 1,564 Torah scrolls, mainly from Jewish villages in Bohemia, and which are in most cases all that remains of places which until the creation of the Nazi 'Protectorate' were an integral, quintessential element in European life.

From the end of the Great War onwards there was always a sense of puzzlement in the West as to why the new post-Habsburg politicians seemed so unreasonable – why the occasional pleasant figure, generally an aristocrat, 'of good will', would so rapidly be submerged by others who seemed little more than wild beasts. Red terrors and White terrors, mass mobilizations, ethnic violence and an obsession on both left and right with military posturing plunged most of the old Empire into a nightmare which, with ever more inventive twists and turns, went on for generations. But these were all figures fighting over a faded and decaying remnant. This can be seen in the coldest way by population figures. Vienna, the great Imperial capital, emptied out, its population dropping by some three hundred thousand in the inter-war period, its vast bureaucratic buildings half empty, its economy in ruins. Budapest, the second Imperial capital, had by contrast a ballooning population, but only because hundreds of thousands of Hungarians fled into the city from Serbian and Romanian reigns of terror in what had just ceased to be southern and eastern Hungary.

These traumas created an immediate nostalgia and a sense that something extremely precious had been lost. It is striking in many of the remarkable novels from the 1930s how many celebrate almost obsessively the broad range of possibilities that had once existed in the former Empire, the geographical sprawl of which had now been replaced by the small and dirty cages of the new nation states. In one of the greatest Hungarian novels, Desző Kosztolányi's charming *Kornél Esti*, the hero waves goodbye to the amusingly named pubs in Budapest (the Torpedo, the Vitriol – 'a low dive') and heads off to the coast. In a magical scene of yearning he travels down through the pre-War Empire, waved on by a friendly Croat guard, to the Hungarian Adriatic port of Fiume, where a Hungarian flag flaps cheerily over the deep blue sea. For the novel's original readers this would have been very hard to read, with the route now filled with implacably hostile and triumphalist new Yugoslav and Fascist Italian owners. Another of Kosztolányi's novels, the wonderful *Skylark*, together with much of the rest of his work, is set in a fictional pre-War southern Hungarian town based on his birthplace of Subotica, now also under Yugoslav rule. Joseph Roth, whose novels tried to embrace as much as possible of the old Empire, shared this pan-European yearning. In *The Emperor's Tomb* the narrator living in Vienna gets together with his chestnut-seller cousin from Slovenia to visit a Jewish coach-driver in Galicia (in Roth's favourite, back-of-beyond, fictional frontier town of Zlotograd). Writers such as Stefan Zweig, Alexander Lernet-Holenia and Miklós Bánffy also fill the 1930s with characters travelling back and forth across the Empire. They celebrate the friendly relations between different nationalities and a sense of tolerance or at least indifference which had now completely vanished in favour of a heavily fanged nationalism. Bánffy's scenes of pre-War young noblemen in Kolozsvár getting friendly policemen to clear the pavement so that they can sing with a gypsy-band beneath the windows of girls they love were crazily impossible in the newly Romanian-ruled city of Cluj at the time he was actually writing.

But of course much of this fiction would shortly in turn be buried under a fresh, even greater wave of horror, which gives the books a painful charm greater than the writers even intended. Indeed, it was perhaps the aristocrats in Bánffy's *Transylvanian Trilogy* who bugged me most as I wandered gloomily through the endless streets of these at-best haggard towns. What I kept coming back to, seeing all these houses whose inhabitants may since 1914 have been scooped out and replaced several times over, is that so much of the critique of the Empire was a genuinely *liberal* one – but liberalism itself ended up as deeply intolerant. The great effort to shake clear of the Empire's creaking, feudal structures meant breaking through into a new world not of tolerance and equality, but of viciousness far greater than anything the old Austro-Hungarian rulers could have dreamed of.

Austro-Hungarian liberalism rapidly splintered with the end of the Empire into mutually enraged forms of exclusionary national-ism or Communism. The numbers of those who remained committed to something even slightly inclusive rapidly dropped to almost zero, leaving only a handful of aristocrats like Bánffy. As soon as the Emperor Karl's rule collapsed there was no model available for a serious democracy – or at best democracy became a casual weapon reached for by a majority group so they could impose themselves on smaller groups. Even Czechoslovakia could not manage its minorities. As with the other successor states a key early move there had been to demolish every trace of the Habsburgs. In the far western German-speaking town of Eger (now Cheb) this meant demolishing the statue of the modernizing, pro-German Joseph II in the main square. Attempts to do this resulted in riots that burned down the only Czech-language school. Czech troops swamped the main square like an occupying army. Once the battered statue had been disposed of, Eger became a hot-bed of German resentment, effectively not part of the Czechoslovak state, with even Czech road signs torn down. In short, Franz Ferdinand's vision of German Bohemia immediately came true. Throughout the

1930s the town noisily celebrated being the place where the
German hero Wallenstein had been killed by Habsburg cowards,
for which could be read the neo-Habsburgs in Prague. With absurd
Wallenstein festivals and marches, with the people of Eger dressed
as soldiers of the Thirty Years War, this all shifted by easy stages
into Sudetenland enthusiasm for Hitler. These people were never
reconciled to the Czechoslovak state. Cheb is now yet another
town entirely filled with new people, another disaster, with every
single German killed or expelled.

So the question that has driven me mad through the years writing this book is the obvious one. Was it inherent in the destruction
of the Habsburg Empire that Nazism would result? In the vast,
endlessly complex nationalist laboratory of the Empire's final
decade, was Hitler himself in fact the quintessential product? So
many of his obsessions, tics and visions seem rooted here and not
in Germany itself. Were his Habsburg obsessions injected into
Germany, much as the German General Staff injected Lenin into
Russia? Like all such questions, in the end it cannot be answered.

A reliable sense of settled gloom can always be had by standing
in the half-complete mess of Heroes' Square in Vienna. It was here
that Hitler had perhaps his greatest triumph, in the spring of 1938.
German Austrians had met the notionally invading Nazi troops in
a delirium of mass joy, their humiliation in the grubby little
Republic of Austria at an end. By the time that Hitler appeared on
the balcony of the Hofburg, looking out onto the square at an
adoring crowd of some two hundred thousand, many thousands of
others (leftists, monarchists, Austrian patriots, Habsburgs) had been
arrested and ferocious anti-Jewish violence had broken out. On
crossing the Austrian border with his motorcade, Hitler had first
gone to visit the graves of his parents in Upper Austria and then
visited Linz, where he had been a student. But it was Vienna
where, as a subject of Franz Joseph, he had spent his early twenties
as a humiliated semi-vagrant. Standing on the hideously ornate
and tacky Hofburg balcony he effectively *became* Franz Joseph, but
a Franz Joseph who would rule a reconstituted Empire just on
behalf of its German element, in grudging cooperation with the

Hungarians – the other 'Nibelung' race – and ending the politics which had dominated pre-1914 Vienna: Jews and Slavs would now once more be put back in their places.

Heroes' Square is a miserable spot. An old barracks and parade-ground cleared into an arena for Imperial splendour, it was only part-built when the Empire ended, leaving just two bathetic statues, one of Prince Eugene, the other of Archduke Charles, and it is now a car park subject to gusts of wind which whirl together dirt and discarded plastic cups. I have always been bothered most by the sight from the square of the huge Nazi-era Flak Tower, lurking like something from *The War of the Worlds* behind the museums. Most of these towers have been demolished, but this one, oddly, has survived – a huge concrete structure used as a high platform for anti-aircraft guns and as an arsenal and bomb-shelter. It was built with these practical purposes in mind, but it was also meant to stand there for ever as a symbol of Viennese fortitude, so that future generations in the Nazi Empire would admire it, just as they admired the statues in Heroes' Square of Vienna's two greatest earlier defenders, or the spot on the Kahlenberg where the princes met before racing down the hill to destroy the Ottoman armies besieging the city. The Flak Tower was meant to be faced with marble, but the marble was marooned in its French quarry as one of the minor casualties of D-Day and then, for obvious reasons, never delivered. Wandering around the square, the Flak Tower is an insistent and nasty presence on the horizon. I remember sitting on the Hofburg steps with my wife on our honeymoon, staring at it – a romantic moment. On every visit since, over some twenty years, I have found myself looking up to see if the Austrians have at last demolished it. But it is still there.

GERMANY

Bautzen ●

Litoměřice ●
Karlovy Vary ●
Prague ●
● Mariánské Lázně ● Kutná Hora

Plzeň ● CZECH REP. ● Olomouc

České Budějovice ● Brno ●
Český Krumlov ●
Linz ● Krems ●
St Pölten ●
Vienna ● ● Bratislava

Salzburg ●
Sopron ●
Bregenz ● AUSTRIA
Innsbruck ● Ják ●
Graz ●
Bolzano ● Klagenfurt ● Maribor ●
Trento ● Ljubljana ● Pécs ●
Gorizia ● SLOVENIA
Venice ● Trieste ● Zagreb ●
Rijeka ● CROATIA

ITALY
BOSNIA-
HERZEGOVINA

A D R I A T I C   Split ●

| 0 | 50 | 100 miles |
| 0 | 50 | 100 | 150 km |

S E A   Dubrovnik ●

MODERN CENTRAL EUROPE

POLAND

UKRAINE

Kraków
Przemyśl
Tarnów
Lviv
Zakopane
Drohobych
Ivano-Frankivsk
SLOVAKIA
Yaremche
Kolomyya
Chernivtsi
Eger
Szentendre
Budapest
Debrecen
Oradea
HUNGARY
Cluj-Napoca
Szekszárd
Szeged
Arad
Alba Iulia
Sighişoara
Viscri
Sibiu
Subotica
Braşov
Novi Sad
Sremski Karlovci
ROMANIA
Belgrade
N
SERBIA
Sarajevo

Former area of Habsburg Empire in 1914

Bibliography

Two books are not listed in the bibliography: Rebecca West's *Black Lamb and Grey Falcon* and Claudio Magris' *Danube*. I adored these books when I read them many years ago and can probably blame them for much of my interest in the region, but I have simply been unable to reread them. They make me feel like a space traveller whose rocket is a sort of dustbin powered by sparklers trying to navigate between Jupiter and Saturn. The gravitational power of these books is just too great: even reading an essay by Geoff Dyer *about* Rebecca West's book was enough to make me feel this whole project was being dragged helplessly into her orbit. So they should not be part of the bibliography, but of course their influence is everywhere, at least at the level of chaotic misrememberings.

I have included a number of titles which I found really interesting but which ended up not directly contributing to the book. I have not included separate listings for all the fiction by Thomas Bernhard, Joseph Roth and Stefan Zweig as it seemed a pointless way to fill up pages: I have just listed a handful of particularly fine examples in the hope that someone somewhere might start with these and then get hooked. Dates are of the editions that I have, therefore not necessarily the first. Spelling of author names is given in the form on the book and is therefore not more broadly consistent.

The real backbone to this book is innumerable tourist information pamphlets, sheets pinned up on church notice boards, pamphlets tucked in with CDs, conversations with individuals vastly better informed than myself, museum booklets and unmanageable piles of evocative, bewildering and entrancing maps – few objects can be more freighted with feeling than a good multilingual map of Transylvania. My two bibles (an obviously contradictory idea) throughout the writing have been a copy of Baedeker's 1911 *Austria-Hungary* guide, generously lent by John Seaton, whose encouragement and friendship have meant so much to me for many years, and Magocsi and Matthews' superb *Historical Atlas of East Central Europe*, which has answered a thousand questions and raised many more.

Charles Allen, *The Buddha and the Sahibs* (London, 2002)

Aharon Appelfeld, trans. Dalya Bilu, *Badenheim 1939* (London, 2005)

Ronald G. Asch, *The Thirty Years War: The Holy Roman Empire and Europe, 1618–48* (Basingstoke, 1997)

Karl Baedeker, *Guide to Austria-Hungary with Excursions to Cetinje, Belgrade and Bucharest* (London and New York, 1911)

Béla Balázs, *The Cloak of Dreams: Chinese Fairy Tales*, trans. Jack Zipes (Princeton, 2010)

Philip Ball, *The Devil's Doctor: Paracelsus and the World of Renaissance Magic and Science* (London, 2006)

Miklós Bánffy, *They Were Counted*, trans. Patrick Thursfield and Katalin Bánffy-Jelen (London, 2000)

Miklós Bánffy, *They Were Divided*, trans. Patrick Thursfield and Katalin Bánffy-Jelen (London, 2001)

Miklós Bánffy, *They Were Found Wanting*, trans. Patrick Thursfield and Katalin Bánffy-Jelen (London, 2000)

Robert Bartlett, *The Making of Europe: Conquest, Colonization and Cultural Change 950–1350* (London, 1993)

Antony Beaumont, *Zemlinsky* (Ithaca, 2000)

Steven Beller, *A Concise History of Austria* (Cambridge, 2006)

David Bellos, *Is That a Fish in Your Ear?* (London, 2011)

Marina Belozerskaya, *The Medici Giraffe and Other Tales of Exotic Animals and Power* (New York, 2006)

Thomas Bernhard, *Extinction*, trans. David McLintock (London, 1996)

Thomas Bernhard, *Old Masters: A Comedy*, trans. E. Osers (London, 2010)

Robert Bireley SJ, *The Refashioning of Catholicism, 1450–1700* (Basingstoke, 1999)

William Blacker, *Along the Enchanted Way: A Story of Love and Life in Romania* (London, 2009)

Paul Blanchard, *The Blue Guide to Northern Italy* (London, 2005)

T. C. W. Blanning, *The Culture of Power and the Power of Culture: Old Regime Europe 1660–1789* (Oxford, 2002)

T. C. W. Blanning (ed.), *The Eighteenth Century* (Oxford, 2000)

T. C. W. Blanning, *Joseph II* (Harlow, 1994)

Tim Blanning, *The Pursuit of Glory: Europe 1648–1815* (London, 2007)

Richard Bonney, *The European Dynastic States, 1494–1660* (Oxford, 1991)

Catherine Wendy Bracewell, *The Uskoks of Senj: Piracy, Banditry, and Holy War in the Sixteenth-Century Adriatic* (Ithaca, 1992)

Vladmir Brnardic, *Imperial Armies of the Thirty Years War: Cavalry* (Botley and Long Island City, 2010)

Vladimir Brnardic, *Imperial Armies of the Thirty Years War: Infantry and Artillery* (Botley and Long Island City, 2009)

Reed Browning, *The War of the Austrian Succession* (New York, 1994)

Rogers Brubaker, Margit Feischmidt, Jon Fox and Liana Grancea, *Nationalist Politics and Everyday Ethnicity in a Transylvanian Town* (Princeton and Oxford, 2006)

Bernd Brunner, *Bears: A Brief History*, trans. Lori Lantz (New Haven, 2007)

Malcolm Bull, *The Mirror of the Gods: Classical Mythology in Renaissance Art* (London 2005)

Tim Burford and Norm Longley, *The Rough Guide to Romania* (London, 2008)

Elias Canetti, *Crowds and Power*, trans. Carol Stewart (London, 1984)

Elias Canetti, *The Human Province*, trans. Joachim Neugroschel (London, 1986)

Elias Canetti, *Kafka's Other Trial*, trans. Christopher Middleton (London, 2012)

Bryan Cartledge, *Mihály Károlyi and István Bethlen* (London, 2009)

Bryan Cartledge, *The Will to Survive: A History of Hungary* (London, 2006)

Holly Case, *Between States: The Transylvanian Question and the European Idea during World War II* (Stanford, 2009)

Kenneth Chalmers, *Béla Bartók* (London, 1995)

Christopher Clark, *The Sleepwalkers: How Europe Went to War in 1914* (London, 2012)

Mark Cornwall (ed.), *The Last Years of Austria-Hungary: A Multi-National Experiment in Early Twentieth-Century Europe* (Exeter, 1990)

Gerald R. Cragg, *The Church and the Age of Reason, 1648–1789* (Harmondsworth, 1960)

Gordon A. Craig, *The Battle of Königgrätz: Prussia's Victory over Austria, 1866* (Philadelphia, 2003)

Kevin Cramer, *The Thirty Years' War and German Memory in the Nineteenth Century* (Lincoln and London, 2007)

Roger Crowley, *Empires of the Sea: The Final Battle for the Mediterranean 1521–1580* (London, 2008)

Norman Davies, *God's Playground: A History of Poland: Volume I: The Origins to 1795* (Oxford, 2005)

Norman Davies, *God's Playground: A History of Poland: Volume II: 1795 to the Present* (Oxford, 2005)

Norman Davies, *Vanished Kingdoms: The History of Half-Forgotten Europe* (London, 2011)

Istvan Deák, *The Lawful Revolutionary: Louis Kossuth and the Hungarians, 1848–1849* (New York, 1979)

Peter Demetz, *Prague in Black and Gold: The History of a City* (London, 1998)

Jeroen Duindam, *Vienna and Versailles: The Courts of Europe's Dynastic Rivals, 1550–1780* (Cambridge, 2003)

Mark Edmundson, *The Death of Sigmund Freud: Fascism, Psychoanalysis and the Rise of Fundamentalism* (London, 2007)

Erich Egg, *Das Grabmal Kaiser Maximilians I.* (Innsbruck, 1993)

Andrew Evans, *The Bradt Guide to Ukraine* (Chalfont St Peter, 2010)

R. J. W. Evans, *Austria, Hungary, and the Habsburgs: Central Europe c. 1683–1867* (Oxford, 2006)

R. J. W. Evans, *The Making of the Habsburg Monarchy 1550–1700* (Oxford, 1979)

R. J. W. Evans, *Rudolf II and His World* (London, 1997)

György Faludy, *My Happy Days in Hell*, trans. Kathleen Szasz (London, 2010)

Niall Ferguson, *The War of the World: History's Age of Hatred* (London, 2006)

David Freedberg, *The Eye of the Lynx: Galileo, His Friends, and the Beginnings of Modern Natural History* (Chicago and London, 2002)

Saul Friedländer, *The Years of Extermination: Nazi Germany and the Jews, 1939–1945* (New York, 2007)

Horst Fuhrmann, *Germany in the High Middle Ages c. 1050–1200* (Cambridge, 1986)

David Gates, *The Napoleonic Wars 1803–1815* (London, 1997)

Misha Glenny, *The Balkans: Nationalism, War and the Great Powers* (London, 1999)

Joscelyn Godwin, *Athanasius Kircher's Theatre of the World* (London and New York, 2009)

Thomas E. Greiss (ed.), *The West Point Atlas for the Wars of Napoleon* (New York, 2003)

Charles Habsburg, *The Autobiography of the Emperor Charles V*, trans. Leonard Francis Simpson (London, 1862 – Kessinger Publishing digital reprint)

Peter Handke, *Repetition*, trans. Ralph Manheim (New York, 1998)

Peter Handke, *A Sorrow Beyond Dreams*, trans. Ralph Manheim (New York, 2002)

Jaroslav Hašek, *The Good Soldier Švejk*, trans. Cecil Parrott (London, 1973)

Peter Heather, *Empires and Barbarians: Migration, Development and the Birth of Europe* (London, 2009)

Charles Hebbert, Norm Longley and Dan Richardson, *The Rough Guide to Hungary* (London, 2005)

Mary Heimann, *Czechoslovakia: The State that Failed* (New Haven and London, 2009)

Holger H. Herwig, *The First World War: Germany and Austria-Hungary 1914–1918* (London and New York, 1997)

Theodor Herzl, *The Jewish State* (London, 2010)

Michael Hochedlinger, *Austria's Wars of Emergence, 1683–1797* (Harlow, 2003)

Amanda Holden with Nicholas Kenyon and Stephen Walsh, *The Viking Opera Guide* (London, 1993)

Peter Hopkirk, *Foreign Devils on the Silk Road: The Search for the Lost Treasures of Central Asia* (London, 1980)

Bohumil Hrabal, *Closely Watched Trains,* trans. Edith Pargeter (Evanston, 1990)

Bohumil Hrabal, *The Death of Mr Baltisberger*, trans. Michael Henry Heim (London, 1990)

Bohumil Hrabal, *Too Loud a Solitude*, trans. Michael Henry Heim (London, 1991)

Rob Humphreys, *The Rough Guide to Austria* (London, 2005)

Rob Humphreys, *The Rough Guide to the Czech Republic* (London, 2009)

Rob Humphreys, *The Real Guide to Czechoslovakia* (New York, 1991)

Agnes Husslein-Arco (ed.), *Anton Romako: Admiral Tegetthoff in the Naval Battle of Lissa* (Vienna, 2010)

Agnes Husslein-Arco and Marie-Louise von Plessen (eds.), *Prince Eugene: General-Philosopher and Art Lover* (Vienna and Munich, 2010)

Charles Ingrao, *The Habsburg Monarchy 1618–1815*, 2nd edition (Cambridge, 2000)

Charles and Barbara Jelavich, *The Establishment of the Balkan National States, 1804–1920* (Seattle, 1977)

Tony Judt, *Postwar: A History of Europe Since 1945* (London, 2007)

Jonathan Keates, *The Siege of Venice* (London, 2005)

Ian Kershaw, *Hitler 1889–1936: Hubris* (London, 1998)

Ian Kershaw, *Hitler 1936–1945: Nemesis* (London, 2001)

Danilo Kiš, *The Encyclopedia of the Dead*, trans. Michael Henry Heim (Evanston, 1997)

Danilo Kiš, *Garden, Ashes*, trans. William J. Hannaher (New York, 1975)

Dezső Kosztolányi, trans. Bernard Adams, *Kornél Esti* (New York, 2011)

Dezső Kosztolányi, trans. Richard Aczel, *Skylark* (New York, 2010)

Paul Koudounaris, *The Empire of Death: A Cultural History of Ossuaries and Charnel Houses* (London and New York, 2011)

Milan Kundera, *Testaments Betrayed: An Essay in Nine Parts*, trans. Linda Asher (London, 1995)

Chris Lavers, *The Natural History of Unicorns* (London, 2009)

Norman Lebrecht, *Why Mahler?: How One Man and Ten Symphonies Changed the World* (London, 2010)

Paul Lendvai, *Inside Austria: New Challenges, Old Demons* (London, 2010)

Alexander Lernet-Holenia, *Baron Bagge / Count Luna*, trans. Richard and Clara Winston and Jane B. Greene (Hygiene, 1980)

Dominic Lieven, *Empire: The Russian Empire and Its Rivals from the Sixteenth Century to the Present* (London, 2002)

Vejas Gabriel Liulevicius, *War Land on the Eastern Front: Culture, National Identity and German Occupation in World War I* (Cambridge, 2000)

Norm Longley, *The Rough Guide to Slovenia* (London, 2007)

John Lukacs, *Budapest 1900: A Historical Portrait of a City and Its Culture* (London, 1993)

C. A. Macartney, *The Hapsburg Empire 1790–1918* (London, 2010)

William O. McCagg, Jr., *A History of the Habsburg Jews 1670–1918* (Bloomington and Indianapolis, 1992)

Diarmaid MacCulloch, *A History of Christianity: The First Three Thousand Years* (London, 2009)

Diarmaid MacCulloch, *Reformation: Europe's House Divided, 1190–1700* (London, 2003)

Richard Mackenney, *Sixteenth Century Europe: Expansion and Conflict* (Basingstoke, 1993)

Gordon McLachlan, *The Rough Guide to Germany* (London, 2004)

Paul Robert Magocsi and Geoffrey J. Matthews, *Historical Atlas of East Central Europe* (Seattle, 1993)

Noel Malcolm, *Bosnia: A Short History* (London, 1994)

William Maltby, *The Reign of Charles V* (Basingstoke, 2002)

Sandor Márai, *Embers*, trans. Carol Brown Janeway (London, 2002)

Peter Marshall, *The Magic Circle of Rudolf II: Alchemy and Astrology in Renaissance Prague* (New York, 2006)

Mark Mazower, *The Balkans: From the End of Byzantium to the Present Day* (London, 2000)

Simon Millar, *Vienna 1683: Christian Europe Repels the Ottomans* (Botley, 2008)

Lieutenant-Colonel J. Mitchell, *The Life of Wallenstein, Duke of Friedland* (London, 1837 – BiblioLife digital reprint)

Laurence Mitchell, *The Bradt Guide to Serbia* (Chalfont St Peter, 2010)

Andrej Mitrović, *Serbia's Great War, 1914–1918* (London, 2007)

Mary Wortley Montagu, *Life on the Golden Horn* (London, 2007)

Simon Sebag Montefiore, *Prince of Princes: The Life of Potemkin* (London, 2000)

Eduard Mörike, *Mozart's Journey to Prague*, trans. David Luke (London, 1997)

Geoff Mortimer, *Wallenstein: The Enigma of the Thirty Years War* (Basingstoke, 2010)

Herta Müller, *The Land of Green Plums*, trans. Michael Hofmann (New York, 1996)

Robert Musil, *Flypaper*, trans. Peter Wortsman (London, 2011)

Robert Musil, *The Man without Qualities*, trans. Eithne Wilkins and Ernst Kaiser (London, 1979)

Ménie Muriel Norman, *A Girl in the Karpathians* (London, 1891 – British Library reprint)

Richard Overy, *The Bombing War: Europe, 1939–1945* (London, 2013)

Geoffrey Parker, *Europe in Crisis 1598–1648*, 2nd edition (Oxford, 2001)

Ota Pavel, *How I Came to Know Fish*, trans. Jindriska Badal and Robert McDowell (London, 2010)

Martyn Rady, *The Emperor Charles V* (Harlow, 1988)

Timothy Reuter, *Germany in the Early Middle Ages 800–1056* (Harlow, 1991)

Gregor von Rezzori, *The Snows of Yesteryear,* trans. H. F. Broch De Rothermann (London, 1989)

Barnaby Rogerson, *The Last Crusaders: The Hundred-Year Battle for the Centre of the World* (London, 2009)

Joseph Roth, *The Emperor's Tomb*, trans. John Hoare (London, 1984)

Joseph Roth, *Flight Without End*, trans. David le Vay in collaboration with Beatrice Musgrave (London, 1984)

Joseph Roth, *Weights and Measures*, trans. David le Vay (London and Chester Springs, 2002)

Ulinka Rublack, *Reformation Europe* (Cambridge, 2005)

Paul W. Schroeder, *The Transformation of European Politics 1763–1848* (Oxford, 1994)

H. M. Scott, *The Birth of the Great Power System, 1740–1815* (Harlow, 2006)

James J. Sheehan, *German History 1770–1866* (Oxford, 1989)

Larry Silver, *Marketing Maximilian: The Visual Ideology of a Holy Roman Emperor* (Princeton, 2008)

Brendan Simms, *Europe: The Struggle for Mastery, 1453 to the Present* (London, 2013)

Brendan Simms, *The Struggle for Mastery in Germany, 1779–1850* (Basingstoke, 1998)

Alan Sked, *The Decline and Fall of the Habsburg Empire, 1815–1918* (Harlow, 1989)

Alan Sked, *The Survival of the Habsburg Empire: Radetzky, the Imperial Army and the Class War, 1848* (London, 1979)

Yuri Slezkine, *The Jewish Century* (Princeton, 2004)

Pamela H. Smith, *The Business of Alchemy: Science and Culture in the Holy Roman Empire* (Princeton, 1994)

Timothy Snyder, *The Reconstruction of Nations: Poland, Ukraine, Lithuania, Belarus 1569–1999* (New Haven and London, 2003)

Martin Sonnabend and Jon Whiteley with Christian Rümelin, *Claude Lorrain: The Enchanted Landscape* (Oxford, 2011)

Jonathan Sperber, *The European Revolutions, 1848–1851* (Cambridge, 1994)

Sybille Steinbacher, *Auschwitz: A History*, trans. Shaun Whiteside (London, 2005)

Zara Steiner, *The Lights That Failed: European International History 1919–1933* (Oxford, 2005)

Rolf Steininger, *South Tyrol: A Minority Conflict of the Twentieth Century* (New Brunswick and London, 2009)

David Stevenson, *1914–1918: The History of the First World War* (London, 2004)

Adalbert Stifter, *The Bachelors*, trans. David Bryer (London, 2008)

Adalbert Stifter, *Brigitta and Other Tales*, trans. Helen Watanabe-O'Kelly (London, 1990)

Adalbert Stifter, *Indian Summer*, trans. Wendell Frye (Bern, 2009)

Adalbert Stifter, *Rock Crystal*, trans. Elizabeth Mayer and Marianne Moore (London, 1999)

Richard Stokes (editor and translator), *The Book of Lieder* (London, 2005)

William Stolzenburg, *Where the Wild Things Were: Life, Death, and Ecological Wreckage in a Land of Vanishing Predators* (New York, 2008)

Norman Stone, *The Eastern Front, 1914–1917* (London, 1975)

Hew Strachan, *The First World War, Volume I: To Arms* (Oxford, 2001)

Peter F. Sugar, *South-Eastern Europe under Ottoman Rule 1354–1804* (Seattle, 1977)

Italo Svevo, *The Nice Old Man and the Pretty Girl*, trans. L. Collison-Morley (Brooklyn, 2010)

Franz A. J. Szabo, *The Seven Years War in Europe 1756–1763* (Harlow, 2008)

Marcus Tanner, *The Raven King: Matthias Corvinus and the Fate of His Lost Library* (New Haven and London, 2009)

A. J. P. Taylor, *The Struggle for Mastery in Europe 1848–1918* (Oxford, 1954)

Keith Thomas, *Religion and the Decline of Magic: Studies in Popular Beliefs in Sixteenth- and Seventeenth-Century England* (London, 1971)

Mark Thompson, *The White War: Life and Death on the Italian Front, 1915–1919* (London, 2008)

John Tincey, *Blenheim 1704: The Duke of Marlborough's Masterpiece* (Oxford, 2004)

H. R. Trevor-Roper, *The European Witch-Craze of the Sixteenth and Seventeenth Centuries* (Harmondsworth, 1969)

Walter Ullmann, *Medieval Political Thought* (Harmondsworth, 1975)

Arminius Vambéry, *The Life and Adventures of Arminius Vambéry* (London and Leipzig, 1883 – Elibron digital reprint)

David Vital, *A People Apart: The Jews in Europe, 1789–1939* (Oxford, 1999)

John Watts, *The Making of Politics, 1300–1500* (Cambridge, 2009)

Geoffrey Wawro, *The Austro-Prussian War: Austria's War with Prussia and Italy in 1866* (Cambridge, 1996)

C. V. Wedgwood, *The Thirty Years War* (London, 1938)

Joachim Whaley, *Germany and the Holy Roman Empire*, two vols. (Oxford, 2012)

Andrew Wheatcroft, *The Enemy at the Gate: Habsburgs, Ottomans and the Battle for Europe* (London, 2008)

Carolinne White (trans.), *The Rule of Benedict* (London, 2008)

Christopher Wickham, *The Inheritance of Rome: A History of Europe from 400 to 1000* (London, 2009)

Peter H. Wilson, *Europe's Tragedy: A New History of the Thirty Years War* (London, 2009)

Peter H. Wilson, *German Armies: War and German Politics, 1648–1806* (London, 1998)

Peter H. Wilson, *The Holy Roman Empire 1495–1806* (Basingstoke, 1999)

Simon Winder, *Germania: A Personal History of Germans Ancient and Modern* (London, 2010)

Larry Wolff, *The Idea of Galicia: History and Fantasy in Habsburg Political Culture* (Stanford, 2010)

Larry Wolff, *Inventing Eastern Europe: The Map of Civilization on the Mind of the Enlightenment* (Stanford, 1994)

Adam Zagajewski, *Two Cities: On Exile, History, and the Imagination*, trans. Lillian Vallee (New York, 1995)

Stefan Zweig, *Amok and Other Stories*, trans. Anthea Bell (London, 2006)

Stefan Zweig, *Beware of Pity*, trans. Phyllis and Trevor Blewitt (London, 1982)

Stefan Zweig, *The Invisible Collection / Buchmendel*, trans. Eden and Cedar Paul (London, 1998)

Illustrations

The title page shows one small detail from the sprawling and wonderful *Triumphal Procession of the Emperor Maximilian I*. This section was created by Hans Burgkmair the Elder in 1515 (*Scala, Florence/BPK, Berlin*). Chapter one: another Burgkmair – a spectacular woodcut from 1507 of the Imperial eagle, creaking with allegory and allusion and with Maximilian enthroned above a sort of giant bird-bath filled with the Nine Muses (*Scala, Florence/BPK, Berlin*). Chapter two: Maximilian in full wizard mode, with the Order of the Golden Fleece around his neck – a seventeenth-century engraving after Lucas van Leyden's 1515 original (*akg-images*). Chapter three: Heavy cavalry armour in the Graz Armoury (*akg-images/Erich Lessing*). Chapter four: *Sour Orange, Terrestrial Mollusc and Larkspur*. In an inspired bit of cultural vandalism Georg Bocskay's immaculate pages of calligraphy for Maximilian II were invaded a generation later by Joris Hoefnagel's fruit, flowers and creatures for Rudolf II. This is a fine example (as well as one of the best titles given to any image) but I can only urge everyone to look at the others on the Getty Museum website – there is one extraordinary work of 'night script' with the black page filled with a sort of lemur or sloth (*Script 1561-62, Illumination 1591-96. Watercolours, gold and silver paint, and ink on parchment. 16.6 x 12.4 cm. The J. Paul Getty Museum, Los Angeles, Ms. 20, fol. 33*). Chapter five: *The Rescue of Slavata and Martinez by the Mother of God*, votive painting, c. 1620, Jindřichův Hradec Castle, Czech Republic. Mary and her minions come to the rescue of the defenestrated Imperial representatives. Just looking at this picture one can understand the rugged nature of the forces the Protestants were now up against. Text illustration page 175: *Demonstration that the Tower of Babel could not have reached the moon* by Athanasius Kircher, from his *Turris Babel* (Amsterdam, 1679) (*Wellcome Library, London. Photo: Wellcome Images*). Chapter six: The Empress Margarita Teresa in fancy dress by Jan Thomas, c. 1667, Schloss Ambras, Innsbruck (*akg-images/Erich Lessing*). Chapter seven: Interior of the Court Library, Hofburg, now known as the State Hall (*Bildarchiv Monheim/akg-images*). Chapter eight: *The Polish Plumb Cake*, c. 1772, an English cartoon by John Lodge, with Russia, France, Prussia and Austria about to tuck in, the devil under the table, with Poland in tears and Turkey indignant (*The Bridgeman Art Library*). Chapter nine: An engraving from the 1830s of Archduke Charles at the Battle of Aspern-Essling (*Universal History Archive/UIG/The Bridgeman Art Library*). Chapter ten: Hungarian patriots being executed by Habsburg troops, an engraving from 1849. These sorts of images circulated widely and, in conjunction with the tireless work of the two great, roving anti-Habsburg orators Kossuth and Garibaldi, made the Habsburg Empire appear irredeemably brutal and backward to much European and American opinion (*Roger-Viollet/Topfoto*). Chapter eleven: a famous photo of the four Habsburg brothers from the early 1860s, exuding what proved to be a misplaced dynastic confidence. From left: Karl Ludwig, the father of Franz Ferdinand and grand-father of Karl I; Franz Joseph I, whose son and heir would commit suicide in 1889; Maximilian, shortly to take the catastrophic decision to accept the crown of Mexico, resulting in his execution in 1867; and Ludwig Viktor, a homosexual transvestite who was ultimately expelled by Franz Joseph from Vienna and lived much of his life monitored closely by Habsburg agents in Salzburg. Ludwig Viktor survived the end of the dynasty by a few days, dying in January 1919. Chapter twelve: The Škoda Engineering Shop, 1890, with some workers just visible (*State Regional Archives, Plzeň*). Chapter thirteen: *Erdődy's Jump* by Karlo Drašković, 1895. I include this picture simply because I have always loved it. Drašković was a member of a Croatian noble family and in his short life made a number of experimental photographs trying to capture movement. István Erdődy, whose athleticism is here preserved for ever, was a member of a family of Hungarian landown-ers in what is now northern Croatia (*Museum of Arts and Crafts, Zagreb*). Chapter fourteen: Franz Ferdinand and Wilhelm II on a hunt near the German town of Springe, 1912 – I think readers can draw their own conclusions from this photo about the steady impressiveness or otherwise of Europe's rulers in this period (*Ullstein/Topfoto*). Chapter fifteen: Antonio Marchisio's painting *The Epilogue*, issued as a postcard. A fine example of the sheer wackiness of nationalism in full cry: the condemned, treacherous, sordid eagle of Austria-Hungary tumbles from its Tyrolean crag, to be replaced by . . . an identical eagle, but with its feathers in better order and backed by a pretty flag. The new nationalist regimes that marched into the Empire's ruins in 1918 and 1919 spread little but misery – the South Tyrol being a small, sad instance (*Castello Museo Storico Italiano della Guerra, Rovereto/De Agostini/akg-images*).

Acknowledgements

Countless hoteliers, fellow train passengers, museum guides, passers-by, waiters, ticket clerks and incredulous bus drivers have made this book possible. Whenever I realized I was totally and fundamentally lost, somebody kind would materialize as though by magic and help me on my way. I finish this book with a sense of utter sadness that I cannot hope ever to return to places which I now know to be exceptionally and often crazily interesting. I cannot enlarge on this without being tiresome, but so often while wandering about Central Europe I would find myself grinning or skipping with excitement in what on the face of it were the simplest of circumstances and can only urge others to go and do the same.

For their invaluable and sometimes cruel comments on some or all of the text I am grateful to Nicholas Blake, Tim Blanning, Christopher Clark, R. J. W. Evans, Christine Jones, Marina Kemp, Tony Lacey, Thomas Penn, Adam Phillips, Norman Stone and Barnaby Winder. For essential help, purloined ideas, encouragement and forbearance I would also like to thank Paul Baggaley, Tracy Bohan, Emma Bravo, Malcolm Bull, the late Peter Carson, Sarah Chalfant, Penny and David Edgar, Niall Ferguson, Helen Fraser, Jonathan Galassi, Eleo Gordon, Jim and Sandy Jones, Barry Langford, Diarmaid MacCulloch, Stefan McGrath, Cecilia Mackay, Mark Mazower, Stuart Proffitt, John Seaton, Brendan Simms, Carole Tonkinson, Adam Tooze, Tom Weldon, Peter Wilson, Stephanie Winder, Elizabeth and Christopher Winder and Andrew Wylie.

My enthusiasm for Central Europe really began at the beginning of 1992 when Christine Jones and I spent our honeymoon in a shockingly cold Vienna and Prague. The last part of the research for this book was done in Kraków and Przemyśl in the company of our now nineteen-year-old son, who could not be a more congenial companion when it comes to examining Jan III Sobieski's tomb sculptures or chained-up remnants of a dragon in the Wawel Cathedral. My family have been tangled up in Habsburg issues therefore for as long as we have been a family and the children – Barnaby, Felix and Martha – continued throughout to be as patient, entertaining and surprising as ever. Christine Jones has been the only person I have wanted to impress for some twenty-three years now. I have gone about this in odd ways – not least through at irregular intervals disappearing to Cluj-Napoca or, worse, sitting in the kitchen listening to folk tunes scored for rustic flute and hoping that somehow she would not mind. I am sure the Hungarians must have a word which would express how much I owe her – there is certainly nothing sufficiently fevered or all-encompassing in English – but as usual I do not know what it is.

Simon Winder
Sequim, Wandsworth Town
2009–13

Index